A THEODICY;

OR,

VINDICATION OF THE DIVINE GLORY,

AS MANIFESTED IN THE

CONSTITUTION AND GOVERNMENT OF THE MORAL WORLD.

BY ALBERT TAYLOR BLEDSOE,

PROFESSOR OF MATHEMATICS AND ASTRONOMY IN THE UNIVERSITY OF MISSISSIPPI.

New-York:

PUBLISHED BY CARLTON & PHILLIPS,

200 MULBERRY-STREET.

1854.

Contents.

INTRODUCTION.

PART I.

PART II.

CONCLUSION.

INTRODUCTION.

OF THE POSSIBILITY OF A THEODICY.

Introduction.

OF THE POSSIBILITY OF A THEODICY.

How, under the government of an infinitely perfect Being, evil could have proceeded from a creature of his own, has ever been regarded as the great difficulty pertaining to the intellectual system of the universe. It has never ceased to puzzle and perplex the human mind. Indeed, so great and so obstinate has it seemed, that it is usually supposed to lie beyond the reach of the human faculties. We shall, however, examine the grounds of this opinion, before we exchange the bright illusions of hope, if such indeed they be, for the gloomy forebodings of despair.

SECTION I.

The failure of Plato and other ancient philosophers to construct a Theodicy, not a ground of despair.

The supposed want of success attending the labours of the past, is, no doubt, the principal reason which has induced so many to abandon the problem of evil in despair, and even to accuse of presumption every speculation designed to shed light upon so great a mystery. But this reason, however specious and imposing at first view, will lose much of its apparent force upon a closer examination.

In every age the same reasoning has been employed to repress the efforts of the human mind to overcome the difficulties by which it has been surrounded; yet, in spite of such discouragements, the most stupendous difficulties have gradually yielded to the progressive developments and revelations of time. It was the opinion of Socrates, for example, that the problem of the natural world was unavoidably concealed from mortals, and that it was a sort of presumptuous impiety, displeasing to the gods, for men to pry into it. If Newton himself had lived in that age, it is probable that he would have entertained the same opinion. It is certain that the problem in question would then have been as far beyond the reach of his powers, as beyond those of the most ordinary individual. The ignorance of the earth's dimensions, the manifold errors respecting the laws of motion, and the defective state of the mathematical sciences, which then prevailed, would have rendered utterly impotent the efforts of a thousand Newtons to grapple with such a problem. The time was neither ripe for the solution of that problem, nor for the appearance of a Newton. It was only after science had, during a period of two thousand years, multiplied her resources and gathered up her energies, that she was prepared for a flight to the summit of the world, whence she might behold and reveal the wonderful art wherewith it hath been constructed by the Almighty Architect. Because Socrates could not conceive of any possible means of solving the great problem of the material world, it did not follow, as the event has shown, that it was forever beyond the reach and dominion of man. We should not then listen too implicitly to the teachers of despair, nor too rashly set limits to the triumphs of the human power. If we may believe "the master of wisdom," they are not the true friends of science, nor of the world's progress. "By far the greatest obstacle," says Bacon, "to the advancement of the sciences, *is to be found in men's despair and idea of impossibility.*"

Even in the minds of those who cultivate a particular branch of knowledge, there is often an internal secret despair of finding the truth, which so far paralyzes their efforts as to prevent them from seeking it with that deep earnestness, without which it is seldom found. The history of optics furnishes a most impressive illustration of the justness of this remark. Previous to the time of Newton, no one seemed to entertain a real hope that this branch of knowledge would ever assume the form and clearness of scientific truth. The laws and properties of so ethereal a substance as light, appeared to elude the grasp of the human intellect; and hence, no one evinced the boldness to grapple directly with them. The whole region of optics was involved in mists, and those who gave their attention to this department of knowledge, abandoned themselves, for the most part, to vague generalities and loose conjectures. In the conflict of manifold opinions, and the great variety of hypotheses which seemed to promise nothing but endless disputes, the highest idea of the science of optics that prevailed, was that of something in relation to light which might be plausibly advanced and confidently maintained. It was reserved for Newton to produce a revolution in the mode of treating this branch of knowledge, as well as that of physical astronomy. Not despairing of the truth, he sternly put away "innumerable fancies flitting on all sides around him," and by searching observation and experiment, brought his mind directly into contact with things themselves, and held it steadily to them, until the clear light of truth dawned. The consequence was, that the dreams of philosophy, falsely so called, gave place to the clear realities of nature. It was to the unconquerable hope, no less than to the profound humility of Newton, that the world is indebted for his most splendid discoveries, as well as for that perfect model of the true spirit of philosophy, which combined the infinite caution of a Butler with the unbounded boldness of a Leibnitz. The lowliest humility, free from the least shadow of despair, united with the loftiest hope, without the least mixture of presumption, both proceeding from an invincible love of truth, are the elements which constituted the secret of that patient and all-enduring thought which conducted the mind of Newton from the obscurities and dreams enveloping the world below into the bright and shining region of eternal truths above. In our humble opinion, Newton has done more for the great cause of knowledge, by the mighty impulse of hope he has given to the powers of the human mind, than by all the sublime discoveries he has made. For, as Maclaurin says: "The variety of opinions and perpetual disputes among philosophers has induced not a few of late, as well as in former times, to think that it was vain labour to endeavour to acquire certainty in natural knowledge, and to ascribe this to some unavoidable defect in the principles of the science. But it has appeared sufficiently, from the discoveries of those who have consulted nature, and not their own imaginations, and particularly from what we learn from Sir Isaac Newton, *that the fault has lain in philosophers themselves, and not in philosophy.*"

We are persuaded the day will come, when it will be seen that the despair of scepticism has been misplaced, not only with regard to natural knowledge, but also in relation to the great problems of the intellectual and moral world. It is true, that Plato failed to solve these problems; but his failure may be easily accounted for, without in the least degree shaking the foundations of our hope. The learned Ritter has said, that Plato felt the necessity imposed upon him, by his system, to reconcile the existence of evil with the perfections of God; but yet, as often as he approached this dark subject, his views became vague, fluctuating, and unsatisfactory. How little insight he had into it on any scientific or clearly defined principle, is obvious from the fact, that he took shelter from its difficulties in the wild hypothesis of the preëxistence of souls. But the impotency of Plato's attempts to solve these difficulties, may be explained without the least disparagement to his genius, or without leading us to hope for light only from the world's possession of better minds.

In the first place, such was the state of mental science when Plato lived, that it would have been impossible for any one to reconcile the existence of evil with the perfections of God. It has been truly said, that "An attention to the internal operations of the human mind, *with a view to analyze its principles*, is one of the distinctions of modern times. Among the ancients scarcely anything of the sort was known."—*Robert Hall.* Yet without a correct analysis of the powers of the human mind, and of the relations they sustain to each other, as well as to external objects and influences, it is impossible to shed one ray of light on the relation subsisting between the existence of moral evil and the divine glory. The theory of motion is "the key to nature." It was with this key that Newton, the great high-priest of nature, entered into her profoundest recesses, and laid open her most sublime secrets to the admiration of mankind. In like manner, the true theory of action is the key to the intellectual world, by which its difficulties are to be laid open and its enigmas solved. Not possessing this key, it was as impossible for Plato, or for any other philosopher, to penetrate the mystery of sin's existence, as it would have been, without a knowledge of the laws of motion, to comprehend the stupendous problem of the material universe.

Secondly, the ancient philosophers laboured under the insuperable disadvantage, that the sublime disclosures of revelation had not been made known to the world. Hence the materials were wanting out of which to construct a Theodicy, or vindication of the perfections of God. For if we could see only so much of this world's drama as is made known by the light of nature, it would not be possible to reconcile it with the character of its great Author. No one was more sensible of this defect of knowledge than Plato himself; and its continuance was, in his view, inconsistent with the goodness of the divine Being. Hence his well-known prediction, that a teacher would be sent from God to clear up the darkness of man's present destiny, and to withdraw the veil from its future glory. The facts of revelation cannot, of course, be logically assumed as verities, in an argument with the atheist; but still, as we shall hereafter see, they may, in connexion with other truths, be made to serve a most important and legitimate function in exploding his sophisms and objections.

SECTION II.

The failure of Leibnitz not a ground of despair.

It is alleged, that since Leibnitz exhausted the resources of his vast erudition, and exerted the powers of his mighty intellect without success, to solve the problem in question, it is in vain for any one else to attempt its solution. Leibnitz, himself, was too much of a philosopher to approve of such a judgment in relation to any human being. He could never have wished, or expected to see "the empire of man, which is founded in the sciences," permanently confined to the boundaries of a single mind, however exalted its powers, or comprehensive its attainments. He finely rebuked the false humility and the disguised arrogance of Descartes, in affirming that the sovereignty of God and the freedom of man could never be reconciled. "If Descartes," says he, "had confessed such an inability for himself alone, this might have savoured of humility; but it is otherwise, when, because he could not find the means of solving this difficulty, he declares it an impossibility for all ages and for all minds." We have, at least, the authority and example of Leibnitz, in favour of the propriety of cultivating this department of knowledge, with a view to shed light on the great problem of the intellectual world.

His failure, if rightly considered, is not a ground for despondency. He approached the problem in question in a wrong spirit. The pride of conquering difficulties is the unfortunate disposition with which he undertook to solve it. His well-known boast, that with him all difficult things are easy, and all easy things difficult, is a proof that his spirit was not perfectly adapted to carry him forward in a contest with the dark enigmas of the universe. Indeed, if we consider what Leibnitz has actually done, we shall perceive, that notwithstanding his wonderful powers, he has rendered many easy things difficult, as well as many difficult things easy. The best way to conquer difficulties is, if we may judge from his example, not to attack them directly, and with the pride of a conqueror, but simply to seek after the truth. If we make a conquest of all the truth, this will make a conquest of all the difficulties within our reach. It is wonderful with what ease a difficulty, which may have resisted the direct siege of centuries, will sometimes fall before a single inquirer after truth, who had not dreamed of aiming at its solution, until this seemed, as if by accident, to offer itself to his mind. If we pursue difficulties, they will be apt to fly from us and elude our grasp; whereas, if we give up our minds to an honest and earnest search after truth, they will come in with their own solutions.

The truth is, that the difficulty in question has been increased rather than diminished by the speculations of Leibnitz. This has resulted from a premature and extreme devotion to system—a source of miscarriage and failure common to Leibnitz, and to most others who have devoted their attention to the origin of evil. On the one hand, exaggerated views concerning the divine agency, or equally extravagant notions on the other, respecting the agency of man, have frequently converted a seeming into a real contradiction. In general, the work of God has been conceived in such a relation to the powers of man, as to make the latter entirely disappear; or else the power of man has been represented as occupying so exalted and independent a position, as to exclude the Almighty from his rightful dominion over the moral world. Thus, the Supreme Being has generally been shut out from the affairs and government of the world by one side, and his energy rendered so all-pervading by the other, as really to make him the author of evil. In this way, the difficulties concerning the origin and existence of evil have been greatly augmented by the very speculations designed to solve them. For if God takes little or no concern in the affairs and destiny of the moral world, this clearly seems to render him responsible for the evil which he might easily have prevented; and, on the other hand, if he pervades the moral world with his power in such a manner as to bring all things to pass, this as clearly seems to implicate him in the turpitude of sin.

After having converted the seeming discrepancy between the divine power and human agency into a real contradiction, it is too late to endeavour to reconcile them. Yet such has been the case with most of the giant intellects that have laboured to reconcile the sovereignty of God and the moral agency of man. It will hereafter be clearly seen, we trust, that it is not possible for any one, holding the scheme of a Calvin, or a Leibnitz, or a Descartes, or an Edwards, to show an agreement between the power of God and the freedom of man; since according to these systems there is an eternal opposition and conflict between them. It is no ground of despair, then, that the mighty minds of the past have failed to solve the problem in question, if the cause of their failure may be traced to the errors of their own systems, and not to the inherent difficulties of the subject.

Those who have endeavoured to solve the problem in question have, for the most part, been necessitated to fail in consequence of having adopted a wrong method. Instead of beginning with observation, and carefully dissecting the world which God has made, so as to rise, by a clear analysis of *things*, to the general principles on which they have been actually framed and put together, they have set out from the lofty region of universal abstractions, and proceeded to reconstruct the world for themselves. Instead of beginning with the actual, as best befits the feebleness of the human intellect, and working their way up into the great system of things, they have taken their position at once in the high and boundless realm of the ideal, and thence endeavoured to deduce the nature of the laws and phenomena of the real world. This is the course pursued by Plato, Leibnitz, Hobbes, Descartes, Edwards, and, indeed, most of those great thinkers who have endeavoured to shed light on the problem in question. Hence each has necessarily become "a sublime architect of words," whose grand and imposing system of shadows and abstractions has but a slight foundation in the real constitution and laws of the spiritual world. Their writings furnish the most striking illustration of the profound aphorism of Bacon, that "the usual method of discovery and proof, by first establishing the most general propositions, then applying and proving the intermediate axioms according to these, is *the parent of error and the calamity of every science.*" He who would frame a real model of the world in the understanding, such as it is found to be, not such as man's reason has distorted, must pursue the opposite course. Surely it cannot be deemed unreasonable, that this course should be most diligently applied to the study of the intellectual world; especially as it has wrought such wonders in the province of natural knowledge, and that too, after so many ages had, according to the former method, laboured upon it comparatively in vain. Because the human mind has not been able to bridge over the impassable gulf between the ideal and the concrete, so as to effect a passage from the former to the latter, it certainly does not follow, that it should forever despair of so far penetrating the apparent obscurity and confusion of real things, as to see that nothing which God has created is inconsistent with the eternal, immutable glory of the ideal: or, in other words, because the real world and the ideal cannot be shown to be connected by a logical dependency, it does not follow, that the actual creation and providence of God, that all his works and ways cannot be made to appear consistent with the idea of an absolutely perfect being and of the eternal laws according to which his power acts: that is to say, because the high *a priori* method, which so magisterially proceeds to pronounce what *must be*, has failed to solve the problem of the moral world, it does not follow, that the inductive method, or that which cautiously begins with an examination of what *is*, may not finally rise to the sublime contemplation of what *ought to be*; and, in the light of God's own creation, behold the magnificent model of the actual universe perfectly conformed to the transcendent and unutterable glory of the ideal.

SECTION III.

The system of the moral universe not purposely involved in obscurity to teach us a lesson of humility.

But the assertion is frequently made, that the moral government of the world is purposely left in obscurity and apparent confusion, in order to teach man a lesson of humility and submission, by showing him how weak and narrow is the human mind. We have not, however, been able to find any sufficient reason or foundation for such an opinion. As every atom in the universe presents mysteries which baffle the most subtle research and the most profound investigation of the human intellect, we cannot see how any reflecting mind can possibly find an additional lesson of humility in the fact, that the system of the universe itself is involved in clouds and darkness. Would it not be strange, indeed, if the mind, whose grasp is not sufficient for the mysteries of a single atom, should be really humbled by the conviction that it is too weak and limited to fathom the wonders of the universe? Does the insignificance of an egg-shell appear from the fact that it cannot contain the ocean?

The truth is, that the more clearly the majesty and glory of the divine perfections are displayed in the constitution and government of the world, the more clearly shall we see the greatness of God and the littleness of man. No true knowledge can ever impress the human mind with a conceit of its own greatness. The farther its light expands, the greater must become the visible sphere of the surrounding darkness; and its highest attainment in real knowledge must inevitably terminate in a profound sense of the vast, unlimited extent of its own ignorance. Hence, we need entertain no fear, that man's humility will ever be endangered by too great attainments in science. Presumption is, indeed, the natural offspring of ignorance, and not of knowledge. Socrates, as we have already seen, endeavoured to inculcate a lesson of humility, by reminding his contemporaries how far the theory of the material heavens was beyond the reach of their faculties. And to enforce this lesson, he assured them that it was displeasing to the gods for men to attempt to pry into the wonderful art wherewith they had constructed the universe. In like manner, the poet, at a much later period, puts the following sentiment into the mouth of an angel :—

> "To ask or search, I blame thee not; for heaven
> Is as the book of God before thee set,
> Wherein to read his wondrous works, and learn
> His seasons, hours, or days, or months, or years:
> This to attain, whether heaven move or earth,
> Imports not if thou reckon right; *the rest*
> *From man or angel the great Architect*
> *Did wisely to conceal, and not divulge*
> *His secrets, to be scann'd by them who ought*
> *Rather admire;* or, if they list to try
> Conjecture, he his fabric of the heavens
> Hath left to their disputes, perhaps to move
> His laughter at their quaint opinions wide
> Hereafter."

All this may be very well, no doubt, for him by whom it was uttered, and for those who may have received it as an everlasting oracle of truth. But the true lesson of humility was taught by Newton, when he solved the problem of the world, and revealed the wonderful art displayed therein by the Supreme Architect. Never before, in the history of the human race, was so impressive a conviction made of the almost absolute nothingness of man, when measured on the inconceivably magnificent scale of the universe. No one, it is well known, felt this conviction more deeply than Newton himself. "I have been but as a child," said he, "playing on the sea-shore; now finding some pebble rather more polished, and now some shell rather more agreeably variegated than another, while the immense *ocean of truth* extended itself *unexplored* before me."

It is, indeed, strangely to forget our littleness, as well as the limits which this necessarily sets to the progress of the understanding, to imagine that the Almighty has to conceal anything with a view to remind us of the weakness of our powers. Indeed, everything around us, and everything within us, brings home the conviction of the littleness of man. There is not a page of the history of human thought on which this lesson is not deeply engraved. Still we do not despair. We find a ground of hope in the very littleness as well as in the greatness of the human powers.

SECTION IV.

The littleness of the human mind a ground of hope.

We would yield to no one in a profound veneration for the great intellects of the past. But let us not be dazzled and blinded by the splendour of their achievements. Let us look at it closely, and see how wonderful it is—this thing called the human mind. The more I think of it, the more it fills me with amazement. I scarcely know which amazes me the more, its littleness or its grandeur. Now I see it, with all its high powers and glorious faculties, labouring under the ambiguity of a word, apparently in hopeless eclipse for centuries. Shall I therefore despise it? Before I have time to do so, the power and the light which is thus shut out from the world by so pitiful a cause, is revealed in all its glory. I see this same intelligence forcing its way through a thousand hostile appearances, resisting innumerable obstacles pressing on all sides around it, overcoming deep illusions, and inveterate opinions, almost as firmly seated as the very laws of nature themselves. I see it rising above all these, and planting itself in the radiant seat of truth. It embraces the plan, it surveys the work of the Supreme Architect of all things. It follows the infinite reason, and recognises the almighty power, in their sublimest manifestations. I rejoice in the glory of its triumphs, and am ready to pronounce its empire boundless. But, alas! I see it again baffled and confounded by the wonders and mysteries of a single atom!

I see this same thing, or rather its mightiest representatives, with a Newton or a Leibnitz at their head, in full pursuit of a shadow, and wasting their wonderful energies in beating the air. They have measured the world, and stretched their line upon the chambers of the great deep. They have weighed the sun, moon, and stars, and marked out their orbits. They have determined the laws according to which all worlds and all atoms move—according to which the very spheres sing together. And yet, when they came to measure "the force of a moving body," they toil for a century at the task, and finally rest in the amazing conclusion, that "the very same thing may have two measures widely different from each other!" Alas! that the same mind, that the same god-like intelligence, which has measured worlds and systems, should thus have wasted its stupendous energies in striving to measure a metaphor!

When I think of its grandeur and its triumphs, I bow with reverence before its power, and am ready to despair of ever seeing it go farther than it has already gone; but when I think of its littleness and its failures, I take courage again, and determine to toil on as a living atom among living atoms. The glory of its triumphs does not discourage me, because I also see its littleness; nor can its littleness extinguish in me the light of hope, because I also see the glory of its triumphs. And surely this is right; for the intellect of man, so conspicuously combining the attributes of the angel and of the worm, is not to be despised without infinite danger, nor followed without infinite caution.

Such, indeed, is the weakness and fallibility of the human mind, even in its brightest forms, that we cannot for a moment imagine, that the inherent difficulties of the dark enigma of the world are insuperable, because they have not been clearly and fully solved by a Leibnitz or an Edwards. On the contrary, we are perfectly persuaded that in the end the wonder will be, not that such a question should have been attempted after so many illustrious failures, but that any such failure should have been made. This will appear the more probable, if we consider the precise nature of the problem to be solved, and not lose ourselves in dark and unintelligible notions. It is not to do some great thing—it is simply to refute the sophism of the atheist. If God were both willing and able to prevent sin, which is the only supposition consistent with the idea of God, says the atheist, he would certainly have prevented it, and sin would never have made its appearance in the world. But sin has made its appearance in the world; and hence, God must have been either unable or unwilling to prevent it. Now, if we take either term of this alternative, we must adopt a conclusion which is at war with the idea of a God.

Such is the argument of the atheist; and sad indeed must be the condition of the Christian world if it be forever unable to meet and refute such a sophism. Yet, it is the error involved in this sophism which obscures our intellectual vision, and causes so perplexing a darkness to spread itself over the moral order and beauty of the world. Hence, in grappling with the supposed great difficulty in question, we do not undertake to remove a veil from the universe—we simply undertake to remove a sophism from our own minds. Though we have so spoken in accommodation with the views of others, the problem of the moral world is not, in reality, high and difficult *in itself*, like the great problem of the material universe. We repeat, it is simply to refute and explode the sophism of the atheist. Let this be blown away, and the darkness which seems to overhang the moral government of the world will disappear like the mists of the morning.

If such be the nature of the problem in question, and such it will be found to be, it is certainly a mistake to suppose that "it must be entangled with perplexities while we see but in part."* It is only while we see amiss, and not while we see in part, that this problem must wear the appearance of a dark enigma. It is clear, that our knowledge is, and ever must be, exceedingly limited on all sides; and if we must understand the whole of the case, if we must comprehend the entire extent of the divine government for the universe and for eternity, before we can remove the difficulty in question, we must necessarily despair of success. But we cannot see any sufficient ground to support this oft-repeated assertion. Because the field of our vision is so exceedingly limited, we do not see why it should be forever traversed by apparent inconsistencies and contradictions. In relation to the material universe, our space is but a point, and our time but a moment; and yet, as that inconceivably grand system is now understood by us, there is nothing in it which seems to conflict with the dictates of reason, or with the infinite perfections of God. On the contrary, the revelations of modern science have given an emphasis and a sublimity to the language of inspiration, that "the heavens declare the glory of the Lord," which had, for ages, been concealed from the loftiest conception of the astronomer.

Nor did it require a knowledge of the whole material universe to remove the difficulties, or to blast the objections which atheists had, in all preceding ages, raised against the perfections of its divine Author. Such objections, as is well known, were raised before astronomy, as a science, had an existence. Lucre-

* Johnson's Works, vol. iv, p. 286.

tius, for example, though he deemed the sun, moon, and stars, no larger than they appear to the eye, and supposed them to revolve around the earth, undertook to point out and declaim against the miserable defects which he saw, or fancied he saw, in the system of the material world. That is to say, he undertook to criticise and find fault with the great volume of nature, before he had even learned its alphabet. The objections of Lucretius, which appeared so formidable in his day, as well as many others that have since been raised on equally plausible grounds, have passed away before the progress of science, and now seem like the silly prattle of children, or the insane babble of madmen. But although such difficulties have been swept away, and our field of vision cleared of all that is painful and perplexing, nay, brightened with all that is grand and beautiful, we seem to be farther than ever from comprehending the whole of the case—from grasping the amazing extent and glory of the material globe. And why may not this ultimately be the case also in relation to the moral universe? Why should every attempt to clear up its difficulties, and blow away the objections of atheism to its order and beauty, be supposed to originate in presumption and to terminate in impiety? Are we so much the less interested in knowing the ways of God in regard to the constitution and government of the moral world than of the material, that he should purposely conceal the former from us, while he has permitted the latter to be laid open so as to ravish our minds? We can believe no such thing; and we are not willing to admit that there is any part of the creation of God in which omniscience alone can cope with the atheist.

SECTION V.

The construction of a Theodicy, not an attempt to solve mysteries, but to dissipate absurdities.

As we have merely undertaken to refute the atheist, and vindicate the glory of the divine perfections, so it would be a grievous mistake to suppose, that we are about to pry into the holy mysteries of religion. No sound mind is ever perplexed by the contemplation of mysteries. Indeed, they are a source of positive satisfaction and delight. If nothing were dark,—if all around us, and above us, were clearly seen,—the truth itself would soon appear stale and mean. Everything truly great must transcend the powers of the human mind; and hence, if nothing were mysterious, there would be nothing worthy of our veneration and worship. It is mystery, indeed, which lends such unspeakable grandeur and variety to the scenery of the moral world. Without it, all would be clear, it is true, but nothing grand. There would be lights, but no shadows. And around the very lights themselves, there would be nothing soothing and sublime, in which the soul might rest and the imagination revel.

Hence it is no part of our object to pry into mystery, but to get rid of absurdity. And in our humble opinion, this would long since have been done, and the difficulty in question solved, had not the friends of truth incautiously given the most powerful protection to the sophism and absurdity of the atheist, by throwing around it the sacred garb of mystery.

SECTION VI.

The spirit in which the following work has been prosecuted, and the relation of the author to other systems.

In conclusion, we offer a few remarks in relation to the manner and spirit in which the following work has been undertaken and prosecuted. In the first place, the writer may truly say, that he did not enter on the apparently dark problem of the moral world with the least hope that he should be able to throw any light upon it, nor with any other set purpose and design. He simply revolved the subject in mind, because he was by nature prone to such meditations. So far from having aimed at things usually esteemed so high and difficult with a feeling of presumptuous confidence, he has, indeed, suffered most from that spirit of despondency, that despair of scepticism, against which, in the foregoing pages, he has appeared so anxious to caution others. It has been patient reflection, and the reading of excellent authors, together with an earnest desire to know the truth, which has delivered him from the power of that spirit, and conducted him to what now so clearly seems "the bright and shining light of truth."

It was, in fact, while engaged in meditation on the powers and susceptibilities of the human mind, as well as on the relations they sustain to each and to other things, and not in any direct attempt to elucidate the origin of evil, that the first clear light appeared to dawn on this great difficulty: and in no other way, he humbly conceives, can the true philosophy of the spiritual world ever be comprehended. For, as the laws of matter had first to be studied and traced out in relation to bodies on the earth, before they could be extended to the heavens, and made to explain its wonderful mechanism; so must the laws and phenomena of the human mind be correctly analyzed and clearly defined, in order to obtain an insight into the intellectual system of the universe. And just in proportion as the clouds and darkness hanging over the phenomena of our own minds are made to disappear, will the intellectual system of the world which God "has set in our hearts," become more distinct and beautiful in its proportions. For it is the mass of real contradictions and obscurities, existing in the little world within, which distorts to our view the great world without, and causes the work and ways of God to appear so full of disorders. Hence, in proportion as these real contradictions and obscurities are removed, will the mind become a truer microcosm, or more faithful mirror, in which the image of the universe will unfold itself, free from the apparent disorders and confusion which seem to render it unworthy of its great Author and Ruler.

Secondly, the relation which the writer sustains to other systems, has been, it appears to himself, most favourable to a successful prosecution of the following speculations. Whether at the outset of his inquiries, he was the more of an Arminian or of a Calvinist, he is unable to say; but if his crude and imperfectly developed sentiments had then been made known, it is probable he would have been ranked with the Arminians. Be this as it may, it is certain that he was never so much of an Arminian, or of anything else, as to imagine that Calvinism admitted of nothing great and good. On the contrary, he has ever believed that the Calvinists were at least equal to any other body of men in piety, which is certainly the highest and noblest of all qualities. And besides, it was a constant delight to him to read the great master-pieces of reasoning which Calvinism had furnished for the instruction and admiration of mankind. By this means he came to believe that the scheme of the Arminians could not be maintained, and his faith in it was gradually undermined.

But although he thus submitted his mind to the dominion of Calvinism, as advocated by Edwards, and earnestly espoused it with some exceptions; he never felt that profound, internal satisfaction of the truth of the system, after which his rational nature continually longed, and which it struggled to realize. He certainly expected to find this satisfaction in Calvinism, if anywhere. Long, therefore, did he pass over every portion of Calvinism, in order to discover, if possible, how its foundations might be rendered more clear and convincing, and all its parts harmonized among themselves as well as with the great undeniable facts of man's nature and destiny. While engaged in these inquiries, he has been more than once led to see what appeared to be a flaw in Calvinism itself; but without at first perceiving all its consequences. By reflection on these apparent defects; nay, by protracted and earnest meditation on them, his suspicions have been confirmed and his opinions changed. If what now so clearly appears to be the truth is so or not, it is certain that it has not been embraced out of a spirit of opposition to Calvinism, or to any other system of religious faith whatever. Its light, whether real or imaginary, has dawned upon his mind while seeking after truth amid the foundations of Calvinism itself; and this light has been augmented more by reading the works of Calvinists themselves, than those of their opponents.

These things are here set down, not because the writer thinks they should have any weight or influence to bias the judgment of the reader, but because he wishes it to be understood that he entertains the most profound veneration for the great and good men whose works seem to stand in the way of the following design to vindicate the glory of God, and which, therefore, he will not scruple to assail in so far as this may be necessary to his purpose. It is, indeed, a matter of deep and inexpressible regret, that in our conflicts with the powers of darkness, we should, however undesignedly, be weakened and opposed by Christian divines and philosophers. But so it seems to be, and we dare not cease to resist them. And if, in the following attempt to vindicate the glory of God, it shall become necessary to call in question the infallibility of the great founders of human systems, this, it is to be hoped, will not be deemed an unpardonable offence.

Thus has the writer endeavoured to work his way through the mingled lights and obscurity of human systems into a bright and beautiful vision of the great harmonious system of the world itself. It is certainly either a sublime truth, or else a glorious illusion, which thus enables him to rise above the apparent disorders and perturbations of the world, as constituted and governed by the Almighty, and behold the real order and harmony therein established. The ideal creations of the poet and the philosopher sink into perfect insignificance beside the actual creation of God. Where clouds and darkness once appeared the most impenetrable, there scenes of indescribable magnificence and beauty are now beheld with inexpressible delight; the stupendous cloud of evil no longer hangs overhead, but rolls beneath us, while the eternal Reason from above permeates its gloom, and irradiates its depths. We now behold the reason, and absolutely rejoice in the contemplation, of that which once seemed like a dark blot on the world's design.

In using this language, we do not wish to be understood as laying claim to the discovery of any great truth, or any new principle. Yet we do trust, that we have attained to a clear and precise statement of old truths. And these truths, thus clearly defined, we trust that we have seized with a firm grasp, and carried as lights through the dark places of theology, so as to expel thence the errors and delusions by which its glory has been obscured. Moreover, if we have not succeeded, nor even attempted to succeed, in solving any mysteries, properly so called, yet may we have removed certain apparent contradictions, which have been usually deemed insuperable to the human mind.

But even if the reader should be satisfied beforehand, that no additional light will herein be thrown on the problem of the moral world, yet would we remind him, that it does not necessarily follow that the ensuing discourse is wholly unworthy of his attention: for the materials, though old, may be presented in new combinations, and much may be omitted which has disfigured and obscured the beauty of most other systems. Although no new fountains of light may be opened, yet may the vision of the soul be so purged of certain films of error as to enable it to reflect the glory of the spiritual universe, just as a single dew-drop is seen to mirror forth the magnificent cope of heaven with all its multitude of stars.

We have sought the truth, and how far we have found it, no one should proceed to determine without having first read and examined. We have sought it, not in Calvinism alone, nor in Arminianism alone, nor in any other creed or system of man's devising. In every direction have we diligently sought it, as our feeble abilities would permit; and yet, we hope, it will be found that the body of truth which we now have to offer is not a mere hasty patchwork of superficial eclecticism, but a living and organic whole. By this test we could wish to be tried; for, as Bacon hath well said, "It is the harmony of any philosophy in itself that giveth it light and credence." And in the application of this test, we could also wish, that the reader would so far forget his sectarian predilections, if he have any, as to permit his mind to be inspired by the immortal words of Milton, which we shall here adopt as a fitting conclusion of these our present remarks:—

"Truth, indeed, came once into the world with her divine Master, and was a perfect shape most glorious to look on; but when he ascended, and his apostles after him were laid asleep, then straight arose a wicked race of deceivers, who, as that story goes of the Egyptian Typhon, with his conspirators, how they dealt with the good Osiris, took the virgin, Truth, hewed her lovely form into a thousand pieces, and scattered them to the four winds. From that time ever since the sad friends of Truth, such as durst appear, imitating the careful search that Isis made for the mangled body of Osiris, went up and down gathering up limb by limb still as they could find them. We have not yet found them all, nor ever shall do, till her Master's second coming; he shall bring together every joint and member, and shall mould them into an immortal feature of loveliness and perfection. Suffer not these licensing prohibitions to stand at every place of opportunity, forbidding and disturbing them that continue seeking, that continue to do our obsequies to the torn body of our martyred saint. We boast our light; but if we look not wisely on the sun itself, it smites us into darkness. Who can discern those planets that are oft combust, and those stars of brightest magnitude, that rise and set with the sun, until the opposite motion of their orbs bring them to such a place in the firmament, where they may be seen morning or evening? The light which we have gained was given us, not to be ever staring on, but by it to discover onward things more remote from our knowledge. It is not the unfrocking of a priest, the unmitring of a bishop, and the removing him from off the Presbyterian shoulders, that will make us a happy nation; no, if other things as great in the Church, and in the rule of life, both economical and political, be not looked into and reformed, we have looked so long upon the blaze that Zuinglius and Calvin have beaconed up to us, that we are stark blind. There be who perpetually complain of schisms and sects, and make it such a calamity that any man dissents from their maxims. It is their own pride and ignorance which causes the disturbing, who neither will hear with meekness, nor can convince, yet all must be suppressed which is not found in their Syntagma. They are the troublers, they are the dividers of unity, who neglect and permit not others to unite those dissevered pieces which are yet wanting to the body of truth. To be still searching what we know not, by what we know, still closing up truth to truth as we find it, (for all her body is homogeneal and proportional,) this is the golden rule in theology as well as in arithmetic, and makes up the best harmony in a Church; not the forced and outward union of cold, and neutral, and inwardly-divided minds."

PART I.

THE EXISTENCE OF MORAL EVIL, OR SIN, CONSISTENT WITH THE HOLINESS OF GOD.

What Time this World's great Workmaister did cast,
  To make all things such as we now behold,
It seems that he before his eyes had plast
  A goodly patterne, to whose perfect mould
He fashion'd them as comely as he could,
That now so fair and seemly they appear,
As naught may be amended anywhere.

That wondrous patterne, wheresoe'er it be,
  Whether in earth laid up in secret store,
Or else in heav'n, that no man may it see
  With sinful eyes, for feare it to deflore,
Is perfect Beautie.

SPENSER.

A THEODICY.

PART I.

CHAPTER I.

THE SCHEME OF NECESSITY DENIES THAT MAN IS RESPONSIBLE FOR THE EXISTENCE OF SIN.

> Ye, who live,
> Do so each cause refer to Heaven above,
> E'en as its motion, of necessity,
> Drew with it all that moves. If this were so,
> Free choice in you were none; nor justice would
> There should be joy for virtue, woe for ill.—DANTE.

THE doctrine of necessity has been, in all ages of the world, the great stronghold of atheism. It is the mighty instrument with which the unbeliever seeks to strip man of all accountability, and to destroy our faith and confidence in God, by tracing up the existence of all moral evil to his agency. "The opinion of necessity," says Bishop Butler, "seems to be the very basis in which infidelity grounds itself." It will not be denied that this opinion seems, at first view, to be inconsistent with the free agency and accountability of man, and that it appears to impair our idea of God by staining it with impurity. Hence it has been used, by the profligate and profane, to excuse men for their crimes. It is against this use of the doctrine that we intend to direct the force of our argument.

But here the question arises: Can we refute the argument against the accountability of man, without attacking the doctrine on which it is founded? If we can meet this argument at all, it must be either by showing that no such consequence flows from the scheme of necessity, or by showing that the scheme itself is false. We cannot meet the sceptic, who seeks to excuse his sins, and to cast dishonour on God, and expose his sophistry, unless we can show that his premises are unsound, or that his conclusions are false. We must do the one or the other of these two things; or, whatever we may think of his moral sensibility, we must acknowledge the superiority of his reason and logic. After long and patient meditation on the subject, we have been forced to the conclusion, that the only way to repel the argument of the sceptic, and cause the intrinsic lustre of man's free-agency to appear, is to unravel and refute the doctrine of necessity.

If we could preserve the scheme of necessity, and at the same time avoid the consequences in question, we may fairly conclude that the means of doing so have been found by some of the illustrious advocates of that scheme. How, then, do they vindicate their own system? How do they repel the frightful consequences which infidelity deduces from it? This is the first question to be considered; and the discussion of it will occupy the remainder of the present chapter.

SECTION I.

The attempts of Calvin and Luther to reconcile the scheme of necessity with the responsibility of man.

Nothing can be more unjust than to bring, as has often been done, the unqualified charge of fatalism against the great Protestant reformers. The manner in which this odious epithet is frequently used, applying it without discrimination to the brightest ornaments and to the darkest specimens of humanity, is calculated to engender far more heat than light. Indeed, under this very ambiguous term, three distinct schemes of doctrine, widely different from each other, are set forth; schemes which every candid inquirer after truth should be careful to distinguish. The first is that scheme of fatalism which rests on the fundamental idea that there is nothing in the universe besides matter and local motion. This doctrine, of course, denies the spirituality of the Divine Being, as well as of all created souls, and strikes a fatal blow at the immutability of moral distinctions. It is unnecessary to say, that in such a sense of the word, neither Calvin nor Luther can be justly accused of fatalism; as it is well known that both of them maintained the spirituality of God, as well as the reality of moral distinctions prior to all human laws.

The second scheme of fatalism rises above the first in point of dignity and purity of character. It proceeds on the idea that all things in heaven and earth are bound together by "an implexed series and concatenation of causes:" it admits the existence of God, it is true, but yet it regards him as merely the greatest and brightest link in the adamantine universal chain of necessity. According to this scheme, as well as to the former, the very idea of moral liberty is inconceivable and impossible. This portentous scheme was perfectly understood and expressly repudiated by Calvin. In reference to this doctrine, which was maintained by the ancient Stoics, he says: "That dogma is falsely and maliciously charged upon us. For we do not, with the Stoics, imagine a necessity arising from a perpetual concatenation and intricate series of causes contained in nature; but we make God the Arbiter and Governor of all things, who, in his own wisdom, has, from all eternity, decreed what he would do, and now by his own power executes what he decreed."

Here we behold the nature of the third scheme, which has been included under the term *fatalism*. It recognises God as the great central and all-controlling power of the universe. It does not deny the possibility of liberty; for it recognises its actual existence in the Divine Being. "If the divine will," says Calvin, "has any cause, then there must be something antecedent, on which it depends; which it is impious to suppose." According to Calvin, it is the uncaused divine will which makes the "necessity of all things." He frequently sets forth the doctrine, that, from all eternity, God decreed whatever should come to pass, not excepting, but expressly including, the deliberations and "volitions of men," and by his own power now executes his decree. As we do not wish to use opprobrious names, we shall characterize these three several schemes of doctrine by the appellations given to them by their advocates. The first we shall call, "materialistic fatalism;" the second, "Stoical fatalism;" and the third we shall designate by the term, "*necessity*."

Widely as these schemes may differ in other respects, they have one feature in common: they all seem to bear with equal stringency on the human will, and deprive it of that freedom which is now conceded to be indispensable to render men accountable for their actions. If our volitions be produced by a series of causes, according to the Stoical notion of fate, or by the omnipotence of God, they would seem to be equally necessitated and devoid of freedom. Hence, in attacking one of these schemes at this point, we really attack them all. We shall first consider the question, then, How does Calvin attempt to reconcile his doctrine with the accountability of man? How does he show, for example, that the first man was guilty and justly punishable for a transgression in which he succumbed to the divine omnipotence?

If a man is really laid under a necessity of sinning, it would certainly seem impossible to conceive that he is responsible for his sins. Nay, it would not only seem impossible to conceive this, but it would also appear very easy to understand, that he could not be responsible for them. In order to remove this difficulty, and repel the attack of his opponents, Calvin makes a distinction between "co-action and necessity." "Now, when I assert," says he, "that the will, being deprived of its liberty, is necessarily drawn or led into evil, I should wonder if any one considered it as a harsh expression, since it has nothing in it absurd, nor is it unsanctioned by the custom of good men. It offends those who know not how to distinguish between necessity and compulsion."* Let us see, then, what is this distinction between necessity and compulsion, or co-action, (as Calvin sometimes calls it,) which is to take off all appearance of harshness from his views. We are not to imagine that this is a distinction without a difference; for, in truth, there is no distinction in philosophy which may be more easily made, or more clearly apprehended. It is this: Suppose a man wills a particular thing, or external action, and it is prevented from happening by any outward restraint; or suppose he is unwilling to do a thing, and he is constrained to do it against his will; he is said to labour under compulsion or co-action. Of course he is not accountable for the failure of the consequence of his will in the one case, nor for the consequence of the force imposed on his body in the other. This kind of necessity is called co-action by Calvin and Luther; it is usually denominated "natural necessity" by Edwards and his followers; though it is also frequently termed compulsion, or co-action, by them.

* Institutes, b. ii, c. iii.

This natural necessity, or co-action, it is admitted on all hands, destroys accountability for external conduct, wherever it obtains. Indeed, if a man is compelled to do a thing against his will, this is not, properly speaking, his act at all; nor is it an omission of his, if he wills to do a thing, and is necessarily prevented from doing it by external restraint. But it should be observed that natural necessity, or co-action, reaches no deeper than the external conduct; and can excuse for nothing else. As it does not influence the will itself, so it cannot excuse for acts of the will. Indeed, it presupposes the existence of a volition, or act of the will, whose natural consequences it counteracts and overcomes. Hence, if the question were—Is a man accountable for his external actions, that is, for the motions of his body, we might speak of natural necessity, or co-action, with propriety; but not so when the question relates to internal acts of the will. All reference to natural necessity, or co-action, in relation to such a question, is wholly irrelevant. No one doubts, and no one denies, that the motions of the body are controlled by the volitions of the mind, or by some external force. The advocates for the inherent activity and freedom of the mind, do not place them in the external sphere of matter, in the passive and necessitated movements of body: they seek not the living among the dead.

But to do justice to these illustrious men, they did not attempt, as many of their followers have done, to pass off this freedom from external co-action for the freedom of the will. Indeed, neither of them contended for the freedom of the will at all, nor deemed such freedom requisite to render men accountable for their actions. This is an element which has been wrought into their system by the subsequent progress of human knowledge. Luther, it is well known, so far from maintaining the freedom of the mind, wrote a work on the "Bondage of the Human Will," in reply to Erasmus. "I admit," says he, "that man's will is free in a certain sense; not because it is now in the same state it was in paradise, *but because it was made free originally, and may, through God's grace, become so again.*"* And Calvin, in his Institutes, has written a chapter to show that "man, in his present state, is despoiled of freedom of will, and subjected to a miserable slavery." He "was endowed

* Scott's Luther and Ref., vol. i, pp. 70, 71.

with free will," says Calvin, " by which, if he had chosen, he might have obtained eternal life."* Thus, according to both Luther and Calvin, man was by the fall despoiled of the freedom of the will.

Though they allow a freedom from co-action, they repudiate the idea of calling this a freedom of the will. "Lombard at length pronounces," says Calvin, "that we are not therefore possessed of free-will, because we have an equal power to do or to think either good or evil, *but only because we are free from constraint.* And this liberty is not diminished, although we are corrupt, and slaves of sin, *and capable of doing nothing but sin.* Then man will be said to possess free-will in this sense, not that he has an equally free election of good and evil, but because he does evil voluntarily, *and not by constraint.* That indeed, is true; but what end could it answer to deck out a thing so diminutive with a title so superb?"† Truly, if Lombard merely meant by the freedom of the will, for which he contended, a freedom from external restraint, or co-action, Calvin might well contemptuously exclaim, "Egregious liberty!"‡ It was reserved for a later period in the history of the Church to deck out this diminutive thing with the superb title of the freedom of the will, and to pass it off for the highest and most glorious liberty of which the human mind can form any conception. Hobbes, it will be hereafter seen, was the first who, either designedly or undesignedly, palmed off this imposture upon the world.

It is a remarkable fact, in the history of the human mind, that the most powerful and imposing arguments used by the early reformers to disprove the freedom of the will have been as confidently employed by their most celebrated followers to establish that very freedom on a solid basis. It is well known, for example, that Edwards, and many other great men, have employed the doctrine of the foreknowledge of God to prove philosophical necessity, without which they conclude there can be no rational foundation for the freedom of the will. Yet, in former times, this very doctrine was regarded as the most formidable instrument with which to overthrow and demolish that very freedom. Thus Luther calls the foreknowledge of God a thunderbolt to dash the doctrine of free-will into atoms. And

* Institutes, b. i, c. xv. † Ibid., b. ii, c. ii. ‡ Ibid.

who can forbear to agree with Luther so far as to say, that if the foreknowledge of God proves anything in opposition to the freedom of the will, it proves that it is under the most absolute and uncontrollable necessity? It clearly seems, that if it proves anything in favour of necessity, it proves everything for which the most absolute necessitarian can contend. Accordingly, a distinguished Calvinistic divine has said, that if our volitions be foreseen, we can no more avoid them "than we can pluck the sun out of the heavens."*

But though the reformers were thus, in some respects, more true to their fundamental principle than their followers have been, we are not to suppose that they are free from all inconsistencies and self-contradiction. Thus, if "foreknowledge is a thunderbolt" to dash the doctrine of free-will into atoms, it destroyed free-will in man before the fall as well as after. Hence the thunderbolt of Luther falls upon his own doctrine, that man possessed free-will in his primitive state, with as much force as it can upon the doctrine of his opponents. He is evidently caught in the toils he so confidently prepared for his adversary. And how many of the followers of the great reformer adopt his doctrine, and wield his thunderbolts, without perceiving how destructively they recoil on themselves! Though they ascribe free-will to man as one of the elements of his pristine glory, yet they employ against it in his present condition arguments which, if good for anything, would despoil, not only man, but the whole universe of created intelligences—nay, the great Uncreated Intelligence himself—of every vestige and shadow of such a power.

It is a wonderful inconsistency in Luther, that he should so often and so dogmatically assert that the doctrine of free-will falls prostrate before the prescience of God, and at the same time maintain the freedom of the divine will. If foreknowledge is incompatible with the existence of free-will, it is clear that the will of God is not free; since it is on all sides conceded that all his volitions are perfectly foreseen by him. Yet in the face of this conclusion, which so clearly and so irresistibly follows from Luther's position, he asserts the freedom of the divine will, as if he were perfectly unconscious of the self-contradiction in which he is involved. "It now then follows," says he, "that

* Dick's Theology.

free-will is plainly a divine term, and can be applicable to none but the Divine Majesty only."* . . . . He even says, If free-will "be ascribed unto men, it is not more properly ascribed, than the divinity of God himself would be ascribed unto them; which would be the greatest of all sacrilege. Wherefore, it becomes theologians to refrain from the use of this term altogether, whenever they wish to speak of human ability, and to leave it to be applied to God only."† And we may add, if they would apply it to God, it becomes them to refrain from all such arguments as would show even such an application of it to be absurd.

In like manner, Calvin admits that the human soul possessed a free-will in its primitive state, but has been despoiled of it by the fall, and is now in bondage to a "miserable slavery." But if the necessity which arises from the power of sin over the will be inconsistent with its freedom, how are we to reconcile the freedom of the first man with the power exercised by the Almighty over the wills of all created beings? So true it is, that the most systematic thinker, who begins by denying the truth, will be sure to end by contradicting himself.

In one respect, as we have seen, Calvin differs from his followers at the present day; the denial of free-will he regards as perfectly reconcilable with the idea of accountability. Although our volitions are absolutely necessary to us, although they may be produced in us by the most uncontrollable power in the universe, yet are we accountable for them, because they are our volitions. The bare fact that we will such and such a thing, without regard to how we come by the volition, is sufficient to render us accountable for it. We must be free from an external *co-action*, he admits, to render us accountable for our external actions; but not from an internal necessity, to render us accountable for our internal volitions. But this does not seem to be a satisfactory reply to the difficulty in question. We ask, How a man can be accountable for his acts, for his volitions, if they are caused in him by an infinite power? and we are told, Because they are *his* acts. This eternal repetition of the fact in which all sides are agreed, can throw no light on the point about which we dispute. We still ask, How can a man be responsible for an act, or volition, which is necessitated

* Bondage of the Will, sec. xxvi. † Ibid.

to arise in his mind by Omnipotence? If any one should reply, with Dr. Dick, that we do not know how he can be accountable for such an act, yet we should never deny a thing because we cannot see how it is; this would not be a satisfactory answer. For, though it is certainly the last weakness of the human mind to deny a thing, because we cannot see how it is; yet there is a great difference between not being able to see *how a thing is*, and being clearly able to see that it *cannot be anyhow at all*,—between being unable to see how two things agree together, and being able to see that two ideas are utterly repugnant to each other. Hence we mean to ask, that if a man's act be necessitated in him by an infinite, omnipotent power, over which he had, and could have, no possible control, can we not see that he *cannot* be accountable for it? We have no difficulty whatever in believing a mystery; but when we are required to embrace what so plainly seems to be an absurdity, we confess that our reason is either weak enough, or strong enough, to pause and reluctate.

SECTION II.

The manner in which Hobbes, Collins, and others, endeavour to reconcile necessity with free and accountable agency.

The celebrated philosopher of Malmsbury viewed all things as bound together in the relation of cause and effect; and he was, beyond doubt, one of the most acute thinkers that ever advocated the doctrine of necessity. From some of the sentiments expressed towards the conclusion of "The Leviathan," which have, not without reason, subjected him to the charge of atheism, we may doubt his entire sincerity when he pretends to advocate the doctrine of necessity out of a zeal for the Divine Sovereignty and the dogma of Predestination. If he hoped by this avowal of his design to propitiate any class of theologians, he must have been greatly disappointed; for his speculations were universally condemned by the Christian world as atheistical in their tendency. This charge has been fixed upon him, in spite of his solemn protestations against its injustice, and his earnest endeavours to reconcile his scheme of necessity with the free-agency and accountability of man.

"I conceive," says Hobbes, "that nothing taketh beginning

from itself, but from the action of some other immediate agent without itself. And that therefore, when first a man hath an appetite or will to something, to which immediately before he had no appetite nor will, the cause of his will is not the will itself, but something else not in his own disposing; so that it is out of controversy, that of voluntary actions the will is the necessary cause, and by this which is said, the will is also caused by other things whereof it disposeth not, it followeth, that voluntary actions have all of them necessary causes, and therefore are necessitated." This is clear and explicit. There is no controversy, he truly says, that voluntary actions, that is, external actions proceeding from the will, are necessitated by the will. And as according to his postulate, the will or volition is also caused by other things of which it has no disposal, so they are also necessitated. In other words, external voluntary actions are necessarily caused by volitions, and volitions are necessarily caused by something else other than the will; and consequently the chain is complete between the cause of volition and its effects. How, then, is man a free-agent? and how is he accountable for his actions? Hobbes has not left these questions unanswered; and it is a mistake to suppose, as is too often done, that his argument in favour of necessity evinces a design to sap the foundations of human responsibility.

He answers these questions precisely as they were answered by Luther and Calvin more than a hundred years before his time. In order to solve this great difficulty, and establish an agreement between necessity and liberty, he insists on the distinction between co-action and necessity. Sir James Mackintosh says, that "in his treatise *de Servo Arbitrio* against Erasmus, Luther states the distinction between co-action and necessity as familiar a hundred and fifty years before it was proposed by Hobbes, or condemned in the Jansenists."* According to his definition of liberty, it is merely a freedom from co-action, or external compulsion. "I conceive liberty," says he, "to be rightly

* Progress of Ethical Philosophy, note O. Indeed, this distinction appears quite as clearly in the writings of Augustine, as it does in those of Luther, or Calvin, or Hobbes. He repeatedly places our liberty and ability in this, that we can "keep the commandments *if we will,*" which is obviously a mere freedom from external co-action. See Part ii, ch. iv, sec. 2.

defined in this manner: Liberty is the absence of all the impediments to action that are not contained in the nature and intrinsical qualities of the agent: as for example, the water is said to descend freely, or to have liberty to descend by the channel of the river, because there is no impediment that way; but not across, because the banks are impediments; and though the water cannot ascend, yet men never say it wants liberty to ascend, but the faculty or power, because the impediment is in the nature of the water and intrinsical." According to this definition, though a man's volitions were thrown out, not by himself, but by some irresistible power working within his mind, say the power of the Almighty, yet he would be free, provided there were no impediments to prevent the external effects of his volitions. This is the liberty which water, impelled by the power of gravity, possesses in descending the channel of a river. It is the liberty of the winds and waves of the sea, which, by a sort of metaphor, is supposed to reign over the dominions of a mechanical and materialistic fate. It is the most idle of all idle things to speak of such a liberty, *or rather, to use the word in such a sense*, when the controversy relates to the freedom of the mind itself. What has such a thing to do with the origin of human volitions, or the nature of moral agency? Is there no difference between the motion of the body and the action of mind? Or is there nothing in the universe of God but mere body and local motion? If there is not, then, indeed, we neither have nor can conceive any higher liberty than that which the philosopher is pleased to allow us to possess; but if there be mind, then there may be things in heaven and earth which are not dreamed of in his philosophy.

The definition which Collins, the disciple of Hobbes, has given of liberty, is the same as that of his master. "I contend," says he, "for liberty, as it signifies a power in man to do as he wills or pleases." The doing here refers to the external action, which, properly speaking, is not an act at all, but merely a change of state in the body. The body merely *suffers* a change of place and position, in obedience to the act of the will; it does not act, nor can it act, because it is passive in its nature. To *do* as one wills, in this sense, is a freedom of the body from co-action; it is not a freedom of the will from internal necessity. Collins says this is "a valuable liberty," and he says truly; for if one were thrown into prison, he could not go wherever he might please, or do as he might will. But the imprisonment of the body does not prevent a man from being a free-agent. He also tells us truly, that "many philosophers and theologians, both ancient and modern, have given definitions of liberty that are consistent with fate and necessity." But then, their definitions, like his own, had no reference to the acts of the mind, but to the motions of the body; and it is a grand irrelevancy, we repeat, to speak of such a thing, when the question relates, not to the freedom of the body, but the freedom of the mind. Calvin truly says, that to call this external freedom from co-action or natural necessity a freedom of the will, is to decorate a most diminutive thing with a superb title; but the philosopher of Malmsbury, and his ingenious disciple, seem disposed to confer the high-sounding title and empty name on us, in order to reconcile us to the servitude and chains in which they have been pleased to bind us.

This idea of liberty, common to Hobbes and Collins, which Mackintosh says was familiar to Luther and Calvin at least a hundred and thirty years before, is in reality of much earlier origin. It was maintained by the ancient Stoics, by whom it is as clearly set forth as by Hobbes himself. The well-known illustration of the Stoic Chrysippus, so often mentioned by Leibnitz and others, is a proof of the correctness of this remark: "Suppose I push against a heavy body," says he: "if it be square, it will not move; if it be cylindrical, it will. What the difference of form is to the stone, the difference of disposition is to the mind." Thus his notion of freedom was derived from matter, and supposed to consist in the absence of friction! The idea of liberty thus deduced from that which is purely and perfectly passive, from an absolutely necessitated state of body, was easily reconciled by him with his doctrine of fate.

Is it not strange that Mr. Hazlitt, after adopting this definition of liberty, should have supposed that he allowed a real freedom to the will? "I prefer exceedingly," says he, "to the modern instances of a couple of billiard-balls, or a pair of scales, the illustration of Chrysippus." We cannot very well see, how the instance of a cylinder is so great an improvement on that of a billiard-ball; especially as a sphere, and not a cylinder, is free to move in all directions.

The truth is, we must quit the region of dead, inert, passive matter, if we would form an idea of the true meaning of the term liberty, as applied to the activity of living agents. Mr. Hazlitt evidently loses himself amid the ambiguities of language, when he says, that "I so far agree with Hobbes and differ from Locke, in thinking that liberty, in the most extended and abstracted sense, is applicable to *material as well as voluntary agents.*" Still this very acute writer makes a few feeble and ineffectual efforts to raise our notion of the liberty of moral agents above that given by the illustration of Chrysippus in Cicero. "My notion of a free agent, I confess," says he, "is not that represented by Mr. Hobbes, namely, one that when all things necessary to produce the effect are present, can nevertheless not produce it; but I believe a free-agent of whatever kind is one which, where all things necessary to produce the effect are present, can produce it; its own operation not being hindered by anything else. The body is said to be free when it has the power to obey the direction of the will; so the will may be said to be free when it has the power to obey the dictates of the understanding."* Thus the liberty of the will is made to consist not in the denial that its volitions are produced, but in the absence of impediments which might hinder its operations from taking effect. This idea of liberty, it is evident, is perfectly consistent with the materialistic fatalism of Hobbes, which is so much admired by Mr. Hazlitt.

SECTION III.

The sentiments of Descartes, Spinoza, and Malebranche, concerning the relation between liberty and necessity.

No one was ever more deeply implicated in the scheme of necessity than Descartes. "Mere philosophy," says he, "is enough to make us know that there cannot enter the least thought into the mind of man, but God must will and have willed from all eternity that it should enter there." His argument in proof of this position is short and intelligible. "God," says he, "could not be absolutely perfect if there could happen anything in this world which did not spring entirely from him." Hence it follows, that it is inconsistent with the absolute per-

* Literary Remains, p. 65.

fections of God to suppose that a being created by him could put forth a volition which does not spring entirely from him, and not even in part from the creature.

Yet Descartes is a warm believer in the doctrine of free-will. On the ground of reason, he believes in an absolute predestination of all things; and yet he concludes from experience that man is free. If we ask how these things can hang together, he replies, that we cannot tell; that a solution of this difficulty lies beyond the reach of the human faculties. Now, it is evident, that reason cannot "make us know" one thing, and experience teach another, quite contrary to it; for no two truths can ever contradict each other. Those who adopt this mode of viewing the subject, generally remind us of the feebleness of human reason, and of the necessary limits to all human speculation. Though, as disciples of Butler, we are deeply impressed with these truths, yet, as disciples of Bacon, we do not intend to despair until we can discover some good and sufficient reason for so doing. It seems to us, that the reply of Leibnitz to Descartes, already alluded to, is not without reason. "It might have been an evidence of humility in Descartes," says he, "if he had confessed his own inability to solve the difficulty in question; but not satisfied with confessing for himself, he does so for all intelligences and for all times."

But, after all, Descartes has really endeavoured to solve the problem which he declared insoluble; that is, to reconcile the infinite perfections of God with the free-agency of man. He struggles to break loose from this dark mystery; but, like the charmed bird, he struggles and flutters in vain, and finally yields to its magical influence. In his solution, this great luminary of science, like others before him, seems to suffer a sad eclipse. "Before God sent us into the world," says he, "he knew exactly what all the inclinations of our wills would be; *it is he that has implanted them in us;* it is he also that has disposed all things, so that such or such objects should present themselves to us at such or such times, by means of which he has known that our free-will would determine us to such or such actions, *and he has willed that it should be so; but he has not willed to constrain us thereto.*" This is found in a letter to the Princess Elizabeth, for whose benefit he endeavoured to reconcile the liberty of man with the perfections of God. It brings us back to the old distinction between necessity and co-action. God brings our volitions to pass; he wills them; they "spring entirely from him;" but we are nevertheless free, because he constrains not our external actions, or compels us to do anything contrary to our wills! We cannot suppose, however, that this solution of the problem made a very clear or deep impression on the mind of Descartes himself, or he would not, on other occasions, have pronounced every attempt at the solution of it vain and hopeless.

In his attempt to reconcile the free-agency of man with the divine perfections, Descartes deceives himself by a false analogy. Thus he supposes that a monarch "*who has forbidden* duelling, and who, certainly knowing that two gentlemen will fight, if they should meet, *employs infallible means to bring them together*. They meet, they fight each other: their disobedience of the laws is an effect of their free-will; they are punishable." "What a king can do in such a case," he adds, "God who has an infinite power and prescience, infallibly does in relation to all the actions of men." But the king, in the supposed case, does not act on the minds of the duellists; their disposition to disobey the laws does not proceed from him; whereas, according to the theory of Descartes, nothing enters into the mind of man which does not spring entirely from God. If we suppose a king, who has direct access to the mind of his subject, like God, and who employs his power to excite therein a murderous intent or any other particular disposition to disobey the law, we shall have a more apposite representation of the divine agency according to the theory of Descartes. Has anything ever been ascribed to the agency of Satan himself which could more clearly render him an accomplice in the sins of men?

From the bosom of Cartesianism two systems arose, one in principle, but widely different in their developments and ultimate results. We allude to the celebrated schemes of Spinoza and Malebranche. Both set out with the same exaggerated view of the sublime truth that God is all in all; and each gave a diverse development to this fundamental position, to this central idea, according as the logical faculty predominated over the moral, or the moral faculty over the logical. Father Malebranche, by a happy inconsistency, preserved the great moral interests of the world against the invasion of a remorseless logic.

Spinoza, on the contrary, could follow out his first principle almost to its last consequence, even to the entire extinction of the moral light of the universe, and the enthronement of blind power, with as little concern, with as profound composure, as if he were merely discussing a theorem in the mathematics.

"All things," says he, "determined to such and such actions, are determined by God; and, if God determines not a thing to act, it cannot determine itself."* From this proposition he drew the inference, that things which are produced by God, could not have existed in any other manner, nor in any other order.† Thus, by the divine power, all things in heaven and earth are bound together in the iron circle of necessity. It required no great logical foresight to perceive that this doctrine shut all real liberty out of the created universe; but it did require no little moral firmness, or very great moral insensibility, to declare such a consequence with the unflinching audacity which marks its enunciation by Spinoza. He repeatedly declares, in various modes of expression, that "the soul is a spiritual automaton," and possesses no such liberty as is usually ascribed to it. All is necessary, and the very notion of a free-will is a vulgar prejudice. "All I have to say," he coolly remarks, "to those who believe that they can speak or keep silence—in one word, can act—by virtue of a free decision of the soul, is, that they dream with their eyes open."‡ Though he thus boldly denies all free-will, according to the common notion of mankind; yet, no less than Hobbes and Collins, he allows that the soul possesses "a sort of liberty." "It is free," says he, in the act of affirming that "two and two are equal to four;" thus finding the freedom of the soul which he is pleased to allow the world to possess in the most perfect type of necessity it is possible to conceive.

But Spinoza does not employ this idea of liberty, nor any other, to show that man is a responsible being. This is not at all strange; the wonder is, that after having *demonstrated* that "the prejudice of men concerning *good* and *evil*, merit and demerit, praise and blame, order and confusion, beauty and deformity," are nothing but dreams, he should have felt bound to defend the position, that we may be justly punished for our

* Ethique, premiere partie, prop. xxvi. † Ibid., prop. xxxiv.

‡ Ethique, Des Passions, prop. ii and Scholium.

offences by the Supreme Ruler of the world. His defence of this doctrine we shall lay before the reader without a word of comment. "Will you say," he replies to Oldenburg, "that God cannot be angry with the wicked, or that all men are worthy of beatitude? In regard to the first point, I perfectly agree that God cannot be angry at anything which happens according to his decree, but I deny that it results that all men ought to be happy; for men can be excusable, and at the same time be deprived of beatification, and made to suffer a thousand ways. A horse is excusable for being a horse, and not a man; but that prevents not that he ought to be a horse, and not a man. He who is rendered mad by the bite of a dog, is surely excusable, and yet we ought to constrain him. In like manner, the man who cannot govern his passions, nor restrain them by the fear of the laws, though excusable on account of the infirmity of his nature, can nevertheless not enjoy peace, nor the knowledge and the love of God; and it is necessary that he should perish."*

It was as difficult for Father Malebranche to restrain his indignation at the system of Spinoza, as it was for him to expose its fallacy, after having admitted its great fundamental principle. This is well illustrated by the facts stated by M. Saisset: "When Mairan," says he, "still young, and having a strong passion for the study of the 'Ethique,' requested Malebranche to guide him in that perilous route; we know with what urgency, bordering on importunity, he pressed the illustrious father to show him the weak point of Spinozism, the precise place where the rigour of the reasoning failed, the *paralogism* contained in the demonstration. Malebranche eluded the question, and could not assign the *paralogism*, after which Mairan so earnestly sought: 'It is not that the paralogism is in such or such places of the *Ethique*, it is everywhere.'"† In this impatient judgment, Father Malebranche uttered more truth than he could very well perceive; the paralogism is truly everywhere, because this whole edifice of words, "this frightful chimera," is really assumed in the arbitrary definition of the term substance. We might say with equal truth, that the fallacy of Malebranche's scheme is also everywhere; for although it stops

* Œuvres de Spinoza, tome ii, 350.

† Introduction to the "Œuvres de Spinoza," by M. Saisset.

short of the consequences so sternly deduced by Spinoza, it sets out from the same distorted view of the sovereignty and dominion of God, from which those consequences necessarily flow.

Spinoza, who had but few followers during his lifetime, has been almost idolized by the most celebrated savans of modern Germany. Whether this will ultimately add to the glory of Spinoza, or detract from that of his admirers, we shall leave the reader and posterity to determine. In the mean time, we shall content ourselves with a statement of the fact, in the language of M. Saisset: "Everything," says he, "appears extraordinary in Spinoza; his person, his style, his philosophy; but that which is more strange still, is the destiny of that philosophy among men. Badly known, despised by the most illustrious of his contemporaries, Spinoza died in obscurity, and remained buried during a century. All at once his name reappeared with an extraordinary eclat; his works were read with passion; a new world was discovered in them, with a horizon unknown to our fathers; and the god of Spinoza, which the seventeenth century had broken as an idol, became the god of Lessing, of Goethe, of Novalis."

"The solitary thinker whom Malebranche called a wretch, Schleiermacher reveres and invokes as equal to a saint. That 'systematic atheist,' on whom Bayle lavished outrage, has been for modern Germany the most religious of men. 'God-intoxicated,' as Novalis said, 'he has seen the world through a thick cloud, and man has been to his troubled eyes only a fugitive mode of Being in itself.' In that system, in fine, so shocking and so monstrous, that 'hideous chimera,' Jacobi sees the last word of philosophy, Schelling the presentiment of the true philosophy."

SECTION IV.

The views of Locke, Tucker, Hartley, Priestley, Helvetius, and Diderot, with respect to the relation between liberty and necessity.

Locke, it is well known, adopted the notions of free-agency given by Hobbes. "In this," says he, "consists freedom, viz., in our being able to act or not to act, according as we shall choose or will."* And this notion of liberty, consisting in a

* Book ii, chapters 21, 27.

freedom from external co-action, has received an impetus and currency from the influence of Locke which it would not otherwise have obtained. Neither Calvin nor Luther, as we have seen, pretended to hold it up as the freedom of the will. This was reserved for Hobbes and his immortal follower, John Locke, who has, in his turn, been copied by a host of illustrious disciples who would have recoiled from the more articulate and consistent development of this doctrine by the philosopher of Malmsbury. It is only because Locke has enveloped it in a cloud of inconsistencies that it has been able to secure the veneration of the great and good.

It is remarkable, that although Locke adopted the definition of free-will given by Hobbes, and which the latter so easily reconciled with the omnipotence and omniscience of God; yet he expressly declares that he had found it impossible to reconcile those attributes in the Divine Being with the free-agency of man. Surely no such difficulty could have existed, if his definition of free-agency, or free-will, be correct; for although omnipotence itself might produce our volitions, we might still be free to act, to move in accordance with our volitions. But the truth is, there was something more in Locke's thoughts and feelings, in the inmost working of his nature, with respect to moral liberty, than there was in his definition. The inconsistency and fluctuation of his views on this all-important subject are fully reflected in his chapter on power.

Both in Great Britain and France, the most illustrious successors of Locke soon delivered themselves from his inconsistencies and self-contradictions. Hartley was not in all respects a follower of Locke, it is true, though he admitted his definition of free-agency. "It appears to me," says Hartley, "that all the most complex ideas arise from sensation, and that *reflection is not a distinct source*, as Mr. Locke makes it." By this mutilation of the philosophy of Locke, it was reduced back to that dead level of materialism in which Hobbes had left it, and from which the former had scarcely endeavoured to raise it. Hence arose the rigid scheme of necessity, for which Hartley is so zealous an advocate. In reading his treatise on the "Mechanism of the Human Mind," we are irresistibly compelled to feel the conviction that the only circumstance which prevents the movements of the soul from being subjected to mathematical calculation, and made a branch of dynamics, is the want of a measure of the force of motives. If this want were supplied, then the philosophy of the mind might be, according to his view of its nature and operations, converted into a portion of mechanics. Yet this excellent man did not imagine for a moment that he upheld a scheme which is at war with the great moral interests of the world. He supposes it is no matter how we come by our volitions, provided our bodies be left free to obey the impulses of the will; this is amply sufficient to render us accountable for our actions, and to vindicate the moral government of God. Thus did he fall asleep with a specious, but most superficial dream of liberty, which has no more to do with the real question concerning the moral agency of man than if it related to the winds of heaven or to the waves of the sea. Accordingly this is the view of liberty which he repeatedly holds up as all-sufficient to secure the great moral interest of the human race.

His great disciple, Dr. Priestley, pursues precisely the same course. "If a man," says he, "be wholly a material being, and the power of thinking the result of a certain organization of the brain, does it not follow that all his functions must be regulated by the laws of mechanism, and that of consequence his actions proceed from an irresistible necessity?" And again, he observes, "the doctrine of necessity is the immediate result of the materiality of man, for mechanism is the undoubted consequence of materialism."* Priestley, however, allows us to possess free-will as defined by Hobbes, Locke, and Hartley.

Helvetius himself could easily admit such a liberty into his unmitigated scheme of necessity, but he did not commit the blunder of Locke and Hartley, in supposing that it bore on the great question concerning the freedom of the mind. "It is true," he says, "we can form a tolerably distinct idea of the word *liberty*, understood in its common sense. *A man is free who is neither loaded with irons nor confined in prison*, nor intimidated like the slave with the dread of chastisement: in this sense the liberty of man consists in the free exercise of his power; I say, of his power, because it would be ridiculous to mistake for a want of liberty the incapacity we are under to pierce the clouds like the eagle, to live under the water like the

* Disquisitions and Introduction, p. 5.

whale, or to become king, emperor, or pope. We have so far a sufficiently clear idea of the word. But this is no longer the case when we come to apply liberty to the will. What must this liberty then mean? We can only understand by it a free power of willing or not willing a thing: but this power would imply that there may be a will without motives, and consequently an effect without a cause. A philosophical treatise on *the liberty of the will* would be a treatise of effects without a cause."*

In like manner, Diderot had the sagacity to perceive that the idea of liberty, as defined by Locke, did not at all come into conflict with his portentous scheme of irreligion, which had grounded itself on the doctrine of necessity. Having pronounced the term liberty, as applied to the will, to be a word without meaning, he proceeds to justify the infliction of punishment on the same grounds on which it is vindicated by Hobbes and Spinoza. "But if there is no liberty," says he, "there is no action that merits either praise or blame, neither vice nor virtue, nothing that ought to be either rewarded or punished. What then is the distinction among men? The doing of good and the doing of evil! The doer of ill is one who must be destroyed, not punished. The doer of good is lucky, not virtuous. But though neither the doer of good nor of ill be free, man is, nevertheless, a being to be modified; it is for this reason the doer of ill should be destroyed upon the scaffold. From thence the good effects of education, of pleasure, of grief, of grandeur, of poverty, &c.; from thence a philosophy full of pity, strongly attached to the good, nor more angry with the wicked than with the whirlwind which fills one's eyes with dust." . . . . . "Adopt these principles if you think them good, or show me that they are bad. If you adopt them, they will reconcile you *too* with others and with yourself: you will neither be pleased nor angry with yourself for being what you are. Reproach others for nothing, and repent of nothing, this is the first step to wisdom. Besides this all is prejudice and false philosophy."

Though these consequences irresistibly flow from the doctrine of necessity, yet the injury resulting from them would be far less if they were maintained only by such men as Helvetius and Diderot. It is when such errors receive the sanction of

* Helvetius on the Mind, p. 44.

Christian philosophers, like Hartley and Leibnitz, and are recommended to the human mind by a pious zeal for the glory of God, that they are apt to obtain a frightful currency and become far more desolating in their effects. "The doctrine of necessity," says Hartley, "has a tendency to abate all resentment against men: *since all they do against us is by the appointment of God, it is rebellion against him to be offended with them.*"

SECTION V.

The manner in which Leibnitz endeavours to reconcile liberty and necessity.

Leibnitz censures the language of Descartes, in which he ascribes all the thoughts and volitions of men to God, and complains that he thereby shuts out free-agency from the world. It becomes a very curious question, then, how Leibnitz himself, who was so deeply implicated in the scheme of necessity, has been able to save the great interests of morality. He does not, for a moment, call in question "the great demonstration from cause and effect" in favour of necessity. It is well known that he has more than once compared the human mind to a balance, in which reasons and inclinations take the place of weights; he supposes it to be just as impossible for the mind to depart from the direction given to it by "the determining cause," as it is for a balance to turn in opposition to the influence of the greatest weight.

Nor is he pleased with Descartes's appeal to consciousness to prove the doctrine of liberty. In reply to this appeal, he says: "The chain of causes connected one with another reaches very far. Wherefore the reason alleged by Descartes, in order to prove the independence of our free actions, by a pretended vigorous internal feeling, has no force.* We cannot, strictly speaking, feel our independence; and we do not always perceive the causes, frequently imperceptible, on which our resolution depends. It is as if a needle touched with the loadstone were sensible of and pleased with its turning toward the north.

* Mr. Stewart says: "Dr. Hartley was, I believe, one of the first (if not the first) who denied that our consciousness is in favour of our free-agency."—*Stewart's Works*, vol. v, Appendix. This is evidently a mistake. In the above passage, Leibnitz, with even more point than Hartley, denies that our consciousness is in favour of free-agency.

For it would believe that it turned itself, independently of any other cause, not perceiving the insensible motions of the magnetic matter."* Thus, he seems to represent the doctrine of liberty as a mere dream and delusion of the mind, and the iron scheme of necessity as a stern reality. Is it in the power of Leibnitz, then, any more than it was in that of Descartes, to reconcile such a scheme with the free-agency and accountability of man? Let us hear him and determine.

Leibnitz repudiates the notion of liberty given by Hobbes and Locke. In his "Nouveaux Essais sur L'Entendement Humain," a work in which he combats many of the doctrines of Locke, the insignificance of his idea of the freedom of the will is most clearly and triumphantly exposed. Philalethe, or the representative of Locke, says: "Liberty is the power that a man has to do or not to do an action *according to his will.*" Theophile, or the representative of Leibnitz, replies: "If men understood only that by liberty, when they ask whether the will is free, their question would be truly absurd." And again: "The question ought not to be asked," says Philalethe, "if the will is free: that is to speak in a very improper manner: but if man is free. This granted, I say that, when any one can, by the direction or choice of his mind, prefer the existence of one action to the non-existence of that action and to the contrary, that is to say, when he can make it exist or not exist, *according to his will*, then he is free. *And we can scarcely see how it could be possible to conceive a being more free than one who is capable of doing what he wills.*" Theophile rejoins: "When we reason concerning the liberty of the will, we do not demand if the man can do what he wills, but if he has a sufficient independence in the will itself; we do not ask if he has free limbs or elbow-room, but if the mind is free, and in what that freedom consists."†

* Essais de Theodicee, p. 99.

† "Hobbes defines a free-agent," says Stewart, "to be 'he that can do if he will, and forbear if he will.' The same definition has been adopted by Leibnitz, by Collins, by Gravezende, by Edwards, by Bonnet, and by all later necessitarians." The truth is, as we have seen, that instead of adopting, Leibnitz has very clearly refuted, the definition of Hobbes. Mr. Harris, in his work entitled "The Primeval Man," has also fallen into the error of ascribing this definition of liberty to Leibnitz. Surely, these very learned authors must have forgotten, that Leibnitz wrote a reply to Hobbes, in which he expressly combats his views of liberty.

Having thus exploded the delusive notion of liberty which Locke had borrowed from Hobbes, Leibnitz proceeds to take what seems to be higher ground. He expressly declares, that in order to constitute man an accountable agent, he must be free, not only from constraint, but also from necessity. In the adoption of this language, Leibnitz seems to speak with the advocates of free-agency; but does he think with them? The sound is pleasant to the ear; but what sense is it intended to convey to the mind? Leibnitz shall be his own interpreter. "All events have their necessary causes," says Hobbes. "Bad," replies Leibnitz: "they have their *determining* causes, by which we can assign a reason for them; but they have not necessary causes." Now does this signify that an event, that a volition, is not absolutely and indissolubly connected with its "determining cause?" Is this the grand idea from which the light of liberty is to beam on a darkened and enslaved world? By no means. We must indulge no fond hopes or idle dreams of the kind. Volition is free from necessity, adds Leibnitz; because "*the contrary could happen without implying a contradiction.*" This is the signification which he attaches to his own language; and it is the only meaning of which it is susceptible in accordance with his system. Thus, Leibnitz saw and clearly exposed the futility of speaking about a freedom from co-action or restraint, when the question is, not whether the body is untrammelled, but whether the mind itself is free in the act of willing. But he did not see, it seems, that it is equally irrelevant to speak of a freedom from a mathematical necessity in such a connexion; although this, as plainly as the other sense of the word, has no conceivable bearing on the point in dispute. If a volition were produced by the omnipotence of God, irresistibly acting on the human mind, still it would not be necessary, in the sense of Leibnitz, since it might and would have been different if God had so willed it; the contrary volition implying no contradiction. Is it not evident, that to suppose the mind may thus be bound to act, and yet be free because the contrary act implies no contradiction, is merely to dream of liberty, and to mistake a shadow for a substance?

As the opposite of a volition implies no contradiction, says Leibnitz, so it is free from an absolute necessity; that is to say, it might have been different, nay, it must have been different, from what it is, provided its determining cause had been different. The same thing may be said of the motions of matter. We may say that they are also free, because the opposite motions imply no contradiction; and we only have to vary the force in order to vary the motion. Hence, freedom in this sense of the word is perfectly consistent with the absolute and uncontrolled dominion of causes over the will; for what can be more completely necessitated than the motions of the body?

The demand of his own nature, which so strongly impelled Leibnitz to seek and cling to the freedom of the mind, as the basis of moral and accountable agency, could not rest satisfied with so unsubstantial a shadow. After all, he has felt constrained to have recourse to the hypothesis of a preëstablished harmony in order to restore, if possible, the liberty which his scheme of necessity had banished from the universe. It is no part of our intention to examine this obsolete fiction; we merely wish to show how essential Leibnitz regarded it to a solution of the difficulty under consideration. "I come now," says he, "to show how the action of the will depends on causes; that there is nothing so agreeable to human nature as this dependence of our actions, and that otherwise we should fall into an absurd and insupportable fatality; that is to say, into the *Mohammedan fate*, which is the worst of all, because it does away with foresight and good counsel. However, it is well to explain how this dependency of our voluntary actions does not prevent that there may be at the bottom of things a marvellous spontaneity in us, which in a certain sense renders the mind, in its resolutions, independent of the physical influence of *all other creatures*. This spontaneity, *but little known hitherto*, which raises our empire over our actions as much as it is possible, *is a consequence of the system of preëstablished harmony*." Thus, in order to satisfy himself that our actions are really free and independent of the physical influence of *other creatures*, he has recourse to a fiction in which few persons ever concurred with him, and which is now universally regarded as one of the vagaries and dreams of philosophy. If we are to be saved from an insupportable fate only by such means, our condition must indeed be one of forlorn hopelessness.

Before we take leave of Leibnitz, there is one view of the difficulty in question which we wish to notice, not because it is peculiar to him, but because it is very clearly stated and confidently relied on by him. It is common to most of the advocates of necessity, and it is exceedingly imposing in its appearance and effect. "Men of all times," says he, "have been troubled by a sophism, which the ancients called the '*raison paresseuse*,' because it induces them to do nothing, or at least to concern themselves about nothing, and to follow only the present inclination to pleasure. For, say they, if the future is necessary, that which is to happen will happen whatever I may do. But the future, say they, is necessary, either because the Divinity foresees all things, and even preëstablishes them in governing the universe; or because all things necessarily come to pass by a concatenation of causes."* Leibnitz illustrated the fallacy of this reasoning in the following manner: "By the same reason (if it is valid) I could say—If it is written in the archives of fate, that poison will kill me at present, or do me harm, this will happen, though I should not take it; and if that is not written, it will not happen, though I should take it; and, consequently, I can follow my inclination to take whatever is agreeable with impunity, however pernicious it may be; which involves a manifest absurdity. . . . This objection staggers them a little, but they always come back to their reasoning, turned in different points of view, until we cause them to comprehend in what the defect of their sophism consists. It is this, that it is false that the event will happen whatever we may do; it will happen, because we do that which leads to it; and if the event is written, the cause which will make it happen is also written. Thus the connexion (*liaison*) of effects and their causes, so far from establishing the doctrine of a necessity prejudicial to practice, serves to destroy it."† The same reply is found more than once in the course of the same great work; and it is employed by all necessitarians in defence of their system. But it is not a satisfactory answer. It overlooks the real difficulty in the case, and seeks to remove an imaginary one. The question is, not whether a necessary connexion between our volitions and their *effects* is a discouragement to practice, but whether a necessary connexion between our volitions and their *causes* is so. It is very true, that no man would be accountable for his external actions or their consequences, if there were no fixed relation

* Essais de Theodicee, pp. 5, 6. † Id., p. 8.

between these and his volitions. If, when a man willed one thing, another should happen to follow which he did not will, of course he would not be responsible for it. And if there were no certain or fixed connexion between his external actions and their consequences, either as they affected himself or others, he certainly would not be responsible for those consequences. This connexion between causes and effects, this connexion between volitions and their consequences, is indispensable to our accountability for such consequences. But for such a connexion, nothing could be more idle and ridiculous than to endeavour to do anything; for we might will one thing, and another would take place.

But must the same necessary connexion exist between the causes of our volitions and the volitions themselves, before we can be accountable for these volitions, for these effects? This is the question. Leibnitz has lost sight of it, and deceived himself by a false application of his doctrine. The doctrine of necessity, when applied to volitions and their effects, is indispensable to build up man's accountability for his external conduct and its consequences. But the same doctrine, when applied to establish a fixed and unalterable relation between the causes of volition and volition itself, really demolishes all responsibility for volition, and consequently for its external results. Leibnitz undertook to show that a necessary connexion between volition and its causes does not destroy man's accountability for his volitions; and he has shown, what no one ever doubted, that a necessary connexion between volition and its effects does not destroy accountability for those effects! Strange as this confusion of things is, it is made by the most celebrated advocates of the doctrine of necessity; which shows, we think, that the doctrine hardly admits of a solid defence. Thus Edwards, for example, insists that the doctrine of necessity is so far from rendering our endeavours vain and useless, that it is an indispensable condition or prerequisite to their success. In illustration of this point, he says: "Let us suppose a real and sure connexion between a man having his eyes open in the clear daylight, with good organs of sight, and seeing; so that seeing is connected with opening his eyes, and not seeing with his not opening his eyes; and also the like connexion between such a man attempting to open his eyes and his actually doing it: the supposed established connexion between these antecedents and consequents, let the connexion be never so sure and necessary, certainly does not prove that it is in vain for a man in such circumstances to attempt to open his eyes, in order to seeing; his aiming at that event, and the use of the means, being the effect of his will, does not break the connexion, or hinder the success."

"So that the objection we are upon does not lie against the doctrine of the necessity of events by a certainty of connexion and consequence: on the contrary, it is truly forcible against the *Arminian* doctrine of contingence and self-determination, which is inconsistent with such a connexion. If there be no connexion between those events wherein virtue and vice consist, and anything antecedent; then there is no connexion between these events and any means or endeavours used in order to them: and if so, then those means must be in vain. The less there is of connexion between foregoing things and following ones, so much the less there is between means and end, endeavours and success; and in the same proportion are means and endeavours ineffectual and in vain."

In like manner, Dr. Chalmers, in his defence of the doctrine of necessity, has in all his illustrations confounded the connexion between a volition and its antecedent, with the relation between a volition and its consequent. To select one such illustration from many, it would be idle, says he, for a man to labour and toil after wealth, if there were no fixed connexion between such exertion and the accumulation of riches.

We reply to all such illustrations,—It is true, there must be a fixed connexion between our endeavours or voluntary exertions and their consequences, in order to render such endeavours or exertions of any avail, or to render us accountable for such consequences. But it should be forever borne in mind, that the question is not whether a fixed connexion obtains between our volitions and their *sequents*, but whether a necessary connexion exists between our volitions and their antecedents. The question is, not whether the will be a power which is often followed by necessitated effects; but whether there be a power behind the will by which its volitions are necessitated. And this being the question, what does it signify to tell us, that the will is a producing power? We deny that volitions and their antecedents are necessarily connected; and our opponents refute us by showing that volitions and their sequents are thus connected! We deny that A and B are necessarily connected; and this position is overthrown and demolished by showing that B and C are thus connected! Is it not truly wonderful that such men as a Leibnitz, an Edwards, and a Chalmers, should, in their zeal to maintain a favourite dogma, commit so great an oversight, and so grievously deceive themselves?

SECTION VI.

The attempt of Edwards to establish free and accountable agency on the basis of necessity—The views of the younger Edwards, Day, Chalmers, Dick, D'Aubigné, Hill, Shaw, and M'Cosh, concerning the agreement of liberty and necessity.

The great metaphysician of New-England insists, that his scheme, and his scheme alone, is consistent with the free-agency and accountability of man. But how does he show this? Does he endeavour to shake the stern argument by which all things seem bound together in the relation of cause and effect? Does he even intimate a doubt with respect to the perfect coherency and validity of this argument? Does he once enter a protest against the doctrine of the Stoics, or of the materialistic fatalists, according to which all things in heaven and earth are involved in an "implex series of causes?" He does not. On the contrary, he has stated and enforced the great argument from cause and effect, in the strongest possible terms. He contends that volition is caused, not by the will nor the mind, but by the strongest motive. This is the cause of volition, and it is impossible for the effect to be loose from its cause. It is an inherent contradiction, a glaring absurdity, to say that motive is the cause of volition, and yet admit that volition may, or may not, follow motive. This is to say, indeed, that motive is the cause, and yet that it is not the cause, of volition; which is a contradiction in terms.* So far from saying anything, then, to extricate the volitions of men from the adamantine circle of necessity, he has exerted his prodigious energies to fasten them therein.

Hence the question arises, Has he left any room for the introduction of that *freedom of the mind*, which it is the great object of his inquiry to establish upon its true foundations?

* Inquiry, part ii, sec. viii.

The liberty for which he contends, is, after all his labours, precisely that advocated by Hobbes and Collins, and no other. It is a freedom from co-action, and not from necessity. But he is entitled to speak for himself, and we shall permit him so to do: "The plain and obvious meaning of the word *freedom* and liberty," says he, "in common speech, is the *power*, opportunity, *or advantage, that any one has, to do as he pleases.* Or, in other words, his being free from hinderance or impediment in the way of doing or conducting in any respect *as he wills.* And the contrary to liberty, whatever name we call it by, is a person being hindered, or unable to conduct as he will, or being necessitated to do otherwise." Here, it will be seen, that liberty, according to this notion of it, has no relation to the manner in which the will arises, or comes into existence; if one's external conduct can only follow his will, he is free.

"There are two things," says he, "contrary to what is called liberty in common speech. One is *constraint*, otherwise called *force*, *compulsion*, and *co-action;* which is a person being necessitated to do a thing *contrary* to his will. The other is *restraint;* which is, his being hindered, and not having power to do *according* to his will. But that which has no will cannot be the subject of these things." This definition, it is plain, presupposes the existence of a volition; and liberty consists in the absence of co-action. It has no relation to the question as to how we come by our volitions, whether they are put forth by the mind itself without being necessitated, or whether they are necessarily produced in us. It leaves this great fundamental question untouched.

On this subject his language is perfectly explicit. There is nothing in Kames, nor Collins, nor Crombie, nor Hobbes, nor any other writer, more perfectly unequivocal. "But one thing more," says he, "I would observe concerning what is vulgarly called liberty, namely, that power and opportunity for one to do and conduct as he will, or according to his choice, is all that is meant by it, without taking into the meaning of the word anything of the cause of that choice, or at all considering how the person came to have such a volition, or internal habit and bias; whether it was determined by some internal antecedent volition, or whether it happened without a cause; whether it were necessarily connected with something foregoing, or not connected. *Let the person come by his choice any how*, yet, if he is able, and there is nothing in the way to hinder his pursuing and executing his will, *the man is perfectly free according to the primary and common notion of freedom.*" Now this is all the definition of liberty with which his "Inquiry" furnishes us; and this, he says, is "sufficient to show what is meant by liberty, according to the common notion of mankind, and in the usual and primary acceptation of the word."

It is easy to see, that there is no difficulty in reconciling liberty, in such a sense, with the most absolute scheme of necessity or fatalism the world has ever seen. Let a man come by his volition ANY HOW; let it be produced in him by the direct and almighty power of God himself; yet, "he is perfectly free," provided there is no external co-action to prevent his volition from producing its natural effects!

President Day is not pleased with the definition contained in the "Inquiry;" and in this particular we think he has discovered a superior sagacity to Edwards. But his extreme anxiety to save the credit of his author has betrayed him, it seems to us, into an apology which will not bear a close examination. "On the subject of liberty or freedom," says he, "which occupies a portion of the fifth section of Edwards's first book, he has been less particular than was to be expected, considering that this is the great object of inquiry in his work. His explanation of what he regards as the proper meaning of the term is applicable to the liberty of outward *action*, to what is called by philosophers *external* liberty." "This is very well as far as it goes. But the professed object of his book, according to the title-page, is an inquiry concerning the freedom of the will, not the freedom of the external conduct. We naturally look for his meaning of this internal liberty. What he has said, in this section, respecting freedom of the will, has rather the appearance of evading such a definition of it as might be considered his own."* Now, is it possible that President Edwards has instituted an inquiry into the freedom of the will, and written a great book in defence of it, and yet has evaded giving his own definition of it? If so, then he may have demolished the views of others on this subject, but he has certainly not established his own in their stead; and hence, for

* Day's Examination of Edwards on the Will, sec. v, pp. 80, 81.

aught we know, he really did not believe in the freedom of the will at all; and, for all his work shows, there may be no such freedom. For how is it possible for any man to establish his views of the freedom of the will, if he is not at sufficient pains to explain his meaning of the terms, and forbears even to give his own definition of them?

But the truth is, the author of the "Inquiry" has placed it beyond all controversy, that he has been guilty of no such omission or evasion. He has left no room to doubt that the definition of liberty, which he says is in conformity "with the common notion of mankind," is his own. He always uses this definition when he undertakes to repel objections against his scheme of necessity. "It is evident," he says, "that such a providential disposing and determining of men's moral actions, though it infers a moral necessity of those actions, *yet it does not in the least infringe the real liberty of mankind, the only liberty that common sense teaches to be necessary to moral agency, which,* AS HAS BEEN DEMONSTRATED, is not inconsistent with such necessity."* He defines liberty in the very words of Collins and Hobbes, to mean the power or opportunity any one has "to do as he pleases;" or, in other words, to do "as he *wills*."† This definition, he says, is according to the primary and common notion of mankind; and now he declares, that "this is the only liberty common sense teaches is necessary to moral agency." It is very strange that any one should have read the great work of President Edwards without perceiving that this is the sense in which he always uses the term when he undertakes to repel the attacks of his adversaries. To select only one instance out of many, he says, "If the Stoics held such a fate as is repugnant to any liberty, consisting in our doing as we please, I utterly deny such a fate. If they held any such fate as is not consistent with the common and universal notions that mankind have of liberty, activity, moral agency, virtue, and vice, I disclaim any such thing, and think I have demonstrated the scheme I maintain is no such scheme."‡ Thus he always has recourse to this definition of liberty, consisting in the power or opportunity any one has "to do as he pleases," or, in other words, "as he wills," whenever he attempts to reconcile his doctrine with the moral agency and accountability of man, or to vindi-

* Inquiry, part iv, sec. 9. † Ibid. ‡ Ibid., sec. 7.

cate it against the attacks of his opponents. We must suppose then, that Edwards has given his own definition of liberty in the Inquiry, or we must conclude that he defended his system by the use of an idea of liberty which he did not believe to be correct; that when he alleged that he "had demonstrated" his doctrine to be consistent with free-agency, he only meant with a false and atheistical notion of free-agency.

We are not surprised that President Day does not like this definition of liberty; but we are somewhat surprised, we confess, that such an idea of liberty should be so unhesitatingly adopted from Edwards, and so confidently set forth as the highest conceivable notion thereof, by Dr. Chalmers. He does not seem to entertain the shadow of a doubt, either that the definition of liberty contained in the Inquiry is that of Edwards himself, or that which is fully founded in truth. He freely concedes, that "we can do as we please," and supposes that the reader may be startled to hear that this is "cordially admitted by the necessitarians themselves!"

But this concession he easily reconciles with the tenet of necessity. "To say that you can do as you please," says he, "is just to affirm one of those sequences which take place in the phenomena of mind—a sequence whereof a volition is the antecedent, and the performance of that volition is the consequent. It is a sequence which no advocate of the philosophical necessity is ever heard to deny. Let the volition ever be formed, and if it point to some execution which lies within the limits we have just adverted to, the execution of it will follow."* Thus, his notion of liberty makes it consist in the absence of external impediments, which might break the connexion of a volition and its consequent, and not in the freedom of the will itself from the absolute dominion of causes. Such an idea of free-will, it must be confessed, is very well adopted by one who intends to maintain "a rigid and absolute predestination" of all events.

The manner in which Edwards attempts to reconcile the free-agency and accountability of man with the great argument from the law of causation, or with his doctrine of necessity, is, as we have seen, precisely the same as that adopted by Hobbes. There is not a shade of difference between them. It is, indeed, easy to demonstrate that liberty, according to this definition of

* Institutes of Theology, vol. ii, part iii, chap. i.

it, is not inconsistent with necessity; and it is just as easy to demonstrate, that it is not inconsistent with any scheme of fate that has ever been heard of among men. The will may be absolutely necessitated in all its acts, and yet the body may be free from external co-action or natural necessity!

But though there is this close agreement between Hobbes and Edwards, there are some points of divergency between Edwards and Calvin. The former comes forward as the advocate of free-will, the latter expressly denies that we have a free-will. Calvin admits that we may be free from co-action or compulsion; but to call this freedom of the will, is, he considers, to decorate a most "diminutive thing with a superb title." And though this is all the freedom Edwards allows us to possess, yet he does not hesitate to declare that his doctrine is perfectly consistent with "the highest degree of liberty that ever could be thought of, or that ever could possibly enter into the heart of man to conceive."

The only liberty we possess, according to all the authors referred to, is a freedom of the body and not of the mind. Though the younger Edwards is a strenuous advocate of his father's doctrine, he has sometimes, without intending to do so, let fall a heavy blow upon it. He finds, for instance, the following language in the writings of Dr. West, "he might have omitted doing the thing if he would," and he is perplexed to ascertain its meaning. "To say that if a man had chosen not to go to a debauch, (for that is the case put by Dr. West,) he would, indeed, have chosen not to go to it, is too great trifling to be ascribed to Dr. West." "Yet to say," he continues, "that the man could have avoided the *external action of going*, &c., if he would, would be equally trifling; for the question before us is concerning the liberty of the *will* or *mind*, and *not* the body." The italics are his own. It seems, then, that in the opinion of the younger Edwards it is very great trifling to speak of the power to do an *external action* in the present controversy, *because it relates to the will or mind, and not to the body.* We believe this remark to be perfectly just, and although it was aimed at the antagonist of President Edwards, it falls with crushing weight on the doctrine of President Edwards himself. Is it not wonderful that so just a reflection did not occur to the younger Edwards, in relation to the definition of liberty contained in the great work he had undertaken to defend?

We have now seen how some of the early reformers, and some of the great thinkers in after-times, have endeavoured to reconcile the scheme of necessity with the free-agency and accountability of man. Before quitting this subject, however, we wish to adduce a remarkable passage from one of the most correct reasoners, as well as one of the most impressive writers that in modern times have advocated the doctrines of Calvinism. "Here we come to a question," says he, "which has engaged the attention, and exercised the ingenuity, and perplexed the wits of men in every age. If God has foreordained whatever comes to pass, the whole series of events is necessary, and human liberty is taken away. Men are passive instruments in the hands of their Maker; they can do nothing but what they are secretly and irresistibly impelled to do; they are not, therefore, responsible for their actions; and God is the author of sin." After sweeping away some attempts to solve this difficulty, he adds: "It is a more intelligible method to explain the subject by the doctrine which makes liberty consist in the power of acting according to the prevailing inclination, or the motive which appears strongest to the mind. Those actions are free which are *the effects of volition. In whatever manner the state of mind which gave rise to volition has been produced, the liberty of the agent is neither greater nor less. It is his will alone which is to be considered, and not the means by which it has been determined.* If God foreordained certain actions, and placed men in such circumstances that the actions would certainly take place agreeably to the laws of the mind, men are nevertheless moral agents, because they act voluntarily and are responsible for the actions which consent has made their own. *Liberty does not consist in the power of acting or not acting, but in acting from choice.* The choice is determined by something in the mind itself, or by something external influencing the mind; but *whatever is the cause*, the choice makes the action free, *and the agent accountable. If this definition of liberty be admitted, you will perceive that it is possible to reconcile the freedom of the will with absolute decrees; but we have not got rid of every difficulty.*" Now this definition of liberty, it is obvious, is precisely the same as that given by

President Edwards, and nothing could be more perfectly adapted to effect a reconciliation between the freedom of the will and the doctrine of absolute decrees. How perfectly it shapes the freedom of man to fit the doctrine of predestination! It is a fine piece of workmanship, it is true; but as the learned and candid author remarks, we must not imagine that we have "got rid of every difficulty." For, "*by this theory*," he continues, "*human actions appear to be as necessary as the motions of matter according to the laws of gravitation and attraction; and man seems to be a machine, conscious of his movements, and consenting to them, but impelled by something different from himself*."* Such is the candid confession of this devoted Calvinist.

We have now seen the nature of that freedom of the will which the immortal Edwards has exerted all his powers to recommend to the Christian world! "Egregious liberty!" exclaimed Calvin. "It merely allows us elbow-room," says Leibnitz. "It seems, after all, to leave us mere machines," says Dick. "It is trifling to speak of such a thing," says the younger Edwards, in relation to the will. "Why, surely, this cannot be what the great President Edwards meant by the freedom of the will," says Dr. Day. He certainly must have evaded his own idea on that point. Is it not evident, that the house of the necessitarian is divided against itself?

Necessitarians not only refute each other, but in most cases each one contradicts himself. Thus the younger Edwards says, it is absurd to speak of a power to act according to our choice, when the question relates, not to the freedom of the body, but to the freedom of the mind itself. He happens to see the absurdity of this mode of speaking when he finds it in his adversary, Dr. West; and yet it is precisely his own definition of freedom. "But if by liberty," says he, "be meant a power of willing and choosing, an exemption from co-action and natural necessity, and power, opportunity, and advantage, to *execute our own choice;* in this sense we hold liberty."† Thus he returns to the absurd idea of free-will as consisting in "elbow-room," which merely allows our choice or volition to pass into effect. Dr. Dick is guilty of the same inconsistency. Though

* Lectures on Theology, by the late Rev. John Dick, D. D.

† Dissertation, p. 41.

he admits, as we have seen, that this definition of liberty does not get rid of every difficulty, but seems to leave us mere "machines;" yet he has recourse to it, in order to reconcile the Calvinistic view of divine grace with the free-agency of man. "The great objection," says he, "against the invincibility of divine grace, is, that it is subversive of the liberty of the will."* But, he replies, "True liberty consists in doing what we do with knowledge and *from choice*."

Yet as if unconscious that their greatest champions were thus routed and overthrown by each other, we see hundreds of minor necessitarians still fighting on with the same weapons, perfectly unmindful of the disorder and confusion which reigns around them in their own ranks. Thus, for example, D'Aubigné says, "It were *easy to demonstrate* that the doctrine of the reformers did not take away from man the liberty of a moral agent, and reduce him to a passive machine." Now, how does the historian so easily demonstrate that the doctrine of necessity, as held by the reformers, does not deny the liberty of a moral agent? Why, by simply producing the old effete notion of the liberty of the will, as consisting in freedom from co-action; as if it had never been, and never could be, called in question. "Every action performed without external restraint," says he, "and in pursuance of the determination of the soul itself, is a free action."† This demonstration, it is needless to repeat, would save any scheme of fatalism from reproach, as well as the doctrine of the reformers.

The scheme of the Calvinists is defended in the same manner in Hill's Divinity: "The liberty of a moral agent," says he, "consists in the power of acting according to his choice; and those actions are free, which are performed without any external compulsion or restraint, in consequence of the determination of his own mind." "According to the Calvinists," says Mr. Shaw, in his Exposition of the Confession of Faith, "the liberty of a moral agent consists in the power of acting according to his choice; and those actions are free which are performed without any external compulsion or restraint, in consequence of the determination of his own mind."‡ Such, if we may believe these learned Calvinists, is the idea of the freedom

* Dick's Lectures, vol. ii, p. 157. † History of the Reformation, b. v.

‡ Hill's Divinity, ch. ix, sec. iii.

of the will which belongs to their system. If this be so, then it must be conceded that the Calvinistic definition of the freedom of the will is perfectly consistent with the most absolute scheme of fatality which ever entered into the heart of man to conceive.

The views of M'Cosh respecting the freedom of the will, seem, at first sight, widely different from those of other Calvinists and necessitarians. The freedom and independence of the will is certainly pushed as far by him as it is carried by Cousin, Coleridge, Clarke, or any of its advocates in modern times. "True necessitarians," says he, "should learn in what way to hold and defend their doctrine. Let them disencumber themselves of all that doubtful argument, derived from man being supposed to be swayed by the most powerful motive."* Again: "The truth is," says he, "it is not motive, properly speaking, that determines the working of the will; but it is the will that imparts the strength to the motive. As Coleridge says, 'It is the man that makes the motive, and not the motive the man.'"† According to this Calvinistic divine, the will is not determined by the strongest motive; on the contrary, it is self-active and self-determined. "Mind is a self-acting substance," says he; "and hence its activity and independence." In open defiance of all Calvinistic and necessitarian philosophy, he even adopts the self-determining power of the will. "Nor have necessitarians," says he, "even of the highest order, been sufficiently careful to guard the language employed by them. Afraid of making admissions to their opponents, we believe that none of them have fully developed the phenomena of human spontaneity. Even Edwards ridicules the idea of the faculty or power of will, or the soul in the use of that power determining its own volitions. Now, we hold it to be an incontrovertible fact, and one of great importance, that the true determining cause of every given volition is not any mere anterior incitement, but the very soul itself, by its inherent power of will."‡ Surely, the author of such a passage cannot be accused of being afraid to make concessions to his opponents. But this is not all. If possible, he rises still higher in his views of the lofty, not to say god-like, independence of the human will. "We rejoice,"

* The Divine Government, Physical and Moral, b. iii, ch. i, sec. iii.

† Id., b. iii, ch. i, sec. ii. ‡ Ibid.

says he, "to recognise such a being in man. We trust that we are cherishing no presumptuous feeling, when we believe him to be free, as his Maker is free. We believe him, morally speaking, to be as independent of external control as his Creator must ever be—as that Creator was when, in a past eternity, there was no external existence to control him."*

Yet, strange as it may seem, Mr. M'Cosh trembles at the idea of "removing the creature from under the control of God;" and hence, he insists as strenuously as any other necessitarian, that the mind, and all its volitions, are subjected to the dominion of causes. "We are led by an intuition of our nature," says he, "to a belief in the invariable connexion between cause and effect; and we see numerous proofs of this law of cause and effect reigning in the human mind as it does in the external world, and reigning in the will as it does in every other department of the mind."† Again: "It is by an intuition of our nature that we believe this thought or feeling could not have been produced without a cause; and that this same cause will again and forever produce the same effects. And this intuitive principle leads us to expect the reign of causation, not only among the thoughts and feelings generally, but among the wishes and volitions of the soul."‡

Now here is the question, How can the soul be self-active, self-determined, and yet all its thoughts, and feelings, and volitions, have producing causes? How can it be free and independent in its acts, and yet under the dominion of efficient causes? How can the law of causation reign in all the states of the mind, as it reigns over all the movements of matter, and yet leave it as free as was the Creator when nothing beside himself existed? In other words, How is such a scheme of necessity to be reconciled with such a scheme of liberty? The author replies, We are not bound to answer such a question §—nor are we. As we understand it, the very idea of liberty, as above set forth by the author, is a direct negative of his doctrine of necessity.

But although he has taken so much pains to dissent from his necessitarian brethren, and to advocate the Arminian notion of free-will, Mr. M'Cosh, nevertheless, falls back upon the old Calvinistic definition of liberty, as consisting in a freedom from

* The Divine Government, Physical and Moral, b. iii, ch. i, sec. ii.

† Ibid. ‡ Ibid. § Ibid.

external co-action, in order to find a basis for human responsibility. It may seem strange, that after all his labour in laying the foundation, he should not build upon it; but it is strictly true. "If any man asserts," says he, "that in order to responsibility, the will must be free—that is, free from physical restraint; free to act as he pleases—we at once and heartily agree with him; and we maintain that in this sense the will is free, as free as it is possible for any man to conceive it to be." And again: "If actions do not proceed from the will, but from something else, from mere physical or external restraint, then the agent is not responsible for them. But if the deeds proceed from the will, then it at once attaches a responsibility to them. Place before the mind a murder committed by a party through pure physical compulsion brought to bear on the arm that inflicts the blow, and the conscience says, here no guilt is attachable. But let the same murder be done with the thorough consent of the will, the conscience stops not to inquire whether *this consent has been caused or no*."* Thus, after all his dissent from Edwards, he returns precisely to Edwards's definition of the freedom of the will as the ground of human responsibility; after all his strictures upon "necessitarians of the first order," he falls back upon precisely that notion of free-will which was so long ago condemned by Calvin, and exploded by Leibnitz, and which relates, as we have so often seen, not to acts of the will at all, but only to the external movements of the body.

SECTION VII.

The sentiments of Hume, Brown, Comte, and Mill, in relation to the antagonism between liberty and necessity.

Mr. Hume has disposed of the question concerning liberty and necessity, by the application of his celebrated theory of cause and effect. According to this theory, the idea of power, of efficacy, is a mere chimera, which has no corresponding reality in nature, and should be ranked among the exploded prejudices of the human mind. "One event follows another," says he; "but we never can observe any tie between them. They seem *conjoined*, but never *connected*."†

* The Divine Government, Physical and Moral, b. iii, ch. i, sec. ii.
† Hume's Works, Liberty and Necessity.

We shall not stop to examine this hypothesis, which has been so often refuted. We shall merely remark in passing, that it owes its existence to a false method of philosophizing. Its author set out with the doctrine of Locke, that all our ideas are derived from sensation and reflection; and because he could not trace the idea of power to either of these sources, he denied its existence. Hence we may apply to him, with peculiar force, the judicious and valuable criticism which M. Cousin has bestowed upon the method of Locke. Though Mr. Hume undertakes, as his title-page declares, to introduce the inductive method into the science of human nature, he departed from that method at the very first step. Instead of beginning, as he should have done, by ascertaining the ideas actually in our minds, and noting their characteristics, and proceeding to trace them up to their sources, he pursued the diametrically opposite course. He first determined and fixed the origin of all our ideas; and every idea which was not seen to arise from this preëstablished origin, he declared to be a mere chimera. He thus caused nature to bend to hypotheses; instead of anatomizing and studying the world of mind according to the inductive method, he pursued the high *a priori* road, and reconstructed it to suit his preëstablished origin of human knowledge. This was not to study and interpret the work of God "in the profound humiliation of the human soul;"* but to re-write the volume of nature, and omit those parts which did not accord with the views and wishes of the philosopher. In the pithy language of Sir William Hamilton, he "did not anatomize, but truncate."

If this doctrine be true, it is idle to talk about free-agency, for there is no such thing as agency in the world. It is true, there is a thing which we call volition, or an act of the mind; but this does not produce the external change by which it is followed. The two events co-exist, but there is no connecting tie between them. "They are *conjoined*, but not connected." In short, according to this scheme, all things are equally free, and all equally necessary. In other words, there is neither freedom nor necessity in the usual acceptation of the terms; and the whole controversy concerning them, which has agitated the learned for so many ages, dwindles down into a mere empty

* Bacon.

and noisy logomachy. Indeed, this is the conclusion to which Mr. Hume himself comes; expressly maintaining that the controversy in question has been a dispute about words. We are not to suppose from this, however, that he forbears to give a definition of liberty. His idea of free-agency is precisely that of Hobbes, and so many others before him. "By liberty," says he, "we can only mean a power of *acting or not acting according to the determination of the will:* that is, if we choose to remain at rest, we may; if we choose to move, we also may."* Such he declares is all that can possibly be meant by the term *liberty;* and hence it follows that any other idea of it is a mere dream. The coolness of this assumption is admirable; but it is fully equalled by the conclusion which follows. If we will observe these two circumstances, says he, and thereby render our definition intelligible, Mr. Hume is perfectly persuaded "that all mankind will be found of one opinion with regard to it." If Mr. Hume had closely looked into the great productions of his own school, he would have seen the utter improbability, that necessitarians themselves would ever concur in such a notion of liberty.†

If Mr. Hume's scheme were correct, it would seem that nothing could be stable or fixed; mind would be destitute of energy to move within its own sphere, or to bind matter in its orbit. All things would seem to be in a loose, disconnected, and fluctuating state. But this is not the view which he had of the matter. Though he denied that there is any connecting link

* Of Liberty and Necessity.

† Although Mr. Hume gives precisely the same definition of liberty as that advanced by Hobbes, Locke, and Edwards, he had the sagacity to perceive that this related not to the freedom of the will, but only of the body. Hence he says, "In short, if motives are not under our power or direction, which is confessedly the fact, we can *at bottom have* NO LIBERTY." We are not at all surprised, therefore, at the reception which Hume gave to the great work of President Edwards, as set forth in the following statement of Dr. Chalmers, concerning the appendix to the "Inquiry." "The history of this appendix," says he, "is curious. It has only been subjoined to the later editions of his work, and did not accompany the first impression of it. Several copies of this impression found their way into this country, and created a prodigious sensation among the members of a school then in all its glory. I mean the metaphysical school of our northern metropolis, whereof Hume, and Smith, and Lord Kames, and several others among the more conspicuous infidels and semi-infidels of that day, were the most distinguished members. They triumphed in the book of Edwards, as that which set a conclusive seal on their principles," &c.—*Institutes of Theology*, vol. ii, ch. ii.

among events, yet he insisted that the connexion subsisting among them is fixed and unalterable. "Let any one define a cause," says he, "without comprehending, as part of the definition, a *necessary connexion* with its effect; and let him show distinctly the origin of the idea expressed by the definition, and I shall readily give up the whole controversy."* This is the philosopher who has so often told us, that events are "conjoined, not connected."

The motives of volition given, for example, and the volition invariably and inevitably follows. How then, may we ask, can a man be accountable for his volitions, over which he has no power, and in which he exerts no power? This question has not escaped the attention of Mr. Hume. Let us see his answer. He admits that liberty "is essential to morality."† For "as actions are objects of our moral sentiment so far only as they are indications of the internal character, passions, and affections, it is impossible that they can give rise either to praise or blame, when they proceed, not from these principles, but are derived altogether from external violence." It is true, as we have seen, that if our external actions, the motions of the body, proceed not from our volitions, but from external violence, we are not responsible for them. This is conceded on all sides, and has nothing to do with the question. But suppose our external actions are inevitably connected with our volitions, and our volitions as inevitably connected with their causes, how can we be responsible for either the one or the other? This is the question which Mr. Hume has evaded and not fairly met.

Mr. Hume's notion about cause and effect has been greatly extended by its distinguished advocate, Dr. Thomas Brown; whose acuteness, eloquence, and elevation of character, have given it a circulation which it could never have received from the influence of its author. Almost as often as divines have occasion to use this notion, they call it the doctrine of Dr. Brown, and omit to notice its true atheistical paternity and origin.

The defenders of this doctrine are directly opposed, in regard to a fundamental point, to all other necessitarians. Though they deny the existence of all power and efficacy, they still hold that human volitions are necessary; while other necessitarians ground their doctrine on the fact, that volitions are produced by

* Of Liberty and Necessity. † Ibid.

the most powerful, the most efficacious motives. They are not only at war with other necessitarians, they are also at war with themselves. Let us see if this may not be clearly shown.

According to the scheme in question, the mind does not act upon the body, nor the body upon the mind; for there is no power, and consequently no action of power, in the universe. Now, it is known that it was the doctrine of Leibnitz, that two substances so wholly unlike as mind and matter could not act upon each other; and hence he concluded that the phenomena of the internal and external worlds were merely "*conjoined*, not *connected*." The soul and body run together—to use his own illustration—like two independent watches, without either exerting any influence upon the movements of the other. Thus arose his celebrated, but now obsolete fiction, of a preëstablished harmony. Now, if the doctrine of Hume and Brown be true, this sort of harmony subsists, not only in relation to mind and body, but in relation to all things in existence. Mind never acts upon body, nor mind upon mind. Hence, this doctrine is but a generalization of the preëstablished harmony of Leibnitz, with the exception that Mr. Hume did not contend that this wonderful harmony was established by the Divine Being. Is it not wonderful that so acute a metaphysician as Dr. Brown should not have perceived the inseparable affinity between his doctrine and that of Leibnitz? Is it not wonderful that, instead of perceiving this affinity, he should have poured ridicule and contempt upon the doctrine of which his own was but a generalization? Mr. Mill, another able and strenuous advocate of Mr. Hume's theory of causation, has likewise ranked the preestablished harmony of Leibnitz, as well as the system of occasional causes peculiar to Malebranche, among the fallacies of the human mind. Thus they are at war with themselves, as well as with their great coadjutors in the cause of necessity.

M. Comte, preëminently distinguished in every branch of science, has taken the same one-sided view of nature as that which is exhibited in the theory under consideration; but he does not permit himself to be encumbered by the inconsistencies observable in his great predecessors. On the contrary, he boldly carries out his doctrine to its legitimate consequences, denying the existence of a God, the free-agency of man, and the reality of moral distinctions.

Mr. Mill also refuses to avail himself of the notion of liberty entertained by Hobbes and Hume, in order to lay a foundation for human responsibility. He sees that it really cannot be made to answer such a purpose. He also sees, that the doctrine of necessity, as usually maintained, is liable to the objections urged against it, that "it tends to degrade the moral nature of man, and to paralyze our desire of excellence."* In making this concession to the advocates of liberty, he speaks from his own "personal experience." The only way to escape these pernicious consequences, he says, is to keep constantly before the mind a clear and unclouded view of the true theory of causation, which will prevent us from supposing, as most necessitarians do, that there is a real connecting link or influence between motives and volitions, or any other events. So strong is the prejudice (as he calls it) in favour of such connection, that even those who adopt Mr. Hume's theory, are not habitually influenced by it, but frequently relapse into the old error which conflicts with the free-agency and accountability of man, and hence an advantage which their opponents have had over them.

These remarks are undoubtedly just. There is not a single writer, from Mr. Hume himself, down to the present day, who has been able either to speak or to reason in conformity with his theory, however warmly he may have embraced it. Mr. Mill himself has not been more fortunate in this respect than many of his distinguished predecessors. It is an exceedingly difficult thing, by the force of speculation, to silence the voice of nature within us. If it were necessary we might easily show, that if we abstract "the common prejudice," in regard to causation, it will be as impossible to read Mr. Mill's work on logic, as to read Mr. Hume's writings themselves, without perceiving that many of its passages have been stripped of all logical coherency of thought. The defect which he so clearly sees in the writings of other advocates of necessity, not excepting those who embrace his own paradox in relation to cause and effect, we can easily perceive in his own.

The doctrine of causation, under consideration, annihilates one of the clearest and most fundamental distinctions ever made in philosophy; the distinction between *action* and *passion*, between

* Mill's Logic, pp. 522, 523.

mind and *matter*. Matter is passive, mind is active. The very first law of motion laid down in the Principia, a work so much admired by M. Comte and Mr. Mill, is based on the idea that matter is wholly inert, and destitute of power either to move itself, or to check itself when moved by anything *ab extra*. This will not be denied. But is mind equally passive? Is there nothing in existence which rises above this passivity of the material world? If there is not, and such is the evident conclusion of the doctrine in question, then all things flow on in one boundless ocean of passivity, while there is no First Mover, no Self-active Agent in the universe. Indeed, Mr. Mill has expressly declared, that the distinction between agent and patient is illusory.* If this be true, we are persuaded that M. Comte has been more successful in delivering the world from the being of a God, than Mr. Mill has been in relieving it from the difficulties attending the scheme of necessity.

SECTION VIII.

The views of Kant and Sir William Hamilton in relation to the antagonism between liberty and necessity.

"To clear up this seeming antagonism between the mechanism of nature and freedom in one and the self-same given action, we must refer," says Kant, "to what was advanced in the critique of pure reason, or what, at least, is a corollary from it, viz., that the necessity of nature which may not consort with the freedom of the subject, attaches simply to a thing standing under the relations of time, i. e., to the modifications of the acting subject as phenomena, and that, therefore, so far (i. e., as phenomena) the determinators of each act lie in the foregoing elapsed time, and are quite beyond his power, (part of which are the actions man has already performed, and the phenomenal character he has given himself in his own eyes,) yet, *e contra*, the self-same subject, being self-conscious of itself as a thing in itself, considers its existence as somewhat detached from the conditions of time, and itself, so far forth, as only determinable by laws given it by its own reason."†

Kant has said, that this "intricate problem, at whose solution centuries have laboured," is not to be solved by "a jargon of

* Mill's Logic, book ii, chap. v, sec. 4.

† Metaphysics of Ethics.

words." If so, may we not doubt whether he has taken the best method to solve it? His solution shows one thing at least, viz., that he was not satisfied with any of the solutions of his predecessors, for his is wholly unlike them. Kant saw that the question of liberty and necessity related to the will itself, and not to the consequences of the will's volitions. Hence he was compelled to reject those weak evasions of the difficulty of reconciling them, and to grapple directly with the difficulty itself. Let us see if this was not too much for him. Let us see if he has been able to maintain the doctrine of necessity, holding it as a "demonstrated truth," and at the same time give the idea of liberty a tenable position in his system.

If we would clear up the seeming antagonism between the mechanism of nature and freedom in regard to the same volition, says he, we must remember, that the volition itself, as standing under the conditions of time, is to be considered as subject to the law of mechanism: yet the mind which puts forth the volition, being conscious that it is a thing somewhat detached from the conditions of time, is free from the law of mechanism, and determinable by the laws of its own reason. That is to say, the volitions of mind falling under the law of cause and effect, like all other events which appear in time, are necessary; while the mind itself, which exists not exactly in time, is free. We shall state only two objections to this view. In the first place, it seems to distinguish the mind from its act, not *modally*, i. e., as a thing from its mode, but *numerically*, i. e., as one thing from another thing. But who can do this? Who regards an act of the mind, a volition, as anything but the mind itself as existing in a state of willing? In the second place, it requires us to conceive, that the act of the mind is necessitated, while the mind itself is free in the act thus necessitated. But who can do this? On the contrary, who can fail to see in this precisely the same seeming antagonism which Kant undertook to remove? To tell us, that volition is necessitated because it exists in time, but the mind is free because it does not exist in time, is, one would think, a very odd way to dispel the darkness which hangs over the grand problem of life. It is to solve one difficulty merely by adding other difficulties to it. Hence, the world will never be much wiser, we are inclined to suspect, with respect to the seeming antagonism between liberty and necessity, in consequence of the speculations of the philosopher of Königsberg, especially since his great admirer, Mr. Coleridge, forgot to fulfil his promise to write the history of a man who existed in "neither time nor space, but a-one side."

Though Kant made the attempt in his Metaphysics of Ethics to overcome the speculative difficulty in question, it is evident that he is not satisfied with his own solution of it, since he has repeatedly declared, that the practical reason furnishes the only ground on which it can be surmounted. "This view of Kant," says Knapp, "implying that freedom, while it is a postulate of our *practical* reason, (i. e., necessary to be assumed in order to moral action,) is yet *inconsistent with our theoretical reason*, (i. e., incapable of demonstration, *and contrary to the conclusions to which the reflecting mind arrives*,) is now very generally rejected."*

In regard to this point, there seems to be a perfect coincidence between the philosophy of Kant and that of Sir William Hamilton. "In thought," says the latter, "we never escape determination and necessity."† If the scheme of necessity never fails to force itself upon our thought, how are we then to get rid of it, so as to lay a foundation for morality and accountability? This question, the author declares, is too much for the speculative reason of man; and being utterly baffled in that direction, we can only appeal to the fact of consciousness, in order to establish the doctrine of liberty. "The philosophy which I profess," says he, "annihilates the theoretical problem—How is the scheme of liberty, or the scheme of necessity, to be rendered comprehensible?—by showing that both schemes are equally inconceivable; but it establishes liberty practically as a fact, by showing that it is either itself an immediate datum, or is involved in an immediate datum of consciousness."‡ We shall hereafter see, why the scheme of necessity always riveted the chain of conviction on the thought of Sir William Hamilton, and compelled him to have recourse to an appeal to consciousness in order to escape its delusive power.

* Knapp's Theology, p. 520. † Reid's Works, note, p. 611. ‡ Id., p. 599, note.

SECTION IX.

The notion of Lord Kames and Sir James Mackintosh on the same subject.

Lord Kames boldly cut the knot which philosophy had failed to unravel for him. Supposing the doctrine of necessity to be settled on a clear and firm basis, he resolved our feelings of liberty into "a deceitful sense" which he imagined the Almighty had conferred on man for wise and good purposes. He concluded that if men could see the truth, in regard to the scheme of necessity, without any illusion or mistake, they would relax their exertions in all directions, and passively submit to the all-controlling influences by which they are surrounded. But God, he supposed, out of compassion for us, concealed the truth from our eyes, in order that we might be induced to take care of ourselves, by the pleasant dream that we really have the power to do so.

We shall not stop to pull this scheme to pieces. We shall only remark, that it is a pity the philosopher undertook to counteract the benevolent design of the Deity, and to expose the cheat and delusion by which he intended to govern the world for its benefit. But the author himself, it is but just to add, had the good sense and candour to renounce his own scheme; and hence we need dwell no longer upon it. It remains at the present day only as a striking example of the frightful contortions of the human mind, in its herculean efforts to escape from the dark labyrinth of fate into the clear and open light of nature.

Sir James Mackintosh, though familiar with the speculations of preceding philosophers, was satisfied with none of their solutions of the great problem under consideration, and consequently he has invented one of his own. This solution is founded on his theory of the moral sentiments, which is peculiar to himself. This theory is employed to show how it is, that although we may come by our volitions according to the scheme of necessity, yet we do not perceive the causes by which they are necessarily produced, and consequently imagine that we are free. Thus, the "feeling of liberty," as he calls it, is resolved into an illusory judgment, and the scheme of necessity is exhibited in all its adamantine strength. "It seems impossible," says he, "for reason to consider occurrences otherwise than as bound together by the connexion of cause and effect; and in this circumstance consists the strength of the necessitarian system."*

We shall offer only one remark on this extraordinary hypothesis. If the theory of Sir James were true, it could only show, that although our volitions are necessarily caused, we do not perceive the causes by which they are produced. But this fact has never been denied: it has always been conceded, that we ascertain the existence of efficient causes, excepting the acts of our minds, only by means of the effects they produce. Both Leibnitz and Edwards long ago availed themselves of this undisputed fact, in order to account for the belief which men entertain in regard to their internal freedom. "Thus," says Edwards, "I find myself possessed of my volitions before I can see the effectual power and efficacy of any cause to produce them, *for the power and efficacy of the cause are not seen but by the effect, and this, for aught I know, may make some imagine that volition has no cause.*" We shall see hereafter that this is a very false account of the genesis of the common belief, that we possess an internal freedom from necessity; but it is founded on the truth which no one pretends to deny, that external efficient causes can only be seen by their effects, and not by any direct perception of the mind. It was altogether a work of supererogation, then, for Sir James Mackintosh to bring forth his theory of moral sentiments to establish the *possibility* of a thing which preceding philosophers had admitted to be a *fact.* It requires no elaborate theory to convince us that a thing might exist without our perceiving it, when it is conceded on all sides, that even if it did exist, we have no power by which to perceive it. With this single remark, we shall dismiss a scheme which resolves our conviction of internal liberty into a mere illusion, and which, however pure may have been the intentions of the author, really saps the foundation of moral obligation, and destroys the nature of virtue.

* Progress of Ethical Philosophy, p. 275.

SECTION X.

The conclusion of Mœhler, Tholuck, and others, that all speculation on such a subject must be vain and fruitless.

Considering the vast wilderness of speculation which exists on the subject under consideration, it is not at all surprising that many should turn away from every speculative view of it with disgust, and endeavour to dissuade others from such pursuits. Accordingly Mœhler has declared, that "so often as, without regard to revelation, *the relation of the human spirit to God hath been more deeply investigated*, men have found *themselves forced . . . . . to the adoption of pantheism, and, with it, the most arrogant deification of man.*"* And Tholuck spreads out the reasoning from effect to cause, by which all things are referred to God, and God himself only made the greatest and brightest link in the chain; and assuming this to be an unanswerable argument, he holds it up as a dissuasive from all such speculations. He believes that reason necessarily conducts the mind to fatalism.

We cannot concur with these celebrated writers, and we would deduce a far different conclusion from the speculations of necessitarians. This sort of scepticism or despair is more common in Germany than it is in this country; for there, speculation pursuing no certain or determinate *method*, has shown itself in all its wild and desolating excesses. But it is sophistry, and not reason, that leads the human mind astray; and we believe that reason, in all cases, is competent to detect and expose the impositions of sophistry. We do not believe that one guide which the Almighty has given us, can, by the legitimate exercise of it, lead us to a different result from that of another guide. We are persuaded that if reason seems to force us into any system which is contradicted by the testimony of our moral nature, or by the truths of revelation, this is unsound speculation: it is founded either on false premises, or else springs from false conclusions, which reason itself may correct, either by pointing out the fallacy of the premises, or the logical incoherency of the argument. We do not then intend to abandon speculation, but to plant it, if we can, on a better foundation, and build it up according to a better method.

* Mœhler's Symbolism, p. 117.

SECTION XI.

The true conclusion from the foregoing review of opinions and arguments.

All the mighty logicians we have yet named have yielded to "the demonstration" in favour of necessity, but we do not know that one of them has ever directed the energies of his mind to pry into its validity. They have all pursued the method so emphatically condemned by Bacon, and the result has verified his prediction. "The usual method," says he, "of discovery and proof by first establishing the most general propositions, then applying and proving the intermediate axioms according to these, is the parent of error and the calamity of every science."* They have set out with the universal law of causality or the principle of the sufficient reason, and thence have proceeded to ascertain and determine the actual nature and processes of things. We may despair of ever being able to determine a single fact, or a single process of nature, by reasoning from truisms; we must begin in the opposite direction and learn "to dissect nature," if we would behold her secrets and comprehend her mysteries.

By pursuing this method it will be seen, and clearly seen, that "the great demonstration" which has led so many philosophers in chains, is, after all, a sophism. We have witnessed their attempts to reconcile the great fact of man's free-agency with this boasted demonstration of necessity. But how interminable is the confusion among them? If a few of them concur in one solution, this is condemned by others, and not unfrequently by the very authors of the solution itself. We entertain too great a respect for their abilities not to believe, that if there had been any means of reconciling these things together, they would long since have discovered them, and come to an agreement among themselves, as well as made the truth known to the satisfaction of mankind. But as it is, their speculations are destitute of harmony—are filled with discordant elements. Instead of the clear and steady light of truth, illuminating the great problem of existence, we are bewildered by the glare of a thousand paradoxes; instead of the sweet voice of harmony, reaching and calling forth a response from the depths of the

* Novum Organum, book i, aph. 69.

human soul, the ear is stunned and confounded with a frightful roar of confused sounds.

We shall not attempt to hold the scheme of necessity, and reconcile it with the fact of man's free-agency. We shall not undertake a task, in the prosecution of which a Descartes, a Leibnitz, a Locke, and an Edwards, not to mention a hundred others, have laboured in vain. But we do not intend to abandon speculation. On the contrary, we intend to show, so clearly and so unequivocally that every eye may see it, that the great boasted demonstration in favour of necessity is a prodigious sophism. We intend to do this; because until the mental vision be purged of the film of this dark error, it can never clearly behold the intrinsic majesty and glory of God's creation, nor the divine beauty of the plan according to which it is governed.

CHAPTER II.

THE SCHEME OF NECESSITY MAKES GOD THE AUTHOR OF SIN.

I told ye then he should prevail, and speed
On his bad errand; man should be seduced,
And flatter'd out of all, believing lies
Against his Maker; no decree of mine
Concurring to necessitate his fall,
Or touch'd with slightest moment of impulse
His free-will, to her own inclining left
In even scale.—MILTON.

THE scheme of necessity, as we have already said, presents two phases in relation to the existence of moral evil; one relating to the agency of man, and the other to the agency of God. In the preceding chapter, we examined the attempts of the most learned and skilful advocates of this scheme to reconcile it with the free-agency and accountability of man. We have seen how ineffectual have been all their endeavours to show that their doctrine does not destroy the responsibility of man for his sins.

It is the design of the present chapter to consider the doctrine of necessity under its other aspect, and to demonstrate that it makes God the author of sin. If this can be shown, it may justly lead us to suspect that the scheme contains within its bosom some dark fallacy, which should be dragged from its hiding-place into the open light of day, and exposed to the abhorrence and detestation of mankind.

In discussing this branch of our subject, we shall pursue the course adopted in relation to the first; for if the doctrine of necessity does not make God the author of sin, we may conclude that this has been shown by some one of its most profound and enlightened advocates. If the attempts of a Calvin, and an Edwards, and a Leibnitz, to maintain such a doctrine, and yet vindicate the purity of God may be shown to be signal failures, we may well doubt whether there is a real agreement between these tenets as maintained by them. Nay, if in order to vindicate their system from so great a reproach, they have been compelled to adopt positions which are clearly inconsistent with the divine holiness, and thus to increase rather than to diminish the reproach; surely their system itself should be more than suspected of error. We shall proceed, then, with this view, to examine their speculations in regard to the agency of God in its connexion with the origin and existence of moral evil.

SECTION I.

The attempts of Calvin and other reformers to show that the system of necessity does not make God the author of sin.

Most of the advocates of divine providence have endeavoured to soften their views, so as to bring them into a conformity with the common sentiments of mankind, by supposing that God merely *permits*, without *producing* the sinful volitions of men. But Calvin rejects this distinction with the most positive disdain. "A question of still greater difficulty arises," says he, "from other passages, where God is said to incline or draw Satan himself and all the reprobate. For the carnal understanding scarcely comprehends how he, acting by their means, and even in operations common to himself and them, is free from any fault, and yet righteously condemns those whose ministry he uses. Hence was invented the distinction between *doing* and *permitting;* because to many persons this has appeared an inexplicable difficulty, that Satan and all the impious are subject to the power and government of God, so that he directs their malice to whatever end he pleases, and uses their crimes for the execution of his judgments. The modesty of those who are alarmed by absurdity, might perhaps be excusable, if they did not attempt to vindicate the divine justice from all accusation by *a pretence utterly destitute of any foundation in truth*."* Here the distinction between God's *permitting* and *doing* in relation to the sins of men, is declared by Calvin to be utterly without foundation in truth, and purely chimerical. So, in various other places, he treats this distinction as "too weak to be supported." "The will of God," says he, "is the supreme and first cause of things;" and he quotes Augustine with approbation to the effect, that "He does not remain an idle spectator, determining to permit anything; there is an

* Institutes, book i, chap. xviii.

intervention of an actual volition, if I may be allowed the expression, which otherwise could never be considered a cause."* According to Calvin, then, nothing ever happens in the universe, not even the sinful volitions of men, which is not caused by God, even by "the intervention of an actual volition" of the supreme will.

It is evident that Calvin scorns to have any recourse to a permissive will in God, in order to soften down the stupendous difficulties under which his system seems to labour. On the contrary, he sometimes betrays a little impatience with those who had endeavoured to mitigate the more rugged features of what he conceived to be the truth. "The fathers," says he, "are sometimes too scrupulous on this subject, and afraid of a simple confession of the truth."† He entertains no such fears. He is even bold and rigid enough in his consistency to say, "that God often actuates the reprobate by the interposition of Satan, but in such a manner that Satan himself acts his part by the divine impulse."‡ And again, he declares that by means of Satan, "God excites the will and strengthens the efforts" of the reprobate.§ Indeed, his great work, whenever it touches upon this awful subject, renders it perfectly clear that Calvin despises all weak evasions in the advocacy of his stern doctrine.

It has been truly said, that Calvin never thinks of "deducing the fall of man from the abuse of human freedom." So far is he from this, indeed, that he seems to lose his patience with those who trace the origin of moral evil to such a source." "They say it is nowhere declared in express terms," says Calvin, "that God decreed Adam should perish by his defection; as though the same God, whom the Scriptures represent as doing whatever he pleases, created the noblest of his creatures without any determinate end. They maintain, that he was possessed of free choice, that he might be the author of his own fate, but that God decreed nothing more than to treat him according to his desert. If so weak a scheme as this be received, what will become of God's omnipotence, by which he governs all things according to his secret counsel, independently of every person or thing besides."‖ The fall of man, says Calvin, was

* Institutes, book i, chap. xvi. † Id., book ii, chap. iv. ‡ Id., book i, chap. xviii. § Id., book iii, chap. xxiii. ‖ Id., book iii, chap. xxiii, sec. 4, 7.

decreed from all eternity, and it was brought to pass by the omnipotence of God. To suppose that Adam was the author of his own fate and fall, is to deny the omnipotence of God, and to rob him of his sovereignty.

Now, if to say that God created man, and then left his sin to proceed wholly from himself, be to rob God of his omnipotence, and to affirm that he made man for no determinate end, the same consequences would follow from the position that God created Satan, and then left his sin and rebellion to proceed wholly from himself. But, strange as it may seem, the very thing which Calvin so vehemently denies in regard to man, he asserts in relation to Satan; and he even feels called upon to make this assertion in order to vindicate the divine purity against the calumny of being implicated in the sin of Satan! "But since the devil was created by God," says he, "we must remark, that this wickedness which we attribute to his nature is not from creation, but from corruption. For whatever evil quality he has, he has acquired by his defection and fall. And of this Scripture apprizes us; but, believing him to have come from God, just as he now is, we shall ascribe to God himself that which is in direct opposition to him. For this reason, Christ declares, that Satan, 'when he speaketh a lie, speaketh of his own;' and adds the reason, 'because he abode not in the truth.' When he says that he abode not in the truth, he certainly implied that he had once been in it; and when he calls him the father of a lie, *he precludes his imputing to God the depravity of his nature, which originated wholly from himself.* Though these things are delivered in a brief and rather obscure manner, yet they are abundantly sufficient to vindicate the majesty of God from every calumny."* Thus, in order to show that God is not the author of sin, Calvin assumes the very positions in regard to the rebellion of Satan which his opponents have always felt constrained to adopt in regard to the transgression of man. What then, on Calvin's own principles, becomes of the omnipotence of God? Does this extend merely to man and not to Satan? Is it not evident that Calvin's scheme in regard to the sin of the first man, is here most emphatically condemned out of his own mouth? Does he not here endorse the very consequence which his adversaries have been accus-

* Institutes, book i, chap. xiv, sec. 16.

tomed to deduce from his scheme of predestination, namely, that it makes God the author of sin?

This scheme of doctrine, it must be confessed, is not without its difficulties. It clothes man, as he came from the hand of his Maker, with the glorious attributes of freedom; but to what end? Is this attribute employed to account for the introduction of sin into the world? Is it employed to show that man, and not God, is the author of moral evil? It is sad to reflect that it is not. The fall of man is referred to the direct "omnipotence of God." The feeble creature yields to the decree and power of the Almighty, who, because he does so, kindles into the most fearful wrath and dooms him and all his posterity to temporal, spiritual, and eternal death. Such is the doctrine which is advanced, in order to secure the omnipotence of God, and to exalt his sovereignty. But is it not a great leading feature of deism itself, that it exalts the power of God at the expense of his infinite moral perfections? So we have understood the matter; and hence, it seems to us, that Christian divines should be more guarded in handling the attribute of omnipotence. "The rigid theologians," says Leibnitz, "have held the greatness of God in higher estimation than his goodness, the latitudinarians have done the contrary; *true orthodoxy has these two perfections equally at heart.* The error which abases the greatness of God should be called *anthropomorphism*, and *despotism* that which divests him of his goodness."*

If Calvin's doctrine be true, God is not the author of sin, inasmuch as he made man pure and upright; but yet, by the same power which created him, has he plunged him into sin and misery. Now, if the creation of man with a sinful nature be inconsistent with the infinite purity of God, will it not be difficult to reconcile with that purity the production of sin in man, after his creation, by an act of the divine omnipotence?

If we ask, How can God be just in causing man to sin, and then punishing him for it? Calvin replies, That all his dealings with us "are guided by equity."† We know, indeed, that all his ways are guided by the most absolute and perfect justice; and this is the very circumstance which creates the difficulty. The more clearly we perceive, and the more vividly we realize,

* Theodice, p. 365. †Institutes, book i, chap. xiv.

the perfection of the divine equity, the more heavily does the difficulty press upon our minds. This assurance brings us no relief; we still demand, if God be just, as in truth he is, how can he deal with us after such a manner? The answer we obtain is, that God is just. And if this does not satisfy us, we are reminded that "it is impossible ever wholly to prevent the petulance and murmurs of impiety."* We seek for light, and, instead of light, we are turned off with reproaches for the want of piety. We have not that faith, we humbly confess, which "from its exaltation looks down on these mists with contempt;"† but we have a reason, it may be "a carnal understanding," which longs to be enlarged and enlightened by faith. Hence, it cannot but murmur when, instead of being enlarged and enlightened by faith, it is utterly overwhelmed and confounded by it. And these murmurings of reason, which we can no more prevent than we could stop the heavings of the mighty ocean from its depths, are met and sought to be quelled with the rebuke, "Who art thou, O man, that repliest against God?" We reply not against God, but against man's interpretation of God's word; and who art thou, O man, that puttest thyself in the place of God? "Men," saith Bacon, "are ever ready to usurp the style, '*Non ego, sed Dominus;*' and not only so, but to bind it with the thunder and denunciation of curses and anathemas, to the terror of those who have not sufficiently learned out of Solomon, that the 'causeless curse shall not come.'"

In relation to the subject under consideration, the amiable and philosophic mind of Melancthon seems to have been more consistent, at one time, than that of most of the reformers. "He laid down," says D'Aubigné, "a sort of fatalism, which might lead his readers to think of God as the author of evil, and which consequently has no foundation in Scripture: 'since whatever happens,' said he, 'happens by necessity, agreeably to divine foreknowledge, it is plain our will hath no liberty whatever.'" It is certainly a very mild expression to say, that the doctrine of Melancthon might lead his readers to think of God as the author of evil. This is a consequence which the logical mind of Melancthon did not fail to draw from his own scheme of necessity. In his commentary on the Epistle to the Romans, in the edition of 1525, he asserted "that God wrought

* Institutes, book iii, ch. xxiii. † Id., book i, ch. xviii.

all things, evil as well as good; that he was the author of David's adultery, and the treason of Judas, as well as of Paul's conversion."

This doctrine was maintained by Melancthon on practical as well as on speculative grounds. It is useful, says he, in its tendency to subdue human arrogance; it represses the wisdom and cunning of human reason. We have generally observed, that whenever a learned divine denounces the arrogancy of reason, and insists on an humble submission to his own doctrines, that he has some absurdity which he wishes us to embrace; he feels a sort of internal consciousness that human reason is arrayed against him, and hence he abuses and vilifies it. But reason is not to be kept in due subordination by any such means. If sovereigns would maintain a legitimate authority over their subjects, they should bind them with wise and wholesome laws, and not with arbitrary and despotic enactments, which are so well calculated to engender hatred and rebellion. In like manner, the best possible way to tame the refractory reason of man, and hold it in subjection, is to bind it with the silken cords of divine truth, and not fetter it with the harsh and galling absurdities of man's invention. Melancthon himself furnished a striking illustration of the justness of this remark; for although, like other reformers, he taught the doctrine of a divine fatality of all events, in order to humble the pride of the human intellect, his own reason afterward rebelled against it. He not only recanted the monstrous doctrine which made God the author of sin, but he openly combatted it.

In the writings of Beza and Zwingle there are passages, in relation to the origin of evil, more offensive, if possible, than any we have adduced from Calvin and Melancthon. The mode in which the reformers defended their common doctrine was, with some few exceptions, the same in substance. They have said nothing which can serve to dispel, or even materially lessen, the stupendous cloud of difficulties which their scheme spreads over the moral government of God.

Considering the condition of the Church, the state of human knowledge, and, in short, all the circumstances of the times in which the reformers lived and acted, it is not very surprising that they should have fallen into such errors. The corruptions of human nature, manifesting themselves in the Romish Church, had so extravagantly exalted the powers of man, and especially of the priesthood, and so greatly depressed or obscured the sovereignty of God, that the reformers, in fighting against these abuses, were naturally forced into the opposite extreme. It is not at all wonderful, we say, that a reaction, which shook the very foundations of the earth, should have carried the authors of it beyond the bounds of moderation and truth. They would have been more than human if they had not fallen into some such errors as these which we have ascribed to them. But the great misfortune is, that these errors should have been stereotyped and fixed in the symbolical books of the Protestant Churches, and made to descend from the reformers to their children's children, as though they were of the very essence of the faith once delivered to the saints. This is the misfortune, the lamentable evil, which has furnished the Romish Church with its most powerful weapons of attack;* which has fortified the strongholds of atheism and infidelity; and which has, beyond all question, fearfully retarded the great and glorious cause of true religion.

If we would examine the most elaborate efforts to defend these doctrines, or rather the great central dogma of necessity from which they all radiate, we must descend to later times; we must turn our attention to the immortal writings of a Leibnitz and an Edwards.

SECTION II.

The attempt of Leibnitz to show that the scheme of necessity does not make God the author of sin.

This philosopher employed all the resources of a sublime genius, and all the stores of a vast erudition, in order to maintain the scheme of necessity, and at the same time vindicate the purity of the Divine Being. That subtle and adroit sceptic, M. Bayle, had drawn out all the consequences of the doctrine of necessity in opposition to the free-agency of man, and to the holiness of God. Leibnitz wrote his great "Essais de Théodicée," for the purpose of refuting these conclusions of Bayle, as well as those of all other sceptics, and of reconciling his system with

* See Mœhler's Symbolism.

the divine attributes. In the preface to his work he says, "We show that evil has another source than the will of God; and that we have reason to say of moral evil, that God only permits it, and that he does not will it. But what is more important, we show that God can not only permit sin, but even concur therein, and contribute to it, without prejudice to his holiness; although, absolutely speaking, he might have prevented it." Such is the task which Leibnitz has undertaken to perform; let us see how he has accomplished it.

"The ancients," says he, "attributed the cause of evil to matter; but where shall we, who derive all things from God, find the source of evil?"* He has more than once answered this question, by saying that the source of evil is to be found in the ideas of the divine mind. "Chrysippus," says he, "has reason to allege that vice comes from the original constitution of some spirits. It is objected to him that God has formed them; and he can only reply, that the imperfection of matter does not permit him to do better. This reply is good for nothing; for matter itself is indifferent to all forms, and besides God has made it. Evil comes rather from forms themselves, but abstract; that is to say, from ideas that God has not produced by an act of his will, no more than he has produced number and figures; and no more, in one word, than all those possible essences which we regard as eternal and necessary; for they find themselves in the ideal region of possibles; that is to say, in the divine understanding. God is then not the author of those essences, in so far as they are only possibilities; but there is nothing actual, but what he discerned and called into existence; and he has permitted evil, because it is enveloped in the best plan which is found in the region of possibles; that plan the supreme wisdom could not fail to choose. It is this notion which at once satisfies the wisdom, the power, and the goodness of God, and yet leaves room for the entrance of evil."†

In reading the lofty speculations of Leibnitz, we have been often led to wonder how one, whose genius was so great, could have permitted himself to rest in conceptions which appear so vague and indistinct. In the above passage we have both light and obscurity; and we find it difficult to determine which predominates over the other. We are clearly told that God is not

* Théodicée, p. 85. † Id., p. 264.

the author of evil, because this proceeds from abstract forms which were from all eternity enveloped in his understanding, and not from any operation of his will. But how does evil proceed from abstract forms; from the ideal region of the possible? Leibnitz does not mean that evil proceeds from abstract ideas, before they are embodied in the creation of real moral agents. Why then did God create beings which he knew from all eternity would commit sin? and why, having created them, did he contribute to their sins by a divine concourse? This is coming down from the *ideal* region of the possible, into the world of *real* difficulties.

According to the philosophy of Leibnitz, God created every intelligent being in the universe with a perfect knowledge of its whole destiny; and there is, moreover, a concourse of the divine will with all their volitions. Now, here we are in the very midst of the concrete world, and here is a difficulty which cannot be avoided by a flight into the ideal region of the possible. How can there be a concourse of the divine will with the human will in one and the same sinful volition, without a stain upon the immaculate purity of God? How can the Father of Lights, by an operation of his will, contribute to our sinful volitions, without prejudice to his holiness? This is the problem which Leibnitz has promised to solve; and we shall, with all patience, listen to his solution.

The solution of this problem, says he, is effected by means of the "privative nature of evil." We shall state this part of his system in his own words: "As to the physical concourse," says he, "it is here that it is necessary to consider that truth which has made so much noise in the schools, since St. Augustine has shown its importance, that evil is a privation, whereas the action of God produces only the positive. This reply passes for a defective one, and even for something chimerical in the minds of many men; but here is an example sufficiently analogous, which may undeceive them."

"The celebrated Kepler, and after him M. Descartes, have spoken of the *natural inertia* of bodies, and that we can consider it as a perfect image, and even as a pattern of the original limitation of creatures, in order to make us see that privation is the formal cause of the imperfections and inconveniences which are found in substance as well as in actions. Suppose that the current of a river carries along with it many vessels which have different cargoes, some of wood, and others of stone; some more, and some less. It will happen that the vessels which are more heavily laden will move more slowly than the others, provided there is nothing to aid their progress . . . Let us compare the force which the current exercises over the vessels and what it communicates to them, with the action of God, who produces and preserves whatever is positive in the creature, and imparts to them perfection, being, and force; let us compare, I say, the inertia of matter with the natural imperfection of creatures, and the slowness of the more heavily laden vessel with the defect which is found in the qualities and in the actions of the creature, and we shall perceive that there is nothing so just as this comparison. The current is the cause of the movement of the vessel, but not of its retardation; God is the cause of the perfection in the nature and the actions of the creature, but the limitation of the receptivity of the creature is the cause of the defect in its actions. Thus the Platonists, St. Augustine, and the schoolmen, have reason to say that God is the material cause of evil, which consists in what is positive, and not the formal cause of it, which consists in privation, as we can say that the current is the material cause of the retardation, without being its formal cause; that is to say, is the cause of the swiftness of the vessel, without being the cause of the bounds of that swiftness. God is as little the cause of sin, as the current of the river is the cause of the retardation of the vessel."* Or as Leibnitz elsewhere says, God is the author of all that is positive in our volitions, and the pravity of them arises from the necessary imperfection of the creature.

We have many objections to this mode of explaining the origin of moral evil, some few of which we shall proceed to state. 1. It is a hopeless attempt to illustrate the processes of the mind by the analogies of matter. All such illustrations are better adapted to darken and confound the subject, than to throw light upon it. If we would know anything about the nature of moral evil, or its origin, we must study the subject in the light of consciousness, and in the light of consciousness alone. Dugald Stewart has conferred on Descartes the proud distinction of having been the first philosopher to teach the

* Théodicée, pp. 89, 90.

true method according to which the science of mind should be studied. "He laid it down as a first principle," says Stewart, "that nothing comprehensible by the imagination can be at all subservient to the knowledge of mind; and that the sensible images involved in all our common forms of speaking concerning its operations, are to be guarded against with the most anxious care, as tending to confound in our apprehensions, two classes of phenomena, which it is of the last importance to distinguish accurately from each other."* 2. The privative nature of evil, as it is called, is purely a figment of the brain; it is an invention of the schoolmen, which has no corresponding reality in nature. When Adam put forth his hand to pluck the forbidden fruit, and ate it, he committed a sinful act. But why was it sinful? Because he knew it was wrong; because his act was a voluntary and known transgression of the command of God. Now, if God had caused all that was positive in this sinful act, that is, if he had caused Adam to will to put forth his hand and eat the fruit, it is plain that he would have been the cause of his transgression. Nothing can be more chimerical, it seems to us, than this distinction between being the author of the substance of an act, and the author of its pravity. If Adam had obeyed, that is, if he had refused to eat the forbidden fruit, such an act would not have been more positive than the actual series of volitions by which he transgressed. 3. If what we call sin, arises from the necessary imperfection of the creature, as the slowness of a vessel in descending a stream arises from its cargo, how can he be to blame for it; or, in other words, how can it be moral evil at all? And, 4. Leibnitz has certainly committed a very great oversight in this attempt to account for the origin of evil. He explains it, by saying that it arises from the necessary imperfection of the creature which limits its receptivity; but does he mean that God cannot communicate holiness to the creature? Does he mean that God endeavours to communicate holiness, and fails in consequence of the necessary imperfection of the creature? If so, what becomes of the doctrine which he everywhere advances, that God can very easily cause virtue or holiness to exist if he should choose to do so? If God can very easily cause this to exist, as Leibnitz contends he can, notwithstanding the necessary imper-

* Progress of Ethical Philosophy, p. 114.

fection of the creature, why has he not done so? Is it not evident, that the philosophy of Leibnitz merely plays over the surface of this great difficulty, and decks it out with the ornaments of fancy, instead of reaching down to the bottom of it, and casting the illuminations of his genius into its depths?

SECTION III.

The maxims adopted and employed by Edwards to show that the scheme of necessity does not make God the author of sin.

"This remarkable man," says Sir James Mackintosh, "the metaphysician of America, was formed among the Calvinists of New-England, when their stern doctrine retained its vigorous authority. His power of subtle argument, perhaps unmatched, certainly unsurpassed among men, was joined, as in some of the ancient mystics, with a character which raised his piety to fervour." It is in his great work on the will, as well as in some of his miscellaneous observations, that Edwards has put forth the powers of his mind, in order to show that the scheme of necessity does not obscure the lustre of the divine perfections. With the exception of the Essais de Théodicée of Leibnitz, it is perhaps the greatest effort the human mind has ever made to get rid of the seeming antagonism between the scheme of necessity and the holiness of God.

According to the system of Edwards, as well as that of his opponents, sin would not have been committed unless it were permitted by God. But in the scheme of Edwards, the agency of God bears a more intimate relation to the origin and existence of sin than is implied by a bare permission of it. "God," says he, disposes "the state of events in such a manner, for wise, holy, and most excellent ends and purposes, that sin, if it be permitted or not hindered, will most certainly and infallibly follow."* And this occurrence of sin, in consequence of his disposing and ordering events, enters into his design. For Edwards truly says, that "If God disposes all events, so that the infallible existence of the events is decided by his providence, then, doubtless, he thus orders and decides things *knowingly* and on *design*. God does not do what he does, nor order what he orders, accidentally and unawares, either *without* or *beside*

* Inquiry, p. 246.

his intention." Thus, we are told, that God so arranges and disposes the events of his providence as to bring sin to pass, and that he does so designedly. This broad proposition is laid down, not merely with reference to sin in general, but to certain great sins in particular. "So that," says Edwards, "what these murderers of Christ did, is spoken of as what God brought to pass or ordered, and that by which he fulfilled his own word." According to Edwards, then, the events of God's providence are arranged with a view to bring all the sinful deeds of men "certainly and infallibly" to pass, as well as their holy acts.

Now, here the question arises, Is this doctrine consistent with the character of God? Is it not repugnant to his infinite holiness? We affirm that it is; Edwards declares that it is not. Let us see, then, if his position does not involve him in insuperable difficulties, and in irreconcilable contradictions.

Edwards supposes that some one may object: "All that these things amount to is, that *God may do evil that good may come;* which is justly esteemed immoral and sinful in men, and therefore may be justly esteemed inconsistent with the perfections of God." This is a fair and honest statement of the objection; now let us hear the reply. "I answer," says Edwards, "that for God to dispose and permit evil in the manner that has been spoken of, is not to do evil that good may come; for it is not to do evil at all." It is not to do evil at all, says he, for the Supreme Ruler of the world to arrange events around one of his creatures in such a manner that they will certainly and infallibly induce him to commit sin. Why is not this to do evil? At first view, it certainly looks very much like doing evil; and it is not at once distinguishable from the temptations ascribed to Satanic agency. Why is it not to do evil, then, when it is done by the Almighty? It is not to do evil, says Edwards, because when God brings sin certainly and infallibly to pass, he does so "for wise and holy purposes." This is his answer: "In order to a thing's being morally evil, there must be one of these two things belonging to it: either it must be a thing *unfit* and *unsuitable* in its own nature, or it must have a *bad tendency*, or it must be done for an evil end. But neither of these things can be attributed to God's ordering and permitting such events as the immoral acts of creatures for good ends."* Let us examine this logic.

We are gravely told, that God designedly brings the sinful acts of men to pass by the use of most certain and infallible means; but this is not to do evil, *because he has a good end in view.* His intention is right; he brings sin to pass for "wise and holy purposes." Let us come a little closer to this doctrine, and see what it is. It will not be denied, that if any being should bring sin to pass without any end at all, except to secure its existence, this would be a sinful agency. If any being should, knowingly and designedly, bring sin to pass in another, without any "wise and holy purposes," all mankind will agree in pronouncing the deed to be morally wrong. But precisely the same deed is not wrong in God, says Edwards, because in his case it proceeds from "a wise and holy purpose," and he has "a good end in view." That is to say, the means, in themselves considered, are morally wrong; but being employed for a wise and holy purpose, for the attainment of a good end, they are sanctified! This is precisely the doctrine, that the end sanctifies the means. Is it not wonderful, that any system should be so dark and despotic in its power as to induce the mind of an Edwards, ordinarily so amazing for its acuteness and so exalted in its piety, to vindicate the character of God upon such grounds?

The defence of Edwards is neither more nor less than a play on the term *evil.* When it is said, that "we may do evil that good may come;" the meaning of the maxim is, that the means in such a case and under such circumstances ceases to be evil. The maxim teaches that "we may do evil," that it is lawful to do evil, with a view to the grand and glorious end to be attained by it. Or, in other words, that it is right to do what would otherwise be morally evil, in order to accomplish a good end. If Edwards had considered the other form of the same odious maxim, namely, that "the end sanctifies the means," he would have found it impossible to evade the force of its application to his doctrine. He could not have escaped from the difficulty of his position by a play upon the word *evil.* He would have seen that he had undertaken to justify the conduct of the Father of Lights, by supposing it to be governed by the most corrupt

* Inquiry, part iv, sec. ix.

maxim of the most corrupt system of casuistry the world has ever seen.

What God does, says Edwards, is not evil at all; because his purpose is holy, because his object is good, his intention is right. In like manner, the maxim says, that when the end is good and holy, "it sanctifies the means." The means may be impure in themselves considered, but they are rendered pure by the cause in which they are employed. This doctrine has been immortalized by Pascal, in his "Provincial Letters;" and we cannot better dismiss the subject than with an extract from the "Provincial Letters." "I showed you," says the jesuitical father, "how servants might, with a safe conscience, manage certain troublesome messages; did you not observe that it is simply taking off their intention from the *sin itself*, and fixing it on the advantage to be gained."* On this principle, stealing, and lying, and murder, may all be vindicated. "Caramuel, our illustrious defender," says the Jesuit, "in his Fundamental Theology," . . . . . . enters into the examination of many new questions resulting from this principle, (of directing the intention,) as, for example, whether the Jesuits may kill the Jansenists? "Alas, father!" exclaimed Pascal, "this is a most surprising point in theology! I hold the Jansenists already no better than dead men by the doctrine of Father Launy." "Aha, sir, you are caught; for Caramuel deduces the very opposite conclusion from the same principles." "How so?" said Pascal. "Observe his words, n. 1146 and 1147, p. 547 and 548. The Jansenists call the Jesuits Pelagians; may they be *killed* for so doing? No—for this plain reason, that the Jansenists are no more able to obscure the glory of our society, than an owl can hide the sun; in fact, they promote it, though certainly against their intention—*occidi non possunt, quia nocere non potuerunt.*" "Alas, father," says Pascal, "and does the existence of the Jansenists depend solely upon their capacity of injuring your reputation? If that be the case, I am afraid they are not in a very good predicament; for if the slightest probability should arise of their doing you any hurt, they may be despatched at once. You can perform the deed logically and in form; for it is only to *direct your intention* right, and you insure a quiet conscience. What a blessedness for those who

* Letter vii.

can endure injuries to know this charming doctrine! But, on the other hand, how miserable is the condition of the offending party! Really, father, it would be better to have to do with people totally devoid of all religion, than with those who have received instructions so far only as to this point, relative to directing the intention. I am afraid the *intention* of the murderer is no consolation to the wounded person. He can have no perception of this secret *direction*—poor man! he is conscious only of the *blow* he receives; and I am not certain whether he would not be less indignant to be cruelly massacred by people in a violent transport of rage, than to be devoutly killed for conscience' sake." Now, we submit it to the candid reader, whether the reasoning here ascribed to the Jesuit by Pascal, is not exactly parallel with that on which Edwards justifies the procedure of the Almighty? If God may choose sin and bring it to pass, without contracting the least impurity, because his *intention is directed aright*, to a wise and good end, may we not be permitted to imitate his example? And again, if God thus employs the creature as an instrument to accomplish his wise and holy purposes, why should he pour out the vials of his wrath upon him for having yielded to the dispensations of his almighty power? In order to save his doctrine from reproach, Edwards has invented a distinction, which next demands our attention. "There is no inconsistence," says he, "in supposing that God may hate a thing as it is in itself, and considered simply as evil, and yet that it may be his will it should come to pass, considering all consequences. I believe there is no person of good understanding who will venture to say, he is certain that it is impossible it should be best, taking in the whole compass and extent of existence, and all consequences in the endless series of events, that there should be such a thing as moral evil in the world. And if so, it will certainly follow, that an infinitely wise Being, who always chooses what is best, must choose that there should be such a thing. And if so, then such a choice is not evil, but a wise and holy choice. And if so, then that Providence which is agreeable to such a choice, is a wise and holy Providence. Men do *will* sin as sin, and so are the authors and actors of it; they love it as sin, and for evil ends and purposes. God does not will sin as sin, or for the sake of anything evil; though it be his pleasure so to order things that, he permitting, sin will come to pass, for the sake of the great good that by his disposal shall be the consequence. His willing to order things so that evil should come to pass for the sake of the contrary good, is no argument that he does not hate evil as evil; and if so, then it is no reason why he may not reasonably forbid evil as evil, and punish it as such."* Here we are plainly told, that although God hates sin as sin, yet, all things considered, he prefers that it should come to pass, and even helps it into existence. But man loves and commits evil *as such*, and is therefore justly punishable for it.

There are several serious objections to this extraordinary distinction. It is not true that men love and commit sin *as sin.* Sin is committed, not for its own sake, but for the pleasure which attends it. If sin did not gratify the appetites, or the passions, or the desires of men, it would not be committed at all; there would be no temptation to it, and it would be seen as it is in its own loathsome nature. Indeed, to speak with philosophical accuracy, sin is never a direct object of our affections or choice; we simply desire certain things, as Adam did the forbidden fruit, and we seek our gratification in them contrary to the will of God. This constitutes our sin. The direct object of our choice is, not disobedience, not sin, but the forbidden thing, the prohibited gratification. We do not love and choose the disobedience, but the thing which leads us to disobey. This is so very plain and simple a matter, that we cannot but wonder that honest men should have lost sight of it in a mist of words, and built up their theories in the dark.

Secondly, the above position, into which Edwards has been forced by the exigencies of his doctrine concerning evil, is directly at war with the great fundamental principle on which his whole system rests, namely, that the will is always determined by the greatest apparent good. For how is it possible that men should commit sin *as sin*, and for its own sake, if they never do anything except what is the most agreeable to them? How is it possible that they pursue moral evil merely *as moral evil*, and yet pursue it as the greatest apparent good? If it should be said that men love sin merely *as sin*, and therefore it pleases them to choose it for its own sake, this reply would be without foundation. For, as we have already seen, there is no

* Inquiry, part iv, sec. ix.

such principle in human nature as the love of sin *as such*, or for its own sake; and consequently sin can never delight or please the human mind as it is in itself. And, besides, it is self-contradictory; for the question is, How can a man commit sin *for its own sake on account of the pleasure it affords him?* It would be an attempt to explain an hypothesis which denies the very fact to be explained by it.

In the third place, if the philosophy of Edwards be true, no good reason can be assigned why men should restrain themselves from the commission of sin: for, all things considered, God prefers the sin which actually exists, and infallibly brings it to pass. He *prefers* it on account of the great good he intends to educe from it. Why then should we not also prefer its existence? God is sovereign; he will permit no more sin than he can and will render subservient to the highest good of the universe; and so much as is for the highest good he will bring into existence. Why, then, should we give ourselves any concern about the matter? Why should we fear that there may be too much sin in the world, or why should we blame other men for their crimes and offences?

The inference which we have just mentioned as necessarily flowing from the doctrine of Edwards, has actually been drawn by some of the most illustrious advocates of that doctrine. Thus says Hartley, as we have already seen, "since all men do against us is by the appointment of God, it is rebellion against him to be offended with them." This is so clearly the logical inference from the doctrine in question, that it is truly wonderful how any one can possibly fail to perceive it.

We are told by Leibnitz and Edwards, that we should not presume to act on the principle of permitting sin in others, or of bringing it to pass, on account of the good that we may educe from it; because such an affair is too high for us. But, surely, we need have no weak fears on this ground; for although it may be too high for us, they do not pretend that it is too high for God. He will allow no more sin to make its appearance in the world, say they, than he will cause to redound to the good of the universe. He prefers it for that reason, and why should we not respond, amen! to his preference? Why should we give ourselves any concern about sin? May we not follow our own inclinations, leaving sin to take its course, and rest quietly in Providence? To this question it will be replied, as Calvin and Edwards repeatedly reply, that the revealed, and not the secret, will of God is the rule of our duty. We do not object to this doctrine; we acknowledge its perfect propriety and correctness: but it is no reply to the consequence we have deduced from the philosophy of Edwards. It only shows that his philosophy leads to a conclusion which is in direct opposition to revelation. So far from objecting that any should turn from the philosophy of Edwards to revelation, in order to find reasons why evil should not be committed by us, we sincerely regret that such a departure from a false philosophy, and return to a true religion, is not more permanent and universal.

The doctrine of Edwards on this subject destroys the harmony of the divine attributes. It represents God as having two wills; or, to speak more correctly, it represents him as having published a holy law for the government of his creatures, which he does not, in all cases, wish them to obey. On the contrary, he prefers that some of them should violate his holy law; and not only so, but he adopts certain and infallible means to lead them to violate and trample it under foot. It is admitted by Edwards, that in this sense God really possesses two wills; but he still denies that this shows any inconsistency in the nature of God.

Edwards says, that the will of God does not oppose sin in the same sense in which it prefers sin, and that, therefore, there is no inconsistency in the case. But let us not deceive ourselves by words. Is it true, that sin is opposed by what is called the revealed will of God, by his command; and yet that it is, all things considered, chosen by his secret and working will? He commands one thing, and yet works to bring another to pass! He prohibits all sin, under the awful penalty of eternal death, and yet secretly arranges and plans things in such a manner as to secure the commission of it!

We have already seen one of these defences. God "hates sin as it is in itself;" and hence he prohibits it by his command. "Yet it may be his will it should come to pass, considering all its consequences;" and hence his secret will is bent on bringing it into existence. There is no inconsistency here, says Edwards, because the divine will relates to two different objects; namely, to "sin considered simply as sin," and to "sin considered in all its consequences." We do not care whether the two propositions contradict each other or not; it is abundantly evident, as we have seen, that it makes God choose that which he hates, even sin itself, as the means of good. It makes the end sanctify the means, even in the eye of the holy God. This doctrine we utterly reject and infinitely abhor. We had rather have "our sight, hearing, and motive power, and what not besides, disputed, and even torn away from us, than suffer ourselves to be disputed into a belief," that the holy God can choose moral evil as a means of good. We had rather believe all the fables in the Talmud and the Koran, than that the ever-blessed God should, by his providence and his power, plunge his feeble creatures into sin, and then punish them with everlasting torments for their transgression. We know of nothing in the Pantheism of Spinoza, or in the atheism of Hobbes, more revolting than this hideous dogma.

The great metaphysician of New-England has made a still further attempt to vindicate the dogma in question. "The Arminians," says he, "ridicule the distinction between the secret and revealed will of God, or, more properly expressed, the distinction between the decree and law of God; because we say he may decree one thing and command another. And so, they argue, we hold a contrariety in God, as if one will of his contradicted another. However, if they will call this a contradiction of wills, we know that there is such a thing; so that it is the greatest absurdity to dispute about it. We and they know it was God's secret will, that Abraham should not sacrifice his son Isaac; but yet his command was, that he should do it."* Such is the instance produced by this acute divine, to show that the secret will of God may prefer the very thing which is condemned by his revealed will or law; and on the strength of it, he is bold to say, "We *know* it, so that *it is the greatest absurdity to dispute about it.*"

We have often seen this passage of Scripture produced by infidels, to show that the Old Testament contains unworthy representations of God. If Edwards had undertaken to refute the infidel ground in relation to this passage, he might have done so with very great ease: but then he would at the same time have refuted himself. The Scriptural account of God's commanding Abraham to offer up his son Isaac, was long ago

* Edwards's Works, vol. vii, p. 406.

employed by the famous infidel Hobbes to show that there are two wills in God. This argument of Hobbes has been refuted by Leibnitz. "Hobbes contends," says Leibnitz, "that God wills not always what he commands, as when he commands Abraham to sacrifice his son:" and he replies, that "God, in commanding Abraham to sacrifice his son, *willed the obedience, and not the action*, which he prevented after having the obedience; for that was not an action which merited in itself to be willed: but such is not the case with those actions which he positively wills, and which are indeed worthy of being the objects of his will; such as piety, charity, and every virtuous action which God commands, and such as the avoidance of sin, more repugnant to the divine perfections than any other thing. It is incomparably better, therefore, to explain the will of God, as we have done it in this work."* It is evident that Leibnitz did not relish the idea of two wills in God; and perhaps few pious minds would do so, if it were presented to them by an atheist. But there was too close an affinity between the philosophy of Leibnitz and that of Hobbes, to permit the former to furnish the most satisfactory refutation of the argument of the latter.

This command to Abraham does not show that there ever was any such contrariety between the revealed and the decretal wills of God, as is contended for by Hobbes and Edwards. God intended, as we are told, to prove the faith of Abraham, in order that it might shine forth and become a bright example to all succeeding ages. For this purpose he commanded him to take his only son, whom he loved, and go into the land of Moriah, and there offer him up as a burnt-offering upon one of the mountains. Abraham obeyed without a murmur. After several days travelling and preparation, Abraham has reached the appointed place, and is ready for the sacrifice. His son Isaac is bound, and laid upon the altar; the father stretches forth his hand to take the knife and slay him. But a voice is heard, saying, "Lay not thine hand on the lad; neither do thou anything unto him." Now, the conduct of Abraham on this memorable occasion, is one of the most remarkable exhibitions of confidence in the wisdom and goodness of God, which the history of the world has furnished. It deserves to be held up to the admiration of mankind, and to be celebrated in all ages

* Théodicée, p. 327.

of the world. We sincerely pity the man, who is so taken up with superficial appearances, or who is so destitute of sympathy with the moral greatness and beauty of soul manifested in this simple narrative, that he can approach it in a little, captious, sneering spirit, rather than in an attitude of profound admiration. But our business, at present, is not so much with the laughing sceptic as with the grave divine.

What evidence, then, does this story furnish that the secret will of God had anything to do with the simple but sublime transaction which it records? God commanded Abraham to repair to the land of Moriah with his son Isaac; but are we informed that his secret will was opposed to the patriarch's going thither, or that it opposed any obstacle to his obedience? Are we told that God so arranged the events of his providence as to render the disobedience of Abraham, in any one particular, certain and infallible? We cannot find the shadow of any such information in the sacred story. And is there the least intimation, that when Abraham was commanded to stay the uplifted knife, the secret will of God was in favour of its being plunged into the bosom of his son? Clearly there is not. Where, then, is the discrepancy between the revealed and the secret wills of God in this case, which we are required to see? Where is this discrepancy so plainly manifested, that we absolutely *know* its existence, so that it is the height of absurdity to dispute against it?

If there is any contrariety at all in this case, it is between the *revealed will* of God in commanding Abraham to offer up his son, and his subsequently *revealed will* to desist from the sacrifice. It does not present even a seeming inconsistency between his secret will and his command, but between two portions of his revealed will. This seeming inconsistency between the command of God and his countermand, in relation to the same external action, has been fully removed by Leibnitz; and if it had not been, it is just as incumbent on the abettors of Edwards's scheme to explain it, as it is upon his opponents. If God had commanded Abraham to do a thing, and yet exerted his secret will to make him violate the injunction, this would have been a case in point: but there is no such case to be found in the word of God.

It may not be improper, in this connexion, to quote the following judicious admonition of Howe: "Take heed," says he, "that we do not oppose the secret and revealed will of God to one another, or allow ourselves so much as to imagine an opposition or contrariety between them. And that ground being once firmly laid and stuck to, as it is impossible that there can be a will against a will in God, or that he can be divided from himself, or against himself, or that he should reveal anything to us as his will that is not his will, (it being a thing inconsistent with his nature, and impossible to him to lie,) that being, I say, firmly laid, (as nothing can be firmer or surer than that,) then measure all your conceptions of the secret will of God by his revealed will, about which you may be sure. But never measure your conceptions of his revealed by his secret will; that is, by what you may imagine concerning that. For you can but imagine while it is secret, and so far as it is unrevealed."*

"It properly belongs," says Edwards, "to the supreme absolute Governor of the universe, to order all important events within his dominions by wisdom; but the events in the moral world are of the most important kind, such as the moral actions of intelligent creatures, and the consequences. These events will be ordered by something. They will either be disposed by wisdom, or they will be disposed by chance; that is, they will be disposed by blind and undesigning causes, if that were possible, and could be called a disposal. Is it not better that the good and evil which happen in God's world should be ordered, regulated, bounded, and determined by the good pleasure of an infinitely wise being, than to leave these things to fall out by chance, and to be determined by those causes which have no understanding and aim? .... It is in its own nature fit, that wisdom, and not chance, should order these things."†

In our opinion, if there be no other alternative, it is better that sin should be left to chance, than ascribed to the high and holy One. But why must sin be ordered and determined by the supreme Ruler of the world, or else be left to chance? Has the great metaphysician forgotten, that there may be such things as men and angels in the universe; or does he mean, with Spinoza, to blot out all created agents, and all subordinate agency, from existence? If not, then certainly God may refuse to be the author of sin, without leaving it to blind chance,

* Howe's Works, p. 1142.

† On the Will, part iv, sec. ix.

which is incapable of such a thing. He may leave it, as we conceive he has done, to the determination of finite created intelligences. If sin is to come into the world, as come it evidently does, it is infinitely better, we say, that it should be left to proceed from the creature, and not be made to emanate from God himself, the fountain of light, and the great object of all adoration. It is infinitely better that the high and holy One should do nothing either by his wisdom or by his decree, by his providence or his power, to help this hideous thing to raise its head amid the inconceivable splendours of his dominion.

Such speculations as those of Edwards and Leibnitz, in our opinion, only reflect dishonour and disgrace upon the cause they are intended to subserve. It is better, ten thousand times better, simply to plant ourselves upon the moral nature of man, and the irreversible dictates of common sense, and annihilate the speculations of the atheist, than to endeavour to parry them off by such invented quibbles and sophisms. They give point, and pungency, and power to the shafts of the sceptic. If we meet him on the common ground of necessity, he will snap all such quibbles like threads of tow, and overwhelm us with the floods of irony and scorn. For, in the memorable words of Sir William Hamilton, "It can easily be proved by those who are able and not afraid to reason, that the doctrine of necessity is subversive of religion, natural and revealed." To perceive this, it requires neither a Bayle, nor a Hobbes, nor a Hume; it only requires a man who is neither unable nor afraid to reason.

SECTION IV.

The attempts of Dr. Emmons and Dr. Chalmers to reconcile the scheme of necessity with the purity of God.

As we have dwelt so long on the speculations of President Edwards concerning the objections in question, we need add but a few remarks in relation to the views of the above-mentioned authors on the same subject. The sentiments of Dr. Emmons on the relation between the divine agency and the sinful actions of men, are even more clearly defined and boldly expressed than those of President Edwards. The disciple is more open and decided than the master. "Since mind cannot act," says he, "any more than matter can move, without a divine agency, it is absurd to suppose that men can be left to the freedom of their own will, to act, or not to act, independently of a divine influence. There must be, therefore, the exercise of a divine agency in every human action, without which it is impossible to conceive that God should govern moral agents, and make mankind act in perfect conformity to his designs."* "He is now exercising his powerful and irresistible agency upon the heart of every one of the human race, and producing either holy or unholy exercises in it."† "It is often thought and said, that nothing more was necessary on God's part, in order to fit Pharaoh for destruction, than barely to leave him to himself. But God knew that no external means and motives would be sufficient of themselves to form his moral character. He determined therefore to operate on his heart itself, and cause him to put forth certain evil exercises in view of certain external motives. When Moses called upon him to let the people go, God stood by him, and moved him to refuse. When the people departed from his kingdom, God stood by him and moved him to pursue after them with increased malice and revenge. And what God did on such particular occasions, he did at all times."‡ It is useless to multiply extracts to the same effect. Could language be more explicit, or more revolting to the moral sentiments of mankind?

If God is alike the author of all our volitions, sinful as well as holy, one wonders by what sort of legerdemain the authors of the doctrine have contrived to ascribe all the glory and all the praise of our holy actions to God, and at the same time all the shame and condemnation of our evil actions to ourselves. In relation to the holy actions of men, all the praise is due to God, say they, because they were produced by his power. Why is not the moral turpitude of their evil actions, then, also ascribed to God, inasmuch as he is said to produce them by his irresistible and almighty agency? We are accountable for our evil acts, say Dr. Emmons and Calvin, because they are *voluntary*. Are not our moral acts, our virtuous acts, also voluntary? Certainly they are; this is not denied; and yet we are not allowed to impute the moral quality of the acts to the agent in such cases. This whole school of metaphysicians, indeed, from Calvin down to Emmons, can make God the author of our evil

*Emmons's Works, vol. iv, p. 372. †Ibid., p. 388. ‡Ibid., p. 327.

acts, by an exertion of his omnipotence, and yet assert that because they are voluntary we are justly blameworthy and punishable for them; but though our virtuous acts are also voluntary, they still insist the praiseworthiness of them is to be ascribed exclusively to Him by whom they were produced. The plain truth is, that as the scheme originated in a particular set purpose and design, so it is one-sided in its views, arbitrary in its distinctions, and full of self-contradictions.

The simple fact seems to be, that if any effect be produced in our minds by the power of God, it is a passive impression, and is very absurdly called a voluntary state of the will. And even if such an impression could be a voluntary state, or a volition, properly so called, we should not be responsible for it, because it is produced by the omnipotence of God. This, we doubt not, is in perfect accordance with the universal consciousness and voice of mankind, and cannot be resisted by the sophistical evasions of particular men, how great soever may be their genius, or exalted their piety.

We shall, in conclusion, add one more great name to the list of those who, from their zeal for the glory of the divine omnipotence, have really and clearly made God the author of sin. The denial of his scheme of "a rigid and absolute predestination," as he calls it, Dr. Chalmers deems equivalent to the assertion, that "things grow up from the dark womb of nonentity, which omnipotence did not summon into being, and which omniscience could not foretell." And again, "At this rate, events would come forth uncaused from the womb of nonentity, to which omnipotence did not give birth, and which omniscience could not foresee."* Now all this is spoken, be it remembered, in relation to the volitions or acts of men. But if there are no such events, except such as omnipotence gives birth to, or summons into being, how clear and how irresistible is the conclusion that God is the author of the sinful acts of the creature? It were better, we say, ten thousand times better, that sin, *that* monstrous birth of night and darkness, should grow up out of the womb of nonentity, if such were the only alternative, than that it should proceed from the bosom of God.

* Institutes of Theology, vol. ii, chap. iii.

CHAPTER III.

THE SCHEME OF NECESSITY DENIES THE REALITY OF MORAL DISTINCTIONS.

Our voluntary service He requires,
Not our necessitated; such with him
Finds no acceptance, nor can find; for how
Can hearts, not free, be tried whether they serve
Willing or no, who will but what they must
By destiny, and can no other choose?—MILTON.

In the preceding chapters we have taken it for granted that there is such a thing as moral good and evil, and endeavoured to show, that if the scheme of necessity be true, man is absolved from guilt, and God is the author of sin. But, in point of fact, if the scheme of necessity be true, there is no such thing as moral good or evil in this lower world; all distinction between virtue and vice, moral good and evil, is a mere dream, and we really live in a non-moral world. This has been shown by many of the advocates of necessity.

SECTION I.

The views of Spinoza in relation to the reality of moral distinctions.

It is shown by Spinoza, that all moral distinctions vanish before the iron scheme of necessity. They are swept away as the dreams of vulgar prejudice by the force of Spinoza's logic; yet little praise is due, we think, on that account, to the superiority of his acumen. The wonder is, not that Spinoza should have drawn such an inference, but that any one should fail to draw it. For if our volitions are necessitated by causes over which we have no control, it seems to follow, as clear as noonday, that they cannot be the objects of praise or blame—cannot be our virtue or vice. So far is it indeed from requiring any logical acuteness to perceive such an inference, that it demands, as we shall see, the very greatest ingenuity to keep from perceiving it. Hence, in our humble opinion, the praise which has been lavished on the logic of Spinoza is not deserved.

His superior consistency only shows one of two things—

either that he possessed a stronger reasoning faculty than his great master, Descartes, or a weaker moral sense. In our opinion, it shows the latter. If his moral sentiments had been vigorous and active, they would have induced him, no doubt, either to invent sophistical evasions of such an inference, or to reject the doctrine from which it flows. If a Descartes, a Leibnitz, or an Edwards, for example, had seen the consequences of the scheme of necessity as clearly as they were seen by Spinoza, his moral nature would have recoiled from it with such force as to dash the premises to atoms. If any praise, then, be due to Spinoza for such triumphs of the reasoning power, it should be given, not to the superiority of his logic, but to the apathy of his moral sentiments. For our part, greatly as we admire sound reasoning and consistency in speculation, we had rather be guilty of ten thousand acts of logical inconsistency, such as those of Edwards, or Leibnitz, or Descartes, than to be capable of resting in the conclusion to which the logic of Spinoza conducted him—that every moral distinction is a vulgar prejudice, and that the existence of moral goodness is a dream.*

SECTION II.

The attempt of Edwards to reconcile the scheme of necessity with the reality of moral distinctions.

It would not be difficult to see, perhaps, that a necessary holiness, or a necessary sin, is a contradiction in terms, if we would only allow reason to speak for itself, instead of extorting testimony from it by subjecting it to the torture of a false logic. For what proposition can more clearly carry its own evidence along with it, than that whatever is necessary to us, that whatever we cannot possibly avoid, is neither our virtue nor our fault? What can be more unquestionable, than that we can be neither to praise nor to blame, neither justly rewardable nor punishable for anything over whose existence we have no power

* Emphatically as this conclusion is stated by Spinoza, and harshly as it is thrust by him against the moral sense of the reader, he could not himself find a perfect rest therein. Nothing can impart this to the reflective and inquiring mind but truth. Hence, even Spinoza finds himself constrained to speak of the duty of love to God, and so forth; all of which, according to his own conclusion, is irrelative nonsense.

or control? Yet this question, apparently so plain and simple in itself, has been enveloped in clouds of metaphysical subtilty, and obscured by huge masses of scholastic jargon. If, on this subject, we have wandered in the dim twilight of uncertain speculation, instead of walking in the clear open day, this has been, it seems to us, because we have neglected the wise admonition of Barrow, that logic, however admirable in its place, was not designed as an instrument "to put out the sight of our eyes."

It shall be our first object, then, to pull down and destroy "the invented quibbles and sophisms" which have so long darkened and confounded the light of reason and conscience in relation to the nature of moral good and evil, to dispel the clouds which have been so industriously thrown around this subject, in order that the bright and shining light of nature may, free and unobstructed, find its way into our minds and hearts.

We say, then, that there never can be virtue or vice in the breast of a moral agent, prior to his own actings and doings. On the contrary, it is insisted by Edwards, that true virtue or holiness was planted in the bosom of the first man by the act of creation. "In a moral agent," says he, "subject to moral obligations, it is the same thing to be perfectly innocent, as to be perfectly righteous. It must be the same, because there can no more be any medium between sin and righteousness, or between being right and being wrong, in a moral sense, than there can be a medium between straight and crooked in a natural."* This is applied to the first man as he came from the hand of the Creator, and is designed to show that he was created with true holiness or virtue in his heart. According to this doctrine, man was made upright, not merely in the sense that he was free from the least bias to evil, or that he possessed all the powers requisite to moral agency, but in the sense that true virtue or moral goodness was planted in his nature by the act of creation. If this be so, the doctrine of a necessary holiness must be admitted; for surely nothing can be more necessary to us, nothing can take place in which we have less to do, than the act by which we are created.

This then is the question which we intend to examine:

* Original Sin, part ii, chap. i, sec. i.

whether that which is concreated with a moral agent, can be his virtue or his vice? Whether, in other words, the dispositions or qualities which Adam derived from the hand of God, partook of the nature of true virtue or otherwise? Edwards assumes the affirmative. To establish his position, he relies upon two arguments, which we shall proceed to examine.

The first argument is designed to show, that unless true virtue, or moral goodness, had been planted in the nature of man by the finger of God, it could never have found its way into the world. To give this argument in his own words, he says: "It is agreeable to the sense of men in all nations and ages, not only that the fruit or effect of a good choice is virtuous, but that the good choice itself, from whence that effect proceeds, is so; yea, also, the antecedent good disposition, temper, or affection of mind, from whence proceeds that good choice, is virtuous. This is the general notion—not that principles derive their goodness from actions, but that actions derive their goodness from the principles whence they proceed; so that the act of choosing what is good is no further virtuous, than it proceeds from a good principle, or virtuous disposition of mind; which supposes that a virtuous disposition of mind may be before a virtuous act of choice; and that, therefore, it is not necessary there should first be thought, reflection, and choice, before there can be any virtuous disposition. If the choice be first, before the existence of a good disposition of heart, what is the character of that choice? There can, according to our natural notions, be no virtue in a choice which proceeds from no virtuous principle, but from mere self-love, ambition, or some animal appetites; therefore, a virtuous temper of mind may be before a good act of choice, as a tree may be before its fruit, and the fountain before the stream which proceeds from it."* Thus, he argues, if there must be choice before a good disposition, or virtue, according to our doctrine, then virtue could not arise at all, or find its way into the world. For all men concede, says he, that every virtuous choice, or act, must proceed from a virtuous disposition; and if this must also proceed from a virtuous act, it is plain there could be no such thing as virtue or moral goodness at all. The scheme which teaches that the act must precede the principle, and the principle the act, reduces the

* Original Sin, part ii, ch. i, sec. i.

very existence of virtue to a plain impossibility. He shows virtue to be possible, and escapes the difficulty, by referring it to the creative energy of the Divine Being, by which the principle of virtue, he contends, was planted in the mind of the first man.

This argument is plausible; but it will not bear a close examination. It might be made to give way, in various directions, before an analysis of the principle on which it is constructed; but we intend to demolish it by easier and more striking arguments. If we had nothing better to oppose to it, we might indeed neutralize its effect by a counter-argument of Edwards himself, which we find in his celebrated work on the will. He there says, that the virtuousness of every virtuous act or choice depends upon its own nature, and not upon its origin or cause. If we must refer every virtuous act, says he, to something in us that is virtuous as its antecedent, we must likewise refer that antecedent to some other virtuous origin or cause; and so on *ad infinitum*. Thus we should be compelled to trace virtue back from step to step, until we had quite driven it out of the world, and excluded it from the universality of things.*

Now this argument seems just as plausible as that which we have produced from the same author, in his work on Original Sin. Let us lay them together, and contemplate the joint result. According to one, the character of every virtuous act depends upon the virtuousness of the principle or disposition whence it proceeds; according to the other, it depends upon its own nature, and not at all upon anything in its origin, or cause, or antecedent. According to one, we must trace every virtuous act to a virtuous principle, and the virtuous principle itself to the necessitating act of God; according to the other, we must look no higher to determine the character of an act than its own nature; and if we proceed to its origin or cause to determine its character, we shall find no stopping-place. We shall not trace it up to God, as before, but we shall banish all virtue quite out of the world, and exclude it from the universality of things. According to one argument, there can be no virtue in the world, unless it be caused to exist, in the first place, by the necessitating, creative act of the Almighty; and according to the other, the virtuousness of every virtuous act depends upon

* Inquiry, part iv, sec. i.

its own nature, and is wholly independent of the question respecting its origin or cause. The solution of these inconsistencies and contradictions, we shall leave to the followers and admirers of President Edwards.*

But we have something better, we trust, to oppose to President Edwards than his own arguments. If his logic be good for anything, it will prove that God is the author of sin as well as of virtue. For it is as much the common notion of mankind that every sinful act must proceed from a sinful disposition or principle, as it is that every virtuous act must proceed from a virtuous disposition or principle; and hence, according to the logic of Edwards, a sinful disposition or principle must have preceded the first sinful act; that an antecedent sinful disposition or principle could not have been introduced by the act of the creature, and consequently it must have been planted in the bosom of the first man by the act of the Creator. This argument, we say, just as clearly shows that sin is impossible, or that it must have been concreated with man, as it shows the same thing in relation to virtue. If we maintain his argument, then, we must either deny the possibility of moral evil or make God the author of it.

After having laid down principles from which the impossibility of moral evil may be demonstrated, it was too late for Edwards to undertake to account for the origin of sin. According to his philosophy, it can have no existence; and hence we are not to look into that philosophy for any very clear account of how it took its rise in the world. Indeed, this point is hurried over by Edwards in a most hasty and superficial manner,

* They are accustomed to boast, that no man ever excelled Edwards in the *reductio ad absurdum*. But we believe no one has produced a more striking illustration of his ability in the use of this weapon, than that which we have just adduced. For if we contend, that every act is to be judged according to its own nature, whether it be good or evil, he will demonstrate, that we render virtue impossible, and exclude it entirely from the world. On the other hand, if we shift our position, and contend that no act is to be judged according to its own nature, but according to the goodness or badness of its origin or cause, he will also reduce this position, diametrically opposite though it be to the former, to precisely the same absurdity; namely, that it excludes all virtue out of the world, and banishes it from the universality of things! Surely, this *reductio ad absurdum* is a most formidable weapon in his hands; since he wields it with such destructive fury against the most opposite principles, and seems himself scarcely less exposed than others to its force.

in which he seems conscious of no little embarrassment. In his great work on the will he devotes one page and a half to this subject; and the greater part of this small space is filled up with the retort upon the Arminians, that their scheme is encumbered with as great difficulties as his own! He lets the truth drop in one place, however, that "the abiding principle and habit of sin" was "first introduced by an evil act of the creature."* Is it possible? How could there be an evil act which did not proceed from an antecedent evil principle or disposition? What becomes of the great common notion of mankind, on which his demonstration is erected? But we must allow the author to contradict himself, since he has now come around to the truth, that an evil act of the creature may and must have preceded the existence of moral evil in the world. If an intelligent creature, however, as it came from the hand of God, can introduce a "principle of sin by a sinful act," why should it be thought impossible for such a creature to introduce a principle of virtue by a virtuous act?

The truth is, that a virtuous act does not require an antecedent virtuous disposition or principle to account for its existence; nor does a vicious act require an antecedent vicious principle to account for its existence. In relation to the rise of good and evil in the world, the philosophy of Edwards is radically defective; and no one can discuss that subject on the principles of his philosophy without finding himself involved in contradictions and absurdities. If his psychology had not been false, he might have seen a clear and steady light where he has only beheld difficulties and confusion. As we have already seen, and as we shall still more fully see, Edwards confounds the power by which we *act* with the susceptibility through which we *feel:* the will with the emotive part of our nature. Every one knows that we may feel without acting; and yet feeling and acting, suffering and doing, are expressly and repeatedly identified in his writings. Having merged the will in sensibility, he regarded virtue and vice as phenomena of the latter, and as evolved from its bosom by the operation of necessitating causes. Hence his views in relation to the nature of moral good and evil, as well as in relation to their origin, became unavoidably dark and confused.

* Inquiry, part iv, sec. x.

If we only bear in mind the distinction between the will and the sensibility, we may easily see how either holiness or sin might have taken its rise in the bosom of the first man, without supposing that either a holy or a sinful principle was planted there by the hand of the Creator. If we will only carry the light of this distinction along with us, it will be no more difficult to account for the rise of the first sin in the bosom of a spotless creature of God, than to account for any other volition of the human mind. The first man, by means of his intelligence, could contemplate the perfection of his Creator, and, doing so, he could not but feel an emotion of admiration and delight. But this *feeling* was not his virtue. It was the natural and the necessary result of the organization which God had given him. He was also so constituted, that certain earthly objects were agreeable to him, and excited his natural appetites and desires. These appetites and desires were not sinful, nor was the sensibility from whose bosom they were evolved: they were the spontaneous workings of the nature which God had bestowed upon him. *But his will was free.* He could turn his mind to God, or he could turn it to earth. He did the latter, and there was no harm in this. But he listened to the voice of the tempter; he fixed his mind on the forbidden fruit; he saw it was pleasant to the eye; he imagined it was good for food, and greatly to be desired to make one wise. Neither the possession of the intellect by which he perceived the beauty of the fruit, nor of the sensibility in which it excited so many pleasurable emotions, was the sin of Adam. They were given to him by the Author of every good and perfect gift. *His will was free.* It was not necessitated to act by his desires. But yet, in direct opposition to the known will of God, he put forth an act of his own free mind, his own unnecessitated will, and plucked the forbidden fruit to gratify his desires. This was his sin—this voluntary transgression of the known will of God. On the other hand, if he had resisted the temptation, and instead of voluntarily gratifying his appetite and desire, had preserved his allegiance to God by acting in conformity with his will, this would have been his virtue. He would have acted in conformity with the rule of duty, and thereby gratified a *feeling* of love to God, instead of the lower feelings of his nature.

Thus, by observing the distinction between the will and the

sensitive part of our nature, we may easily see how either holiness or sin might have arisen in the bosom of the first man, though he had neither a holy nor a sinful principle planted in his nature by the hand of the Creator. We may easily see that he had all the powers requisite to moral agency, and that he was really capable of either a holy or a sinful act, without any antecedent principle of holiness or sin in his nature.

We have now said enough, we think, to show the fallacy of Edwards's first great argument in favour of a necessary holiness. We have seen, that we need not suppose the existence of a virtuous principle in the first man, in order to account for his first virtuous act, or to render virtue possible. We might point out many other errors and inconsistencies in which that argument is involved; but to avoid, as far as possible, becoming prolix and tiresome, we shall proceed to consider his second argument in favour of a necessary or concreated holiness.

His second argument is this: "Human nature must have been created with some dispositions—a disposition to relish some things as good and amiable, and to be averse to others as odious and disagreeable; otherwise it must be without any such thing as inclination or will; perfectly indifferent, without preference, without choice, or aversion, towards anything as agreeable or disagreeable. But if it had any concreated dispositions at all, they must be either right or wrong, either agreeable or disagreeable to the nature of things. If man had at first the highest relish of things excellent and beautiful, a disposition to have the quickest and highest delight in those things which were most worthy of it, then his dispositions were morally right and amiable, and never can be excellent in a higher sense. But if he had a disposition to love most those things that were inferior and less worthy, then his dispositions were vicious. And it is evident there can be no medium between these."

It is thus that Edwards seeks and finds virtue in the emotion, and not in the voluntary element of man's nature. The natural concreated disposition of Adam, he supposes, was morally right in the highest sense of the word, because he was so made as to relish and delight in the glorious perfections of the divine nature. Our first answer to this is, that it is contradicted by the reason and moral judgment of mankind in general, and, in particular, by the reason and moral judgment of Edwards himself.

It is agreeable to the voice of human reason, that nothing can be *our virtue*, in the true sense of the word, which was planted in us by the act of creation, and in regard to the production of which we possessed no knowledge, exercised no agency, and gave no consent. And if we listen to the language of Edwards, when the peculiarities of his system are out of the question, we shall find that this moral judgment was as agreeable to him as it is to the rest of mankind. For example: human nature is created with a disposition to be grateful for favours; and this disposition, according to Edwards, must either be agreeable or disagreeable to the nature of things, that is, it must be either morally right or wrong in the highest sense of the word. There can be no medium between these two—it must partake of the nature of virtue or of vice. Now, which of the terms of this alternative does Edwards adopt? Does he pronounce this natural disposition our virtue or our vice? We do not know what Edwards would have said, if this question had been propounded to him in connexion with the argument now under consideration; but we do know what he has said of it in other portions of his works. This natural concreated disposition is, says he, neither our virtue nor our vice! "That ingratitude, or the want of natural affection," says he, "shows a high degree of depravity, does not prove that all gratitude and natural affection possesses the nature of true virtue or saving grace."* "We see, in innumerable instances, that mere nature is sufficient to excite gratitude in men, or to affect their hearts with thankfulness to others for favours received."† "Gratitude being thus a natural principle, ingratitude is so much the more vile and heinous; because it shows a dreadful prevalence of wickedness, which even overbears and suppresses the better principles of human nature. It is mentioned as a high degree of wickedness in many of the heathen, that they were without natural affection. Rom. ii, 31. But that the want of gratitude, or natural affection, is evidence of a great degree of *vice*, is no argument that all gratitude and natural affection has the nature of *virtue* or saving grace."

Here, as well as in various other places, Edwards speaks of

* Religious Affections, part iii, sec. ii. † Ibid.

gratitude and other natural affections as the better principles of our nature; to be destitute of which he considers a horrible deformity. But, however amiable and lovely, he denies to these natural affections, or dispositions, the character of virtue; because they are merely natural or concreated dispositions. They are innocent; that is, they are neither our virtue nor our vice, but a medium between moral good and evil. Nothing can be more reasonable than this, and nothing more inconsistent with the logic of the author. Such is the testimony of Edwards himself, when he escapes from the shadows of a dark system, and the trammels of a false logic, and permits his own individual mind, in the clear open light of nature, to work in full unison with the universal mind of man.

According to the author's own definition of "true virtue," it "is the beauty of those qualities and acts of the mind that are of a moral nature, i. e., such as are attended with desert of *praise* or *blame*." Surely, Adam could have deserved no praise for the qualities bestowed on him by the act of creation; and hence, according to the author's own definition, they could not have been his virtue. In regard to the "new creation" of the soul, Edwards contends that all the praise is due to God, and no part of it to man; because the whole work is performed by divine grace, without human coöperation. Now, we admit that if the whole work of regeneration is performed by God, then man is not to be praised for it; that is to say, it is not his virtue. Here again the author sets forth the true principle; but how does it agree with his logic in relation to the first man? Was not his creation wholly and exclusively the work of God? If so, then all the praise is due to God, and no part of it to man. But, according to the author's own definition, when there is no praiseworthiness there is no virtue; and hence, as Adam deserved no praise on account of what he received at his creation, so such endowments partook not of the nature of true virtue.

But we have a still more fundamental objection to the argument in question. It proceeds on the supposition that *true virtue* consists in mere *feeling*. This view of the nature of virtue is admirably adapted to make it agree and harmonize with the scheme of necessity; but it is not a sound view. If an object is calculated to excite a certain feeling or emotion in the mind, that feeling or emotion will necessarily arise in view of such object. If the glorious perfections of the divine nature, for example, had been presented to the mind of Adam, no doubt he would have been necessarily compelled to "love, relish, and delight in them." But this feeling of love and delight, thus necessarily evolved out of the bosom of his natural disposition, however exquisite and enrapturing, would not have been his virtue or holiness. It would have been the spontaneous and irresistible development of the nature which God had given him We may admire it as the most beautiful unfolding of that nature, but we cannot applaud it as the virtue or moral goodness of Adam. We look upon it merely as the excellency and glory of the divine work of creation. We could regard the glory of the heavens, or the beauty of the earth, with a sentiment of moral approbation, as easily as we could ascribe the character of moral goodness to the noble qualities with which the Almighty had been pleased to adorn the nature of the first man.

The beautiful feeling or emotion of love is merely the blossom which precedes the formation of true virtue in the heart. This consists, not in holy feelings, as they are called, but in holy exercises of the will. It is only when the will, in its workings, coalesces with a sense of right and a feeling of love to God, that the blossom gives place to the fruit of virtue. A virtuous act is not a spontaneous and irresistible emotion of the sensibility; it is a voluntary exercise and going forth of the will in obedience to God.

It is a strange error which makes virtue consist in "the spontaneous affections, emotions, and desires that arise in the mind in view of its appropriate objects." If these necessarily arise in us, "and do not wait for the bidding of the will,"* how can they possibly be our virtue? how can they form the objects of moral approbation in us? Yet is it confidently asserted, that the denial of such a doctrine "stands in direct and palpable opposition to the authority of God's word."† The word of God, we admit, says that holiness consists in love; but does it assert that it consists in the *feeling* of love merely? or in any feeling which spontaneously and irresistibly arises in the mind? If the Scripture had been written expressly to refute such a moral heresy, it could not have been more pointed or explicit.

Holiness consists in love. But what is the meaning of the

* Dr. Woods. † Ibid.

term love, as set forth in Scripture? We answer, "This is the love of God," that we "*keep* his commandments." "Let us not love in word, neither in tongue, but in *deed* and in truth." "Whosoever heareth these sayings of mine and *doeth* them, I will liken him unto a wise man who built his house upon a rock." "He that hath my commandments, and *keepeth* them, he it is that loveth me." Here, as well as in innumerable other places, are we told that true love is not a mere evanescent feeling of the heart, but an inwrought and abiding habit of the will. It is not a *suffering*, it is a *doing*. The most lively emotions, the most ecstatic feelings, if they lead not the will to action, can avail us nothing; for the tree will be judged, not by its blossoms, but by its fruits.

If we see our brother in distress, we cannot but sympathize with him, unless our hearts have been hardened by crime. The feeling of compassion will spontaneously arise in our minds, in view of his distress; but let us not too hastily imagine therefore that we are virtuous, or even humane. We may possess a tender feeling of compassion, and yet the feeling may have no corresponding act. The opening fountain of compassion may be shut up, or turned aside from its natural course, by a wrong habit of the will; and hence, with all our weeping tenderness of feeling, we may be destitute of any true humanity. We may be merely as sounding brass, or a tinkling cymbal. "Whoso hath this world's goods, and seeth his brother have need, and shutteth up his bowels of *compassion* from him, how dwelleth the love of God in him?" It is this *loving in work*, and not in *feeling* merely, which the word of God requires of us; and when, at the last day, all nations, and kindreds, and tongues, shall stand before the throne of heaven, we shall be judged, not according to the feelings we have experienced, but according to the deeds done in the body. Hence, the doctrine which makes true virtue or moral goodness consist in the spontaneous and irresistible feelings of the heart, "stands in direct and palpable opposition to the authority of God's word."

Feeling is one thing; obedience is another. This counterfeit virtue or moral goodness, which begins and terminates in feeling, is far more common than true virtue or holiness. Who can reflect, for instance, on the infinite goodness of God, without an emotion or feeling of love? That man must indeed be uncommonly hard-hearted and sullen, who can walk out on a fine day and behold the wonderful exhibitions of divine goodness on all sides around him, without being warmed into a feeling of admiration and love. When all nature is music to the ear and beauty to the eye, it requires nothing more than a freedom from the darker stains and clouds of guilt within, to lead a sympathizing heart to the sunshine of external nature, as it seems to rejoice in the smile of Infinite Beneficence. The heart may swell with rapture as it looks abroad on a happy universe, replenished with so many evidences of the divine goodness; nay, the story of a Saviour's love, set forth in eloquent and touching language, may draw tears from our eyes, and the soul may rise in gratitude to the Author of such boundless compassion; and yet, after all, we may be mere sentimentalists in religion, whose wills and whose lives are in direct opposition to all laws, both human and divine. Infidelity itself, in such moments of deep but transitory feeling, may exclaim with an emotion known but to few Christian minds, "Socrates died like a philosopher, but Jesus Christ like a God," and its iron nature still retain "the unconquerable will."

We may now safely conclude, we think, that the mists raised by the philosophy and logic of Edwards have not been able to obscure the lustre of the simple truth, that true virtue or holiness cannot be produced in us by external necessitating causes. Whatsoever is thus produced in us, we say, cannot be our virtue, nor can we deserve any praise for its existence. This seems to be a clear dictate of the reason of man; and it would so seem, we have no doubt, to all men, but for certain devices which to some have obscured the light of nature. The principal of these devices we shall now proceed to examine.

SECTION III.

Of the proposition that "The essence of the virtue and vice of dispositions of the heart and acts of the will, lies not in their cause, but in their nature."[*]

For the sake of greater distinctness, we shall confine our attention to a single branch of this complex proposition; namely, that the essence of virtuous acts of the will lies not in their

[*] Inquiry of President Edwards, part iv, sec. 1.

cause, but their nature. Our reasoning in relation to this point, may be easily applied to the other branches of the proposition.

We admit, then, that the essence of a virtuous act lies in its nature. If this means that the nature of a virtuous act lies in its nature, or its essence lies in its essence, it is certainly true; and even if the author attached different ideas to the terms *essence* and *nature*, we do not care to search out his meaning; as we may very safely admit his proposition, whatever may be its signification. We are told by the editor, that the whole proposition is very important on account of "the negative part," namely, that "the essence of virtue and vice lies not in their *cause.*" We are also willing to admit, that the essence of everything lies in its own nature, *and not in its cause.* But why is this proposition brought forward? What purpose is it designed to serve in the philosophy of the author?

This question is easily answered. He contends that true virtue may be, and is, necessitated to exist by powers and causes over which we have no control. If we raise our eyes to such a source of virtue, its intrinsic lustre and beauty seem to fade from our view. The author, indeed, endeavours to explain why it is, that the scheme of necessity seems to be inconsistent with the nature of true virtue. The main reason is, says he, because we imagine that the essence of virtue and vice consists, not in their nature, but in their origin and cause. Hence this persuasion not to busy ourselves about the origin or cause of virtue and vice, but to estimate them according to their nature.

We are fully persuaded. If any can be found who will assert "that the virtuousness of the dispositions or acts of the will, consists not in the nature of these dispositions or acts of the will, but wholly in the origin or cause of them," we must deliver them up to the tender mercies of President Edwards. Or if any shall talk so absurdly as to say, "that if the dispositions of the mind, or acts of the will, *be never so good*, yet if the cause of the disposition or act be not our virtue, there is nothing virtuous or praiseworthy in it," we have not one word to say in his defence; nor shall we ever raise our voice in favour of any one, who shall maintain, that "if the will, in its inclinations or acts, *be never so bad*, yet, unless it arises from something that is our vice or fault, there is nothing vicious or blameworthy in it." For we are firmly persuaded, that if the acts of the will be good, then they are good; and if they be bad, then they are bad; whatever may have been their origin or cause. We shall have no dispute about such truisms as these.

We insist, indeed, that the first virtuous act of the first man was so, because it partook of the nature of virtue, and not because it had a virtuous origin or cause in a preceding virtuous disposition of the mind. But, in his work on Original Sin, Edwards contends otherwise. He there contends, that no act of Adam could have been virtuous, unless it had proceeded from a virtuous origin or cause in the disposition of his heart; and that this could have had no existence in the world, unless it had proceeded from the power of the Creator. Thus he looked beyond the nature of the act itself, even to its origin and cause, in order to show upon what its moral nature depended; but now he insists that we should simply look at its own nature, and not to its origin or cause, in order to determine this point. He ascends from acts of the will to their origin or cause, in order to show that virtue can only consist with the scheme of necessity; and yet he denies to us the privilege of ascending with him, in order to show that the nature of virtue cannot at all consist with the scheme of necessity!

We admit that the virtuousness of every virtuous act lies, not in its origin or cause, but in itself. But still we insist that a virtuous act, as well as everything else, may be traced to a false origin or cause that is utterly inconsistent with its very nature. A horse is undoubtedly a horse, come from whence it may; but yet if any one should tell us that horses grow up out of the earth, or drop down out of the clouds, we should certainly understand him to speak of mere phantoms, and no real horses, or we should think him very greatly mistaken. In like manner, when we are told that virtue may be, and is, necessitated to exist in us by causes over which we have no control; that we may be to praise for any gift bestowed upon us by the divine power; we are constrained to believe that he has given a false genealogy of moral goodness, and one that is utterly inconsistent with its nature. Nor can we be made to blink this truth, which so perfectly accords, as we have seen, with the universal sentiment of mankind, by being reminded that moral goodness consists, not in its origin or cause, but in its own nature. Virtue is always virtue, we freely admit, proceed from what quarter of the universe it may; yet do we insist that it can no more be produced in us by an extraneous agency than it can grow up out of the earth, or drop down out of the clouds of heaven. That which is produced in us by such an agency, be it what it may, is not our virtue, nor is any praise therefor due to us. To mistake such effects or passive impressions for virtue, is to mistake phantoms for things, shadows for substances, and dreams for realities.

SECTION IV.

The scheme of necessity seems to be inconsistent with the reality of moral distinctions, not because we confound natural and moral necessity, but because it is really inconsistent therewith.

Let us then look at this matter, and see if we are really so deplorably blinded by the ambiguity of a word, that we cannot contemplate the glory of the scheme of moral necessity as it is in itself. The distinction between these two things, *natural* and *moral* necessity, is certainly a clear and a broad one. Let us see, then, if we may not find our way along the line of this distinction, without that darkness and confusion by which our judgment is supposed to be so sadly misled and perverted.

It is on all sides conceded, that natural necessity is inconsistent with the good or ill desert of human actions. If a man were commanded, for example, to leap over a mountain, or to lift the earth from its centre, he would be justly excusable for the nonperformance of such things, because they lie beyond the range of his natural power. "There is here a limit to our power," as Dr. Chalmers says, "beyond which we cannot do that which we please to do; and there are many thousand such limits."* This is natural necessity, in one of its branches. It circumscribes and binds our natural power. It limits the external sphere beyond which the effects or consequences of our volitions cannot be projected. It reaches not to the interior sphere of the will itself, and has no more to do with its freedom than has the influence of the stars. We may please to do a thing, nay, we may freely will it, and yet a natural necessity may cut off and prevent the external consequence of the act.

Again, if by a superior force, a man's limbs or external

*Institutes of Theology, part iii, chap. i.

bodily organs should be used as instruments of good or evil, without his concurrence or consent, he would be excusable for the consequences of such use. This is the other branch of natural necessity. It is evident that it has no relation to the freedom or to the acts of the will, but only to the external movements of the body. It interferes merely with that external freedom of bodily motion, about which we heard so much in the first chapter of this work, and which the advocates of necessity have, for the most part, so industriously laboured to pass off upon the world for the liberty of the will itself. As this natural necessity, then, trenches not upon the interior sphere of the will, so it merely excuses for the performance or non-performance of external actions. It leaves the great question with respect to man's accountability for the acts of the will itself, from which his external actions proceed, wholly untouched and undetermined.

Far different is the case with respect to moral necessity. This acts directly upon the will itself, and absolutely controls all its movements. Within its own sphere it is conceded to be "as absolute as natural necessity,"* and "as sure as fatalism."† It absolutely and unconditionally determines the will at all times, and in all cases. Yet we are told that we are accountable for all the acts thus produced in us, because they are the acts of our own wills! Nothing is done against our wills, as in the case of natural necessity; (they should rather say, against the external effects of our wills;) but our wills always follow, and we are accountable therefor, though they cannot but follow. Moral necessity is not irresistible, because this implies resistance, and our wills never resist that which makes us willing. It is only invincible; and invincible it is indeed, since with the mighty, sovereign power of the Almighty it controls all the thoughts, and feelings, and volitions of the human mind. Now we see this scheme as it is in itself, in all its nakedness, just as it is presented to us by its own most able and enlightened defenders. And seeing it thus removed from all contact with the scheme of natural necessity, we ask, whether agents can be justly held accountable for acts thus determined and controlled by the power of God, or by those invincible causes which his omnipotence marshalleth?

* President Edwards. † Dr. Chalmers.

We speak not of external acts; and hence we lay aside the whole scheme of natural necessity. We speak of the acts of the will; and we ask, if these be not free from the dominion of moral necessity, from necessitating causes over which we have no control, can we be accountable for them? Can we be to praise or to blame for them? Can they be our virtue or our vice? These questions, we think, we may safely submit to the impartial decision of every unbiassed mind. And to such minds we shall leave it to determine, whether the scheme of moral necessity has owed its hold upon the reason of man to a dark confusion of words and things, or whether its glory has been obscured by the misconception of its opponents?

In conclusion, we shall simply lay down, in a few brief propositions, what we trust has now been seen in relation to the nature of virtue and vice:—1. No necessitated act of the mind can be its virtue or its vice. 2. In order that any act of the will should partake of a moral nature, it must be free from the dominion of causes over which it has no control, or from whose influence it cannot depart. 3. Virtue and vice lie not in the passive state of the sensibility, nor in any other necessitated states of the mind, but in acts of the will, and in habits formed by a repetition of such free voluntary acts. Whatever else may be said in relation to the nature of virtue and of vice, and to the distinction between them, these things appear to be clearly true; and if so, then the scheme of moral necessity is utterly inconsistent with their existence, and saps the very foundation of all moral distinctions.

CHAPTER IV.

THE MORAL WORLD NOT CONSTITUTED ACCORDING TO THE SCHEME OF NECESSITY.

> I made him just and right;
> Sufficient to have stood, though free to fall.
> Such I created all the ethereal powers
> And spirits, both them who stood and them who fail'd;
> Freely they stood who stood, and fell who fell.—MILTON.

WE have already witnessed the strange inconsistencies into which the most learned and ingenious men have fallen, in their attempts to reconcile the doctrine of necessity with the accountability of man, and the glory of God. Having involved themselves in that scheme, on what has appeared to them conclusive evidence, they have seemed to struggle in vain to force their way out into the clear and open light of nature. They have seemed to torment themselves, and to confound others, in their gigantic efforts to extricate themselves from a dark labyrinth, out of which there is absolutely no escape. Let us see, then, if we may not refute the pretended demonstration in favour of necessity, and thereby restore the mind to that internal satisfaction which it so earnestly desires, and which it so constantly seeks in a perfect unity and harmony of principle.

SECTION I.

The scheme of necessity is based on a false psychology.

There are three great leading faculties or attributes of the human mind; namely, the *intelligence*, the *sensibility*, and the *will*. By means of these we *think*, we *feel*, and we *act*. Now, the phenomena of thinking, feeling, and acting, will be found, on examination, to possess different characteristics; of which we must form clear and fixed conceptions, if we would extricate the philosophy of the will from the obscurity and confusion in which it has been so long involved. Let us proceed then to examine them, to interrogate our consciousness in relation to them.

Suppose, for example, that an apple is placed before me. I fix my attention upon it, and consider its form: *it is round.* This judgment, or decision of the mind, in relation to the form of the apple, is a state of the intelligence. It does not depend on any effort of mine, whether it shall appear round to me or not: I could not possibly come to any other conclusion if I would: I could as soon think it as large as the globe as believe it to be square, or of any other form than round. Hence this judgment, this decision, this state of the intelligence, is necessitated. The same thing is true of all the other perceptions or states of the intelligence. M. Cousin has truly said: "Undoubtedly different intellects, or the same intellect at different periods of its existence, may sometimes pass different judgments in regard to the same thing. Sometimes it may be deceived; it will judge that which is false to be true, the good to be bad, the beautiful to be ugly, and the reverse: but at the moment when it judges that a proposition is true or false, an action good or bad, a form beautiful or ugly, at that moment it is not in the power of the intellect to pass any other judgment than that it passes. It obeys laws it did not make. It yields to motives which determine it independent of the will. In a word, the phenomenon of intelligence, comprehending, judging, knowing, thinking, whatever name be given to it, is marked with the characteristic of necessity."*

Once more I fix my attention on the apple: an agreeable sensation arises in the mind; a desire to eat it is awakened. This desire or appetite is a state of the sensibility. Whether I shall feel this appetite or desire, does not depend upon any effort or exertion of my will. The mind is clearly passive in relation to it; the desire, then, is as strongly marked with the characteristic of necessity, as are the states of the intelligence. The same is true of all our feelings; they are necessarily determined by the objects in view of the mind. There is no controversy on these points; it is universally agreed that every state of the intelligence and of the sensibility is necessarily determined by the evidence and the object in view of the mind. It is not, then, either in the intelligence or in the sensibility that we are to look for liberty.

But once more I fix my attention on the apple: the desire is

* Psychology, p. 247.

awakened, and I conclude to eat it. Hitherto I have done nothing except in fixing my attention on the apple. I have experienced the judgment that it is round, and felt the desire to eat it. But now I conclude to eat it, and I make an effort of the mind to put forth my hand to take the apple and eat it. It is done. Now here is an entirely new phenomenon; it is an *effort*, an *exertion*, an *act*, a *volition* of the mind. The name is of no importance; the circumstances under which the phenomenon arises have called attention to it, and the precise thing intended is seen in the light of consciousness. Let us look at it closely, and mark its characteristic well, being careful to see neither more nor less than is presented by the phenomenon itself.

We are conscious, then, of the existence of an act, of a volition: everybody can see what this is. We must not say, as the advocates of free-agency usually do, that when we put forth this act or volition we are conscious of a power to do the contrary; for this position may be refuted, and the foundation on which we intend to raise our superstructure undermined. We are merely conscious of the existence of the act itself, and not even of the power by means of which we act; the existence of the power is necessarily inferred from its exercise. This is the only way in which we know it, and not from the direct testimony of consciousness. Much less if we had refused to act, should we have been conscious of the power to withhold it; much less again are we conscious of the power to withhold the act, as we do not in the case supposed exercise this power. But certainly we are conscious of the act itself; all men will concede this, and this is all our argument really demands.

Here then we are conscious of an act, of an effort, of the mind. Look at it closely. Is the mind passive in this act? No; we venture to answer for the universal intelligence of man. If this act had been produced in us by a necessitating cause, would not the mind have been passive in it? In other words, would it not have been a passive impression, and not an act, not an effort of the mind at all? Yes; we again venture to answer for the unbiassed reason of man. But it is not, we have seen, a passive impression; it is an act of the mind, and hence it is not necessitated. It is not necessitated, because it is not stamped with the characteristic of necessity. The universal reason of man declares that the will has not necessarily yielded like the intelligence and the sensibility, to motives over which it had no control. It does not bear upon its face the mark of any such subjection "to the power and action" of a cause. It is marked with the characteristic, not of necessity, but of liberty.

We would not say, with Dr. Samuel Clarke, that "action and liberty are identical ideas;" but we will say, that the idea of action necessarily implies that of liberty; for if we duly reflect on the nature of an act we cannot conceive it as being necessitated. This consideration furnishes an easy and satisfactory solution of a problem, by which necessitarians are sadly perplexed. They endeavour in various ways to account for the fact that we believe our volitions to be free, or not necessarily caused. Some resolve this belief and feeling of liberty into a deceitful sense; some imagine that we are deceived by the ambiguities of language; and some resort to other methods of explaining the phenomenon. "It is true," says President Edwards, "I find myself possessed of my volitions before I can see the effectual power of any cause to produce them, for the power and efficacy of the cause is not seen but by the effect; and this, for aught I know, may make some imagine that volition has no cause, or that it produces itself." But this is not a satisfactory account of the *imagination*, as he would term it. We also find ourselves possessed of our judgments and feelings before we perceive the effectual power of the cause which produces them. Why then do we refer these to the operation of a necessary cause, and not our volitions? If the power and efficacy of the cause is seen only by the effect in the one case, it is only seen in the same manner in the other. Why then do we differ in our conclusions with respect to them? Why do we refer the judgment and the feeling to necessary causes, and fail to do the same in relation to the volition? The reason is obvious. The mind is passive in judging and feeling, and hence these phenomena necessarily demand the operation of causes to account for them; but the mind is active in its volitions, and this necessarily excludes the idea of causes to produce them. The mind clearly perceives, by due reflection, and at all times sees dimly, at least, that an act or volition is different in its nature from a passive impression or a produced effect; and hence it knows and feels that it is exempt from the power and efficacy of a producing cause in its volitions. This fact of our consciousness it is not in the power of sophistry wholly to conceal, nor in the power of human nature to evade. Hence we carry about with us the irresistible conviction that we are free; that our wills are not absolutely subject to the dominion of causes over which we have no control. Hence we see and know that we are self-active.

Having completed our analysis, in as far as our present purpose demands, we may proceed to show that the system of necessity is founded on a false psychology,—on a dark confusion of the facts of human nature. It is very remarkable that all the advocates of this system, from Hobbes down to Edwards, will allow the human mind to possess only two faculties, the understanding and the will. The will and the sensibility are expressly identified by them. Locke distinguished between will and desire, between the *faculty* of willing and the *susceptibility* to feeling; but Edwards has endeavoured to show that there is no such distinction as that for which Locke contends. We shall not arrest the progress of our remarks in order to point out the manner in which Edwards has deceived himself by an appeal to logic rather than to consciousness, because the threefold distinction for which we contend is now admitted by necessitarians themselves. Indeed, after the clear and beautiful analysis by M. Cousin, they could not well do otherwise than recognise this threefold distinction; but they have done so, we think it will be found, without perceiving all the consequences of such an admission to their system. It is an admission which, in our opinion, will show the scheme of necessity to be insecure in its foundation, and disjointed in all its parts.

With the light of this distinction in our minds, it will be easy to follow and expose the sophistries of the necessitarian. He often declaims against the idea of liberty for which we contend, on the ground that it would be, not a perfection, but a very great imperfection of our nature to possess such a freedom. But in every such instance he confounds the will with one of the passive susceptibilities of the mind. Thus, for example, Collins argues that liberty would be a great imperfection, because "nothing can be more irrational and absurd than to be able to refuse our assent to what is evidently true to us, and to assent to what we see to be false." Now, all this is true, but it is not to the purpose; for no one contends that the intelligence is free in assenting to, or in dissenting from, the evidence in view of the mind. No rational being, we admit, could desire such a freedom; could desire to be free, for example, from the conviction that two and two make four. M. Lamartine, we are aware, expresses a very lively abhorrence of the mathematics, because they allow not a sufficient *freedom of thought*—because they exercise so great a *despotism over the intellect.* But the circumstance which this flowery poet deems an imperfection in the mathematics, every enlightened friend of free-agency will regard as their chief excellency and glory.

The same error is committed by Spinoza: "We can consider the soul under two points of view," says he, "as thought and as desire." Here the will is made to disappear, and we behold only the two susceptibilities of the soul, which are stamped with the characteristic of necessity. Where, then, will Spinoza find the freedom of the soul? Certainly not in the will, for this has been blotted out from the map of his psychology. Accordingly he says: "The free will is a chimera of the species, flattered by our pride, and founded upon our ignorance." He must find the freedom of the soul then, if he find it at all, in one of its passive susceptibilities. This, as we have already seen, is exactly what he does; he says the soul is free in the affirmation that two and two are four! Thus he finds the liberty of the soul, not in the exercises of its will, of its active power, but in the bosom of the intelligence, which is absolutely necessitated in all its determinations.

In this particular, as well as in most others, Spinoza merely reproduces the error of the ancient Stoics. It was a principle with them, says Ritter, "that the will and the desire are one with thought, and may be resolved into it."* Thus, by the ancient Stoics, as well as by Hobbes, and Spinoza, and Collins, and Edwards, the will is merged in one of the passive elements of the mind, and its real characteristic lost sight of. "By the freedom of the soul," says Ritter, "the Stoics understood simply that assent which it gives to certain ideas."† Thus the ancient Stoics endeavoured to find the freedom of the soul, where Spinoza and so many modern necessitarians have sought to find it, in the passive, necessitated states of the intelligence. This was

* History of Ancient Philosophy, vol. iii, p. 555. † Ibid.

indeed to impose upon themselves a mere shadow for a substance,—a dream for a reality.

"By whatever name we call the act of the will," says Edwards, "choosing, refusing, approving, disapproving, liking, disliking, embracing, rejecting, determining, directing, commanding, forbidding, inclining or being averse, being pleased or displeased with—all may be reduced to this of choosing."* Thus, in the vocabulary and according to the psychology of this great author, the phenomena of the sensibility and those of the will are identified, as well as the faculties themselves. *Pleasing* and *willing*, liking and acting, are all one with him. His psychology admits of no distinction, for example, between the pleasant impression made by an apple on the sensibility, and the act of the will by which the hand is put forth to take it. "The will and the affections of the soul," says he, "are not two faculties; the affections are not essentially distinct from the will, nor do they differ from the mere actings of the will and inclination, but only in the liveliness and sensibility of exercise."† And again, "I humbly conceive that the affections of the soul are not properly distinguished from the will, as though there were two faculties."‡ And still more explicitly, "all acts of the will are truly acts of the affections."§ Is it not strange, that one who could exhibit such wonderful discrimination when the exigences of his system demanded the exercise of such a power, should have confounded things so clearly distinct in their natures as an act of the will and an agreeable impression made on the sensibility?

It is not possible for any mind, no matter how great its powers, to see the nature of things clearly when it comes to the contemplation of them with such a confusion of ideas. Even President Edwards is not exempt from the common lot of humanity. His doctrine is necessarily enveloped in obscurity. We can turn it in no light without being struck with its inconsistencies or its futility. He repeatedly says, the will is always determined by the strongest affection, or appetite, or passion; that is, by the most agreeable state of the sensibility. But if the will and the sensibility are identical, as his language expressly makes them; or if the states of the one are not dis-

* President Edwards's Works, vol. ii, p. 16.
† Id., vol. v, pp. 10, 11.
‡ Id., vol. iv, p. 82.
§ Ibid.

tinguishable from the states of the other, then to say that the will is always determined by the sensibility, or an act of the will by the strongest affection of the sensibility, is to say that a thing is determined by itself. It is to say, in fact, that the will is always determined by itself; a doctrine against which he uniformly protests. Nay, more, that an act of the will causes itself; a position which he has repeatedly ascribed to his opponents, and held up to the derision of mankind.

It is very remarkable, that Edwards seems to have been conscious, at times, that he laid himself open to the charge of such an absurdity, when he said that the will is determined by the greatest apparent good, or by what seems most agreeable to the mind. For he says, "I have chosen rather to express myself thus, that the will always is as the greatest apparent good, or as what appears most agreeable, than to say the will is determined by the greatest apparent good, or by what seems most agreeable; *because an appearing most agreeable to the mind, and the mind's preferring, seem scarcely distinct.*" We have taken the liberty to emphasize his words. Now here he tells us that the "mind's preferring," by which word he has explained himself to mean willing,* is scarcely distinct from "an appearing most agreeable to the mind." Here he returns to his psychology, and identifies the most agreeable impression made on the sensibility with an act of the will. He does not like to say, that the act of the will is caused by the most agreeable sensation, because this seems to make a thing the cause of itself.

In this he does wisely; but having shaped his doctrine to suit himself more exactly, in what form is it presented to us? Let us look at it in its new shape, and see what it is. The will is not determined by the greatest apparent good, because a thing is not determined by itself; but the will is always as the greatest apparent good! Thus the absurdity of saying a thing is determined by itself is avoided; but surely, if an appearing most agreeable to the mind is not distinct from the mind's acting, then to say that the mind's acting is always as that which appears most agreeable to it is merely to say, that the mind's acting is always as the mind's acting! or, in other words, that a thing is always as itself! Thus, his great fundamental propo-

* Inquiry, p. 17.

sition is, in one form, a glaring absurdity; and in the other, it is an insignificant truism; and there is no escape from this dilemma except through a return to a better psychology, to a sounder analysis of the great facts of human nature.

When Edwards once reaches the truism that a thing is always as itself, he feels perfectly secure, and defies with unbounded confidence the utmost efforts of his opponents to dislodge him. "As we observed before," says he, "nothing is more evident than that, when men act voluntarily, and do what they please, then they do what appears most agreeable to them; and to say otherwise, would be as much as to affirm, that men do not choose what appears to suit them best, or what seems most pleasing to them; or that they do not choose what they prefer—*which brings the matter to a contradiction.*" True; this brings the matter to a contradiction, as he has repeatedly told us; for choosing, and preferring, or willing, are all one. But if any one denies that a man does what he pleases when he does what he pleases; or if he affirms that he pleases without pleasing, or chooses without choosing, or prefers without preferring, we shall leave him to the logic of the necessitarian and the physician. We have no idea that he will ever be able to refute the volumes that have been written to confound him. President Edwards clearly has the better of him; for he puts "the soul in a state of choice," and yet affirms that it "has no choice." He might as well say, indeed, that "a body may move while it is in a state of rest," as to say that "the mind may choose without choosing," or without having a choice. He is very clearly involved in an absurdity; and if he can read the three hundred pages of the Inquiry, without being convinced of his error, his case must indeed be truly hopeless.

Edwards is far from being the only necessitarian who has fallen into the error of identifying the sensibility with the will; thus reducing his doctrine to an unassailable truism. In his famous controversy with Clarke, Leibnitz has done the same thing. "Thus," says he, "in truth, the motives comprehend all the dispositions which the mind can have to act voluntarily; for they include not only reasons, but also the inclinations and passions, or other preceding impressions. Wherefore if the mind should prefer a weak inclination to a strong one, *it would act against itself, and otherwise than it is disposed to act.*"

Now is it not wonderful, that so profound a thinker, and so acute a metaphysician, as Leibnitz, should have supposed that he was engaged in a controversy to show that the mind never acts otherwise than it acts; that it never acts against itself? Having reduced his doctrine to this truism, he says, this "shows that the author's notions, contrary to mine, are superficial, and appear to have no solidity in them, when they are well considered." True, the notions of Clarke were superficial, and worse than superficial, if he supposed that the mind ever acts contrary to its act, or otherwise than it really acts. But Clarke distinguished between the disposition and the will.

In like manner Thummig, the disciple of Leibnitz, has the following language, as quoted by Sir William Hamilton: "It is to philosophize very crudely concerning mind, and to image everything in a corporeal manner, to conceive that actuating reasons are something external, which make an impression on the mind, and *to distinguish motives from the active principle itself.*" Now this language, it seems, is found in Thummig's defence of the last paper of Leibnitz (who died before the controversy was terminated) against the answer of Clarke. But, surely, if it is a great mistake, as the author insists it is, to distinguish motives from the active principle itself; then to say that the active principle is determined by motives, is to say that the active principle is determined by itself. And having reached this point, the disciple of Leibnitz finds himself planted precisely on the position he had undertaken to overthrow, namely, that the will is determined by itself. And again, if it be wrong to distinguish the motive from the active principle itself, then to say that the active principle never departs from the motive, is to affirm that a thing is always as itself.

The great service which a false psychology has rendered to the cause of necessity is easily seen. For having identified an act of the will with a state of the sensibility, which is universally conceived to be necessitated, the necessitarian is delivered from more than half his labours. By merging a phenomenon or manifestation of the will in a state of the sensibility, it seems to lose its own characteristic, which is incompatible with the scheme of necessity, and to assume the characteristic of feeling, which is perfectly reconcilable with it; nay, which demands the scheme of necessity to account for its existence. Thus, the system of necessity is based on a false psychology, on which it has too securely stood from the earliest times down to the present day. But the stream of knowledge, ever deepening and widening in its course, has been gradually undermining the foundations of this dark system.

SECTION II.

The scheme of necessity is directed against a false issue.

As we have seen in the last section, the argument of the necessitarian is frequently directed against a false issue; but the point is worthy of a still more careful consideration.

We shall never cease to admire the logical dexterity with which the champions of necessity assail and worry their adversaries. They have said, in all ages, that "nothing taketh beginning from itself;" but who ever imagined or dreamed of so wild an absurdity? It is conceded by all rational beings. Motion taketh not beginning from itself, but from action; action taketh not beginning from itself, but from mind; and mind taketh not beginning from itself, but from God. It is false, however, to conclude that because nothing taketh beginning from itself, it is brought to pass "by the action of some immediate agent without itself." The motion of body, as we have seen, is produced by the action of some immediate agent without itself; but the action of mind is produced, or brought to pass, by no action at all. It taketh beginning from an agent, and not from the action of an agent. This distinction, though so clearly founded in the nature of things, is always overlooked by the logic of the necessitarian. They might well adopt the language of Bacon, that the subtilty of nature far surpasseth that of our logic.

Hobbes was content to rest on a simple statement of the fact, that nothing can produce itself; but it is not every logician who is willing to rely on the inherent strength of such a position. Ask a child, Did you make yourself? and the child will answer, No. Propound the same question to the roving savage, or to the man of mere common sense, and he will also answer, No. Appeal to the universal reason of man, and the same emphatic No, will come up from its profoundest depths. But your redoubtable logicians are not satisfied to rely on such testimony alone: they dare not build on such a foundation unless it be first secured and rendered firm by the aid of the syllogistic process. I know "I did not make myself," says Descartes, "for if I had made myself, I should have given myself every perfection." Now this argument in true syllogistic form stands thus: If I had made myself, I should have endowed myself with every perfection; I am not endowed with every perfection; therefore I did not make myself. Surely, after so clear a process of reasoning, no one can possibly doubt the proposition that Descartes did not make himself! In the same way we might prove that he did not make his own logic: for if he had made his logic, he would have endowed it with every possible perfection; but it is not endowed with every possible perfection, and therefore he did not make it.

But President Edwards has excelled Descartes, and every other adept in the syllogistic art, except Aristotle in his physics, in his ability to render the light of perfect day clearer by a few masterly strokes of logic. He has furnished the reason why some persons imagine that volition has no cause of its existence, or "that it produces itself." Now, by the way, would it not have been as well if he had first made sure of the fact, before he undertook to explain it? But to proceed: let us see how he has proved that volition does not produce itself,—that it does not arise out of nothing and bring itself into existence.

He does this in true logical form, and according to the most approved methods of demonstration. He first establishes the general position, that no existence or event whatever can give rise to its own being,* and he then shows that this is true of volition in particular.† And having reached the position, that volition does not arise out of nothing, but must "have some antecedent" to introduce it into being; he next proceeds to prove that there is a necessary connexion between volition and the antecedents on which it depends for existence. This completes the chain of logic, and the process is held up by his followers to the admiration of the world as a perfect demonstration. Let us look at it a little more closely, and examine the nature and mechanism of its parts.

If the huge frame of the earth, with all its teeming population and productions, could rise up out of nothing, he argues,

* Inquiry, part i, sec. iii.

† Id., part i, sec. iv.

and bring itself into being without any cause of its existence, then we could not prove the being of a God. All this is very true. For, as he truly alleges, if one world could thus make itself, so also might another and another, even unto millions of millions. The universe might make itself, or come into existence without any cause thereof, and hence we could never know that there is a God. But surely, if any man imagined that even one world could create itself, it is scarcely worth while to reason with him. It is not at all likely that he would be frightened from his position by such a *reductio ad absurdum.* We should almost as soon suspect a sane man of denying the existence of God himself, as of doubting the proposition that "nothing taketh beginning from itself."

Having settled it to his entire satisfaction, by this and other arguments, that no effect whatever can produce itself, he then proceeds to show that this proposition is true of volitions as well as of all other events or occurrences. "If any should imagine," says he, "there is something in the sort of event that renders it possible to come into existence without a cause, and should say that the free acts of the will are existences of an *exceeding different nature* from other things, by reason of which they may come into existence without *previous ground or reason of it,* though other things cannot; if they make this objection in good earnest, it would be an evidence of their strangely forgetting themselves; for it would be giving some account of the existence of a thing, when, at the same time, they would maintain there is no ground of its existence."* True, if any man should suppose that a volition rises up in the world "without any ground or reason of its existence," and afterward endeavour to assign a ground or reason of it, he would certainly be strangely inconsistent with himself; but we should deem his last position, that there must be a ground or reason of its existence, to be some evidence of *his coming to himself*, rather than of his having forgotten himself. But to proceed with the argument. "Therefore I would observe," says he, "that the particular nature of existence, be it never so diverse from others, can lay no foundation for that thing coming into existence without a cause; because, to suppose this, would be to suppose the *particular nature* of existence to be a thing prior to existence,

* Inquiry, pp. 54, 55.

without a cause or reason of existence. But that which in any respect makes way for a thing coming into being, or for any manner or circumstance of its first existence, must be prior to existence. The distinguished nature of the effect, which is something belonging to the effect, cannot have influence backward to act before it is. The peculiar nature of that thing called volition, can do nothing, can have no influence, while it is not. And afterward it is too late for its influence: for then the thing has made sure of its existence already without its help."* After all this reasoning, and more to the same effect, we are perfectly satisfied that volition, no matter what its nature may be, cannot produce itself; and that it must have some ground or reason of its existence, some antecedent without which it could not come into being.

We shall not do justice to this branch of our subject, if we leave it without laying before the reader one or two more specimens of logic from the celebrated Inquiry of President Edwards. He is opposing "the hypothesis," he tells us, "of acts of the will coming to pass without a cause." Now, according to his definition of the term *cause*, as laid down at the beginning of the section under consideration, it signifies any antecedent on which a thing depends, in whole or in part, for its existence, or which constitutes the reason why it is, rather than not.† His doctrine is, then, that nothing ever comes to pass without some "ground or reason of its existence," without some antecedent which is necessary to account for its coming into being. And those who deny it are bound to maintain the strange thesis, that something may come into existence without any antecedent to account for it; that it may rise from nothing and bring itself into existence. It is against this thesis that his logic is directed.

"If it were so," says he, "that things only of one kind, viz., acts of the will, seemed to come to pass of themselves; and it were an event that was continual, and that happened in a course whenever were found subjects capable of such events; this very thing would demonstrate there was some cause of them, which made such a difference between this event and others. For contingency is blind, and does not pick and choose a particular sort of events. Nothing has no choice. This no-cause, which causes no existence, cannot cause the existence which

* Inquiry, p. 55. † Id., p. 50.

comes to pass to be of one particular sort only, distinguished from all others. Thus, that only one sort of matter drops out of heaven, even water; and that this comes so often, so constantly and plentifully, all over the world, in all ages, shows that there is some cause or reason of the falling of water out of the heavens, and that something besides mere contingence had a hand in the matter."* We do not intend to comment on this passage; we merely wish to advert to the fact, that it is a laboured and logical effort to demolish the hypothesis that acts of the will do not bring themselves into existence, and to show that there must be some antecedent to account for their coming into being. We shall only add, "it is true that nothing has no choice;" but who ever pretended to believe that *nothing* puts forth volitions? that there is no mind, no motive, no ground or reason of volition? Is it not wonderful that the great metaphysician of New-England should thus worry himself and exhaust his powers in grappling with shadows and combatting dreams, which no sane man ever seriously entertained for a moment?

"If we should suppose non-entity to be about to bring forth," he continues, "and things were coming into existence without any cause or *antecedent* on which the existence, or kind or manner of existence depends, or which could at all determine whether the things should be stones or stems, or beasts or angels, or human bodies or souls, or only some new motion or figure in natural bodies, or some new sensation in animals, or new idea in the human understanding, or new volition in the will, or anything else of all the infinite number of possibles,—then it certainly would not be expected, although many millions of millions of things were coming into existence in this manner all over the face of the earth, that they should all be only of one particular kind, and that it should be thus in all ages, and that this sort of existences should never fail to come to pass when there is room for them, or a subject capable of them, and that constantly whenever there is occasion."† Now all these words are put together to prove that non-entity cannot bring forth effects, at least such effects as we see in the world; for if non-entity brought them forth, that is, to come to the point in dispute, if non-entity brought forth our volitions, they would not be always of one particular sort of effects. But they are of one

* Inquiry, p. 54. † Id., p. 55.

articular sort, and hence there must be some antecedent to ccount for this uniformity in their nature, and they could not ave been brought forth by nonentity! Surely if anything an equal the fatuity of the hypothesis that nonentity can bring orth, or that a thing can produce itself, it is a serious attempt o refute it. How often, while poring over the works of neces-itarians, are we lost in amazement at the logical mania which eems to have seized them, and which, in its impetuous efforts o settle and determine everything by reasoning, leaves reason tself neither time nor opportunity to contemplate the nature of hings themselves, or listen to its own most authoritative and rreversible mandates.

But lest we should be suspected of doing this great metaphy-ician injustice, we must point out the means by which he has o grossly deceived himself. According to his definition of notive, as the younger Edwards truly says, it includes every ause and condition of volition. If anything is merely a condi-on, without which a volition could not come to pass, though exerts no influence, it is called a cause of that volition, and laced in the definition of motive. And if anything exerts a ositive influence to produce volition, this is also a cause of it, nd is included in the same definition. In short, this definition mbraces every conceivable antecedent on which volition in ny manner, either in whole or in part, either negatively or ositively, depends. Thus the most heterogeneous materials are rowded together under one and the same term,—the most dif-rent ideas under one and the same definition. Is it possible conceive of a better method of obscuring a subject than such course? When Edwards merely means a condition, why does e not say so? and when he means a producing cause, why does e not use the right word to express his meaning? If he had arried on the various processes of his reasoning with some one lear and distinct idea before his mind, we might have expected reat things from him; but he has not chosen to do so. It is ith the term *cause* that he operates, against the ambiguities f which he has not guarded himself or his reader.

"Having thus explained what I mean by cause," says he, I assert that nothing ever comes to pass without a cause." Ve have seen his reasoning on this point. He labours through age after page to establish his very ambiguous proposition, in a sense in which nobody ever denied it; unless some one has affirmed that a thing may come into being without any ground or reason of its existence,—may arise out of nothing and help itself into existence. Having sufficiently established his fundamental proposition in this sense, he proceeds to show that every effect and volition in particular, is necessarily connected with its cause. "It must be remembered," says he, "that it has been already shown, that nothing can ever come to pass without a cause or a reason;"* and he then proceeds to show, that "the acts of the will must be connected with their cause." In this part of his argument, he employs his ambiguous proposition in a different sense from that in which he established it. In the establishment of it he only insists that there must be some antecedent sufficient to account for every event; and in the application of it he contends, that the antecedent or cause must produce the event. These ideas are perfectly distinct. There could be no act of the mind unless there were a mind to act, and unless there were a motive in view of which it acts; but it does not follow that the mind is compelled to act by motive. But let us see how he comes to this conclusion.

"For an event," says he, "to have a cause and ground of its existence, and yet not be connected with its cause, is an inconsistency. For if the event be not connected with its cause, it is not dependent on the cause: *its existence is, as it were, loose from its influence, and may attend it or may not.*"† "Dependence on the influence of a cause is the very notion of an effect."‡ Again, "to suppose there are some events which have a cause and ground of their existence, that yet are not necessarily connected with their cause, is to suppose that they have a cause which is not their cause. Thus, if the effect be not necessarily connected with the cause, with its influence and influential circumstances, then, as I observed before, *it is a thing possible and supposable that the cause may sometimes exert the same influence under the same circumstances, and yet the effect not follow.*"§ He has much other similar reasoning to show that it is absurd and contradictory to say that motive is the cause of volition, and yet admit that volition may be loose from the influence of motive, or that "the cause is not sufficient to produce the effect."‖ In all this he uses the term in its most nar-

* Inquiry, p. 77. † Ibid. ‡ Ibid. § Id., p. 78. ‖ Id., p. 79.

row and restricted sense. It is no longer a mere antecedent or antecedents, which are sufficient to account for the existence of the phenomena of volition; it is an efficient cause which produces volitions. Thus he establishes his ambiguous proposition in one sense, and builds on it in another. He explains the term *cause* to signify any antecedent, in order, he tells us, to prevent objection to his doctrine, when he alleges that nothing ever comes to pass without some cause of its existence; and yet, when he applies this fundamental proposition to the construction of his scheme, he returns to the restricted sense of the word, in which it signifies, "that which has a positive efficacy or influence to produce a thing." It is thus that the great scheme of President Edwards is made up of mere words, having no intrinsic coherency of parts, and appearing consistent throughout, only because its disjointed fragments seem to be united, and its huge chasms concealed by means of the ambiguities of language.

SECTION III.

The scheme of necessity is supported by false logic.

One reason why the advocates of necessity deceive themselves, as well as others, is, that there is great want of precision and distinctness in their views and definitions. We are told by them that the will is always determined by the strongest motive; that this is invariably the cause of volition. But what is meant by the term *cause?* We have final causes, instrumental causes, occasional causes, predisposing causes, efficient causes, and many others. Now, in which of these senses is the word used, when we are informed that motive is the cause of volition? On this point we are not enlightened. Neither Leibnitz nor Edwards is sufficiently explicit. The proposition, as left by them, is vague and obscure.

Leibnitz inclined to the use of the word *reason*, because he carried on a controversy with Bayle and Hobbes, who were atheists; though he frequently speaks of a chain of causes which embrace human volitions.* While Edwards, who opposed the Arminians, generally employs the more rigid term *cause;* though he, too, frequently represents motive as "the ground and reason" of volition. The one softens his language, in places, as he con-

* Théodicée.

tends with those who had rendered themselves obnoxious to the Christian world by an advocacy of the doctrine of necessity in connexion with atheistical sentiments. The other appears to prefer the stronger expression, as he puts forth his power against antagonists whose views of liberty were deemed subversive of the tenets of Calvinism. But the law of causality, as stated by Edwards, and the principle of the sufficient reason, as defined and employed by Leibnitz, are perfectly identical.

When we are told that motive is the cause of volition, it is evident we cannot determine whether to deny or to assent to the proposition, unless we know in what sense the term *cause* is used. We might discuss this perplexed question forever, by the use of such vague and indefinite propositions, without progressing a single step toward the end of the controversy. We must bring a more searching analysis to the subject, if we hope to accomplish anything. We must take the word cause or *reason*, in each of its significations, in order to discover in what particulars the contending parties agree, and in what particulars they disagree, in order to see how far each party is right, and how far it is wrong. This is the only course that promises the least prospect of a satisfactory result.

If we mean by the cause of volition, that which wills or exerts the volition, there is no controversy; for in this sense the advocates of necessity admit that the mind is the cause of volition. Thus says Edwards: "The acts of my will are my own; i. e., they are acts of my will."* It is universally conceded that it is the mind which wills, and nothing else in the place of it; and hence, in this sense of the word, there is no question but that the mind is the cause of volition. But the advocates of necessity cannot be understood in this sense; for they deny that the mind is the cause of volition, and insist that it is caused by motive.

The term *cause* is very often used to designate the condition of a thing, or that without which it could not happen or come to pass. Thus we are told by Edwards, that he sometimes uses "the word cause to signify any *antecedent*" of an event, "whether it has any influence or not," in the production of such event.† If this be the meaning, when it is said that motive is the cause of volition, the truth of the proposition is conceded by the advocates of free-agency. In speaking of arguments and

* Inquiry, p. 277. † Id., pp. 50, 51.

motives, Dr. Samuel Clarke says: "Occasions indeed there may be, and are, upon which that substance in man, wherever the self-moving principle resides, freely exerts its active power."* Herein, then, there is a perfect agreement between the contending parties. The fact that the mind requires certain conditions or occasions, on which to exercise its active power, does not at all interfere with its freedom; and hence the advocates of free-agency have readily admitted that motives are the occasional causes of volition. We must look out for some other meaning of the term, then, if we would clearly and distinctly fix our minds on the point in controversy.

We say that an antecedent is the cause of its consequent, when the latter is produced by the action of the former. For example, a motion of the body is said to be caused by the mind; because it is produced by an act of the mind. This seems to be what is meant by an "*efficient cause.*" It is, no doubt, the most proper sense of the word; and around this it is that the controversy still rages, and has for centuries raged.

The advocates of necessity contend, not only that volition is the effect of motive, but also that "to be an effect implies *passiveness*, or the being subject to the power and action of its cause."† Such precisely is the doctrine of Edwards, and Collins, and Hobbes. In this sense of the word it is denied that motive is the cause of volition, and it is affirmed that mind is the cause thereof. Thus, says Dr. Samuel Clarke, in his reply to Collins, "'T is the self-moving principle, and not at all the reason or motive, which is the *physical* or *efficient* cause of action;" by which we understand him to mean volition, as that is the thing in dispute. Now, when the advocates of free-agency insist that motive is not the efficient cause of volition, and that mind is the efficient cause thereof, we suppose them to employ the expression, *efficient cause*, in one and the same sense in both branches of the proposition. This is the only fair way of viewing their language; and if they wished to be understood in any other manner, they should have taken the pains to explain themselves, and not permit us to be misled by an ambiguity. Here the precise point in dispute is clearly presented; and let us hear the contending parties, before we proceed to decide between them.

* Remarks upon Collins's Philosophical Inquiry. † Inquiry, p. 198.

You are in error, says the necessitarian to his opponents, in denying that motive, and in affirming that mind, is the efficient cause of volition. For if an act of the mind, or a volition, is caused by the mind, it must be produced by a preceding act of the mind, and this act must be produced by another preceding act of the mind, and so on *ad infinitum;* which reduces the matter to a plain impossibility. Now, if the necessitarian has not been deceived by an unwarrantable ambiguity on the part of his adversary, he has clearly reduced his doctrine to the absurdity of an infinite series of acts: that is to say, if the advocate of free-agency does not depart from the ordinary meaning of words, when he affirms that mind is the *efficient cause* of volition; and if he does not use these terms "*efficient cause,*" in different senses in the same sentence, then we feel bound to say that he is fairly caught in the toils of his adversary. But we are not yet in condition to pass a final judgment between the parties.

The necessitarian contends that "volition, or an act of the mind, is the effect of motive, and that it is subject to the power and action of its cause."* The advocate of free-will replies, If we must suppose an action of motive on the mind to account for its act, we must likewise suppose another action to account for the action of motive; and so on *ad infinitum.* Thus the necessitarian seems to be fairly caught in his own toils, and entrapped by his own definition and arguments.

Our decision (for the correctness of which we appeal to the calm and impartial judgment of the reader) is as follows: If the term *cause* be understood in the first or the second sense above mentioned, there is no disagreement between the contending parties; and if it be understood in the third sense, then both parties are in error. If, in order to account for an act of the mind, we suppose it is caused by an action of motive, we are involved in the absurdity of an infinite series of actions; and on the other hand, if we suppose it is caused by a preceding act of the mind itself, we are forced into the same absurdity. Hence, we conclude, that an act of the mind, or a volition, is not produced by the action of either mind or motive, but takes its rise in the world without any such efficient cause of its existence.

* Edwards's Inquiry, p. 178.

Each party has refuted his adversary, and in the enjoyment of his triumph he seems not to have duly reflected on the destruction of his own position. Both are in the right, and both are in the wrong; but, as we shall hereafter see, not equally so. If we adopt the argument of both sides, in so far as it is true, we shall come to the conclusion that action must take its rise somewhere in the universe without being caused by preceding action. And if so, where shall we look for its origin? in that which by nature is endowed with active power, or in that which is purely and altogether passive?

We lay it down, then, as an established and fundamental position, that the mind acts or puts forth its volitions without being efficiently caused to do so,—without being impelled by its own prior action, or by the prior action of anything else. The conditions or occasions of volition being supplied, the mind itself acts in view thereof, without being subject to the power or action of any cause whatever. All rational beings must, as we have seen, either admit this exemption of the mind in willing from the power and action of any cause, or else lose themselves in the labyrinth of an infinite series of causes. It is this exemption which constitutes the freedom of the human soul.

We are now prepared to see, in a clear light, the sophistical nature of the pretended demonstration of the scheme of necessity. "It is impossible to consider occurrences," says Sir James Mackintosh, otherwise than as bound together in "*the relation of cause and effect.*" Now this relation, if we interpret it according to the nature of things, and not according to the sound of words, is not one, but two.

The motions of the body are caused by the mind, that is, they are produced by the action of the mind; this constitutes one relation: but acts of the mind are caused, that is, they are produced by the action of nothing; and this is a quite different relation. In other words, the motions of body are produced by preceding action, and the acts of the mind are not produced by preceding action. Hence, the first are necessitated, and the last are free: the first come under "the relation of cause and effect," and the last come under a very different relation. The relation of cause and effect connects the most remote consequences of volition with volition itself; but when we reach volition, there a new relation arises: it is the relation which subsists between an agent and its act. We may trace changes in the external world up to the volitions or acts of mind, and perceive no diversity in the chain of dependencies; but precisely at this point the chain of cause and effect ceases, and agency begins. The surrounding circumstances may be conditions, may be occasional causes, may be predisposing causes, but they are not, and cannot be, producing or efficient causes. Here, then, the iron chain terminates, and freedom commences. In the ambiguity which fails to distinguish between "the relation of cause and effect," and the relation which volition bears to its antecedents, "consists the strength of the necessitarian system." Let this distinction be clearly made and firmly borne in mind, and the great boasted adamantine scheme of necessity will resolve itself into an empty, ineffectual sound.

Hence, if we would place the doctrine of liberty upon solid grounds, it becomes necessary to modify the categories of M. Cousin. All things, says he, fall under the one or the other of the two following relations: the relation between subject and attribute, or the relation between cause and effect. This last category, we think, should be subdivided, so as to give two relations; one between cause and effect, properly so called, and the other between agent and action. Until this be done, it will be impossible to extricate the phenomena of the will from the mechanism of cause and effect.

We think we might here leave the stupendous sophism of the necessitarian; but as it has exerted so wonderful an influence over the human mind, and obscured, for ages, the glory of the moral government of God, we may well be permitted to pursue it further, and to continue the pursuit so long as a fragment or a shadow of it remains to be demolished.

SECTION IV.

The scheme of necessity is fortified by false conceptions.

One of the notions to which the cause of necessity owes much of its strength, is a false conception of liberty, as consisting in "a power over the determinations of the will." Hence it is said that this power over the will can do nothing, can cause no determination except by acting to produce it. But accord ing to this notion of liberty, this causative act cannot be free unless it be also caused by a preceding act; and so on *ad infinitum.* Such is one of the favourite arguments of the necessitarian. But in truth the freedom of the mind does not consist in its possessing a power over the determinations of its own will, for the true notion of freedom is a negative idea, and consists in the absence of every power over the determinations of the will. The mind is free because it possesses a power of acting, over which there is no controlling power, either within or without itself.

It must be admitted, it seems to us, that the advocates of free-agency have too often sanctioned this false conception of liberty, and thereby strengthened the cause of their opponents. Cudworth, Clark, Stuart, Coleridge, and Reid, all speak of this supposed power of the mind over the determinations of the will, as that which constitutes its freedom. Thus says Reid, for example: "By the liberty of a moral agent, I understand a power over the determinations of his own will." Now, it is not at all strange that this language should be conceived by necessitarians in such a manner as to involve the doctrine of liberty in the absurd consequence of an infinite series of acts, since it is so understood by some of the most enlightened advocates of free-agency themselves. "A power over the determinations of our will," says Sir William Hamilton, "supposes an act of the will that our will should determine so and so; for we can only exert power through a rational determination or volition. *This definition of liberty is right.* But the question upon question remains, (and this *ad infinitum*)—have we a power (a will) over such anterior will? and until this question be definitively answered, which it never can, we must be *unable to conceive the possibility of the fact of liberty.* But, though inconceivable, this fact is not therefore false." True, we are unable to conceive the possibility of the fact of liberty, if this must be conceived as consisting in a power over the determinations of the will; but, in our humble opinion, this definition of liberty is *not* right. It seems more correct to say, that the freedom of the will consists in the absence of a power over its determinations, than in the presence of such a power.

There is another false conception which has given great apparent force to the cause of necessity. It is supposed that the states of the will, the volitions, are often necessitated by the necessitated states of the sensibility. In other words, it is supposed that the appetites, passions, and desires, often act upon the will, and produce its volitions. But this seems to be a very great mistake, which has arisen from viewing the subtle operations of the mind through the medium of those mechanical forms of thought that have been derived from the contemplation of the phenomena of the material world. In truth, the feelings do not act at all, and consequently they cannot act upon the will. It is absurd, as Locke and Edwards well say, to ascribe power, which belongs to the agent himself, to the properties of an agent. Hence, it is absurd to suppose that our feelings, appetites, desires, and passions, are endowed with power, and can act. They are not agents—they are merely the properties of an agent. It is the mind itself which acts, and not its passions. These are but passive impressions made upon the sensibility; and hence, "it is to philosophize very crudely concerning mind, and to image everything in a corporeal manner," to conceive that they act upon the will and control its determinations, just as the motions of body are caused and controlled by the action of mind.*

This conception, however, is not peculiar to the necessitarian. It has been most unfortunately sanctioned by the greatest advocates of free-agency. Thus says Dr. Reid, in relation to the appetites and passions: "Such motives are not addressed to the rational powers. Their influence is *immediately* upon the will." "When a man is acted upon by contrary motives of this kind, he finds it easy to yield to the strongest. *They are like two forces pushing him in contrary directions. To yield to the strongest he needs only be passive.*" If this be so, how can Dr. Reid maintain, as he does, that "the determination was made by the *man*, and not by the motive?" To this assertion Sir William Hamilton replies: "But was the *man* determined by no motive to that determination? Was his specific volition to this or to that without a cause? On the supposition that the sum of the influences (motives, dispositions, tendencies) to volition A is equal to 12, and the sum of counter volition B, equal to 8—can we conceive that the determination of volition A should not be necessary? We can only conceive the voli

* See Examination of Edwards on the Will.

tion B to be determined by supposing that the man *creates* (calls from nonexistence into existence) a certain supplement of influences. But this creation as actual, or in itself, is inconceivable; and even to conceive the possibility of this inconceivable act, we must suppose some cause by which the man is determined to exert it. We thus *in thought*, never escape determination and necessity. It will be observed that I do not consider this inability to notion any disproof of the fact of free-will."

It is true, that if we suppose, according to the doctrine of Sir William and Dr. Reid, that two counter influences act upon the will, the one being as 12 and the other as 8, then the first must necessarily prevail. But if this supposition be correct, we are not only unable to conceive the fact of liberty, we are also able to conceive that it cannot be a fact at all. There is a great difference, we have been accustomed to believe, between being unable to conceive how a thing is, and being able to conceive that it cannot be anyhow at all: the first would leave it a mere mystery,—the last would show it to be an absurdity. In the one case, the thing would be above reason, and in the other, contrary to reason. Now, to which of these categories does the fact of liberty, as left by Sir William Hamilton, belong? Is it a mystery, or is it an absurdity? Is it an inconceivable fact, or is it a conceived impossibility? It seems to us that it is the latter; and that if we will only take the pains to view the phenomena of mind as they exist in consciousness, and not through the medium of material analogies, we shall be able to untie the knot which Sir William Hamilton has found it necessary to cut.

The doctrine of liberty, if properly viewed, is perfectly conceivable. We can certainly conceive that the omnipotence of God can put forth an act without being impelled thereto by a power back of his own; and to suppose otherwise, is to suppose a power greater than God's, and upon which the exercise of his omnipotence depends. By parity of reason, we should be compelled to suppose another power still back of that, and so on *ad infinitum*. This is not only absurd, but, as Calvin truly says, it is impious. Here, then, we have upon the throne of the universe a clear and unequivocal instance of a self-active power,—a power whose goings forth are not impelled by any power without itself. It goes forth, it is true, in the light of the Eternal Reason, and in pursuit of the ends of the Eternal Goodness; but yet in itself it possesses an infinite fulness, being self-sustained, self-active, and wholly independent of all other powers and influences whatsoever.

Now, if such a Being should create at all, it is not difficult to conceive that he would create subordinate agents, bearing his own image in this, namely, the possession of a self-active power. It is not difficult to conceive that he should produce spiritual beings like himself, who can act without being necessitated to act, like the inanimate portions of creation, as well as those of an inferior nature. Nor is it more difficult to conceive that man, in point of fact, possesses such a limited self-active power, than it is to conceive that God possesses an infinite self-active power. Indeed we must and do conceive this, or else we should have no type or representative in this lower part of the world, by and through which to rise to a contemplation of its universal Lord and Sovereign. We should have a temple without a symbol, and a universe without a God. But God has not thus left himself without witness; for he has raised man above the dust of the earth in this, that he is endowed with a self-active power, from whence, as from an humble platform, he may rise to the sublime contemplation of the Universal Mover of the heavens and the earth. But for this ray of light, shed abroad in our hearts by the creative energy of God, the nature of the divine power itself would be unknown to us, and its eternal, immutable glories shrouded in impenetrable darkness. The idea of an omnipotent power, moving in and of itself in obedience to the dictates of infinite wisdom and goodness, would be forever merged and lost in the dark scheme of an implexed series and concatenation of causes, binding all things fast, God himself not excepted, in the iron bonds of fate.

If liberty be a *fact*, as Sir William Hamilton contends it is, then no such objections can be urged against it as those in which he supposes it to be involved. We are aware of what may be said in favour of such a mode of viewing subjects of this kind, as well as of the nature of the principles from which it takes its rise. But we cannot consider those principles altogether sound. They appear to be too sceptical, with respect to the powers of the human mind, and the destiny of human knowledge. The sentiment of Leibnitz seems to rest upon a more solid foundation. "It is necessary to come," says he, "to the grand question which M. Bayle has recently brought upon the carpet, to wit, whether a truth, and especially a truth of faith, can be subject to unanswerable objections. That excellent author seems boldly to maintain the affirmative of this question: he cites grave theologians on his side, and even those of Rome, who appear to say what he pretends; and he adduces philosophers who have believed *that there are even philosophical truths, the defenders of which cannot reply to objections made against them.*" "For my part," says Leibnitz, "I avow that I cannot be of the sentiment of those who maintain that a truth can be liable to invincible objections; for what is an *objection* but an argument of which the conclusion contradicts our thesis? and is not an invincible argument a demonstration?" "It is always necessary to yield to demonstrations, whether they are proposed for our adoption, or advanced in the form of objections. And it is unjust and useless to wish to weaken the proofs of adversaries, under the pretext that they are only objections; since the adversary has the same right, and can reverse the denominations, by honouring his arguments with the name of *proofs*, and lowering yours by the disparaging name of objections."*

There is another false conception, by which the necessitarian fortifies himself in his opposition to the freedom of the will. As he identifies the sensibility and the will, so when the indifference of the latter is spoken of, the language is understood to mean that the mind is indifferent, and destitute of all feeling or emotion. But this is to view the doctrine of liberty, not as it is held by its advocates, but as it is seen through the medium of a false psychology. We might adduce a hundred examples of the truth of this remark, but one or two must suffice. Thus, Collins supposes that the doctrine of liberty implies, that the mind is "indifferent to good and evil;" "indifferent to what causes *pleasure* or *pain*;" "indifferent to all objects, and swayed by no motives." Gross as this misrepresentation of the doctrine of free-agency is, it is frequently made by its opponents. It occurs repeatedly in the writings of President Edwards and Presi-

* Discours de la Conformitè de la Foi avec la Raison.

dent Day.* The freedom of the *will*, indeed, no more implies an indifference of the *sensibility* than the power of a bird to fly implies the existence of a vacuum.

SECTION V.

The scheme of necessity is recommended by false analogies.

It is insisted that there is no difficulty in conceiving of a caused action or volition; but this position is illustrated by false and deceptive analogies. Thus says an advocate of necessity: "The term passive is sometimes employed to express the relation of an effect to its cause. In this sense, it is so far from being inconsistent with activity, that activity may be the very effect which is produced. A cannonshot is said to be passive, with respect to the charge of powder which impels it. But is there no activity given to the ball? Is not the whirlwind active when it tears up the forest?"† Not at all, in any sense pertaining to the present controversy. The tremendous power, whatever it may be, which sets the whirlwind in motion, is active; the wind itself is perfectly passive. The air is acted on, and it merely *suffers* a change of place. If it tears up the forest, this is not because it exercises an active power, but because it is body coming into contact with body, and both cannot occupy the same space at one and the same time. It tears up the forest, not as an agent, but as an instrument.

The same is true of the cannonball. This does not *act;* it merely *moves.* It does not put forth a volition, or an exercise of power; it merely suffers a change of place. In one word, there is no sort of resemblance between an act of mind and the motion of body. This has no active power, and cannot be made to act: it is passive, however, and may be made to move. If the question were, Can a body be made to move? these illustrations would be in point; but as it relates to the possibility of causing the mind to put forth a volition, they are clearly irrelevant. And if they were really apposite, they would only show that the mind may be caused to act like a cannonball, a whirlwind, a clock, or any other piece of machinery. This is the only kind of *action* they serve to prove may be caused; and

* See Examination of Edwards on the Will, sec. ix.

† President Day on the Will, p. 160.

such action, as it is called, has far more to do with machinery than with human agency.

President Edwards also has recourse to false analogies. To select only one instance: "It is no more a contradiction," says he, "to suppose that action may be the effect of some other cause besides the agent, or being that acts, than to suppose that life may be the effect of some other cause besides the being that lives."* Now, as we are wholly passive in the reception of life, so it may be wholly conferred upon us by the power and agency of God. The very reason why we suppose an act cannot be caused is, that it is a voluntary exercise of our own minds; whereas, if it were caused, it would be a necessitated passive impression. How can it show the fallacy of this position, to refer to the case of a caused life, in regard to which, by universal consent, we do not and cannot act at all?

The younger Edwards asserts, that "to say that an agent that is acted upon cannot act, is as groundless as to say that a body acted upon cannot move." Again: "My actions are *mine;* but in what sense can they be properly called mine, if I be not the efficient cause of them?—Answer: my thoughts and all my perceptions and feelings are *mine;* yet it will not be pretended that I am the efficient cause of them."† But in regard to all our thoughts and feelings, we are, as we have seen, altogether passive; and these are ours, because they are necessarily produced *in us.* Is it only in this sense that our acts are ours? Are they ours only because they are necessarily caused to exist in our minds? If so, then indeed we understand these writers; but if they are not merely passive impressions, why resort to states of the intelligence and the sensibility, which are conceded to be passive, in order to illustrate the reasonableness of their scheme, and to expose the unreasonableness of the opposite doctrine? We admit that every passive impression is caused; but the question is, Can the mind be caused to act? As we lay all the stress on the *nature of an act,* as seen in the light of consciousness, what does it signify to tell us that another thing, which possesses no such nature, may be efficiently caused? All such illustrations overlook the essential difference between action and passion, between *doing* and *suffering.*

* Inquiry, p. 203. † Dissertation, p. 181.

SECTION VI.

The scheme of necessity is rendered plausible by a false phraseology.

The false psychology, of which we have spoken, has been greatly strengthened and confirmed in its influences by the phraseology connected with it. As Mr. Locke distinguished between will and desire, partially at least, so he likewise distinguished a preference of the mind from a volition. But President Edwards is not satisfied with this distinction. "*The instance he mentions*," says Edwards, "does not prove there is anything else in *willing* but merely preferring."* This may be very true; but is there nothing in willing, in *acting*, but merely *preferring?* This last term, however it may be applied, seems better adapted to express a state of the intelligence, than an act of the will. Two objects are placed before the mind: one affects the sensibility in a more agreeable manner than the other, and therefore the intelligence pronounces that one is more to be desired than the other. This seems to be precisely what is meant by the use of the term preference. One prefers an orange to an apple, for instance, because the orange affects his sensibility more agreeably than the apple; and the intelligence perceiving this state of the sensibility, declares in favour of the orange. This decision of the judgment is what is usually meant by the use of the term preference, or choice. To prefer, is merely to judge, in view of desire, which of two objects is more agreeable. But judging and desiring are, as we have seen, both necessitated states of the mind. Why, then, apply the term preference, or choice, to acts of the will? Why apply a term, which seems to express merely a state of the intelligence, which all concede is necessitated, to an act of the will? Is it not evident, that by such a use of language the cause of necessity gains great apparent strength?

There is another way in which the language of the necessitarian deceives. The language he employs often represents the facts of nature, but not facts as they would be, if his system were true. Hence, when this system is attacked, its advocates repel the attack by the use of words which truly represent nature, but not their errors. This gives great plausibility

* Inquiry of Edwards, p. 222.

to their apologies. Thus, when it is objected that the scheme of necesssity "makes men no more than mere machines," they are always ready to reply, "that notwithstanding this doctrine, man is entirely, perfectly, and unspeakably different from a machine." But how? Is it because his volitions, as they are called, are not necessarily determined by causes? No. Is it because his will may be loose from the influence of motives? No. Is it because he may follow the strongest motive, or may not follow it? No. Nothing of the kind is hinted. How does the man, then, differ so entirely from a machine? Why, "in that he has reason and understanding, with a faculty of will, and so is capable of volition and choice." True, a machine has no reason or understanding; but suppose it had, would it be a person? By no means. We have seen that the understanding, or the intelligence, is necessarily determined; all its states are necessitated as completely as the movements of a machine. This constitutes an essential likeness, and it is what is always meant, when it is said that necessity makes men mere machines. But it seems that man also has "a faculty of will, and so is capable of volition or choice."* Yes, he can *act.* Now this language means something according to the system of nature; but what does it mean according to the system of necessity? It merely means that the human mind is susceptible of being necessitated to undergo a change by the "power and action of a cause," which the advocates of that system are pleased to call an act. They never hint that we are not machines, because we have any power by which we are exempt from the most absolute dominion of causes. They never hint that we are not machines, because our volitions, or acts, are not as necessarily produced *in us*, as the motions of a clock are produced in it. Now, if this scheme were true, there would be no such things as acts or volitions in us: all the phenomena of our minds would be passive impressions, like our judgments and feelings. When they speak of the will, then, which is capable of volitions, or acts, they deceive by using the language of nature, and not of their false scheme.

* Edwards's Inquiry, p. 222.

SECTION VII.

The scheme of necessity originates in a false method, and terminates in a false religion.

This system, as we have seen, has been built up, not by an analysis of the phenomena of the human mind, but by means of universal abstractions and truisms. It takes its rise, not from the facts of nature, but from the conceptions of the intellect. In other words, instead of anatomizing the world which God has made so as to exhibit the actual plan according to which it has been constituted, it sets out from certain identical propositions, such as that every effect must have a cause, and proceeds to inform us how the world *must* have been constituted. This "usual method of discovery and proof," as Bacon says, "by first establishing the most general propositions, then applying and proving the intermediate axioms according to these, is the parent of error and the calamity of every science." Nowhere, it is believed, can a more striking illustration of the truth of these pregnant words be found, than in the method adopted by necessitarians. They begin with the universal proposition, that every effect must have a cause, as a self-evident truth, and then proceed, not to examine and discover how the world is made, but to demonstrate how it *must* have been constructed. This is not to "interpret," it is to "anticipate" nature.

By this high *a priori* method the freedom of the human mind is demonstrated, as we have seen, to be an impossibility, and the accountability of man a dream. Man is not responsible for sin, or rather, there is no such thing as moral good and evil in the lower world; since God, the only efficient fountain of all things and events, is the sole responsible author of all evil as well as of all good. Such, as we have seen, are the inevitable logical consequences of this boasted scheme of necessity.

But we have clearly shown, we trust, that the grand demontration of the necessitarian is a sophism, whose apparent force is owing to a variety of causes:—First, it seeks out, and lays its foundation in, a false psychology; identifying the feelings, or affections, and the will. Secondly, by viewing the opposite scheme through the medium of this false psychology, it reduces its main position to the pitiful absurdity that a thing may produce itself, or arise out of nothing, and bring itself into existence; and then demolishes this absurdity by logic! Thirdly, it reduces itself to the truism, that a thing is always as it is; and being entrenched in this stronghold, it gathers around itself all the common sense and all the reason of mankind, as well it may, and looks down with sovereign contempt on the feeble attacks of its adversaries. Fourthly, it fortifies itself by a multitude of false conceptions, arising from a hasty application of its universal truism, and not from a severe inspection and analysis of things. Fifthly, it decorates itself in false analogies, and thereby assumes the imposing appearance of truth. Sixthly, it clothes itself in deceptive and ambiguous phraseology, by which it speaks the language of truth to the ear, but not to the sense. And, seventhly, it takes its rise in a false method, and terminates in a false religion.

These are some of the hidden mysteries of the scheme of necessity; which having been detected and exposed, we do not hesitate to pronounce it a grand imposition on the reason of mankind. As such, we set aside this stupendous sophism, whose dark shadow has so long rested on the beauty of the world, obscuring the intrinsic majesty and glory of the infinite goodness therein displayed. We put away and repudiate this vast assemblage of errors, which has so sadly perplexed our mental vision, and so frightfully distorted the real proportions of the world, as to lead philosophers, such as Kant and others, to pronounce a Theodicy impossible. We put them aside utterly, in order that we may proceed to vindicate the glory of God, as manifested in the constitution and government of the moral world.

CHAPTER V.

THE RELATION BETWEEN THE HUMAN WILL AND THE DIVINE AGENCY.

Thou art the source and centre of all minds,
Their only point of rest, eternal Word!
From Thee departing, they are lost and rove
At random, without honour, hope, or peace.
From Thee is all that soothes the life of man,—
His high endeavour and his glad success,
His strength to suffer and his will to serve.—COWPER.

And God proclaim'd from heaven, and by an oath
Confirm'd, that each should answer for himself;
And as his own peculiar work should be
Done by his proper self, should live or die.—POLLOK.

THE evils of haste and precipitancy in the formation of opinions are, perhaps, nowhere more deplorably exhibited, than in regard to the relation between human and divine agency. Indeed, so many rash judgments have been put forth on this important subject, that the very act of approaching it has come to be invested, in the minds of many persons, with the character of rashness and presumption. Hence the frequent warnings to turn our attention from it, as a subject lying beyond the range of all sober speculation, and as unsuited to the investigation of our finite minds. If this be a wise conclusion, it would be well to leave it to support itself, instead of attempting to bolster it up with the reasons frequently given for it.

SECTION I.

General view of the relation between the divine and the human power.

It is frequently said, for example, that it is impossible to reconcile the agency of God with that of man; because we do not know how the divine power operates upon the human mind. But, if we examine the subject closely, we shall find that the manner in which the Spirit of God operates, is not what we want to know, in order to remove the great difficulty in question. If such knowledge were possessed in the greatest possible perfection, we have no reason to believe that our insight into the relation between the human and the divine power would be at all improved. For aught we can see, our notions on this point would remain as dim and feeble as if we possessed no such knowledge. If we could ascertain, however, precisely what is done by the power of man, then we should see whether there be any real inconsistency or conflict between them or not. This is the point on which we need to be enlightened, in order to clear up the difficulty in question; and on this point the most satisfactory light may be attained. If we must wait to understand the *modus operandi* of the divine Spirit, before we can dispel the clouds and darkness which his influence casts over the free-agency of man, then must we indeed defer this great mystery to another state of being, and perhaps forever. Those who have looked in this direction for light, may well deplore our inability to see it. But let us look in the right direction: let us consider, not the *modus operandi* of the divine power, but the effects produced by it, and then, perhaps, we may behold the beautiful harmony subsisting between the agency of God and the freedom of man.

The reason why the views of most persons concerning this relation are so vague and indistinct is, that they do not possess a sufficiently clear and perfect analysis of the human mind. The powers and susceptibilities of the mind, as well as the laws which govern its phenomena, seem blended together in their minds in one confused mass; and hence the relations they bear to each other, and to the divine agency, are as dim and fluctuating as an ill-remembered dream. In this confusion of laws and phenomena, of powers and susceptibilities, of facts and fancies, it is no wonder that so many crude conceptions and vague hypotheses have sprung up and prevailed concerning the great difficulty under consideration. In the dim twilight of mental science, which has shown all things distorted and nothing in its true proportions, it is no wonder that the beautiful order and perspective of the moral world should have been concealed from our eyes. It was to have been expected, that every attempt to delineate this order, would, under such circumstances, prove premature, and aggravate rather than lessen the apparent disorders prevailing in the spiritual world. Accordingly, such attempts generally terminate, either in the denial of the free-agency of man, or of the sovereignty of God;

and those who have maintained both of these tenets in reality, as well as in name, have usually refused to allow themselves to be troubled by the apparent contradictions in which they are involved. While they recognise the two spheres of the human and of the divine agency, they have left them so shadowy and indistinct, and so distorted from their real proportions, that they have inevitably seemed to clash with each other. Hence, to describe these two spheres with clearness and precision, and to determine the precise point at which they come into contact without intersecting each other, is still a desideratum in the science of theology. We shall endeavour to define the human power and the divine sovereignty, and to exhibit the harmony subsisting between them, in such a manner as to supply, in some small degree at least, this great *desideratum* which has so long been the reproach of the most sublime of all the sciences.

But this is not to be done by planting ourselves upon any one particular platform, and dogmatizing from thence, as if that particular point of view necessarily presented us with every possible phase of the truth. There has been, indeed, so much of this one-sided, exclusive, and dogmatizing spirit manifested in relation to the subject in question, as to give a great appearance of truth to the assertion of an ingenious writer, that inasmuch as different minds contemplate the divine and human agency from different points of view, the predominant or leading idea presented to them can never be the same; and hence they can never agree in the same representation of the complex whole. The one, says he, "necessarily gives a greater prominence to the divine agency, and the other to the scope and influence of the human will, and consequently they pronounce different judgments; just as a man who views a spherical surface from the inside will forever affirm it to be concave, while he who contemplates it from the outside will as obstinately assert that it is convex." But although this has been the usual method of treating the subject in question, such weakness and dogmatizing is self-imposed, and not an inevitable condition of the human mind. We may learn wisdom from the errors of the past, no less than from its most triumphant and glorious discoveries.

In the discussion of this subject, it is true that opposite parties have confined themselves to first appearances too much, and rested on one-sided views. But are we necessarily tied down to such inadequate conceptions? The causes which separate men in opinion, and the obstacles which keep them asunder, are indeed powerful; but we hope they do not form an eternal barrier between the wise and good. In regard to doctrines so fundamental and so vital as the divine sovereignty and human freedom, it is to be hoped that all good men will some day unite, and perfectly harmonize with each other.

As we are rational beings, so we are not tied down to that appearance of things which is presented to one particular point of view. If this were the case, the science of astronomy would never have had an existence. Even the phenomena of that noble science are almost inconceivably different from those presented to the mind of man at his particular point of view. From the small shining objects which are brought to our knowledge by the sense of sight, the reason rises to the true dimensions of those tremendous worlds. And after the human mind has thus furnished itself with the facts of the solar system, it has proceeded but a small way toward a knowledge of the system itself. It has also to deduce the laws of the material world from its first appearances, and, armed with these, it must transport itself from the earth to the true centre of the system, from which its wonderful order and beauty may be contemplated, and revealed to the world. Then these innumerable twinkling points of light, which sparkle in the heavens like so many atoms, become to the eye of reason the stupendous suns and centres of other worlds and systems.

If we should judge from first appearances, indeed, if we could not emancipate ourselves from phenomena as they are exhibited to us from one particular point of view, then should we never escape the conclusion, that the earth is the fixed centre of the universe, around which its countless myriads of worlds perform their eternal revolutions. But, fortunately, we are subject to no such miserable bondage. The mind of man has already raised itself from the planet to which his body is confined, and, planting itself on the true centre of the system, has beheld the sublime scheme planned by the infinite reason, and executed by the almighty power of the Divine Architect. Surely the mind which can do, and has done, all this, has the capacity to understand, place it where you will, that although the inside of a sphere is concave, the outside may be convex; as well as some other things which may perhaps have been placed beyond its power, without due consideration. But in every attempt to emancipate ourselves from first appearances, and to reach a knowledge of the truth, "not as reflected under a single angle," but as seen in all its fulness and beauty, it is indispensable to contemplate it on all sides, and to mark the precise boundaries of all its phases.

Hence we shall not plant ourselves on the fact of man's power alone, and, viewing the subject exclusively from thence, enlarge the sphere of human agency to such an extent as to shut the divine agency quite out of the intellectual and moral world. Nor, on the other hand, shall we permit ourselves to become so completely absorbed in the contemplation of the majesty of God, to dwell so warmly on his infinite sovereignty and the littleness of man, as to cause the sphere of human power to dwindle down to a mere point, and entirely disappear. We shall endeavour to find the true medium between these two extreme opinions. That such a medium exists *somewhere*, will not be denied by many persons. The only question will be, as to where and how the line should be drawn to strike out this medium. In most systems of theology, this line is not drawn at all, but left completely in the dark. We are shown some things on both sides of this line, but we are not shown the line itself. We are made to see, for example, the fact of human existence as something distinct from God, that we may not err with Spinoza, in reducing man to a mere fugitive mode of the Divine Being, to a mere shadow and a dream. And on the other side, we are made to contemplate the omnipotence of God, that we may not call in question his sovereignty and dominion over the moral world. But between these two positions, on which the light of truth has thus been made to fall, there is a tract of dark and unexplored territory, a *terra incognita*, which remains to be completely surveyed and delineated, before we can see the beauty of the whole scene. In the attempt to map out this region, to define the precise boundary of that *imperium in imperio*, of which Spinoza and others entertained so great a horror, we should endeavour to follow the wise maxim of Bacon, "to despise nothing, and to admire nothing."

In other words, we should endeavour to "prove all things,

and to hold fast that which is good," without yielding a blind veneration to received dogmas, or a blind admiration to the seductive charms of novelty. Hence, we shall first stand on the same platform with Pelagius, and endeavour to view the subject with his eyes; to see all that he saw, as well as to correct the errors of his observation. And having done this, we shall then transport ourselves to the platform of Augustine, and contemplate the subject from his point of view, so as to possess ourselves of his great truths, and also to correct the errors of his observation. Having finished these processes, it will not be found difficult to combine the truths of these two conflicting schemes in a complete and harmonious system, which shall exhibit both the human and the divine elements of religion in their true proportions and just relations to each other.

SECTION II.

The Pelagian platform, or view of the relation between the divine and the human power.

The doctrine of Pelagius was developed from his own personal experience, and moulded, in a great measure, by his opposition to the scheme of Augustine. According to the historian, Neander, as well as to the testimony of Augustine himself, the life of Pelagius was, from beginning to end, one "earnest moral effort." As his character was gradually formed by his own continued and unremitted exertions, without any sudden or violent revolution in his views or feelings, so the great fact of human agency presented itself to his individual consciousness with unclouded lustre. This fact was the great central position from which his whole scheme developed itself. And, as the history of his opinion shows, he was led to give a still greater predominance to this fact, in consequence of his opposition to the system of Augustine, by which it seemed to him to be subverted, and the interests of morality threatened.

The great fact of free-will, of whose existence he was so well assured by his own consciousness, was so imperfectly interpreted by him, that he was led to exclude other great facts from his system, which might have been perfectly harmonized with his central position. Thus, as Neander well says, he denied the operation of the divine power in the renovation of the soul,* because he could not reconcile its influence with the free-agency of man. This was the weak point in the philosophy of Pelagius, as it has been in the system of thousands who have lived since his time. To reject the one of two facts, both of which rest upon clear and unequivocal evidence, is an error which has been condemned by Butler and Burlamaqui, as well as by many other celebrated philosophers. But this error, so far as we know, has been by no one more finely reproved than by Professor Hodge, of Princeton. "If the evidence of the constant revolution of the earth round its axis," says he, "were presented to a man, it would certainly be unreasonable in him to deny the fact, merely because he could not reconcile it with the stability of everything on the earth's surface. Or if he saw two rays of light made to produce darkness, must he resist the evidence of his senses, because he knows that two candles give more light than one? Men do not act thus irrationally in physical investigations. They let each fact stand upon its own evidence. They strive to reconcile them, and are happy when they succeed. But they do not get rid of difficulties by denying facts.

"If in the department of physical knowledge we are obliged to act upon the principle of receiving every fact upon its own evidence, even when unable to reconcile one with another, it is not wonderful that this necessity should be imposed upon us in those departments of knowledge which are less within the limits of our powers. It is certainly irrational for a man to reject all the evidence of the spirituality of the soul, because he cannot reconcile this doctrine with the fact that a disease of the body disorders the mind. Must I do violence to my nature in denying the proof of design afforded by the human body, because I cannot account for the occasional occurrence of deformities of structure? Must I harden my heart against all the evidence of the benevolence of God, which streams upon me in a flood of light from all his works, because I may not know how to reconcile that benevolence with the existence of evil? Must I deny my free-agency, the most intimate of all convic-

* A different view of the Pelagian doctrine on this point is given by Wiggers, and yet we suppose that both authors are in the right. The truth seems to me, that Pelagius, as usually happens to those who take one-sided views of the truth, has asserted contradictory positions.

tions, because I cannot see the consistency between the freeness of an act and the frequency of its occurrence? May I deny that I am a moral being, the very glory of my nature, because I cannot change my character at will?"*

If this judicious sentiment had been observed by speculatists, it had been well for philosophy, and still better for religion. The heresy of Pelagius, and the countless forms of kindred errors, would not have infested human thought. But this sentiment, however just in itself, or however elegantly expressed, should not be permitted to inspire our minds with a feeling of despair. It should teach us caution, but not despondency; it should extinguish presumption, but not hope. For if "we strive to reconcile the facts" of the natural world, "and are happy when we succeed," how much more solicitous should we be to succeed in such an attempt to shut up and seal the very fountains of religious error?

Nothing is more wonderful to my mind, than that Pelagius should have such followers as Reimarus and Lessing, not to mention hundreds of others, who deny the *possibility* of a divine influence, because it seems to them to conflict with the intellectual and moral nature of man.† To assert, as these philosophers do, that the power of God cannot act upon the human mind without infringing upon its freedom, betrays, as we venture to affirm, a profound and astonishing ignorance of the whole doctrine of free-agency. It proceeds on the amazing supposition that the will is the only power of the human mind, and that volitions are the only phenomena ever manifested therein; so that God cannot act upon it at all, unless it be to produce volitions. But is it true, that God must do all things within us, or he can do nothing? that if he produce a change in our mental state, then he must produce all conceivable changes therein? In order to refute so rash a conclusion, and explode the wild supposition on which it is based, it will be necessary to recur to the threefold distinction of the intelligence, the sensibility, and the will, already referred to.

In the perception of truth, as we have seen, the intelligence is perfectly passive. Every state of the intelligence is as completely necessitated as is the affirmation that two and two are

* The Way of Life, chap. iii, sec. ii.

† Knapp's Theology, vol. ii, p. 471. Note by the translator.

equal to four. The decisions of the intelligence, then, are not free acts; indeed, they are not acts at all, in the proper sense of the word. They are passive states of the intellect. They are usually called acts, it is true; and this use of language is, no doubt, one of the causes which has given rise to so many errors and delusions in regard to moral and accountable agency. With every decision or state of the intelligence, with every perception of truth by it, there is intimately associated, it is true, an act of the mind, a state of the will, a volition, by which the attention is directed to the subject under consideration; and it is this intimate association in which the two states or mental phenomena seem blended into one, which has led so many to regard the passive susceptibility, called the intelligence, as an active power, and its states as free acts of the mind. A more correct analysis, a finer discrimination of the real facts of consciousness, must prevail on this subject, before light can be let in upon the philosophy of free and accountable agency. The dividing knife must be struck between the two *phenomena* in question, between an active state of the will and the passive states of the intelligence, and the obstinate association be severed in our imagination, before the truth can be seen otherwise than through distorting films of error.

As every state of the intelligence is necessitated, so God may act upon this department of our mental frame without infringing upon the nature of man in the slightest possible degree. As the law of necessity is the law of the intelligence, so God may absolutely necessitate its states, by the presentation of truth, or by his direct and irresistible agency in connexion with the truth, without doing violence to the laws of our intellectual and moral nature. Nay, in so acting, he proceeds in perfect conformity with those laws. Hence, no matter how deep a human soul may be sunk in ignorance and stupidity, God may flash the light of truth into it, in perfect accordance with the laws of its nature. And, as has been well said, "The first effect of the divine power in the new, as in the old creation, is light."

This is not all. Every state of the sensibility is a passive impression, a necessitated phenomenon of the human mind. No matter what fact, or what truth, may be present to the mind, either by its own voluntary attention or by the agency of God, or by the coöperation of both, the impression it makes upon the sensibility is beyond the control of the will, except by refusing to give the attention of the mind to it. Hence, although truth may be vividly impressed upon the intelligence, although the glories of heaven and the terrors of hell may be made to shine into it, yet the sensibility may remain unaffected by them. It may be dead. Hence, God may act upon this, may cause it to melt with sorrow or to glow with love, without doing violence to any law of our moral nature. There is no difficulty, then, in conceiving that the second effect of the divine power in the new creation is "a new heart."

Having done all this, he may well call on us to "work out our salvation with fear and trembling, for God worketh in us to will and to do of his own good pleasure." We have seen that the state of the will, that a volition is not necessitated by the intelligence or by the sensibility; and, hence, it may "obey the heavenly vision," or it may "resist and do despite to the Spirit of grace." If it obey, then the vivifying light and genial shower have not fallen upon the soul in vain. The free-will coalesces with the renovated intelligence and sensibility, and the man "has root in himself." The blossom gradually yields to the fruit, and the germ of true holiness is formed in the soul. This consists in the voluntary exercise of the mind, in obedience to the knowledge and the love of God, and in the permanent habit formed by the repetition of such exercises. Hence, in the great theandric work of regeneration, we see the part which is performed by God, and the part which proceeds from man.

This shows an absolute dependence of the soul upon the agency of God. For without knowledge the mind can no more perform its duty than the eye can see without light; and without a feeling of love to God, it is as impossible for it to render a spiritual obedience, as it would be for a bird to fly in a vacuum. Yet this dependence, absolute as it is, does not impair the free-agency of man. For divine grace supplies, and must supply, the indispensable conditions of holiness; but it does not produce holiness itself. It does not produce holiness itself, because, as we have seen, a necessary holiness is a contradiction in terms.

Is it not evident, then, that those who assert the impossibility of a divine influence, on the ground that it would destroy the free-agency of man, have proceeded on a wonderful confusion of the phenomena of the human mind? Is it not evident that they have confounded those states of the intelligence and the sensibility, which are marked over with the characteristics of necessity, with those states of the will which inevitably suggest the ideas of freedom and accountability? But, strange as it may seem, the philosophers who thus shut the influence of the Divine Being out of the spiritual world, because they cannot reconcile it with the moral agency of man, do not always deny the influence of created beings over the mind. On the contrary, it is no uncommon thing to see philosophers and theologians, who begin by denying the influence of the Divine Spirit upon the human mind, in order to save the freedom of the latter, end by subjecting it to the most absolute dominion of facts, and circumstances, and motives.

SECTION III.

The Augustinian Platform, or view of the relation between the divine agency and the human.

The doctrine of Augustine, like that of Pelagius, was developed from the individual experience and consciousness of its author. The difference between them was, that the sensible experience of the one furnished him with only the human element of religion, which was unduly magnified by him; while the divine element was the great prominent fact in the consciousness of the other, who accordingly rendered it too exclusive in the formation of his views. The one elevated the human element of religion at the expense of the divine; the other permitted the majesty of the divine to overshadow the human, and cause it to disappear.

The causes which induced Augustine to take this sublime but one-sided view of religion may be easily understood. In the early part of his life, he abandoned himself to vicious excesses; being hurried away, to use a metaphor, by the violence of his appetites and passions. His conscience, no doubt, often reproved him for such a course of life, and gave rise to many resolutions of amendment. But experience taught him that he could not transform and mould his own character at pleasure. He lacked those views of truth, and those feelings of reverence and love to God, without which true obedience is impossible. Hence he struggled in vain. He felt his own impotency. He still yielded to the importunities of appetite and passion. Of a sudden, however, he finds his views of divine things changed, and his religious sensibilities awakened. He knows this marvellous transformation is not effected by himself. He ascribes it, and he truly ascribes it, to the power of God; by which he has been brought from a region of darkness to light. Old things had passed away, and all things become new.

But now observe the precise manner in which the error of Augustine takes its rise in his mind. He, too, as well as Pelagius, confounds the passive susceptibility of the heart with a voluntary state of the will. The intelligence and the sensibility are the only elements in his psychology; the states of them, which are necessitated, constitute all the phenomena of the human mind. Holiness, according to him, consists in a feeling of love to God. He knows this is derived from the divine agency; and hence he concludes, that the whole work of conversion is due to God, and no part of it is performed by himself. I know, says he, that I did not make myself love God, by which he means a feeling of love; and this he takes to be true holiness, which has been wrought in his heart by the power of God. "Love is the fulfilling of the law; but love to God is not shed abroad in our hearts by the law, but by the Holy Ghost." He is sure the whole work is from God, because he is sure that the intelligence and the sensibility are the whole of man. How many excellent persons are there, who, taking their stand upon the same platform of a false psychology, proceed to dogmatize with Augustine as confidently as if the only possible ground of difference from them was a want of the religious experience of the Christian consciousness, by which they have been so eminently blessed. We deny not the reality of their Christian experience; but we do doubt the accuracy of their interpretation of it.

Thus, the complex fact of consciousness, consisting in a state of the sensibility and a state of the will, was viewed from opposite points by Pelagius and Augustine. The voluntary phase of it was seen by Pelagius, and hence he became an exclusive and one-sided advocate of free-agency; the passive side was beheld by Augustine, and hence he became a one-sided and exclusive advocate of divine grace. If we would possess the truth, and the whole truth, we must view it on all sides, and give a better interpretation of the natural consciousness of the one, as well as the supernatural consciousness of the other, than they themselves were enabled to give. Then shall we not instinctively turn to one-sided views of revelation. Then shall we not always repeat with Pelagius, "Work out your own salvation with fear and trembling," nor always exclaim with Augustine, that "God worketh in us to will and to do of his good pleasure;" but we shall with equal freedom and readiness approach and appropriate both branches of the truth.

SECTION IV.

The views of those who, in later times, have symbolized with Augustine.

Those divines who have adopted, in the main, the same leading views with Augustine, have generally admitted the fact of free-agency; but, because they could not reconcile it with their leading tenet, they have, as we have seen, explained it away. The only freedom which they allow to man, pertains, as we have shown, not to the will at all, but only to the external sphere of the body. They have maintained the great fact in words, but rejected it in substance. Though they have seen the absurdity of rejecting one fact because they could not reconcile it with another, yet their internal struggle after a unity and harmony of principle has induced them to deny, in reality, what they have seemed to themselves to preserve and maintain. We have seen, in the first chapter of this work, in what manner this has been done by them; it now remains to take a view of the subject, in connexion with the point under consideration.

The man who confounds the sensibility with the will should, indeed, have no difficulty in reconciling the divine agency with the human. If the state of the mind in willing is purely passive, like a state of the mind in feeling; then to say that it is produced by the power of God, would create no difficulty whatever. Hence, the great difficulty of reconciling the human with the divine agency, which has puzzled and perplexed so many, should not exist for one who identifies the will with the sensibility; and it would exist for no one holding this psychology, if there were not more in the operations of his nature than in the developments of his system. Perhaps no one ever more completely lost sight of the true characteristic of the manifestations of the will, by thrusting them behind the phenomena of the sensibility, than President Edwards; and hence the difficulty in question seemed to have no existence for him. So far from troubling himself about the line which separates the human agency from the divine, he calmly and quietly speaks as if such a line had no existence. According to his view, the divine agency encircles all, and man is merely the subject of its influence. It is true, he uses the terms active and actions, as applicable to man and his exertions; but yet he regards his very acts, his volitions, as being produced by God. "In efficacious grace," says he, "God does all, and we do all. God produces all, and we act all. For that is what he produces; namely, our own acts." Now I think Edwards could not have used such language, if he had attached any other idea to the term act, than what really belongs to it when it is applied, as it often is, to the passive states of the intelligence and the sensibility. An *act* of the intellect, or an *act* of the affections, may be produced by the power of God; but not an act of the will. For, as the Princeton Review well says, "a necessary volition is an absurdity, a thing inconceivable."

It is scarcely necessary to add, that in causing all real human agency to disappear before the divine sovereignty, Edwards merely reproduced the opinion of Calvin; which he endeavoured to establish, not by a fierce, unreasoning dogmatism, but upon the principles of reason and philosophy. "The apostle," says Calvin, "ascribes everything to the Lord's mercy, *and leaves nothing to our wills or exertions*."* He even contends, that to "suppose man to be a coöperator with God, so that the validity of election depends on his consent," is to make the "will of man superior to the counsel of God;"† as if there were no possible medium between nothing and omnipotence.

* Institutes, b. iii, ch. xxiv. † Ibid.

SECTION V.

The danger of mistaking distorted for exalted views of the divine sovereignty.

There is no danger, it is true, that we shall ever form too exalted conceptions of the divine majesty. All notions must fall infinitely below the sublime reality. But we may proceed in the wrong direction, by making it our immediate aim and object to exalt the sovereignty of God. An object so vast and overwhelming as the divine omnipotence, cannot fail to transport the imagination, and to fill the soul with wonder. Hence, in our passionate, but always feeble, endeavours to grasp so wonderful an object, our vision may be disturbed by our emotions, and the glory of God badly reflected in our minds. Our utmost exertions may thus end, not in exalted, but in distorted views of the divine sovereignty. Is it not better, then, for feeble creatures like ourselves, to aim simply to acquire a knowledge of the truth, which, we may depend upon it, will not fail to exhibit the divine sovereignty in its most beautiful lights?

If such be our object, we shall find, we think, that God is the author of our spiritual views in religion, as well as those genuine feelings of reverence and love, without which obedience is impossible; and that man himself is the author of the volitions by which his obedience is consummated. This shows the precise point at which the divine agency ceases, and human agency begins; the precise point at which the sphere of human power comes into contact with the sphere of omnipotence, without intersecting it and without being annihilated by it. It shows at once the absolute dependence of man upon God, without a denial of his free and accountable agency; and it asserts the latter, without excluding the Divine Being from the affairs of the moral world. It renders unto Cæsar the things which are Cæsar's, and unto God the things which are God's. At the same time that it combines and harmonizes these truths, it shows the errors of the opposite extremes, and places the doctrines of human and divine agency upon a solid and enduring basis, by preventing each from excluding the other.

In all our inquiries, truth, and truth alone, should be our grand object. All by-ends and contracted purposes, all party schemes and sectarian zeal, will be almost sure to defeat their own objects, by seeking them with *too direct and exclusive an aim.* These, even when noble and praiseworthy, must be sought and reached, if reached at all, by seeking and finding the truth. Thus, for instance, would we exalt the sovereignty of God, then must we not directly seek to exalt that sovereignty, but put away from us all the forced contrivances and factitious lights which have been invented for that purpose. It is the light of truth alone, sought for its own sake, and therefore clearly seen, that can reveal the sublime proportions, and the intrinsic moral loveliness, of this awful attribute of the Divine Being. On the other hand, would we vindicate the freedom of man, and break into atoms the iron law of necessity, which is supposed to bind him to the dust, then again must we seek the truth without reference to this particular aim or object. We must study the great advocates of that law with as great earnestness and fairness as its adversaries. For it is by the light of truth alone, that the real position man occupies in the moral world, or the orbit his power moves in, can be clearly seen, free from the manifold illusions of error; and until it be thus seen, the liberty of the human mind can never be successfully and triumphantly vindicated. If we would understand these things, then, we must struggle to rise above the foggy atmosphere and the refracted lights of prejudice, into the bright region of eternal truth.

CHAPTER VI.

THE EXISTENCE OF MORAL EVIL, OR SIN, RECONCILED WITH THE HOLINESS OF GOD.

> One doubt remains,
> That wrings me sorely, if I solve it not.
> ° ° ° ° ° ° ° ° ° ° °
> The world, indeed, is even so forlorn
> Of all good, as thou speakest it, and so swarms
> With every evil. Yet, beseech thee, point
> The cause out to me, that myself may see
> And unto others show it: for in heaven
> One places it, and one on earth below.—Dante.

Theology teaches that God is a being of infinite perfections. Hence, it is concluded, that if he had so chosen, he might have secured the world against the possibility of evil; and this naturally gives rise to the inquiry, why he did not thus secure it? Why he did not preserve the moral universe, as he had created it, free from the least impress or overshadowing of evil? Why he permitted the beauty of the world to become disfigured, as it has been, by the dark invasion and ravages of sin? This great question has, in all ages, agitated and disturbed the human mind, and been a prolific source of atheistic doubts and scepticism. It has been, indeed, a dark and perplexing enigma to the eye of faith itself.

To solve this great difficulty, or at least to mitigate the stupendous darkness in which it seems enveloped, various theories have been employed. The most celebrated of these are the following: 1. The hypothesis of the soul's preëxistence; 2. The hypothesis of the Manicheans; and, 3. The hypothesis of optimism. It may not be improper to bestow a few brief remarks on these different schemes.

SECTION I.

The hypothesis of the soul's preëxistence.

This was a favourite opinion with many of the ancient philosophers. In the Phædon of Plato, Socrates is introduced as maintaining it; and he ascribes it to Orpheus as its original author. Leibnitz supposes that it was invented for the purpose of explaining the origin of evil;* but the truth seems to be, that it arose from the difficulty of conceiving how the soul could be created out of nothing, or out of a substance so different from itself as matter. The hypothesis in question was also maintained by many great philosophers, because they imagined that if the past eternity of the soul were denied, this would shake the philosophical proof of its future eternity.† There can be no doubt, however, that after the idea of the soul's preëxistence had been conceived and entertained, it was very generally employed to account for the origin of evil.

But it must be conceded that this hypothesis merely draws a veil over the great difficulty it was designed to solve. The difficulty arises, not from the circumstance that evil exists in the present state of our being, but from the fact that it is found to exist anywhere, or in any state, under the moral administration of a perfect God. It is as difficult to conceive why such a being should have permitted the soul to sin in a former state of existence, even if such a state were an established reality, as it is to account for its rise in the present world. To remove the difficulty out of sight, by transferring the origin of evil beyond the sphere of visible things, is a poor substitute for a solid and satisfactory solution of it. The great problem of the moral world is not to be illuminated by any such fictions of the imagination; and we had better let it alone altogether, if we have nothing more rational and solid to advance.

SECTION II.

The hypothesis of the Manicheans.

Though this doctrine is ascribed to Manes, after whom it is called, it is of a far more early origin. It was taught, says Plutarch, by the Persian Magi, whose views are exhibited by him in his celebrated treatise of Isis and Osiris. "Zoroaster," says he, "thought that there are two gods, contrary to each other in their operations—a good and an evil principle. To the former he gave the name of Oromazes, and to the latter that of Arimanius. The one resembles light and truth, the other darkness and ignorance." We do not allude to this theory for

* Essais de Théodicée.

† Cudworth's Intellectual System.

the purpose of combatting it; we suppose it would scarcely find a respectable advocate at the present day. This, like many other inventions of the great intellects of antiquity, has entirely disappeared before the simple but sublime doctrines of the religion of Jesus.

M. Bayle, it is true, has exhausted the resources of his genius, as well as the rich stores of his learning, in order to adorn the doctrine of Manes, and to render it more plausible, if possible, than any other which has been employed to explain the origin and existence of evil. But this was not because he sincerely believed it to be founded in truth. He merely wished to show its superiority to other schemes, in order that by demolishing it he might the more effectually inspire the minds of men with a dark feeling of universal scepticism. It was decorated by him, not as a system of truth, but as a sacrifice to be offered up on the altar of atheism. True to the instincts of his philosophy, he sought on this subject, as well as on all others, to extinguish the light of science, and manifest the wonders of his power, by hanging round the wretched habitation of man the gloom of eternal despair.

Though this doctrine is now obsolete in the civilized world, it was employed by a large portion of the ancient philosophers to account for the origin of evil. This theory does not, it is true, relieve the difficulty it was designed to solve; but it shows that there was a difficulty to be solved, which would not have been the case if evil could have been ascribed to the Supreme God as its author. If those philosophers could have regarded him as a Being of partial goodness, they would have found no difficulty in explaining the origin and existence of evil; they would simply have attributed the good and the evil in the world to the good and the evil supposed to pertain to his nature. But they could not do this, inasmuch as the human mind no sooner forms an idea of God, than it regards him as a being of unlimited and unmixed goodness. It has shown a disposition, in all ages, to adopt the most wild and untenable hypotheses, rather than entertain the imagination that evil could proceed from the Father of Lights. The doctrine of Manes, then, as well as the other hypotheses employed to explain the origin of evil, demonstrates how deep is the conviction of the human mind that God is light, and in him there is no darkness at all.

In searching after the fountain of evil, it turns from the great source of life and light, and embraces the wildest extravagancies, rather than indulge a dark suspicion respecting the goodness of its Maker.

SECTION III.

The hypothesis of optimism.

"The fundamental principle of the optimist is," says Dugald Stewart, "that all events are ordered for the best; and that evils which we suffer are parts of a great system conducted by almighty power under the direction of infinite wisdom and goodness." Leibnitz, who is unquestionably one of the greatest philosophers the world has produced, has exerted all his powers to adorn and recommend the scheme of optimism. We have, in a former chapter, considered the system of Leibnitz; but we have not denied its fundamental principle, which is so well expressed in the above language of Mr. Stewart. If he had confined himself to that principle, without undertaking to explain *how* it is that God orders all things for the best, his doctrine would have been free from objections, except for a want of clearness and precision.

Dr. Chalmers has said that the scheme of optimism, as left by Leibnitz, is merely an hypothesis. He insists, however, that even as an hypothesis, it may be made to serve a highly important purpose in theology. "If it be not an offensive weapon," says he, "with which we may beat down and demolish the strongholds of the sceptic, it is, at least, an armour of defence, with which we may cause all his shafts to fall harmless at our feet." This remark of Dr. Chalmers seems to be well founded. The objection of the sceptic, as we have seen, proceeds on the supposition that if a Being of infinite perfections had so chosen, he might have made a better universe than that which actually exists. But we have as good reasons to make suppositions as the sceptic. Let us suppose, then, that notwithstanding the evil which reigns in the world, the universe is the best possible universe that even infinite wisdom, and power, and goodness, could have called into existence. Let us suppose that this would be clearly seen by us, if we only knew the whole of the case; if we could only view the present condition of man in all its connexions and relations to God's infinite plans for the universe and for eternity. In other words, let us suppose, that if we were only omniscient, our difficulty would vanish, and where we now see a cloud over the divine perfections, we should behold bright manifestations of them. This is a mere supposition, it is true, but it should be remembered that the objection in question is based on a mere supposition. When it is asked, why God permitted evil if he had both the power and the will to prevent it? it is assumed that the prevention of evil is better, on the whole, than the permission of it, and consequently more worthy of the infinite wisdom and goodness ascribed to God. But as this is a mere supposition, which has never been proved by the sceptic, we do not see why it may not be sufficiently answered by a mere supposition.

This is an important idea. In many a good old writer, it exists in the dark germ; in Dr. Chalmers it appears in the expanded blossom. Its value may be shown, and its beauty illustrated, by a reference to the affairs of human life; for many of the most important concerns of society are settled and determined by the application of this principle. If a man were on trial for his life, for example, and certain facts tending to establish his guilt were in evidence against him, no enlightened tribunal would pronounce him guilty, provided any hypothesis could be framed, or any supposition made, by which the facts in evidence could be reconciled with his innocence. "Evidence," says a distinguished legal writer, "is always insufficient, where, assuming all to be proved which the evidence tends to prove, some other hypothesis may still be true; for it is the actual exclusion of any other hypothesis which invests mere circumstances with the force of proof."* This is a settled principle of law. If any supposition can be made, then, which would reconcile the facts in evidence with a man's innocence, the law directs that he shall be acquitted. Any other rule of decision would be manifestly unjust, and inconsistent with the dictates of a sound policy.

This principle is applicable, whether the accused bear a good or a bad moral character. As, according to the hypothesis, he might be innocent; so no tribunal on earth could fairly determine that he was guilty. The hardship of such a conclusion

* Starkie on Evidence.

would be still more apparent in regard to the conduct of a man whose general character is well known to be good. In such a case, especially, should the facts be of such a nature as to exclude every favourable hypothesis, before either truth or justice would listen to an unfavourable decision and judgment.

Such is the rule which human wisdom has established, in order to arrive at truth, or at least to avoid error, in relation to the acts and intentions of men. Hence, is it not reasonable, we ask, that we should keep within the same sacred bounds, when we come to form an estimate of the ways of God? No one can fairly doubt that the world is replete with the evidences of his goodness. If he had so chosen, he might have made every breath a sigh, every sensation a pang, and every utterance of man's spirit a groan; but how differently has he constituted the world within us, and the glorious world around us! Instead of swelling every sound with discord, and clothing every object with deformity, he has made all nature music to the ear and beauty to the eye. The full tide of his universal goodness flows within us, and around us on all sides. In its eternal rounds, it touches and blesses all things living with its power. We live, and move, and have our very being in the goodness of God. Surely, then, we should most joyfully cling to an hypothesis which is favourable to the character of such a Being. Hence, we infinitely prefer the warm and generous theory of the optimist, which regards the actual universe as the best possible, to the dark and cold hypothesis of the sceptic, which calls in question the boundless perfections of God.

In the foregoing remarks, we have concurred with Dr. Chalmers in viewing the doctrine of Bayle as a mere unsupported hypothesis; but have we any right to do so? It has not been proved, it is true; but there are some things which require no proof. Is not the doctrine of Bayle a thing of this kind? It certainly seems evident that if God hates sin above all things, and could easily prevent it, he would not permit it to appear in his dominions. This view of the subject recommends itself powerfully to the human mind, which has, in all ages, been worried and perplexed by it. It seems to carry its own evidence along with it; to shake the mind with doubt, and overspread it with darkness. Hence, we should either expose its fallacy or else fairly acknowledge its power.

On the other hand, the theory of Leibnitz, or rather the great fundamental idea of his theory, is more than a mere hypothesis. It rests on the conviction of the human mind that God is infinitely perfect, and seems to flow from it as a necessary consequence. For how natural, how irresistible the conclusion, that if God be absolutely perfect, then the world made by him must be perfect also! But while these two hypotheses seem to be sound, it is clear that both cannot be so: there is a real conflict between them, and the one or the other must be made to give way before our knowledge can assume a clearly harmonious and satisfactory form.

The effects of the hypothesis of the sceptic may be neutralized by opposing to it the hypothesis of the theist. But we are not satisfied to stop at this point. We intend, not merely to neutralize, but to explode, the theory of the sceptic. We intend to wrest from it the element of its strength, and grind it to atoms. We intend to lay our finger precisely upon the fallacy which lies so deeply concealed in its bosom, and from which it derives all its apparent force and conclusiveness. We shall drag this false principle from its place of concealment into the open light of day, and thereby expose the utter futility, the inherent absurdity, of the whole atheistical hypothesis, to which it has so long imparted its deceptive power. If Leibnitz did not detect this false principle, and thereby overthrow the theory of Bayle, it was because he held this principle in common with him. We must eliminate this error, common to the scheme of the atheist and to that of the theist, if we would organize the truths which both contain, and present them together in one harmonious and symmetrical system; into a system which will enable us, not merely to stand upon the defensive, and parry off the attacks of the sceptic, but to enter upon his own territory, and demolish his strongholds; not merely to oppose his argument by a counter-argument, but to explode his sophism, and exhibit the cause of God in cloudless splendour.

This false principle, this concealed fallacy, of which the atheist has been so long allowed to avail himself, has been the source of many unsuspected errors, and many lamentable evils. It has not only given power and efficacy to the weapons of the sceptic, but to the eye of faith itself has it cast clouds and darkness over the transcendent glory of the moral government of God. It has prevented a Leibnitz from refuting the sophism of a Bayle, and induced a Kant to declare a theodicy impossible. It has, indeed, as we shall see, crept into and corrupted the whole mass of religious knowledge; converting the radiant and clearly-defined body of truth into a dark, heterogeneous compound of conflicting elements. Hence we shall utterly demolish it, that neither a fragment nor a shadow of it may remain to darken and delude the minds of men.

SECTION IV.

The argument of the atheist—The reply of Leibnitz and other theists—The insufficiency of this reply.

Sin exists. This is the astounding fact of which the atheist avails himself. He has never ceased to contend, that as God has permitted sin to exist, he was either unable or unwilling to prevent it. God might easily have prevented sin, says he, if he had chosen to do so; but he has not chosen to do so, and therefore his love of virtue is not infinite, his holiness is not unlimited. Now, we deny this conclusion, and assert the infinite holiness of God.

This assertion may be true, says Voltaire, and hence God would have prevented all sin, if his power had not been limited. The only conceivable way, says he, to reconcile the existence of sin with the purity of God, is "to deny his omnipotence." We insist, on the contrary, that the power of God is absolutely without bounds or limits. Though sin exists, we still maintain, in opposition to every form of atheism, that this fact implies no limitation of any of the perfections of God.

Before proceeding to establish this position, we shall consider the usual reply of the theist to the great argument of the atheist. "The greatest love which a ruler can show for virtue," says Bayle, "is to cause it, if he can, to be always practised without any mixture of vice. If it is easy for him to procure this advantage to his subjects, and he nevertheless permits vice to raise its head in his dominions, intending to punish it after having tolerated it for a long time, his affection for virtue is not the greatest of which we can conceive; *it is then not infinite.*" This has been the great standing argument of atheism in all ages of the world. This argument, as held by the atheists of antiquity, is presented by Cudworth in the following words: "The supposed Deity and Maker of the world was either willing to abolish all evils, but not able; or he was able but not willing; or else, lastly, he was both able and willing. This latter is the only thing that answers fully to the notion of a God. Now that the supposed Creator of all things was not thus both able and willing to abolish all evils, is plain, because then there would have been no evils at all left. Wherefore, since there is such a deluge of evils overflowing all, it must needs be that either he was willing, and not able to remove them, and then he was impotent; or else he was able and not willing, and then he was envious; or, lastly, he was neither able nor willing, and then he was both impotent and envious." This argument is, in substance, the same as that presented by Bayle, and relied upon by atheists in all subsequent times.

To the argument of Bayle, the following reply is given by Leibnitz: "When we detach things that are connected together, —the parts from the whole, the human race from the universe, the attributes of God from each other, his power from his wisdom,—we are permitted to say that *God can cause virtue to be in the world without any mixture of vice, and even that he may easily cause it to be so.*"* But he does not cause virtue to exist without any mixture of vice, says Leibnitz, because the good of the whole universe requires the permission of moral evil. How the good of the universe requires the permission of evil, he has not shown us; but he repeatedly asserts this to be the fact, and insists that if God were to prevent all evil, this would work a greater harm to the whole than the permission of some evil. Now, is this a sufficient and satisfactory reply to the argument of the atheist?

It certainly seems to possess weight, and is entitled to serious consideration. Bayle contends, that as evil exists, the Creator and Governor of the world cannot be absolutely perfect. He should have concluded with me, Leibnitz truly says, that as God is absolutely perfect, the existence of evil is necessary to the perfection of the universe, or is an unavoidable part of the best world that could have been created. It is thus that he neutralizes, without demolishing, the argument of the atheist, and each person is left to be more deeply affected by the argu-

* Théodicée.

ment of Leibnitz, or by that of Bayle, as his faith in the unlimited goodness of God is strong or weak. If the theist, by such means, should gain a complete victory, this would be due to the faith of the vanquished, rather than to the superiority of the logic by which he is subdued.

To this argument of Leibnitz we may then well apply his own remarks upon another celebrated philosopher. Descartes met the argument of the necessitarian, not by exposing its fallacy, but by repelling the conclusion of it on extraneous grounds. "This was to cut the Gordian knot," says Leibnitz, who was himself a necessitarian, "and to reply to the conclusion of one argument, not by resolving it, but by opposing to it a contrary argument; which is not conformed to the laws of philosophical controversy." The reply of Leibnitz to Bayle is clearly open to the same objection. It does not analyze the sophism of the sceptic, or resolve it into its elements, and point out its error; it merely opposes its conclusion by the presentation of a contrary argument. Hence it is not likely to produce very great effect; for, as Leibnitz himself says, in relation to this mode of attacking sceptics, "It may arrest them a little, but they will always return to their reasoning, presented in different forms, until we cause them to comprehend wherein the defect of their sophism consists." Leibnitz has, then, according to his own canons of criticism, merely cut the Gordian knot of atheism, which he should have unravelled. He has merely arrested the champions of scepticism "a little," whom he should have overthrown and demolished.

His reply is not only incomplete, in that it does not expose the sophistry of the atheist; it is also unsound. It carries in its bosom the elements of its own destruction. It is self-contradictory, and consequently untenable. It admits that it is easy for God to cause virtue to exist, and yet contends that, in certain cases, he fails to do so, because the highest good of the universe requires the existence of moral evil. But how is this possible? It will be conceded that the good of the individual would be promoted, if God should cause him to be perfectly holy and happy. This would be for the good of each and every individual moral agent in the universe. How, then, is it possible for such an exercise of the divine power to be for the good of all the parts, and yet not for the good of the whole?

So far from being able to see how these things can hang together, it seems evident that they are utterly repugnant to each other.

The highest good of the universe, we are told, requires the permission of evil. What good? Is it the holiness of moral agents? This, it is said, can be produced by the agency of God, without the introduction of evil, and produced, too, in the greatest conceivable degree of perfection. Why should evil be permitted, then, in order to attain an end, which it is conceded can be perfectly attained without it? Is there any higher end than the perfect moral purity of the universe, which God seeks to accomplish by the permission of sin? It certainly is not the happiness of the moral universe; for this can also be secured, in the highest possible degree, by the agency of the Divine Being, without the permission of moral evil. What good is there, then, beside the perfect holiness and happiness of the universe, to the production of which the existence of moral evil is necessary? There seems to be no such good in reality. It appears to be a dream of the imagination, a splendid fiction, which has been recommended to the human mind by its horror of the cheerless gloom of scepticism.

SECTION V.

The sophism of the atheist exploded, and a perfect agreement shown to subsist between the existence of sin and the holiness of God.

Supposing God to possess perfect holiness, he would certainly prevent all moral evil, says the atheist, unless his power were limited. This inference is drawn from a false premiss; namely, that if God is omnipotent, he could easily prevent moral evil, and cause virtue to exist without any mixture of vice. This assumption has been incautiously conceded to the atheist by his opponent, and hence his argument has not been clearly and fully refuted. To refute this argument with perfect clearness, it is necessary to show two things: first, that it is no limitation of the divine omnipotence to say that it cannot work contradictions; and secondly, that if God should cause virtue to exist in the heart of a moral agent, he would work a contradiction. We shall endeavour to evince these two things, in order to refute the grand sophism of the sceptic, and lay a solid foundation for a genuine scheme of optimism, against which no valid objection can be urged.

In the first place, then, it is not a limitation of the divine omnipotence to say, that it cannot work contradictions. There will be little difficulty in establishing this point. Indeed, it will be readily conceded; and if we offer a few remarks upon it, it is only that we may leave nothing dark and obscure behind us, even to those whose minds are not accustomed to such speculations.

As contradictions are impossible in themselves, so to say that God could perform them, would not be to magnify his power, but to expose our own absurdity. When we affirm, that omnipotence cannot cause a thing to be and not to be at one and the same time, or cannot make two and two equal to five, we do not set limits to it; we simply declare that *such things are not the objects of power*. A circle cannot be made to possess the properties of a square, nor a square the properties of a circle. Infinite power cannot confer the properties of the one of these figures upon the other, not because it is less than infinite power, but because it is not within the nature, or province, or dominion of power, to perform such things, to embody such inherent and immutable absurdities in an actual existence. In regard to the doing of such things, or rather of such absurd and inconceivable nothings, omnipotence itself possesses no advantage over weakness. Power, from its very nature and essence, is confined to the accomplishment of such things as are possible, or imply no contradiction. Hence it is beyond the reach of almighty power itself to break up and confound the immutable foundations of reason and truth. God possesses no such miserable power, no such horribly distorted attribute, no such inconceivably monstrous imperfection and deformity of nature, as would enable him to embody absurdities and contradictions in actual existence. It is one of the chief excellencies and glories of the divine nature, that its infinite power works within a sphere of light and love, without the least tendency to break over the sacred bounds of eternal truth, into the outer darkness of chaotic night!

The truth of this remark, as a general proposition, will be readily admitted. In general terms, it is universally acknowledged; and its application is easy where the impossibility is plain, or the contradiction glaring. But there are things which really imply a contradiction, without being suspected to do so. We may well ask, in relation to such things, why God does not produce them, without being sensible of the absurdity of the inquiry. The production of virtue, or true holiness, in the breast of a moral agent, is a thing of this kind.*

This conducts us to our second position; namely, that if God should cause virtue to exist in the breast of a moral agent, he would work a contradiction. In other words, the production of virtue by any extraneous agency, is one of those impossible conceits, those inherent absurdities, which lie quite beyond the sphere of light in which the divine omnipotence moves, and has no existence except in the outer darkness of a lawless imagination, or in the dim regions of error, in which the true nature of moral goodness has never been seen. It is absurd, we say, to suppose that moral agents can be governed and controlled in any other way than by moral means. All physical power is here out of the question. By physical power, in connexion with wisdom and goodness, a moral agent may be created, and endowed with the noblest attributes. By physical power, a moral agent may be caused to glow with a *feeling* of love, and armed with an uncommon energy of will; but such effects, though produced by the power of God, are not the virtue of the moral agent in whom they are produced. This consists, not in the possession of moral powers, but in the proper and obedient exercise of those powers.† If infinite wisdom, and goodness, and power, should muster all the means and appliances in the universe, and cause them to bear with united energy on a single mind, the effect produced, however grand and beautiful, would not be the virtue of the agent in whom it is produced. Nothing can be his virtue which is produced by an extraneous agency. This is a dictate of the universal reason and consciousness of mankind. It needs no metaphysical refinement for its support, and no scholastic jargon for its illustration. On this broad principle, then, which is so clearly deduced, not from the confined darkness of the schools, but the open light of nature, we intend to take our stand in opposition to the embattled ranks of atheism.

The argument of the atheist assumes, as we have seen, that a

* See chapter iii. † Compare chap. iii.

Being of infinite power could easily prevent sin, and cause holiness to exist. It assumes that it is possible, that it implies no contradiction, to create an intelligent moral agent, and place it beyond all liability to sin. But this is a mistake. Almighty power itself, we may say with the most profound reverence, cannot create such a being, and place it beyond the possibility of sinning. If it could not sin, there would be no merit, no virtue, in its obedience. That is to say, it would not be a moral agent at all, but a machine merely. The power to do wrong, as well as to do right, is included in the very idea of a moral and accountable agent, and no such agent can possibly exist without being invested with such a power. To suppose such an agent to be created, and placed beyond all liability to sin, is to suppose it to be what it is, and not what it is, at one and the same time; it is to suppose a creature to be endowed with a power to do wrong, and yet destitute of such a power, which is a plain contradiction. Hence, Omnipotence cannot create such a being, and deny to it a power to do evil, or secure it against the possibility of sinning.

We may, with the atheist, conceive of a universe of such beings, if we please, and we may suppose them to be at all times prevented from sinning by the omnipotent and irresistible energy of the Divine Being; and having imagined all this, we may be infinitely better pleased with this ideal creation of our own than with that which God has called into actual existence around us. But then we should only prefer the absurd and contradictory model of a universe engendered in our own weak brains, to that which infinite wisdom, and power, and goodness have actually projected into being. Such a universe, if freed from contradictions, might be also free from evil, nay, from the very possibility of evil; but only on condition that it should at the same time be free from the very possibility of good. It admits into its dominions moral and accountable creatures, capable of knowing and serving God, and of drinking at the purest fountain of uncreated bliss, only by being involved in irreconcilable contradiction. It may appear more delightful to the imagination, before it comes to be narrowly inspected, than the universe of God; and the latter, being compared with it, may seem less worthy of the infinite perfections of its Author; but, after all, it is but a weak and crazy thing, a contradictious and impossible conceit. We may admire it, and make it the standard by which to try the work of God; but, after all, it is but an "idol of the human mind," and not "an idea of the Divine Mind." It is a little, distorted image of human weakness, and not a harmonious manifestation of divine power. Among all the possible models of a universe, which lay open to the infinite mind and choice of God, a thing so deformed had no place; and when the sceptic concludes that the perfections of the Supreme Architect are limited, because he did work after such a model, he only displays the impotency of his own wisdom, and the blindness of his own presumption.

Hence, the error of the atheist is obvious. He does not consider that the only way to place all creatures beyond a liability to sin, is to place them below the rank of intelligent and accountable beings. He does not consider that the only way to prevent "sin from raising its head" is to prevent holiness from the possibility of appearing in the universe. He does not consider that among all the ideal worlds present to the Divine Mind, there was not one which, if called into existence, would have been capable of serving and glorifying its Maker, and yet incapable of throwing off his authority. Hence, he really finds fault with the work of the Almighty, because he has not framed the world according to a model which is involved in the most irreconcilable contradictions. In other words, he fancies that God is not perfect, because he has not embodied an absurdity in the creature. If God, he asks, is perfect, why did he not render virtue possible, and vice impossible? Why did he not create moral agents, and yet deny to them the attributes of moral agents? Why did he not give his creatures the power to do evil, and yet withhold this power from them? He might just as well have demanded, why he did not create matter without dimensions, and circles without the properties of a circle. Poor man! he cannot see the wisdom and power of God manifested in the world, because it is not filled with moral agents which are not moral agents, and with glorious realities that are mere empty shadows!

If the above remarks be just, then the great question, why has God permitted sin, which has exercised the ingenuity of man in all ages, is a most idle and insignificant inquiry. The only real question is, why he created such beings as men at all; and not why he created them, and then permitted them to sin. The first question is easily answered. The second, though often propounded, seems to be a most unmeaning question. It is unmeaning, because it seeks to ascertain the *reason why* God has permitted a thing, which, in reality, he has not permitted at all. Having created a world of moral agents, that is, a world endowed with a power to sin, it was impossible for him to prevent sin, so long as they retained this power, or, in other words, so long as they continued to exist as moral agents. A universe of such agents given, its liability to sin is not a matter for the will of God to permit; this is a necessary consequence from the nature of moral agents. He could no more deny peccability to such creatures than he could deny the properties of the circle to a circle; and if he could not prevent such a thing, it is surely very absurd to ask why he permitted it.

On the supposition of such a world, God did not permit sin at all; it could not have been prevented. It would be considered a very absurd inquiry, if we should ask, why God permitted two and two to be equal to four, or why he permitted the three angles of a triangle to be equal to two right angles. But all such questions, however idle and absurd, are not more so than the great inquiry respecting the permission of moral evil. If this does not so appear to our minds, it is because we have not sufficiently reflected on the great truth, that a necessary virtue is a contradiction in terms, an inherent and utter impossibility. The full possession of this truth will show us, that the cause of theism has been encumbered with great difficulties, because its advocates have endeavoured to explain the reason *why* God has permitted a thing, which, in point of fact, he has not permitted. Having attempted to explain a fact which has no existence, it is no wonder that they should have involved themselves in clouds and darkness. Let us cease then, to seek the reason of that which is *not*, in order that we may behold the glory of that which *is*.

We have seen that it is impossible for Omnipotence to create moral agents, and yet prevent them from possessing an ability to sin or transgress the law of God. In other words, that the Almighty cannot give agents a power to sin, and at the same time deny this power to them. To expect such things of him, is to expect him to work contradictions; to expect him to cause a thing to be what it is, and not what it is, at one and the same time. Thus, although sin exists, we vindicate the character of God, on the ground that it is an inherent impossibility to exclude all evil from a moral universe. This is the high, impregnable ground of the true Christian theist.

We have already said, that the only real question is, not why God permitted evil, but why he created beings capable of sinning. Such creatures are, beyond all question, the most noble specimens of his workmanship. St. Augustine has beautifully said, that the horse which has gone astray is a more noble creature than a stone which has no power to go astray. In like manner, we may say, a moral agent that is capable of knowing, and loving, and serving God, though its very nature implies an ability to do otherwise, is a more glorious creature than any being destitute of such a capacity. If God had created no such beings, his work might have represented him "as a house doth the builder," but not "as a son doth his father." If he had created no such beings, there would have been no eye in the universe, except his own, to admire and to love his works. Traces of his wisdom and goodness might have been seen here and there, scattered over his works, provided any eye had been lighted up with intelligence to see them; but nowhere would his living and immortal image have been seen in the magnificent temple of the world. It will be conceded, then, that there is no difficulty in conceiving why God should have preferred a universe of creatures, beaming with the glories of his own image, to one wholly destitute of the beauty of holiness and the light of intelligence. But having preferred the noblest order of beings, its inseparable incident, a liability to moral evil, could not have been excluded.

Hence God is the author of all good, and of good alone; and evil proceeds, not from him nor from his permission, but from an abuse of those exalted and unshackled powers, whose nature and whose freedom constitute the glory of the moral universe.

This, then, is the sublime purpose of God, to give and continue existence to free moral agents, and to govern them for their good as well as for his own glory. This is the decree of the Almighty, to call forth from nothing into actual existence, the universe which now shines around us, and spread over it the dominion of his perfect moral law. He does not cause sin.

He does not permit sin. He sees that it will raise its hideous head, but he does not say—*so let it be.* No! sin is the thing which God hates, and which he is determined, by all the means within the reach of his omnipotence, utterly to root out and destroy. The word has gone forth, "Offences must needs come, but woe unto the man by whom they come!" His omnipotence is pledged to wipe out the stain and efface the shadow of evil, in as far as possible, from the glory of his creation. But yet, so long as the light and glory of the moral universe is permitted to shine, may the dark shadow of evil, which moral agents cast upon its brightness and its beauty, continue to exist and partially obscure its divine perfections. And would it not be unworthy of the divine wisdom and goodness to remove this partial shadow, by an utter extinction of the universal light?

SECTION VI.

The true and only foundation of optimism.

Though few have been satisfied with the details of the system of optimism, yet has the great fundamental conception of that system been received by the wise and good in all ages. "The atheist takes it for granted," says Cudworth, "that whosoever asserts a God, or a perfect mind, to be the original of all things, does therefore *ipso facto* suppose all things to be well made, and as they should be. And this, doubtless, was the sense of all the ancient theologers," &c.* This distingushed philosopher himself maintains, as well as Leibnitz, that the intellectual world could not have been made better than it is, even by a being of infinite power and goodness. "To believe a God," says he, "is to believe the existence of all *possible* good and perfection in the universe; it is to believe that things are as they should be, and that the world is so well framed and governed, as that the whole system thereof could not possibly have been better."†

But while this fundamental principle has been held by philosophers, both ancient and modern, it has been, as we have seen, connected with other doctrines, by which it is contradicted, and its influence impaired. The concession which is universally made to the sceptic, that if God is omnipotent, he

* Intellectual System, vol. ii, p. 328. † Id., vol. ii, p. 149.

can easily cause virtue to exist without any mixture of vice, is fatal to the great principle that lies at the foundation of optimism. It resolves the whole scheme, which regards the world as the best that could possibly be made, into a loose, vague, and untenable hypothesis. It is true, the good man would infinitely prefer this hypothesis to the intolerable gloom of atheism; but yet our rational nature demands something more solid and clear on which to repose. Indeed, the warmest supporters of optimism have supplied us with the lofty sentiments of a pure faith, rather than with substantial and satisfactory views. The writings of Plato, Leibnitz, Cudworth, and Edwards, all furnish illustrations of the justness of this remark. But nowhere is its truth more clearly seen than in the following passage from Plotinus: "God made the *whole* most beautiful, entire, complete, and sufficient," says he; "all agreeing friendly with itself and its parts; both the nobler and the meaner of them being alike congruous thereunto. Whosoever, therefore, from the parts thereof, will blame the whole, is an absurd and unjust censurer. For we ought to consider the parts not alone by themselves, but in reference to the whole, whether they be harmonious and agreeable to the same; otherwise we shall not blame the universe, but some of its parts taken by themselves."*

The theist, however, who maintains this beautiful sentiment, is accustomed to make concessions by which its beauty is marred, and its foundation subverted. For if God could easily cause virtue to exist without any mixture of vice, it is demonstrable that the universe might be rendered more holy and happy than it is, in each *and every one of its parts, and consequently in the whole.* But if we assume the position, as in truth we may, that a necessary virtue is a contradiction in terms, then we can vindicate the infinite perfections of God, by showing that sin may enter into the best possible world. This great truth, then, that "a necessary holiness is a contradiction in terms," which has been so often uttered and so seldom followed out to its consequences, is the precise point from which we should contemplate the world, if we would behold the power and goodness of God therein manifested. This is the secret of the world by which the dark enigma of evil is to be solved.

* Cudworth's Intellectual System, vol. ii, p. 338.

This is the clew, by which we are to be conducted from the dark labyrinth of atheistical doubt and scepticism, into the clear and open light of divine providence. This is the great central light which has been wanting to the scheme of optimism, to convert it from a mere but magnificent hypothesis, into a clearly manifested and glorious reality.

God governs everything according to the nature which he has given it. Indeed, it would be as impossible to necessitate true and genuine obedience by the application of power, as it would be to convert a stone into a moral agent by the application of motives and persuasion. As sin is possible, then, though omnipotence be pledged to prevent its existence, it is clear that it cannot be regarded as a limitation of the divine power. This cuts off the objection of Voltaire, and explodes the grand sophism on which it is based. God hates sin above all things, and is more than willing to prevent it; and he actually does so, in so far as this is possible to infinite wisdom and power. This refutes the objection of Bayle, and leaves his argument without the shadow of a foundation. God does not choose sin, or permit it as a means of the highest good, as if there could be any higher good than absolute and universal holiness; but it comes to pass, because God has created a world of moral agents, and they have transgressed his law. This removes the high and holy God infinitely above the contamination of all evil, above all contact with the sin of the world, and shows an impassable gulf between the purity of the Creator and the pravity of the creature. By revealing the true connexion of sin with the moral universe, and its relation to God, it clearly shows that its existence should not raise the slightest cloud of suspicion respecting his infinite goodness and power, and thus reconciles the fact of sin's existence with the adorable perfections of the Governor of the world.

It may be said, that although God could not cause holiness to prevail universally, by the exercise of his power, yet he might employ means and influences sufficient to prevent the occurrence of sin. To this there are two satisfactory answers. First, it is a contradiction to admit that God cannot necessitate virtue, because such a thing is impossible; and yet suppose that he could, in all cases, secure the existence of it, without any chance of failure. It both asserts and denies at the same time, the idea of a necessary holiness. Secondly, the objection in question proceeds on the supposition, that there are resources in the stores of infinite wisdom and goodness, which might have been successfully employed for the good of the universe, and which God has failed to employ. But this is a mere gratuitous assumption. It never has been, and it never can be proved. It has not even the appearance of reason in its favour. Let the objector show wherein the Almighty could have done more than he has actually done to prevent sin, and secure holiness, without attempting violence to the nature of man, and then his objection may have some force, and be entitled to some consideration. But if he cannot do this, his objection rests upon a mere unsupported hypothesis. It is very easy to conceive that more light might have been imparted to men, and greater influences brought to bear on their feelings; but it will not follow that such additional inducements to virtue would have been good for them. For aught we know, it might only have added to their awful responsibilities, without at all conducing to their good. For aught we know, the means employed by God for the salvation of man from sin and misery have, both in kind and degree, been precisely such as to secure the *maximum* of good and the *minimum* of evil.

Let the sceptic frame a more perfect moral law for the government of the world than that which God has established; let him show where more tremendous sanctions might be found to enforce that law; let him show how the Almighty might have made a more efficacious display of his majesty, and power, and goodness, than he has actually exhibited to us; let him refer to more powerful influences, consistent with the free-agency and accountability of man, than those exerted by the Spirit of God; let him do all this, we say, and then he may have some right to object and find fault. In one word, let him meet the demand of the Most High, "what more could have been done to my vineyard, that I have not done in it," and show it to be without foundation, and then there will be some appearance of reason in his objection.

SECTION VII.

The glory of God seen in the creation of a world, which he foresaw would fall under the dominion of sin.

It may be said that we have not yet gone to the bottom of the difficulty; that although omnipotence could not deny the capacity to commit sin to a moral agent, yet God could prevent moral evil, by refusing to create any being who he foreknew would transgress his law. As God might have prevented the rise of evil in our world, by refusing to create man, why, it may be asked, did he not do so? Why did he not, in this way, spare the universe that spectacle of crime and suffering which has been presented in the history of our fallen race? To this we answer, that God did not choose to prevent sin in this way, but to create the world exactly as he did, though he foresaw the fall and all its consequences; *because the highest good of the universe required the creation of such a world.* We are now prepared to see this great truth in its true light.

The highest good of the universe may, no doubt, be promoted in various ways by the redemption of our fallen race, of which we have no conception in our present state of darkness and ignorance. But we are furnished with some faint glimpses of the true source of that admiration and wonder with which the angels of God are inspired, as they contemplate the manifestation of his glory in reconciling the world to himself. The felicity of the angels, and no doubt of all created intelligences, must be found in the enjoyment of God. No other object is sufficiently vast to fill and satisfy the unlimited desires of the mind. And as the character of God must necessarily constitute the chief happiness of his creatures, so every new manifestation of the glory of that character must add to their supreme felicity.

Now, if there had been no such thing as sin, the compassion of God would have been forever concealed from the eyes of his intelligent creatures. They might have adored his purity; but of that tender compassion which calls up the deepest and most pleasurable emotions in the soul, they could have known absolutely nothing. They might have witnessed his love to sinless beings; but they could never have seen that love in its omnipotent yearnings over the ruined and the lost. The attribute of mercy or compassion would have been forever locked up and concealed in the deep recesses of the Divine Mind; and the blessing, and honour, and glory, and dominion, which shall be ascribed by the redeemed unto Him that sitteth upon the throne, and unto the Lamb, forever and ever, would not have been heard in the universe of God. The chord which now sends forth the sweetest music in the harmony of heaven, filling its inhabitants with deep and rapturous emotions of sympathy and delight, would never have been touched by the finger of God.

How far such a display of the divine character is necessary to the ends of the moral government of God can be known only to himself. We are informed in his word, that it is by the redemption of the world, through Christ, that the ends of his moral government are secured. It pleased the Father, saith St. Paul, that in Christ all fulness should dwell; and having made peace through the blood of his cross, by him to reconcile all things unto himself, whether they be things in earth, or things in heaven. Thus we are told that all things in heaven are reconciled unto God, by the blood of the cross. But it may be asked, How was it possible to reconcile those beings unto God who had never sinned against him, nor been estranged from him? According to the original, God is not exactly said to reconcile, but *to keep together*, all things, by the mediation and work of Christ. The angels fell from heaven, and man sinned in paradise; but the creatures of God are secured from any further defection from him, by the all-controlling display of his character, and by the stupendous system of moral agencies and means which have been called forth in the great work of redemption.

In this view of the passage in question we are happy to find that we are confirmed by so enlightened a critic as Dr. Macknight. In relation to these words, "And by him to reconcile all things," he says, "Though I have translated the ἀποκαταλλάζαι to reconcile, which is its ordinary meaning, *I am clearly of opinion* that it signifies here to *unite* simply; because the good angels are said, in the latter part of the verse, to be reconciled with Christ, who never were at enmity with him. I therefore take the apostle's meaning to be this: 'It pleased the Father, by Christ, to unite all things to Christ, namely, as their Head and

Governor.'" (Col. i, 20.) The same sublime truth is revealed in other portions of Scripture, as in the fifteenth chapter of First Corinthians, where it is said, that it is the design of God to subject all things to Christ, and exception is made only of Him by whom this universal subjection and dominion is established.

The accomplishment of such an object, it will be admitted, is one of unspeakable importance. For no government, however perfect and beautiful in other respects, can be of much value unless it be so constructed as to secure its own permanency. This grand object, revelation informs us, has been attained by the redemption of the world through Christ. But for his work, those blessed spirits now bound together in everlasting society with God, by the sacred ties of confidence and love, might have fallen from him into the outer darkness, as angels and archangels had fallen before them. The ministers of light, though having drunk deeply of the goodness of God, and rejoiced in his smile, were not satisfied with their condition, and, striving to better it, plucked down ruin on their heads. So, man in paradise, not content with his happy lot, but vainly striving to raise himself to a god, forsook his allegiance to his Maker, and yielded himself a willing servant to the powers of darkness. But an apostle, though born in sin, having tasted the bitter fruits of evil, and the sweet mercies of redeeming love, felt such confidence in God, that in whatsoever state he was, he could therewith be content. Not only in heaven—not only in paradise—but in a dungeon, loaded with irons, and beaten with stripes, he could rejoice and give glory to God. This firm and unshaken allegiance in a weak and erring mortal to the throne of the Most High God, presents a spectacle of moral grandeur and sublimity to which the annals of eternity, but for the existence of sin, had presented no parallel.

It is by the scheme of Christianity alone that the confidence of the creature in his God has been rendered too strong for the gates of hell to prevail against him. But for this scheme, the moral government of God might have presented scenes of mutability and change, infinitely more appalling than the partial evil which we behold in our present state. Or if God had chosen to prevent this, to render it absolutely impossible, by the creation of no beings who he foreknew would rebel against him, this might have contracted his moral empire into the most insignificant limits. Thus, by the creation of the world, God has prepared the way to extend the boundaries of his empire, and to secure its foundations. Christ is the corner-stone of the spiritual universe, by which all things in heaven and earth are kept from falling away from God, its great centre of light and life. No wonder, then, that when this crowning event in the moral government of the universe was about to be accomplished, the heavenly host should have shouted, "Glory to God in the highest!"

This view of the subject of moral evil, derived from revelation, harmonizes all the phenomena of the moral world with the perfections of God, as well as warms and expands the noblest feelings of the human heart. St. Paul ascribes the stability of all things in heaven to the manifestation of the divine character in the redemption of our fallen race. If this be the case, then those who so confidently assert that God might have preserved the world in holiness, without impairing the free-agency of man, as easily as he keeps the angels from falling, are very much mistaken. This assertion is frequently made; but, as we conceive, without authority either from reason or revelation. It is said by a learned divine, "That God has actually preserved some of the angels from falling; and that he has promised to preserve, and will, therefore, certainly preserve the spirits of just men made perfect; and that this has been, and will be, done without infringing at all on their moral agency. Of course, he could just as easily have preserved Adam from falling, without infringing on his moral agency."* This argument is pronounced by its author to be conclusive and "unanswerable." But if God preserves one portion of his creatures from falling, by the manner in which he has dealt with those who have fallen, it does not follow that he could just as easily have kept each and every portion of them from a defection. If a ruler should prevent a part of his subjects from rebellion, by the way in which he has dealt with those who have rebelled, does it follow that he might just as easily have secured obedience in the rebels? It clearly does not; and hence there is a radical defect in the argument of these learned divines and the school to which they belong. Let them show that all things in heaven are not secured in their eternal allegiance to God by the

* Dwight's Sermons, vol. i, pp. 254–412. Dick's Lec., p. 248.

work of Christ, and then they may safely conclude, that man might have been as certainly and infallibly secured against a defection as angels and just men made perfect. If God binds the spiritual universe to himself, by the display of his unbounded mercy to a fallen race, it does not follow that he could, by the same means, have preserved that race itself, and every other order of beings, from a defection. For, on this supposition, there would have been no fallen race to call forth his infinite compassion, and send its binding influences over angels and the spirits of just men made perfect.

According to the sublime idea of revelation, it is the transcendent glory of the cross that it exerts moral influences, which have bound the whole intelligent creation together in one harmonious society with God, its sovereign and all-glorious head. For aught we know, the stability of the spiritual universe could not possibly have been secured in any other way; and hence, if there had been no fall, and no redemption, the grand intellectual system which is now so full of confidence and joy, might have been without a secure foundation. We have seen that its foundation could not, from the very nature of things, have been established and fixed by mere power; for this could not have kept a single moral agent from the possibility of sinning, much less a boundless universe of such beings.

The Christian believer, then, labours under no difficulty in regard to the existence of evil, which should in the least oppress his mind. If he should confine his attention too narrowly to the nature of evil as it is in itself, he may, indeed, perplex his brain almost to distraction; but he should take a freer and wider range, viewing it in all its relations, dependencies, and ultimate results. If he should consider the origin of evil exclusively, he may only meet with impenetrable obscurity and confusion, as he endeavours to pry into the dark enigma of the world; but all that is painful in it will soon vanish, if he will only view it in connexion with God's infinite plans for the good of the universe. He will then see, that this world, with all its wickedness and woe, is but a dim speck of vitality in a boundless dominion of light, that is necessary to the glory and perfection of the whole.

The believer should not, for one moment, entertain the low view, that the atonement confers its benefits on man alone.

The plan of redemption was not an after-thought, designed to remedy an evil which the eye of omniscience had not foreseen; it was formed in the counsels of infinite wisdom long before the foundations of the world were laid. The atonement was made for man, it is true; but, in a still higher sense, man was made for the atonement. All things were made *for* Christ. God, whose prerogative it is to bring good out of evil, will turn the short-lived triumph of the powers of darkness into a glorious victory, and cause it to be a universal song of rejoicing to his great name throughout the endless ages of eternity.

Who would complain, then, that he is subject to the evils of this life, since he has been subjected in hope? Everything around us is a type and symbol of our high destiny. All things shadow forth the glory to be revealed in us. The insignificant seed that rots in the earth does not die. It lives, it germinates, it grows, it springs up into the stately plant, and is crowned with beauty. The worm beneath our feet, though seemingly so dead, is, by the secret all-working power of God, undergoing changes to fit it for a higher life. In due time it puts off its form of death, and rises, "like a winged flower," from the cold earth into a warm region of life and light. In like manner, the bodies we inhabit, wonderfully and fearfully as they are made, are destined to moulder in the grave, and become the food of worms, before they are raised like unto Christ's glorified body, clothed with power and immortality. Nature itself, with all its teeming forms of beauty, must decay, till "pale concluding winter comes at last, and shuts the scene." But the scene is closed, and all its magnificence shut in, only that it may open out again, as it were, into all the wonders of a new creation. Even so the human soul, although it be subjected to the powers of darkness for a season, may emerge into the light and blessedness of eternity. Such is the destiny of man; and upon himself, under God, it depends whether this high destiny be fulfilled, or his bright hopes blasted. "I call heaven and earth this day to witness," saith the Lord, "that I have set before you life and death, blessing and cursing; therefore choose life."

SECTION VIII.

The little, captious spirit of Voltaire, and other atheizing minute philosophers.

It will be objected, no doubt, that in the foregoing vindication of the divine holiness, we have taken for granted the Christian scheme of redemption; but it should be remembered, that we do not propose "to justify the ways of God to man" on deistical principles. We are fully persuaded, that if God had merely created the world, and remained satisfied to look down as an idle spectator upon the evils it had brought upon itself, his character and glory would not admit of vindication; and we should not have entered upon so chimerical an enterprise. We have attempted to reconcile the government of the world, as set forth in the system we maintain, and in no other, with the perfections of God; and whoever objects that this cannot be done, is bound, we insist, to take the system as it is in itself, and not as it is mangled and distorted by its adversaries. We freely admit, that if the Christian religion does not furnish the means of such a reconciliation, then we do not possess them, and are necessarily devoted to despair.

Here we must notice a very great inconsistency of atheists. They insist that if the world had been created by an infinitely perfect Being, he would not have permitted the least sin or disorder to arise in his dominions; yet, when they hear of any interposition on his part for the good of the world, they pour ridicule upon the idea of such intervention as wholly unworthy of the majesty of so august a Being. So weak and wavering are their notions, that it agrees equally well with their creed, that it becomes an infinitely perfect Being to do all things, and that it becomes him to do nothing! Can you believe that an omnipotent God reigns, says M. Voltaire, since he beholds the frightful evils of the world without putting forth his arm to redress them? Can you believe, asks the same philosopher, that so great a being, even if he existed, would trouble himself about the affairs of so insignificant a creature as man?

Such inconsistencies are hardly worthy of a philosopher, who possesses a wisdom so sublime, and a penetration so profound, as to authorize him to sit in judgment on the order and harmony of the universe. They are perfectly worthy, however, of the author of Candidus. The poison of this work consists, not in its argument, but in its ridicule. Indeed, it is not even an attempt at argument or rational criticism. The sole aim of the author seems to be to show the brilliancy of his wit, at the expense of "the best of all possible worlds;" and it must be confessed that he has shown it, though it be in the worst of all possible causes.

Instead of attempting to view the existence of evil in the light of any principle whatever, he merely accumulates evil upon evil; and when the mass has become sufficiently terrific, with the jeering mockery of a small fiend, he delights in the contemplation of the awful spectacle as a conclusive demonstration that the Ruler of the world is unequal to the government of his creatures. His book is merely an appeal to the ignorance and feelings of the reader, and can do no mischief, except when it may happen to find a weak head in union with a corrupt heart. For what does it signify that the castle of the Baron Thunder-ten-trock was not the most perfect of all possible castles; does this disprove the skill of the great Architect of the universe? Or what does it signify that Dr. Pangloss lost an eye; does this extinguish a single ray of the divine omniscience, or depose either of the great lights which God ordained to rule the world? Lastly, what does it signify that M. Voltaire, by a horrible abuse of his powers, should have extinguished the light of reason in his soul; does this disprove the goodness of that Being by whom those powers were given for a higher and a nobler purpose? A fracture in the dome of St. Paul's would, no doubt, present as great difficulties to an insect lost in its depths, as the disorders of this little world presented to the captious and fault-finding spirit of M. Voltaire; and would as completely shut out the order and design of the whole structure from its field of vision, as the order and design of the magnificent temple of the world was excluded from the mind of this very minute philosopher.

CHAPTER VII.

OBJECTIONS CONSIDERED.

Heaven seeth all, and therefore knows the sense
Of the whole beauteous frame of Providence.
His judgment of God's kingdom needs must fail,
Who knows no more of it than this dark jail.—BAXTER.

One part, one little part, we dimly scan,
Through the dark medium of life's feverish dream;
Yet dare arraign the whole stupendous plan,
If but that little part incongruous seem.—BEATTIE.

THOUGH we have taken great pains to obviate objections by the manner in which we have unfolded and presented our views, yet we cannot but foresee that they will have to run the gauntlet of adverse criticism. Indeed, we could desire nothing more sincerely than such a thing, provided they be subjected to the test of principle, and not of prejudice. But how can such a thing be hoped for? Is all theological prejudice and bigotry extinct, that an author may hope to have a perfectly fair hearing, and impartial decision? Experience has taught us that we must expect to be assailed by a great variety of cavils, and that the weakest will often produce as great an effect as the strongest upon the minds of sectarians. Hence, we shall endeavour to meet all such objections as may occur to us, provided they can be supposed to exert any influence over the mind.

SECTION I.

It may be objected that the foregoing scheme is "new theology."

If nothing more were intended by such an objection, than to put the reader on his guard against the prejudice in favour of novelty, we could not complain of it. For surely every new opinion which comes into collision with received doctrines, should be held suspected, until it is made to undergo the scrutiny to which its importance and appearance of truth may entitle it. No reasonable man should complain of such a precaution. Certainly, the present writer should not complain of such treatment, for it is precisely the treatment which he has received from himself. He well remembers, that when the great truths, as he now conceives them to be, first dawned upon his own mind, how sadly they disturbed and perplexed his blind veneration for the past. As he was himself, then, so ready to shrink from his own views as "new theology," he surely cannot censure any one else for so doing, provided he will but give them a fair and impartial hearing before he proceeds to scout them from his presence.

It is true, after the writer had once fairly made the discovery that "old theology" is not necessarily true theology, he could proceed with the greater freedom in his inquiries. He did not very particularly inquire whether *this* or *that* was old or new, but whether it was true. He felt assured, that if he could only be so fortunate as to find the truth, the defect of novelty would be cured by lapse of time, and he need give himself no very great concern about it.

Not many centuries ago, as everybody knows, Galileo was condemned and imprisoned for teaching "new theology." He had the unbounded audacity to put forth the insufferable heresy, "directly against the very word of God itself," that the sun does not revolve around the earth. The Vatican thundered, and crushed Galileo; but it did not shake the solar system. This stood as firm in its centre, and rolled on as calmly and as majestically in its course, as if the Vatican had not uttered its anathema. Its thunders are all hushed now. Nay, it has even reversed its former decree, and concluded to permit the orbs of light to roll on in the paths appointed for them by the mighty hand that reared this beautiful fabric of the heavens and the earth. Even so will it be, in relation to all sound views pertaining to the constitution and government of the moral world; and those who may deem them unsound, will have to give some more solid reason than an odious epithet, before they can resist their progress.

We do not pretend that they have not, or that they cannot give, more solid reasons for this opposition to what is called "new theology." We only mean, that an *objection*, which, entirely overlooking the truth or the falsehood of an opinion, appeals to prejudice by the use of an odious name, is unworthy of a serious and candid inquirer after truth, and therefore should be laid aside by all who aspire to such a character.

SECTION II.

It may be imagined that the views herein set forth limit the omnipotence of God.

This objection has already been sufficiently answered; but it may be well to notice it more distinctly and by itself, as it is one upon which great reliance will be placed. It is not denying the omnipotence of God, as all agree, to say that he cannot work contradictions; but, as we have seen, a necessitated volition is a contradiction in terms. Hence, it does not deny or limit the divine omnipotence, to say, it cannot produce or necessitate our volitions. It is absurd to say, that that is a voluntary exercise of power, which is produced in us by the power of God. Both of these principles are conceded by those who will be among the foremost, in all probability, to deny the conclusion which necessarily flows from them. Thus, the Princeton Review, for example, admits that God cannot work contradictions; and also that "a necessary volition is an absurdity, a thing inconceivable." But will it say, that God cannot work a volition in the human mind? that omnipotence cannot work this particular absurdity? If that journal should speak on this subject at all, we venture to predict it will be seen that it has enounced a great truth, without perceiving its bearing upon the Princeton school of theology.

If this objection has any solidity, it lies with equal force against the scheme of Leibnitz, Edwards, and other philosophers and divines, as well as against the doctrine of the foregoing treatise. For they affirm, that God chooses sin as the necessary means of the greatest good; and that he could not exclude sin from the universe, without causing a greater evil than its permission. This sentiment is repeatedly set forth in the Essais de Théodicée of Leibnitz; and it is also repeatedly avowed by Edwards. Now, here is an inherent impossibility; namely, the prevention of sin without producing a greater evil than its permission, which it is assumed God cannot work. In other words, when it is asserted, that he chooses sin as the necessary means of the greatest good, it is clearly intended that he *cannot* secure the greatest good without choosing that sin should exist. Hence if the doctrine of this discourse limits the omnipotence of God, no less can be said of that to which it is opposed.

But both schemes may be objected to on this ground, and both be set aside as limiting the perfections of God. Indeed, it has been objected against the scheme of Leibnitz, "that it seems to make something which I do not know how to express otherwise than by the ancient stoical fate, antecedent and superior even to God himself. I would therefore think it best to say, with the current of orthodox divines, that God was perfectly free in his purpose and providence, and that there is no reason to be sought for the one or the other beyond himself."* We do not know what reply Leibnitz would have made to such an objection; but we should be at no loss for an answer, were it urged against the fundamental principle of the preceding discourse. We should say, in the first place, that it was a very great pity the author could not find a better way of expressing his objection, "than by the ancient stoical fate, antecedent and superior even to God himself." To say that God cannot work contradictions, is not to place a stoical fate, nor any other kind of fate, above him. And if it is, this impiety is certainly practised by "the current of orthodox divines," even in the author's own sense of the term; for they all affirm that God cannot work contradictions.

If such an objection has any force against the present treatise, it might be much better expressed than by an allusion to "the ancient stoical fate." Indeed, it is much better expressed by Luther, in his vindication of the doctrine of consubstantiation. When it was urged against that doctrine, that it is a mathematical impossibility for the same corporeal substance to be in a thousand different places at one and the same time, the great reformer resisted the objection as an infringement of the divine sovereignty: "God is above mathematics," he exclaimed: "I reject reason, common-sense, carnal arguments, and mathematical proofs."† There is no doubt but the orthodox divines of the present day will be disposed to smile at this specimen of Luther's pious zeal for the sovereignty of God; and although

* Witherspoon, as quoted in "New and Old Theology," issued by the Presbyterian Board of Publication.

† D'Aubigne's History of the Reformation, book xiii.

they may not be willing to admit that God is above all reason and common-sense, yet will they be inclined to think that, in some respects, Luther was a little below them. But while they smile at Luther, might it not be well to take care, lest they should display a zeal of the same kind, and equally pleasant in the estimation of posterity?

In affirming that *omnipotence* cannot work contradictions, we are certainly very far from being sensible that we place a "stoical fate" above God, or any other kind of fate. We would not place mathematics above God; much less would we place him below mathematics. Nor would we say anything which would seem to render him otherwise than "perfectly free in his purpose, or in his providence." To say that he cannot make two and two equal to five, is not, we trust, inconsistent with the perfection of his freedom. If it would be a great imperfection in mortals, as all orthodox divines will admit, to be able to affirm and believe that two and two are equal to five; then it would be a still greater imperfection in God, not only to be able to affirm such a thing, but to embody it in an actual creation. In like manner, if it would be an imperfection in us to be able to affirm so great "an absurdity," a thing so "inconceivable" as a "necessary volition;" then it could not add much to the glory of the Divine Being, to suppose him capable of producing such a monstrosity in the constitution and government of the world.

There is a class of theologians who reject every explication of the origin of evil, on the ground that they limit the divine sovereignty; and to the question why evil is permitted to exist, they reply, "We cannot tell." If God can, as they insist he can, easily cause holiness to shine forth with unclouded, universal splendour, no wonder they cannot tell why he does not do so. If, by a single glance of his eye, he can make hell itself clear up and shine out into a heaven, and fix the eternal glories of the moral universe upon an immovable foundation, no wonder they can see no reason why he refuses to do so. The only wonder is that they cannot see that, on this principle, there is no reason at all for such refusal, and the permission of moral evil. For if God can do all this, and yet permits sin "to raise its hideous head in his dominions," then there is, and must be, something which he loves more than holiness, or abhors more than sin. And hence, the reason why they cannot tell is, in our humble opinion, because they have already *told too much*,—more than they know. To doubt in the right place, is often the best cure for doubt; and to dogmatize in the wrong place, is often the most certain road to scepticism.

SECTION III.

The foregoing scheme, it may be said, presents a gloomy view of the universe.

If we say that God cannot necessitate our volitions, or necessarily exclude all evil from a moral system, it will be objected, that, on these principles, "we have no certainty of the continued obedience of holy, angelic, and redeemed spirits."* This is true, if the scheme of necessity affords the only ground of certainty in the universe. But we cannot see the justness of this assumption. It is agreed on all sides, that a fixed habit of acting, formed by repeated and long-continued acts, is a pretty sure foundation for the certainty of action. Hence, there may be some little certainty, some little stability in the moral world, without supposing all things therein to be necessitated. Perhaps there may be, on this hypothesis, as great certainty therein, as is actually found to exist. In the assertion so often made, that if all our volitions are not controlled by the divine power, but left to ourselves, then the moral world will not be so well governed as the natural, and disorders will be found therein; the *fact* seems to be overlooked, that there is actually disorder and confusion in the moral world. If it were our object to find an hypothesis to overturn and refute the *facts* of the moral world, we know of none better adapted to this purpose than the doctrine of necessity; but if it be our aim, not to deny, but to explain the phenomena of the moral world, then must we adopt some other scheme.

But it has been eloquently said, that "if God could not have prevented sin in the universe, he cannot prevent believers from falling; he cannot prevent Gabriel and Paul from sinking at once into devils, and heaven from turning into a hell. And were he to create new races to fill the vacant seats, they might turn to devils as fast as he created them, in spite of anything that he could do short of destroying their moral agency. He

* Old and New Theology, p. 38.

is liable to be defeated in all his designs, and to be as miserable as he is benevolent. This is infinitely the gloomiest idea that was ever thrown upon the world. It is gloomier than hell itself." True, there might be a gloomier spectacle in the universe than hell itself; and for this very reason it is, as we have seen, that God has ordained hell itself, that such gloomier spectacle may never appear in the universe to darken its transcendent and eternal glories. It is on this principle that we reconcile the infinite goodness of God with the awful spectacle of a world lying in ruins, and the still more awful spectacle of an eternal hell beyond the grave.

It is true, there might be a gloomier *idea* than hell itself; there might be two such *ideas*. Nay, there *might* be two such things; but yet, so far as we know, there is only one. We beg such objectors to consider, there are some things which, even according to our scheme, will not take place quite so fast as they may be pleased to imagine them. It is true, for example, that a man, that a rational being, *might* take a copper instead of a guinea, if both were presented for his selection; but although we may conceive this, it does not follow that he will actually take the copper and leave the guinea. It is also true, that a man *might* throw himself down from the brink of a precipice into a yawning gulf; yet he may, perhaps, refuse to do so. This may be merely a gloomy *idea*, and may never become a gloomy fact. In like manner, as one world fell away from God, so *might* another, and another. But yet this imagination may never be realized. Indeed, the Supreme Ruler of all things has assured us that it will not be the case; and in forming our views of the universe, we feel more disposed to look at facts than at fancies.

We need not frighten ourselves at "gloomy ideas." There are gloomy facts enough in the universe to call forth all our fears. Indeed, if we should permit our minds to be directed, not by the reality of things, but by the relative gloominess of ideas, we should altogether deny the eternity of future torments, and rejoice in the contemplation of the bright prospects of the universal holiness and happiness of created beings. We believe, however, that when the truth is once found, it will present the universe of God in a more glorious point of view, than it can be made to display by any system of error whatever. Whether the foregoing scheme possesses this characteristic of truth or not, the reader can now determine for himself. He can determine whether it does not present a brighter and more lovely spectacle to contemplate God, the great fountain of all being and all light, as doing all that is possible, in the very nature of things, for the holiness and happiness of the universe, and actually succeeding, through and by the coöperation of his creation, in regard to all worlds but this; than to view him as possessing the power to shut out all evil from the universe, for time and for eternity, and yet absolutely refusing to do so.

But let me insist upon it, that the first and the all-important inquiry is, "What is truth?" This is the only wise course; and it is the only safe course for the necessitarian. For no system, when presented in its true colours, is more gloomy and appalling than his own. It represents the great God, who is seated upon the throne of the universe, as controlling all the volitions of his rational creatures by the omnipotence of his will. The first man succumbs to his power. At this unavoidable transgression, God kindles into the most fearful wrath, and dooms both himself and his posterity to temporal and eternal misery. If this be so, then let me ask the reader, if the *fact* be not infinitely "gloomier than hell itself?"

SECTION IV.

It may be alleged, that in refusing to subject the volitions of men to the power and control of God, we undermine the sentiments of humility and submission.

This objection is often made: it is, indeed, the great practical ground on which the scheme of necessity plants itself. The object is, no doubt, a most laudable one; but every laudable object is not always promoted by wise means. Let us see, then, if it be wise thus to assert the doctrine of a necessitated agency, in order to abase the pride of man, and teach him a lesson of humility.

If we set out from this point of view, it will be found exceedingly difficult, if not impossible, to tell when and where to stop. In fact, those who rely upon this kind of argument, often carry it much too far; and if we look around us, we shall find that the only means of escaping the charge of pride, is to swallow all the doctrines which the teachers of humility may be pleased to present to us. Thus, for example, Spinoza would have us to believe that man is not a person at all, but a mere fugitive mode of the Divine Being. Nothing is more ridiculous, in his eyes, than that so insignificant a thing as a man should aspire to the rank of a distinct, personal existence, and assume to himself the attribute of free-will. "The free-will," says he, "is a chimera of the same kind, flattered by our pride, and in reality founded upon our ignorance." Now it may not be very humble in us, but still we beg leave to protest against this entire annihilation of our being.

Even M. Comte, who in his extreme modesty, denies the existence of a God, insists that it is nothing but the fumes of pride and self-conceit, the intoxication of vanity, which induces us to imagine that we are free and accountable beings. No doubt he would consider us sufficiently humble and submissive, provided we would only forswear all the light which shines within us and around us, and swallow his atheistical dogmas. But there is something more valuable in the universe, if we mistake not, than even a reputation for humility.

But no one will expect us to go so far in self-abasement and humility, as to submit our intellects to all sorts of dogmas. It will be amply sufficient, if we only go just far enough to receive the dogmas of his particular creed. Thus, for example, if you assail the doctrine of necessity, on which, as we have seen, Calvinism erects itself, the Puseyite will clasp his hands, and cry out, "Well done!" But if you turn around and oppose any of his dogmas, then what pride and presumption to set up your individual opinion against "the decisions of the mother Church!"* And he will be sure to wind up his lesson of humility with that of St. Vincentius: "*Quod ubique, quod semper, quod ab omnibus.*" Seeing, then, that a reputation for humility is not the greatest good in the universe, and that the only possibility of obtaining it, even from one party, is by a submission of the intellect to its creed; would it not be as well to leave such a reputation to take care of itself, and use all exertions to search out and find the truth?

Tell a carnal, unregenerate man, it is said, that though God had physical power to create him, he has not moral power

* The writer here speaks from personal experience.

to govern him, and you could not furnish his mind with better aliment for pride and rebellion. Should you, after giving this lesson, press upon him the claims of Jehovah, you might expect to be answered, as Moses was by the proud oppressor of Israel: "Who is the Lord, that I should obey his voice?"* He must, indeed, be an exceedingly *carnal man*, who should draw such an inference from the doctrine in question. But we should not tell him that "God had no moral power to govern him." We should tell him, that God could not control all his volitions; that he could not govern him as a machine is governed, without destroying his free-agency; but we should still insist that he possessed the most absolute and uncontrollable power to govern him; that God can give him a perfect moral law, and power to obey it, with the most stupendous motives for obedience; and then, if he persist in his disobedience, God can, and will, shut him up in torments forever, that others, seeing the awful consequences of rebellion, may keep their allegiance to him. Is this to deny the power of God to govern his creatures?

But is it not wonderful that a Calvinist should undertake to test a doctrine by the consequences which a "proud oppressor," or "a carnal man," might draw from it? If we should tell such a man, that God possesses the absolute power to control his volitions, and that nothing ever happens on earth but in perfect accordance with his good will and pleasure, might we not expect him to conclude, that he would then leave the matter with God, and give himself no trouble about it?

If we may judge from the practical effect of doctrines, then the authors of the objection in question do not take the best method to inculcate the lesson of humility. They take the precise course pursued by Melancthon, and often with the same success. This great reformer, it is well known, undertook to frame his doctrine so as to teach humility and submission: with this view he went so far as to insist, that man was so insignificant a thing, that he could not act at all, except in so far as he was acted upon by the Divine Being. Having reached this position, he not only saw, but expressly adopted the conclusion, that God is the author of all the volitions of men; that he was the author of David's adultery as well as of Saul's conversion.

* Old and New Theology, p. 40.

Now, it is true, if the human mind could abase itself so low as to embrace such a doctrine, it would give a most complete, if not a most pleasing example of its submissiveness. But it cannot very well do so. For even amid the ruins of our fallen nature, there are some fragments left, which raise the intellect and moral nature of man above so blind and so abject a submission to the dominion of error. Hence it was, that Melancthon himself could not long submit to his own doctrine; and he who had undertaken to teach others humility, became one of the most illustrious of rebels. This suggests the profound aphorism of Pascal: "It is dangerous to make us see too much how near man is to the brutes, without showing him his greatness. It is also dangerous to make him see his greatness without his baseness. It is still more dangerous to leave him ignorant of both. But it is very advantageous to represent to him both the one and the other."*

The fact is, that nothing can teach the human intellect a genuine submission but the light of evidence: this, and this alone, can rivet upon our speculative faculty the chains of inevitable conviction, and bind it to the truth. Those who teach error, then, may preach humility with success to the blind and the unthinking; but wherever men may be disposed to think for themselves, they must expect to find rebels. How many at the present day have begun, like Melancthon, by the preaching of submission, and ended by the practice of rebellion against their own doctrines. It is wonderful to observe the style of criticism usually adopted by the faithful, as one illustrious rebel after another is seen to depart from their ranks. The moment he is known to doubt a single dogma of the established faith, the awful suspicion is set afloat, "there is no telling where he will end." Alas! this is but too true; for when a man has once discovered that what he has been taught all his life to regard and reverence as a great mystery, is in reality an absurdity and an imposition on his reason, there is no telling where he will end. The reaction may be so great, indeed, as to produce an entire shipwreck of his faith. But in this case, let us not chide our poor lost brother with pride and presumption, as if we ourselves were unstained with the same sin. Let us remember, that the fault may be partly our own, as well as

* Pensées, I. Partie, art. iv, sec. vii.

his. Let us remember, that the sin of not even every unwarrantable innovation, is exclusively imputable to the innovator himself. For, as Lord Bacon says, "A froward retention of customs is a great innovator."

If those who, some centuries ago, formed the various creeds of the Christian world, were fallible men, and if they permitted serious errors to creep into the great mass of religious truth contained in those creeds, then the best way to prevent innovation is, not to preach humility and submission, but to bring those formularies into a conformity with the truth. For, if the "Old Theology" be unsound, the "New Theology" will have the audacity to show itself. And who, among the children of men, will set bounds to the progress of the human mind, either in the direction of God's word or his work, and say, Hitherto shalt thou come, and here shall thy proud waves be stayed? Who will lash the winds into submission, or bind the raging ocean at his feet?

SECTION V.

The foregoing treatise may be deemed inconsistent with gratitude to God.

"Such reflections," it has been urged, "afford as little ground for gratitude as for submission. Why do we feel grateful to God for those favours which are conferred on us by the agency of our fellow-men, except on the principle that they are instruments in *his* hand, who, without 'offering the least violence to their wills, or taking away the liberty or contingency of second causes,' hath most sovereign dominion over them, to do by them, and upon them, whatsoever himself pleaseth? On any other ground, *they* would be worthy of the principal, and He of the secondary praise."* True, if men are "*only instruments in his hand*," we should give him all the praise; but we should never feel grateful to our earthly friends and benefactors. As we should not, on this hypothesis, be grateful for the greatest benefits conferred on us by our fellow-men; so, in the language of Hartley, and Belsham, and Diderot, we should never resent, nor censure, the greatest injuries committed by the greatest criminals. But on our principles, while we have infinite ground for gratitude to God, we also have some little room for gratitude to our fellow-men.

* Old and New Theology.

SECTION VI.

It may be contended, that it is unfair to urge the preceding difficulties against the scheme of necessity; inasmuch as the same, or as great, difficulties attach to the system of those by whom they are urged.

This is the great standing objection with all the advocates of necessity. Indeed, we sometimes find it conceded by the advocates of free-agency; of which concessions the opposite party are ever ready and eager to avail themselves. In the statement of this fact, I do not mean to complain of a zeal which all candid minds must acknowledge to be commendable on the part of the advocates of necessity. It is a fact, however, that the following language of Archbishop Whately, in relation to the difficulty of accounting for the origin of evil, is often quoted by them: "Let it be remembered, that it is not peculiar to any one theological system: let not therefore the Calvinist or the Arminian urge it as an objection against their respective adversaries; much less an objection clothed in offensive language, which will be found to recoil on their own religious tenets, as soon as it shall be perceived that both parties are alike unable to explain the difficulty; let them not, to destroy an opponent's system, rashly kindle a fire which will soon extend to the no less combustible structure of their own."

No one can doubt the justice or wisdom of such a maxim; and it would be well if it were observed by all who may be disposed to assail an adversary's scheme with objections. Every such person should first ask himself whether his objection might not be retorted, or the shaft be hurled back with destructive force at the assailant. But although the remark of Archbishop Whately is both wise and just, it is not altogether so in its application to Archbishop King, or to other Arminians. For example, it is conceded by Dr. Reid, that he had not found the means of reconciling the existence of moral evil with the perfections of God; but is this any reason why he should not shrink with abhorrence from the doctrine of necessity which so clearly appeared to him to make God the direct and proper cause of moral evil? "We acknowledge," says he, "that nothing can happen under the administration of the Deity which he does not permit. The permission of natural and moral evil is a phenomenon which cannot be disputed. To account for this phenomenon under the government of a Being of infinite goodness, has, in all ages, been considered as difficult to human reason, whether we embrace the system of liberty or that of necessity." But because he could not solve this difficulty, must he therefore embrace, or at least cease to object against every absurdity which may be propounded to him? Because he cannot comprehend why an infinitely good Being should permit sin, does it follow that he should cease to protest against making God the proper cause and agent of all moral evil as well as good? In his opinion, the scheme of necessity does this; and hence he very properly remarks: "This view of the divine nature, the only one consistent with the scheme of necessity, appears to me much more shocking than the permission of evil upon the scheme of liberty. It is said, that it requires only *strength of mind* to embrace it: to me it seems to require much strength of countenance to profess it." In this sentiment of Dr. Reid the moral sense and reason of mankind will, I have no doubt, perfectly concur. For although we may not be able to clear up the stupendous difficulties pertaining to the spiritual universe, this is no reason why we may be permitted to deepen them into absurdities, and cause them to bear, in the harshest and most revolting form, upon the moral sentiments of mankind.

The reason why Dr. Reid and others could not remove the great difficulty concerning the origin of evil is, as we have seen, because they proceeded on the supposition that God could create a moral system, and yet necessarily exclude all sin from it. This mistake, it seems to me, has already been sufficiently refuted, and the existence of moral evil brought into perfect accordance and harmony with the infinite holiness of God.

But it is strenuously insisted, in particular, that the divine foreknowledge of all future events establishes their necessity; and thus involves the advocates of that sublime attribute in all the difficulties against which they so loudly declaim. As I have examined this argument in another place,* I shall not dwell upon it here, but content myself with a few additional remarks. The whole strength of this argument in favour of necessity arises from the assumption, that if God foresees the future volitions of men, they must be bound together with other

* Examination of Edwards on the Will.

things according to the mechanism of cause and effect; that is to say that God could not foresee the voluntary acts of men, unless they should be necessitated by causes ultimately connected with his own will. Accordingly, this bold position is usually assumed by the advocates of necessity. But to say that God could not foreknow future events, unless they are indissolubly connected together, seems to be a tremendous flight for any finite mind; and especially for those who are always reminding us of the melancholy fact of human blindness and presumption. Who shall set limits to the modes of knowledge possessed by an infinite, all-comprehending mind? Who shall tell *how* God foresees future events? Who shall say it must be in this or that particular way, or it cannot be at all?

Let the necessitarian prove his assumption, let him make it clear that God could not foreknow future events unless they are necessitated, and he will place in the hands of the sceptic the means of demonstrating, with absolute and uncontrollable certainty, that God does not foreknow all future events at all, that he does not foresee the free voluntary acts of the human mind. For we do know, as clearly as we can possibly know anything, not even excepting our own existence, or the existence of a God, that we are free in our volitions, that they are not necessitated; and hence, according to the assumption in question, God could not foresee them. If the sceptic could see what the necessitarian affirms, he might proceed from what he *knows*, by a direct and irresistible process, to a denial of the foreknowledge of God, in relation to human volitions.

But fortunately the assumption of the necessitarian is not true. By the fundamental laws of human belief, we know that our acts are not necessitated; and hence, we infer that as God foresees them all, he may do so without proceeding from cause to effect, according to the method of finite minds. We thus reason from the *known* to the *unknown;* from the clear light of facts around us up to the dark question concerning the possibility of the modes in relation to the divine prescience. We would not first settle this question of possibility, we would not say that God cannot foreknow except in one particular way, and then proceed to reason from such a postulate against the clearest facts in the universe. No logic, and especially no logic based upon so obscure a foundation, shall ever be permitted to extinguish for us the light of facts, or convert the universal intelligence of man into a falsehood.

Those who argue from foreknowledge in favour of necessity, usually admit that there is neither *before* nor *after* with God. This is emphatically the case with the Edwardses. Hence, foreknowledge infers necessity in no other sense than it is inferred by present or concomitant knowledge. This is also freely conceded by President Edwards. In what sense, then, does present knowledge infer necessity? Let us see. I know a man is now walking before me; does this prove that he could not help walking? that he is necessitated to walk? It is plain that it infers no such thing. It infers the necessary connexion, not between the act of the man in walking and the causes impelling him thereto, but between my knowledge of the fact and the existence of the fact itself. This is a necessary connexion between two ideas, or propositions, and not between two events. This confusion is perpetually made in the "great demonstration" from foreknowledge in favour of necessity. It proves nothing, except that the greatest minds may be deceived and misled by the ambiguities of language.

This argument, we say, only shows a necessary connexion between two ideas or propositions. This is perfectly evident from the very words in which it is often stated by the advocates of necessity. "I freely allow," says President Edwards, "that foreknowledge does not prove a thing necessary any more than after-knowledge; but the after-knowledge, which is certain and infallible, proves that it is now become impossible but that the proposition known should be true." Now, here we have a necessary connexion between the certain and infallible knowledge of a thing, and the infallible certainty of its existence! What has this to do with the question about the will? If any man has ever undertaken to assert its freedom, by denying the necessary connexion between two or more ideas, propositions, or truths, this argument may be applied to him; we have nothing to do with it.

Again: "To suppose the future volitions of moral agents," says President Edwards, "not to be necessary events; or, which is the same thing, events which are not impossible but that they may not come to pass; and yet to suppose that God certainly foreknows them, and knows all things, is to suppose God's knowledge to be inconsistent with itself. For to say, that God certainly, and without all conjecture, knows that a thing will infallibly be, which at the same time he knows to be so *contingent* that it may possibly not be, is to suppose his knowledge inconsistent with itself; or that one thing he knows is utterly inconsistent with another thing he knows. It is the same thing as to say, he now knows a proposition to be of certain infallible truth which he knows to be of contingent uncertain truth." Now all this is true. If we affirm God's foreknowledge to be certain and at the same time to be uncertain, we contradict ourselves. But what has this necessary connexion between the elements of the divine foreknowledge, or between our propositions concerning them, to do with the necessary connexion among *events?*

The question is not whether all future events will certainly come to pass; or, in other words, whether all future events are future events; for this is a truism, which no man in his right mind can possibly deny. But the question is, whether all future events will be determined by necessitating causes, or whether they may not be, in part, the free unnecessitated acts of the human mind. This is the question, and let it not be lost sight of in a cloud of logomachy. If all future events are necessitated, then all past events are necessitated. But if we know anything, we know that all present events are not necessitated, and hence, all future events will not be necessitated. We deem it always safer to reason thus *from the known to the unknown*, than to invert the process.

But suppose that foreknowledge proves that all human volitions are under the influence of causes, in what sense does it leave them free? Does it leave them free to depart from the influence of motives? By no means. It would be a contradiction in terms, according to this argument, to say that they are certainly and infallibly foreknown, and yet that they may possibly not come to pass. Hence, if the argument proves anything, it proves the absolute fatality of all human volitions. It leaves not a fragment nor a shadow of moral liberty on earth.

If this argument prove anything to the purpose, then Luther was right in declaring that "the foreknowledge of God is a thunderbolt to dash the doctrine of free-will into atoms;" and

Dr. Dick is right in affirming, "that it is as impossible to avoid them" (our volitions) "as it is to pluck the sun out of the firmament."* It either proves all the most absolute necessitarian could desire, or it proves nothing. In our humble opinion it proves the latter.

On this point the testimony of Dr. Dick himself is explicit: "Whatever is the foundation of his foreknowledge," says he, "what he does foreknow will undoubtedly take place. Hence, then, *the actions of men are as unalterably fixed from eternity, as if they had been the subject of an immutable decree.*"† But to dispel this grand illusion, it should be remembered, that the actions of men will not come to pass because they are foreknown; but they are foreknown because they will come to pass. The free actions of men are clearly reflected back in the mirror of the divine omniscience—they are not projected forward from the engine of the divine omnipotence.

Since the argument in question proves so much, if it proves anything, we need not wonder that it was employed by Cicero and other ancient Stoics to establish the doctrine of an absolute and unconditional fate. "If the will is free," says he, "then fate does not rule everything, then the order of all causes is not certain, and the order of things is no longer certain in the prescience of God; if the order of things is not certain in the prescience of God, then things will not take place as he foresees them; and if things do not take place as he foresees, there is no foreknowledge in God." Thus, by a *reductio ad absurdum*, he establishes the position that the will is not free, but fate rules all things. Edwards and Dick, however, would only apply this argument to human volitions. But are not the volitions of the divine mind also foreknown? Certainly they are; this will not be denied. Hence, the very men who set out to exalt the power of God and abase the glory of man, have, by this argument, raised a dominion, not only over the power of man, but also over the power of God himself. In other words, if this argument proves that we cannot act unless we be first acted upon, and impelled to act, it proves no less in relation to God; and hence, if it show the weakness and dependence of men, it also shows the weakness and dependence of God. So apt are men to adopt arguments which defeat

* Theology, vol. i, p. 358. † Ibid.

their own object, whenever they have any other object than the discovery of truth.

It is frequently said, as we have seen, that it is a contradiction to affirm that a thing is foreknown, or will certainly come to pass, and that it may possibly not come to pass. This position is at least as old as Aristotle. But let it be borne in mind, that if this be a contradiction, then future events are placed, not only beyond the power of man, but also beyond the power of God itself; for it is conceded on all hands, that God cannot work contradictions. This famous argument entirely overlooks the question of power. It simply declares the thing to be a contradiction, and as such, placed above all power. In other words, if it be absurd or self-contradictory to say, that a future event is foreknown, and, at the same time, *might* not come to pass, this proposition is true of the volitions of the divine no less than of the human mind; for they are all alike foreknown. That is to say, if the argument from foreknowledge proves that the volitions of man *might* not have been otherwise than they are, it proves precisely the same thing in regard to the volitions of God. Thus, if this argument proves anything to the purpose, it reaches the appalling position of Spinoza, that nothing in the universe could possibly be otherwise than it is. And if this be so, then let the Calvinist decide whether he will join with the Pantheist and fatalist, or give some little quarter to the Arminian. Let him decide whether he will continue to employ an argument which, if it proves anything, demonstrates the dependency of the divine will as well as of the human; and instead of exalting the adorable sovereignty of God, subjects him to the dominion of fate.

PART II.

THE EXISTENCE OF NATURAL EVIL, OR SUFFERING, CONSISTENT WITH THE GOODNESS OF GOD.

The path of sorrow, and that path alone,
Leads to the land where sorrow is unknown.

* * * * * *

But He, who knew what human hearts would prove,
How slow to learn the dictates of his love,
That, hard by nature and of stubborn will,
A life of ease would make them harder still,
In pity to the souls his grace design'd
For rescue from the ruin of mankind,
Call'd forth a cloud to darken all their years,
And said, "Go, spend them in the vale of tears."

COWPER.

PART II.

CHAPTER I.

GOD DESIRES AND SEEKS THE SALVATION OF ALL MEN.

Love is the root of creation,—God's essence.
Worlds without number
Lie in his bosom, like children: he made them for this purpose only,—
Only to love, and be loved again. He breathed forth his Spirit
Into the slumbering dust, and, upright standing, it laid its
Hand on its heart, and felt it was warm with a flame out of heaven.

TEGNER.

THE attentive reader has perceived before this time, that one of the fundamental ideas, one of the great leading truths, of the present discourse is, that a necessary holiness is a contradiction in terms,—an inherent and utter impossibility. This truth has shown us why a Being of infinite purity does not cause virtue to prevail everywhere, and at all times. If virtue could be necessitated to exist, there seems to be no doubt that such a Being would cause it to shine out in all parts of his dominion, and the blot of sin would not be seen upon the beauty of the world. But although moral goodness cannot be necessitated to exist, yet God has attested his abhorrence of vice and his approbation of virtue, by the dispensation of natural good and evil, of pleasure and pain. Having marked out the path of duty for us, he has made such a distribution of natural good and evil as is adapted to keep us therein. The evident design of this arrangement is, as theologians and philosophers agree, to prevent the commission of evil, and secure the practice of virtue. The Supreme Ruler of the world adopts this method to promote that moral goodness which cannot be produced by the direct omnipotency of his power.

Hence, it must be evident, that although God desires the happiness of his rational and accountable creatures, he does not bestow happiness upon them without regard to their moral character. The great dispensation of his natural providence, as well as the express declaration of his word, forbids the inference that he desires the happiness of those who obstinately persist in their evil courses. If we may rely upon such testimony, he desires *first* the *holiness* of his intelligent creatures, and *next* their *happiness*. Hence, it is well said by Bishop Butler, that the "divine goodness, with which, if I mistake not, we make very free in our speculations, *may not be a bare, single disposition to produce happiness*, but a disposition to make the good, the faithful, the honest man happy."*

He desires the holiness of all, that all may have life. This great truth is so clearly and so emphatically set forth in revelation, and it so perfectly harmonizes with the most pleasing conceptions of the divine character, that one is filled with amazement to reflect how many crude undigested notions there are in the minds of professing Christians, which are utterly inconsistent with it. "As I live, saith the Lord God, I have no pleasure in the death of the wicked, but that the wicked turn from his way, and live. Turn ye, turn ye, for why will ye die?" This solemn asseveration that God desires not the death of the sinner, but that he should turn from his wickedness and live, one would suppose should satisfy every mind which reposes confidence in the divine origin of revelation. And yet, until the minds of men are purged from the films of a false philosophy and sectarian prejudice, they seem afraid to look at the plain, obvious meaning of this and other similar passages of Scripture. They will have it, that God desires the ultimate holiness and happiness of only a portion of mankind, and the destruction of all the rest; that upon some he bestows his grace, causing them to become holy and happy, and appear forever as the monuments of his mercy; while from some he withholds his saving grace, that they may become the fearful objects of his indignation and wrath. Such a display of the divine character seems to be equally unknown to reason and to revelation.

* Butler's Analogy, part i, chap. ii.

SECTION I.

The reason why theologians have concluded that God designs the salvation of only a part of mankind.

The reason why so many theologians come to so frightful a conclusion is, that they imagine God could very easily cause virtue in the breast of every moral agent, if he would. Hence arises in their minds the stupendous difficulty, "How can God really desire the holiness and happiness of all, since he refuses to make all holy and happy? Is he really in earnest, in pleading with sinners to turn from their wickedness, since he might so easily turn them, and yet will not do it? Is the great God really sincere in the offer of salvation to all, and in the grand preparations he hath made to secure their salvation, since he will not put forth his mighty, irresistible hand to save them?" Such is the great difficulty which has arisen from the imagination in question, and confounded theology for ages, as well as cast a dark shadow upon the Christian world. It is only by getting rid of this unfounded imagination, this false supposition, that this stupendous difficulty can be solved, and the glory of the divine government clearly vindicated.

We have before us Mr. Symington's able and plausible defence of a limited atonement, in which he says, that "*the event is the best interpreter of the divine intention.*" Hence he infers, that as all are not actually saved, it was not the design of God that all should be saved, and no provision is really made for their salvation. This argument is plausible. It is often employed by the school of theologians to which the author belongs, and employed with great effect. But is it sound? No doubt it has often been shown to be unsound *indirectly;* that is, by showing that the conclusion at which it arrives comes into conflict with the express declarations of Scripture, as well as with our notions of the perfections of God. But this is not to analyze the argument itself, and show it to be a sophism. Nor can this be done, so long as the principle from which the conclusion necessarily follows be admitted. If we admit, then, that God could very easily cause virtue or moral goodness to exist everywhere, we must conclude that "*the event is the best interpreter* of the divine intention;" and that the atonement and all other provisions for the salvation of men are limited in extent by the design of God. That is to say, if we admit the premiss assumed by Mr. Symington and his school, we cannot consistently deny their conclusion.

Nor could we resist a great many other conclusions which are frightful in the extreme. For if God could easily make all men holy, as it is contended he can, then the event is the best evidence of his real intention and design. Hence he really did not design the salvation of all men. When he gave man a holy law, he really did not intend that he should obey and live, but that he should transgress and die. When he created the world, he really did not intend that all should reach the abodes of eternal bliss, but that some should be ruined and lost forever. Such are some of the consequences which necessarily flow from the principle, that holiness may be caused to exist in the breast of every moral agent. This is not all. We have before us another book, which insists that since the world was created, the law of God has never been violated, because his will cannot be resisted. Hence, it is seriously urged, that if theft, or adultery, or murder, be perpetrated, it must be in accordance with the will of God, and consequently no sin in his sight. "The whole notion of sinning against God," this book says, "is perfectly puerile." Now all this vile stuff proceeds on the supposition, that "the event is the best interpreter of the divine intention;" and it rests upon that supposition with just as great security, as does the argument in favour of a limited atonement. Though we may well give such stuff to the winds, or trample it under foot with infinite scorn, as an outrage against the moral sentiments of mankind; yet we cannot meet it on the arena of logic, if we concede that holiness may be everywhere caused to exist, and universal obedience to the divine will secured.

The only principle, it clearly seems to us, on which we can reconcile such glaring discrepancies between the express will of God and the event, is, that the event is of such a nature that it is not an object of power, or cannot be caused to exist by the Divine Omnipotence. For his "secret will," or rather his executive will, is always in perfect harmony with his revealed will. It is from an inattention to the foregoing principle, that theologians have not been able to see and vindicate the sincerity of God, in the offer of salvation to all men. We have examined their efforts to remove this difficulty, and been constrained to agree with Dr. Dick, that "we may pronounce these attempts to reconcile the universal call of the gospel with the sincerity of God, to be a faint struggle to extricate ourselves from the profundities of theology." But on looking into those solutions again, in which for some years we found a sort of rest, we could clearly perceive why theology had struggled in vain to deliver itself from its profound embarrassments on this subject, as well as on many others. These solutions admit the very principle which necessarily creates the difficulty, and renders a satisfactory answer impossible. Discard this false principle, substitute the truth in its stead, and the sincerity of God will come out from every obscurity, and shine with unclouded splendour.

SECTION II.

The attempt of Howe to reconcile the eternal ruin of a portion of mankind with the sincerity of God in his endeavours to save them.

To illustrate the justness of the remark just made, we shall select that solution of the difficulty in question which has been deemed the most profound and satisfactory. We mean the solution of "the wonderful Howe."* This celebrated divine clearly saw the impossibility of reconciling the sincerity of God with the offer of salvation to all, on the supposition that he does anything to prevent the salvation, or promote the ruin of those who are finally lost. He rejects the scheme of necessity, or a concurrence of the divine will, in relation to the sinful volitions of men, as aggravating the difficulty which he had undertaken to solve. This was one great step towards a solution. But it still remained to "reconcile God's prescience of the sins of men with the wisdom and sincerity of his counsels, exhortations, and whatsoever means he uses to prevent them." Let us see how he has succeeded in his attempt to accomplish this great object.

He admits in this very attempt, "that the universal, continued rectitude of all intelligent creatures had, we may be sure, been willed with a peremptory, efficacious will, if it had been best." He expressly says, that God might have prevented sin from

* Robert Hall, a profound admirer of Howe, has pronounced his attempt to reconcile the sincerity of God with the universal offer of salvation, to be one of his great master-pieces of thought and reasoning.

raising its head in his dominions, if he had chosen to do so. "Nor was it less easy," says he, "by a mighty, irresistible hand, universally to expel sin, than to prevent it." Now, having made this concession, was it possible for him to vindicate the sincerity and wisdom of God in the use of means to prevent sin, which he foresaw must fail to a very great extent?

After having made such an admission, or rather after having assumed such a position, we think it may be clearly shown that the author was doomed to fail; and that he has deceived himself by false analogies in his gigantic efforts to vindicate the character of God. He says, for example: "We will, for discourse's sake, suppose a prince endowed with the gift or spirit of prophecy. This most will acknowledge a great perfection, added to whatsoever other of his accomplishments. And suppose this his prophetic ability to be so large as to extend to most events which fall out in his dominions. Is it hereby become unfit for him to govern his subjects by laws, or any way admonish them of their duty? Hath this perfection so much diminished him as to depose him from his government? It is not, indeed, to be dissembled, that it were a difficulty to determine, whether such foresight were, for himself, better or worse. Boundless knowledge seems only in a fit conjunction with an unbounded power. But it is altogether unimaginable that it should destroy his relation to his subjects; as what of it were left, if it should despoil him of his legislative power and capacity of governing according to laws made by it? And to bring back the matter to the Supreme Ruler: let it for the present be supposed only, that the blessed God hath, belonging to his nature, the universal prescience whereof we are discoursing; we will surely, upon that supposition, acknowledge it to belong to him as a perfection. And were it reasonable to affirm, that by a perfection he is disabled from government? or were it a good consequence, 'He foreknows all things—he is therefore unfit to govern the world?'"

This way of representing the matter, it must be confessed, is exceedingly plausible and taking at first view; but yet, if we examine it closely, we shall find that it does not touch the real knot of the difficulty. The cases are not parallel. The prince is endowed with a foreknowledge of offences, which it is not in his power wholly to prevent. Hence it may be perfectly consistent with his wisdom and sincerity, to use all the means in his power to prevent them, though he may see they will fail in some cases, while they will succeed in others. But God, according to the author, might prevent all sin, or exclude it all from his dominions by "his mighty, irresistible hand." Hence it may not be consistent with his wisdom and sincerity to use means which he foresees will have only partial success, when he might so easily obtain universal and perfect success. It seems evident, then, that this is a deceptive analogy. It overlooks the root, and grapples with the branches of the difficulty. Let it be seen, that no power can cause the universal, continued moral rectitude of intelligent creatures, and then the two cases will be parallel; and God may well use all possible means to prevent sin and cause holiness, though some of his subjects may resist and perish. Let this principle, which we have laboured to establish, be seen, and then may we entirely dispel the cloud which has so long seemed to hang over the wisdom and sincerity of the Supreme Ruler of the world. We might offer strictures upon other passages of the solution under consideration; but as the same error runs through all of them, the reader may easily unravel its remaining obscurities and embarrassments for himself.

If holiness cannot be caused by a *direct* application of power, it follows that there is no want of wisdom in the use of *indirect* means, or of sincerity in the use of the most efficacious means the nature of the case will admit: but if universal holiness may be caused to exist by a mere word, then indeed it seems to be clearly inconsistent with wisdom to resort to means which must fail to secure it, and with sincerity to utter the most solemn and vehement asseverations that it is the will of God to secure it; for how obvious is the inquiry, If he so earnestly desire it, and can so easily secure it, why does he not do it?

In rejecting the principle for which we contend, Howe has paid the usual penalty of denying the truth; that is, he has contradicted himself. "It were very unreasonable to imagine," says he, "that God cannot, in any case, extraordinarily oversway the inclinations and determine the will of such a creature, in a way agreeable enough to its nature, (though we particularly know not, and we are not concerned to know, or curiously to inquire in what way,) and highly reasonable to suppose that in many cases he doth." Here he affirms, that our wills may be overruled and determined in perfect *conformity to our natures*, in some way or other, though we know not how. Why, then, does not God so overrule our wills in all cases, and secure the existence of universal holiness? Because, says he, "it is manifest to any sober reason, that it were very incongruous this should be the ordinary course of his conduct to mankind, or the same persons at all times; that is, that the whole order of intelligent creatures should be moved only by inward impulses; *that God's precepts, promises, and comminations, whereof their nature is capable, should be all made impertinences*, through his constant overpowering those that should neglect them; that the faculties, whereby men are capable of moral government, should be rendered to this purpose, *useless and vain;* and that they should be tempted to expect to be constantly managed *as mere machines that know not their own use.*"

What strange confusion and self-contradiction! The wills of men may be, and often are, swayed by the mighty, irresistible hand of God, and in a way *agreeable to their nature;* and yet this is not done in all cases, lest men should be governed as *mere machines!* The laws, promises, and threatenings of God, are not to be rendered vain and useless in all cases, but only in some cases! Indeed, if we would escape such inconsistencies and self-contradictions, we must return to the position that a necessary holiness is a contradiction in terms,—that no power can cause it. From this position we may clearly see, that the laws, promises, and comminations; the counsels, exhortations, and influences of God, which are employed to prevent sin, are not a system of grand impertinences,—are not a vast and complicated machinery to accomplish what might be more perfectly, easily, and directly accomplished without them. We may see, that God really desires the holiness and happiness of all men, although some may be finally lost; that he is in earnest in the great work of salvation; and when he so solemnly declares that he has no pleasure in the death of the sinner, but would rather he should turn and live, he means precisely what he says, without the least equivocation or mental reservation. This position it is, then, which shows the goodness of God in unclouded glory, and reconciles his sincerity with the final result of his labours.

But we have not yet got rid of every shade of difficulty. For it may still be asked, why God uses means to save those who he foresees will be lost? why he should labour when he foresees his labour will be in vain? To this we answer, that it does not follow his labour will be in vain, because some may be pleased to rebel and perish. This would be the case in regard to such persons, provided his only object in what he does be to save them; but although this is one great end and aim of his agency, it does not follow that it is his only object. For if any perish, it is certainly desirable that it be from their own fault, and not from the neglect of God to provide them with the means of salvation. It is his object, as he tells us, to vindicate his own character, and to stop every mouth in regard to the lost, as well as to save the greatest possible number. But this object could not be accomplished, if some should be permitted to perish without even a possibility of salvation. Hence he gives to all the means, power, and opportunity to turn and live; and this fact is nearly always alluded to in relation to the finally impenitent and lost. Thus says our Saviour, with tears of commiseration and pity: "O Jerusalem, Jerusalem, how often would I have gathered thy children together, even as a hen gathereth her chickens under her wings, and ye would not! Behold, your house is left unto you desolate." Now the tears of the Redeemer thus wept over lost souls, and this eloquent vindication of his own and his Father's goodness and compassion, would be a perfect mockery, if salvation had never been placed within their reach, or if their obedience, their real spiritual obedience and submission, might have been secured. But as it is, there is not even the shadow of a ground for suspecting the sincerity of the Redeemer, or his being in earnest in the great work of saving souls.

Again the impenitent are addressed in the following awful language: "Turn ye at my reproof: behold, I will pour out my spirit upon you, I will make known my words unto you. Because I have called, and ye refused; I have stretched out my hand and no man regarded; but ye have set at naught all my counsel and would none of my reproof: I also will laugh at your calamity: I will mock when your fear cometh." Thus the proceeding of the Almighty, in the final rejection of the impenitent, is placed on the ground, that they had obstinately resisted the means employed for their salvation. This seems to remove every shade of difficulty. But how dark and enigmatical, nay, how self-contradictory, would all such language appear, if they might have been very easily rendered holy and happy! Thus, by bearing in mind that a necessary holiness is a contradiction, an absurd and impossible conceit, the goodness of God is vindicated in regard to the lost, and his sincerity is evinced in the offer of salvation to all.

SECTION III.

The views of Luther and Calvin respecting the sincerity of God in his endeavours to save those who will finally perish.

On any other principle, we must forever struggle in vain to accomplish so desirable and so glorious an object. If we proceed on the assumption that holiness may be very easily caused by an omnipotent, extraneous agency, we shall never be able to vindicate the sincerity of the Almighty, in the many solemn declarations put forth by him that he desires the salvation of all men. The only sound, logical inference for such premises, is that drawn by Luther, namely, that when God exhorts the sinner, who he foresees will remain impenitent, to turn from his wickedness and live, he does so merely in the way of mockery and derision; just "as if a father were to say to his child, 'Come,' while he knows that he cannot come."*

The representation which Calvin, starting from the same point of view, gives of the divine character, is not more amiable or attractive than that of Luther. He maintains that "the most perfect harmony" exists between these two things: "God's having appointed from eternity on whom he will bestow his favour and exercise his wrath, and his proclaiming salvation indiscriminately to all."† But how does he maintain this position? How does he show this agreement? "There is more apparent plausibility," says he, "to the objection [against predestination] from the declaration of Peter, that 'the Lord is not willing that any should perish, but that all should come to repentance.' But the second clause furnishes an immediate solution of the difficulty; for the willingness to come to repent-

* Hagenbach's History of Doctrines, vol. ii, p. 259.

† Institutes, book iii, chap. xxiv, sec. xvii.

ance must be understood in consistence with the general tenor of Scripture."* Now what is the general tenor of Scripture, which is to overrule this explicit declaration that "God is not willing that any should perish?" The reader will be surprised, perhaps, that it is not Scripture at all, but the notion that God might easily convert the sinner if he would. "Conversion is certainly in the power of God;" he adds, "let him be asked, whether he wills the conversion of all, when he promises a few individuals to give them 'a heart of flesh,' while he leaves them with 'a heart of stone.'" Thus the very clearest light of the divine word is extinguished by the application of a false metaphysics. God tells us that he "is not willing that any should perish:" Calvin tells us, that this declaration must, in conformity with the general tenor of Scripture, be so understood as to allow us to believe that he is not only willing that many should perish, but also that their destruction is preördained and forever fixed by an eternal and immutable decree of God. Nay, that they are, and were, created for the express purpose of being devoted to death, spiritual and eternal. Is this to interpret, or to refute the divine word?

The view which Calvin, from this position, finds himself bound to take of the divine character, is truly horrible, and makes one's blood run cold. The call of the gospel, he admits, is universal—is directed to the reprobate as well as to the elect; but to what end, or with what design, is it directed to the former? "He directs his voice to them," if we may believe Calvin, "but it is that they may become more deaf; he kindles a light, but it is that they may be made more blind; he publishes his doctrine, but it is that they may be more besotted; he applies a remedy, but it is that they may not be healed. John, citing this prophecy, declares that the Jews could not believe, because the curse of God was upon them. Nor can it be disputed, that to such persons as God determines not to enlighten, he delivers his doctrine involved in enigmatical obscurity, that its only effect may be to increase their stupidity."†

In conclusion, we would add that it is this idea of a necessitated holiness which gives apparent solidity to the arguments of the Calvinist, and which neutralizes the attacks of their opponents. To select only one instance out of a thousand: the

* Institutes, book iii, chap. xxiv, sec. xvi. † Id., sec. xiii.

Calvinist insists that if God had really intended the salvation of all men, then all would have been saved; since nothing lies beyond the reach of his omnipotence. To this the Arminian cries out with horror, that if God does not desire the salvation of all, but is willing that a portion should sin and be eternally lost, then his goodness is limited, and his glory obscured. In perfect conformity with these views, the one contends for a limited atonement, insisting that it is confined either in its original design, or in its application, to a certain, fixed, definite number of mankind; while the other maintains, with equal earnestness, that such is the goodness of God that he has sent forth his Son to make an atonement for the sins of the whole world. To design and prepare it for all, says the Calvinist, and then apply it only to a few, is not consistent with either the wisdom or goodness of God; and that he does savingly apply it only to a small number of the human race is evident from the fact that only a small number are actually saved. However the doctrine of a limited atonement, or, what is the same thing in effect, the limited application of the atonement, may be exclaimed against and denounced as dishonourable to God, all must and do admit the fact, that it is efficaciously applied to only a select portion of mankind; which is to deny and to admit one and the same thing in one and the same breath.

Now, in this contest of arms, it is our humble opinion that each party gets the better of the other. Each overthrows the other; but neither perceives that he is himself overthrown. Hence, though each demolishes the other, neither is convinced, and the controversy still rages. Nor can there ever be an end of this wrangling and jangling while the arguments of the opposite parties have their roots in a common error. Let the work of Mr. Symington, or any other which advocates a limited atonement, be taken up, its argument dissected, and let the false principle, that God could easily make all men holy if he would, be eliminated from them, and we venture to predict that they will lose all appearance of solidity, and resolve themselves into thin air.*

* We do not intend to investigate the subject of a limited atonement in the present work, because it is merely a metaphysical off-shoot from the doctrine of election and reprobation, and must stand or fall with the parent trunk. The strength of this we purpose to try in a subsequent chapter.

CHAPTER II.

NATURAL EVIL, OR SUFFERING, AND ESPECIALLY THE SUFFERING OF INFANTS RECONCILED WITH THE GOODNESS OF GOD.

> Sweet Eden was the arbour of delight;
> Yet in his lovely flowers our poison blew:
> Sad Gethsemane, the bower of baleful night,
> Where Christ a health of poison for us drew;
> Yet all our honey in that poison grew:
> So we from sweetest flowers could suck our bane,
> And Christ, from bitter venom, could again
> Extract life out of death, and pleasure out of pain.
>
> GILES FLETCHER.

IF, as we have endeavoured to show, a necessary holiness is a contradiction in terms, then the existence of natural evil may be easily reconciled with the divine goodness, in so far as it may be necessary to punish and prevent moral evil. Indeed, the divine goodness itself demands the punishment of moral evil, in order to restrain its prevalence, and shut out the disorders it tends to introduce into the moral universe. Nor is it any impeachment of the infinite wisdom and goodness of God, if the evils inflicted upon the commission of sin be sufficiently great to answer the purpose for which they are intended—that is, to stay the frightful progress and ravages of moral evil. Hence it was that the sin of one man brought "death into the world, and all our woe." Thus the good providence of God, no less than his word, speaks this tremendous lesson to his intelligent creatures: "Behold the awful spectacle of a world lying in ruins, and tremble at the very thought of sin! A thousand deaths are not so terrible as one sin!"

SECTION I.

All suffering not a punishment for sin.

We should not conclude from this, however, that all suffering or natural evil bears the characteristic of a punishment for moral evil. This seems to be a great mistake of certain theologians, who pay more attention to the coherency of their system than to the light of nature or of revelation. Thus, says Dr.

Dick: "If our antagonists will change the meaning of words, they cannot alter the nature of things. Pain and death are evils, and when inflicted by the hand of a just God, *must be punishments:* for although the innocent may be harassed and destroyed by the arbitrary exercise of human power, none but the guilty suffer under his administration. To pretend that, although death and other temporal evils have come upon us through the sin of Adam, yet these are not to be regarded as a punishment, is neither more nor less than to say,—they must not be called a punishment, because this would not agree with our system. If we should concede that they are a punishment, we should be compelled to admit that the sin of the first man is imputed to his posterity, and that he was their federal head. We deny, therefore, that the labours and sorrows of the present life, the loss of such joys as are left to us at its close, and the dreadful agonies and terrors with which death is often attended, have the nature of a penalty. In like manner, a man may call black white, and bitter sweet, because it will serve his purpose; but he would be the veriest simpleton who should believe him."

Now, we do not deny that the agonies and terrors of death are sometimes a punishment for sin: this is the case in regard to all those who actually commit sin, and sink into the grave amid the horrors of a guilty conscience. But the question is, Do suffering and death never fall upon the innocent under the administration of God? We affirm that they do; and also that they may fall upon the innocent, in perfect accordance with the infinite goodness of God. In the first place, we reply to the confident assertions of Dr. Dick, and of the whole school to which he belongs, as follows: To pretend that death and other temporal evils are *always punishments*, is neither more nor less than to say, "they *must* be called punishments, because this would agree with our system. If we should concede that they are *not* a punishment, we should be compelled to admit that the sin of the first man is not imputed to his posterity, and that he was *not* their federal head. If our antagonists," &c. Surely it is not very wise to use language which may be so easily retorted.

Secondly, it is true, the change of a word cannot alter the nature of things; but it may alter, and very materially too, our view of the nature of things. Besides, if to refuse to call suffering in certain cases a *punishment*, be merely to change a word, why should so great an outcry be made about it? Why may we not use that word which sounds the most pleasantly to the ear, and sits the most easily upon the heart?

Thirdly, we do not arbitrarily and blindly reject the term *punishment*, "because it does not agree with our system." We not only reject the term, but also the very idea and the thing for which it stands. We mean to affirm, that the innocent do sometimes suffer under the administration of God; and that all suffering is not a punishment for sin. The very idea of punishment, according to Dr. Dick himself, is, that it is suffering inflicted on account of sin in the person upon whom it is inflicted; and hence, wherever pain or death falls under the administration of God, we must there find, says he, either actual or imputed sin. Now, in regard to certain cases, we deny both the name and the thing. And we make this denial, as it will be seen, not because it agrees with our system merely, but because it agrees with the universal voice and reason of mankind, except where that voice has been silenced, and that reason perverted, by dark and blindly-dogmatizing schemes of theology.

Fourthly, there is a vast difference, in reality, between regarding some sufferings as mere calamities, and all suffering as *punishment*. If we regard all suffering as punishment, then we need look no higher and no further in order to vindicate the character of God in the infliction of them. For, according to this view, they are the infliction of his retributive justice, merited by the person upon whom they fall, and adapted to prevent sin; and consequently here our inquiries may terminate; just as when we see the criminal receive the penalty due to his crimes. On the other hand, if we may not view all suffering as punishment, then must we seek for other grounds and principles on which to vindicate the goodness of God; then must we look for other ends, or final causes, of suffering under the wise economy of divine providence. And this search, as we shall see, will lead us to behold the moral government of the world, not as it is darkly distorted in certain systems of theology, but as it is in itself, replete with light and ineffable beauty.

But before we undertake to show this by direct arguments, let us pause and consider the predicament to which the greatest divines have reduced themselves, by their advocacy of such an imputation of the sin of one man. Dr. Dick affirms, as we have seen, that every evil brought upon man under the good providence of God, must be a punishment for sin; and hence, as infants do not actually sin, they are exposed to divine wrath on account of the sin of Adam, which is imputed to them. But is not this imputation, which draws after itself pain and death, also an evil? How has it happened, then, that in the good providence of God, this tremendous evil, this frightful source of so many evils, has been permitted to fall on the infant world? Must there not be some other sin imputed to justify the infliction of such an evil, and so on *ad infinitum?* Will Dr. Dick carry out his principle to this consequence? Will he require, as in consistency he is bound to require, that the tremendous evil of the imputation of sin shall not fall upon any part of God's creation, except as a punishment for some antecedent guilt? No, indeed: at the very second step his great principle, so confidently and so dogmatically asserted, completely breaks down under him. The imposition of this evil is justified, not by any antecedent guilt, but by the divine constitution, according to which Adam is the federal head and representative of the human race. Thus, after all, Dr. Dick has found some principle or ground on which to justify the infliction of evil, beside the principle of guilt or ill-desert. Might there not possibly be, then, such a divine constitution of things, as to bring suffering upon the offspring of Adam in consequence of his sin, without resorting to the dark and enigmatical fiction of the imputation of his transgression? If there be a divine constitution, as Dr. Dick contends there is, which justifies the imputation of moral evil, with all its frightful consequences, both temporal and eternal death, may it not be possible, in the nature of things, to suppose a divine constitution to justify suffering without the imputation of sin? How can the one of these things be so utterly repugnant to the divine character, and the other so perfectly agreeable to it? Until this question be answered, we may suspect the author himself of having assumed positions and made confident assertions, "because they agree with his system."

"We say, then," says Dr. Dick, "that by his sin his posterity became liable to the punishment denounced against himself. They became guilty through his guilt, which is imputed to them, or placed to their account; so that they are treated as if they had personally broken the covenant." Thus all the posterity of Adam, not excepting infants, became justly obnoxious to the "penalty of the covenant of works,—death, temporal, spiritual, and eternal." Now, we would suppose that this scheme of imputation is attended with at least as great a difficulty as the doctrine that the innocent do sometimes suffer under the good providence of God. Indeed, the author does not deny that it is attended with difficulties, which have never been answered. In regard to the imputation of sin, he says: "Candour requires me to add, that we are not competent fully to assign the reasons of this dispensation. After the most mature consideration of the subject, it appears *mysterious* that God should have placed our first parent in such circumstances, that while he might insure, he might forfeit, his own happiness and that of millions of beings who were to spring from his loins. We cannot tell why he adopted this plan with us and not with angels, each of whom was left to stand or fall for himself."* Now, when it is affirmed that the innocent may suffer for wise and good purposes, why is all this candour and modesty forgotten? Why is it not admitted, "It may be so;" "We cannot tell?" Why is the fact, of which these writers so often and so eloquently remind us, that the human intellect is a poor, blind, weak thing, quite unfit to pry into mysteries, then sunk in utter oblivion, and a tone of confident dogmatism assumed? Why not act consistently with the character of the sceptic or the dogmatist, and not put on the one or the other by turns, according to the exigencies of a system?

If we ask, why infants are exposed to death, we are told, that it is a punishment for Adam's sin imputed to them. We are told that this *must* be so; since "none but the guilty ever suffer under the administration of God," who is not an arbitrary and cruel tyrant to cause the innocent to suffer. Why then, we ask, does he impute sin to them? To this it is replied, "We cannot tell." No wonder; for if there must always be antecedent guilt to justify God in imposing evil upon his sub-

* Lectures on Theology, vol. i, p. 458.

jects, then there can be no reason for such a dispensation for imposing the tremendous evil of the imputation of sin. The advocates of it themselves have laid down a principle, which shows it to be without a reason. Hence they may well say, "We cannot tell." Thus suffering is justified by the imputation of guilt; the imputation of guilt by the divine constitution; and the divine constitution, by nothing! If this is all that can be done, would it not have been just as well to have begun, as well as ended, in the divine constitution of things? But, no! even the most humble of men must have some explanation, some little mitigation of their difficulties, if it be only to place the world upon the back of an elephant, the elephant upon the back of a tortoise, and the tortoise upon nothing.

It seems to be inconceivably horrible to Dr. Dick, and others of his school, that the innocent should ever be made to suffer under the providence of God; but yet they earnestly insist that the same good providence plunges the whole human race—infants and all—into unavoidable guilt, and then punishes them for it! To say that the innocent may be made to suffer is monstrous injustice—is horrible; but to say that they are made sinners, and then punished, is all right and proper! To say that the innocent can suffer under the administration of God, is to shock our sense of justice, and put out the light of the divine goodness; but it is all well if we only say that the punishment due to Adam's sin is made, by the same good administration, to fall upon all his posterity *in the form of moral evil, and that then they are justly punished for this punishment!* Alas, that the minds of the great and the good, born to reflect the light of the glorious gospel of God upon a darkened world, should be so sadly warped, so awfully distorted, by the inexorable necessities of a despotic system!

SECTION II.

The imputation of sin not consistent with the goodness of God.

This point has been already indirectly considered, but it is worthy of a more direct and complete examination. It is very remarkable that although Dr. Dick admits he cannot reconcile the scheme of imputation with the character of God, or remove its seeming hardships, not to say cruelty, he yet positively affirms that "it is a proof of the goodness of God."* Surely, if the covenant of works, involving the imputation of sin, as explained by Dr. Dick, be a "*proof* of the divine goodness," it cannot but appear to be too severe. But as this point, on which he scarcely dwells at all, is more elaborately and fully discussed by President Edwards, we shall direct our attention to him.

"It is objected," says Edwards, "that appointing Adam to stand in this great affair as the moral head of his posterity, and so treating them as *one* with him, is injurious to them." "To which," says he, "I answer, it is demonstrably otherwise; that such a constitution was so far from being *injurious* to Adam's posterity any more than if every one had been appointed to stand for himself personally, that it was, in itself considered, attended with a more eligible *probability* of a *happy* issue than the latter would have been; and so is a constitution that truly expresses the goodness of its Author." Now, let us see how this is *demonstrated.*

"There is a *greater tendency* to a happy issue in such an appointment," says he, "than if every one had been appointed to stand for himself; especially on these accounts: (1.) That Adam had *stronger motives to watchfulness* than his posterity would have had; in that, not only his own eternal welfare lay at stake, but also that of all his posterity. (2.) Adam was in a state of complete *manhood* when his trial began."† In the first place, then, the constitution for which Edwards contends is "an expression of the divine goodness," because it presented stronger motives to obedience than if it had merely suspended the eternal destiny of Adam alone upon his conduct. The eternal welfare of his posterity was staked upon his obedience; and, having this stupendous motive before him, he would be more likely to preserve his allegiance than if the motive had been less powerful. The magnitude of the motive, says Edwards, is the grand circumstance which evinces the goodness of God in the appointment of such a constitution. If this be true, it is very easy to see how the Almighty might have made a vast improvement in his own constitution for the government of the world. He might have made the motive still stronger, and thereby made the appointment or covenant still better: instead of suspending merely the eternal destiny of the human race upon the conduct

* Lectures on Theology, p. 458. † Edwards's Works, vol. ii, p. 548.

of Adam, he might have staked the eternal fate of the universe upon it. According to the argument of Edwards, what a vast, what a wonderful improvement would this have been in the divine constitution for the government of the world, and how much more conspicuously would it have displayed the goodness of its Divine Author!

Again, the scheme of Edwards is condemned out of his own mouth. If this scheme be better than another, because its motives are *stronger*, why did not God render it still more worthy of his goodness, by rendering its motives still more powerful and efficacious? Edwards admits, nay, he insists, that God might easily have rendered the motives of his moral government perfectly efficacious and successful. He repeatedly declares that God could have prevented all sin, "by giving such influences of his Spirit as would have been absolutely effectual to hinder it." If the goodness of a constitution, then, is to be determined by the strength of its motives, as the argument of Edwards supposes, then we are bound, according to his principles, to pronounce that for which he contends unworthy of the goodness of God, as being radically unsound and defective. This is emphatically the case, as the Governor of the world might have strengthened the motives to obedience *indefinitely*, not by augmenting the danger, but by increasing the security of his subjects; that is to say, not by making the penalty more terrific, but by giving a greater disposition to obedience.

The same thing may be clearly seen from another point of view. Let us suppose, for instance, that God had established the constitution or covenant, that if Adam had persevered in obedience, then all his posterity should be confirmed in holiness and happiness; and that if he fell, he should fall for himself alone. Would not such an appointment, we ask, have been more likely to have been attended with a happy issue than that for which Edwards contends? Let us suppose again, that after such a constitution had been established, its Divine Author had really secured the obedience of Adam; would not this have made a "happy issue" perfectly certain? Why then was not such a constitution established? It would most assuredly have been an infinitely clearer and more beautiful expression of the divine goodness than that of Edwards. Hence, the philosophy of Edwards easily furnishes an unspeakably better constitution for the government of the world, than that which has been established by the wisdom of God! Is it not evident, that the advocates of such a scheme should never venture before the tribunal of reason at all? Is it not evident, that their only safe policy is to insist, as they sometimes do, that we do not know what is consistent, or *inconsistent*, with the attributes of God, in his arrangements for the government of the world? Is it not evident, that their truest wisdom is to be found in habitually dwelling on the littleness, weakness, misery, and darkness of the human mind, and in rebuking its arrogance for presuming to pry into the *mysteries* of their system?

The vindication of the divine goodness by Edwards, is, we think it must be conceded, exceedingly weak. All it amounts to is this,—that this scheme is an expression of the goodness of God, because, in certain respects, it is better than a scheme which might have been established. So far from showing it to be the best possible scheme, his philosophy shows it might be greatly improved in the *very respects* in which its excellency is supposed to consist. In other words, he contends that God has displayed his goodness in the appointment of such a constitution, on the ground that he might have made a worse; though, according to his own principles, it is perfectly evident that he might have made a better! Is this to express, or to deny, the absolute, infinite goodness of God? Is it to manifest the glory of that goodness to the eye of man, or to shroud it in clouds and darkness?

Edwards also says, that "the goodness of God in such a constitution with Adam appears in this: that if there had been no *sovereign, gracious* establishment at all, but God had proceeded on the basis of mere *justice*, and had gone no farther than this required, he might have demanded of Adam and all his posterity, that they should have performed *perfect, perpetual obedience*." The italics are all his own. On this passage, we have to remark, that it is built upon unfounded assumptions. It is frequently said, we are aware, that if it had not been for the redemption of the world by a "sovereign, gracious" dispensation, the whole race of man might have been justly exposed to the torments of hell forever. But where is the proof? Is it found in the word of God? This tells us what *is*, what *has been*, and what *will be;* but it is not given to speculate upon what *might* be. For aught we know, if there had been no salvation through Christ, as a part of the actual constitution and system of the world, then there would have been no other part of that system whatever. We are not told, and we do not know, what it would have been consistent with the justice of God to do in relation to the world, if there had been no remedy provided for its restoration. Perhaps it might never have been created at all. The work of Christ is the great sun and centre of the system as *it is;* and if this had never been a part of the original grand design, we do not know that the planets would have been created to wander in eternal darkness. We do not know that even the justice of God would have created man, and permitted him to fall, wandering everlastingly amid the horrors of death, without hope and without remedy. We find nothing of the kind in the word of God; and in our nature it meets with no response, except a wail of unutterable horror. We like not, we confess, those vindications of God's goodness, which consist in drawing hideous, black pictures of his justice, and then telling us that it is not so dark as these. We want not to know whether there might not be darker things in the universe than God's love; we only want to know if there could be anything brighter, or better, or more beautiful.

The most astounding feature of this vindication of the divine goodness still remains to be noticed. We are told that the constitution in question is good, because it was so likely to have had a "happy issue." And when this constitution was established by the sovereign will and pleasure of God, the conduct of Adam, it is conceded, was perfectly foreseen by him. At the very time this constitution was established, its Divine Author foresaw with perfect absolute certainty what would be the issue. He knew that the great federal head, so appointed by him, would transgress the covenant, and bring down the curse of "death, temporal, spiritual, and eternal," upon all his posterity. O, wonderful goodness! to promise eternal life to the human race on a condition which he certainly foreknew would not be performed! Amazing grace! to threaten eternal death to all mankind, on a condition which he certainly foreknew would be fulfilled!

This cannot be evaded, by asserting that the same difficulty attaches to the fact, that God created Adam foreseeing he would fall. His foreknowledge did not necessitate the fall of Adam. It left him free as God had created him. Life and death were set before him, and he had the power to stand, as well as the power to fall. He had no right to complain of God, then, if, under such circumstances, he chose to rebel, and incur the penalty. But if the scheme of Edwards be true, the descendants of Adam did not have their fate in their own hands. It did not depend on their own choice. It was necessitated, even prior to their existence, by the divine constitution which had indissolubly connected their awful destiny, their temporal and eternal ruin, with an event already foreseen. And the constitution binding such awful consequences to an event already foreseen, is called an expression of the goodness of God!

Suppose, for example, that a great prince should promise his subjects that on the happening of a certain event, over which they had no control, he would confer unspeakable favours upon them. Suppose also, that at the same time he should declare to them, that if the event should not happen, he would load them with irons, cast them into prison, and inflict the greatest imaginable punishments upon them during the remainder of their lives. Suppose again, that at the very time he thus made known his *gracious intentions* to them, he knew perfectly well that the event on which his favour was suspended would not happen. Then, according to his certain foreknowledge, the event fails, and the penalty of the covenant or appointment is inflicted upon his subjects:—they are cast into prison; they are bound in chains, and perpetually tormented with the greatest of all imaginable evils:—not because they had transgressed the appointment or sovereign constitution, but because an event had taken place over which they had no control. Now, who would call such a ruler a good prince? Who could conceive, indeed, of a more cruel or deceitful tyrant? But we submit it to the candid reader, if he be not more like the prince of predestination, than the great God of heaven and earth?

This scheme of imputation, so far from being an expression of infinite goodness, were indeed an exhibition of the most frightful cruelty and injustice. It would be a useful, as well as a most curious inquiry, to examine the various contrivances of ingenious men, in order to bring the doctrine of imputation into harmony with the justice of God. We shall briefly allude to only two of these wonderful inventions,—those of Augustine and Edwards. Neither of these celebrated divines supposed that a foreign sin, properly so called, is ever imputed to any one; but that the sin of Adam, which is imputed to his descendants, is their own sin, as well as his.* But here the question arises, How could they make Adam's sin to be the sin of his descendants, many of whom were born thousands of years after it was committed?

Augustine, as is well known, maintained the startling paradox, that all mankind were present in Adam, and sinned in him. In this way, he supposed that all men became partakers in the guilt of Adam's sin, and consequently justly liable to the penalty due to his transgression. Augustine was quite too good a logician not to perceive, that if all men are responsible for Adam's sin, because they were in him when he transgressed, then, it follows, that we are also responsible for the sins of all our ancestors, from whom we are more immediately descended. This follows from that maxim of jurisprudence, from that dictate of common-sense, that a rule of law is coëxtensive with the reason upon which it is based. Hence, as Wiggers remarks: "Augustine thought it not improbable that the sins of ancestors *universally* are imputed to their descendants."† This conclusion is clearly set forth in the extracts made by the translator of Wiggers.‡ If this scheme be true, we know indeed that we are all guilty of Adam's sin; but who, or how many of the human race, were the perpetrators of Cain's murder beside himself, we cannot determine. Indeed, if this frightful hypothesis be well founded, if it form a part of the moral constitution of the world, no man can possibly tell how many thefts, murders, or treasons, he may have committed in his ancestors. One thing is certain, however, and that is, that the man who is born later in the course of time, will have the more sins to answer for, and the more fearful will be the accumulation of his guilt; as all the transgressions of all his ancestors, from Adam down to his immediate parents, will be laid upon his head.

Clearly as this consequence is involved in the fundamental prin-

* Edwards on Original Sin, part iv, chap. iii, p. 543.

† Encheir., c. 46, 47. See also remarks by the American editor and translator.

‡ See p. 284.

ciple of Augustine's theory, the good father could not but reel and stagger under it. "Respecting the sins of the other parents," says he, "the progenitors from Adam down to one's own immediate father, *it may not improperly be debated*, whether the child is implicated in the evil acts and multiplied original faults of *all*, so that each one is the worse in proportion as he is later; or that, in respect to the sins of their parents, God threatens posterity to the third and fourth generation, because, *by the moderation of his compassion*, he does not further extend his anger in respect to the faults of progenitors, lest those on whom the grace of regeneration is not conferred, *should be pressed with too heavy a burden in their own eternal damnation*, if they were compelled to contract by way of origin (*originaliter*) the *sins* of *all* their preceding parents from the commencement of the human race, and *to suffer the punishment due to them*.* Whether, on so great a subject, anything else can or cannot be found, by a more diligent reading and scrutiny of the Scriptures, I dare not hastily affirm."†

Thus does the sturdy logician, notwithstanding his almost indomitable hardihood, seem to stand appalled before the consequences to which his principles would inevitably conduct him. Having followed those principles but a little way, the scene becomes so dark with his representations of the divine justice, that he feels constrained to retrace his steps, and arbitrarily introduce the divine mercy, in order to mitigate the indescribable horrors which continually thicken around him. Such hesitation, such wavering and inconsistency, is the natural result of every scheme which places the decisions of the head in violent conflict with the indestructible feelings of the heart.

In his attempt to reconcile the scheme of imputation with the justice of God, Edwards has met with as little success as Augustine. For this purpose, he supposed that God had constituted an identity between Adam and all his posterity, whereby the latter became partakers of his rebellion. "I think it would go

* If God, out of the abundance of his compassion, imputes the sins of parents only to the third or fourth generation, how has it happened that Adam's transgression is imputed to all his posterity, and punished throughout all generations? Is there any consistency, or harmony, in such views respecting the government of the world?

† Wiggers's Presentation, note by translator, p. 285.

far toward directing us to the more clear conception and right statement of this affair," says he, in reference to imputation, "were we steadily to bear this in mind, that God, in every step of his proceedings with Adam, in relation to the covenant or constitution established with him, looked on his posterity as being *one with him*. And though he dealt more immediately with Adam, it yet was as the *head* of the whole body, and the *root* of the whole tree; and in his proceedings with him, he dealt with all the branches as if they had been then existing in their root. From which it will follow, that both guilt, or exposedness to punishment, and also depravity of heart, came upon Adam's posterity just as they came upon him, as much as if he and they had all coëxisted, like a tree with many branches; allowing only for the difference necessarily resulting from the place Adam stood in as head or root of the whole. Otherwise, it is as if, in every step of proceeding, every alteration in the root had been attended at the same instant with the same alteration throughout the whole tree, in each individual branch. I think this will naturally follow on the supposition of their being a constituted *oneness* or *identity* of Adam and his posterity in this affair."* As the sap of a tree, Edwards has said, spreads from the root of a tree to all its branches, so the original sin of Adam descends from him through the generations of men.

In the serious promulgation of such sentiments, it is only forgotten that sin is not the sap of a tree, and that the whole human race is not really one and the same person. Such an idea of personal identity is as utterly unintelligible as the nature of the sin and the responsibility with which it is so intimately associated. Surely these are the dark dreams of men, not the bright and shining lights of eternal truth.

Before we take leave of President Edwards, we would remark, that he proceeds on the same supposition with Calvin,† Bates,‡ Dwight,§ Dick, and a host of others, that suffering is always a punishment of sin, and of "sin in them who suffer."‖ "The light of nature," says Edwards, "or tradition from ancient revelation, led the heathen to conceive of death as in a peculiar manner an evidence of divine vengeance. Thus we have an

* Edwards on Original Sin, part iv, ch. iii.

† Institutes, book ii, ch. i.

‡ Divine Attributes.

§ Sermon on Original Sin.

‖ Original Sin, part i, ch. ii.

account, that when the barbarians saw the venomous beast hang on Paul's hand, they said among themselves, 'No doubt, this man is a murderer, whom, though he hath escaped the seas, yet vengeance suffereth not to live.'"* We think that the barbarians concluded rashly: it is certain that St. Paul was neither a murderer nor a god. Nor, indeed, if the venomous beast had taken his life, would this have proved him to be a murderer, any more than its falling off into the fire proved him to be a god, according to the rash judgment of the barbarians. There is a better source of philosophy, if we mistake not, than the rash, hasty, foolish judgments of barbarians.

SECTION III.

The imputation of sin not consistent with human, much less with the divine goodness.

There are few persons whose feelings will allow them to be consistent advocates of the doctrine of the imputation of Adam's sin. "To many other divines," says Bishop Burnet, "this seems a harsh and inconceivable opinion: it seems repugnant to the justice and goodness of God to reckon men guilty of sin which they never committed, and to punish them in their souls eternally for that which is no act of theirs."† It certainly "seems very hard," as the author says, "to apprehend how persons who have never sinned, but are only unhappily descended, should be, in consequence of that, under so great a misery." But how to escape the pressure of this stupendous difficulty is the question. There are many who cannot endure it; or rather, there are very few who can endure it; but, as Bishop Burnet says, they find no difficulty in the idea of temporal punishment on account of Adam's sin. "This, they think, is easily enough reconcilable with the notions of justice and goodness, since this is only a temporary *punishment* relating to men's persons."‡ But do they not sacrifice their logic to their feelings? Let us see.

This view of a limited imputation, and a limited *punishment*, is not confined to the Church of England. It prevails to a greater or less extent in all denominations. But President Edwards has, we think, unanswerably exposed the inconsistency

* Original Sin, part i, ch. ii.

† Exposition of the Thirty-nine Articles, article ix.

‡ Ibid.

of its advocates. "One of them supposes," says he, "that this sin, though truly imputed to INFANTS, so that thereby they are exposed to a proper *punishment*, yet is not imputed to them in such a *degree*, as that upon this account they should be liable to *eternal* punishment, as Adam himself was, but only to *temporal death*, or *annihilation;* Adam himself, the immediate actor, being made infinitely more guilty of it than his posterity. On which I would observe, that to suppose God imputes, not *all* the guilt of Adam, but only *some little part* of it, relieves nothing but his *imagination*. To think of poor little infants bearing such torments for Adam's sin, as they sometimes do in this world, and these torments ending in death and annihilation, may sit easier on the imagination, than to conceive of their suffering eternal misery for it; but it does not at all relieve one's *reason*. There is no rule of reason that can be supposed to lie against imputing a sin in the *whole* of it, which was committed by one, to another who did not personally commit it, but will also lie against its being so imputed and punished in *part;* for all the reasons (if there be any) lie against the *imputation*, not the *quality* or *degree* of what is imputed. If there be any rule of reason that is strong and good, lying against a proper derivation or communication of guilt from one that acted to another that did not act, then it lies against all that is of that nature .... If these reasons are good, all the difference is this: that to bring a *great* punishment on infants for Adam's sin, is a *great* act of injustice, and to bring a comparatively *smaller* punishment is a smaller act of injustice; but not, that this is not as truly and demonstrably an act of injustice as the other."*

We hold this to be a solid and unanswerable argument; and we hold also, that God can no more commit a small act of injustice than a great one. Hence, in the eye of *reason*, there is no medium between rejecting the whole of the imputation of Adam's sin, and ceasing to object against the imputation of the whole of it, as inconsistent with the justice and goodness of God. We may arbitrarily wipe out a portion of it in order to relieve our *imagination;* but this brings no relief to the calm and passionless reason. It may still the wild tumults of emotion, but it cannot silence the voice of the intellect. Why not relieve

* Edwards on Original Sin, part iv, ch. iii.

both the *imagination* and the *reason?* Why not wipe out the whole dark film of imputation, and permit the glad eye to open on the bright glory of God's infinite goodness?

The wonder is, that when Edwards had carried out his logic to such a conclusion, he did not regard his argument as a perfect *reductio ad absurdum.* The wonder is, that when he had carried out his logic to the position, that it might well consist with the justice of God to impute the whole of Adam's sin to "poor little infants," as he calls them, and then cause them to endure "eternal torments for it," his whole nature did not recoil from such a conclusion with indescribable horror. For our part, highly as we value logical consistency, we should prefer a little incoherency in our reasoning, a little flexibility in our logic, rather than bear even one "poor little infant" on the hard, unyielding point of it into the torments of hell forever.

St. Augustine was the great founder of the doctrine of the imputation of sin. But although he did more than any other person to give this doctrine a hold upon the mind of the Christian world, it never had a perfect hold upon his own mind. So far from being able to reconcile it with the divine goodness, he could not reconcile it with his own goodness. For this purpose, he employed the theory that all the posterity of Adam were, in the most literal sense, already *in him*, and sinned in him—in his person; and that Adam's sin is therefore justly imputed to all his posterity.* He also appeals to revelation. "St. Augustine," as Father Almeyda truly says, "and the fathers who follow him, take the fundamental principle of their doctrine (which affirms that infants without baptism will endure eternal pain) from the sentence which the Supreme Judge is to pronounce at the last day. We know that the Lord, dividing the human race into two portions, will put the elect on the right hand, and the reprobate on the left; and he will say to those on the left, Depart into eternal fire. St. Augustine then argues, that infants will not be on the right, because Jesus Christ has positively excluded all those who shall not *be born again of water* and of the Holy Spirit: then they will be on the left; and thus they will be comprehended in the damnation of eternal fire, which the Lord will pronounce against those who shall

* See Knapp's Theology, vol. ii, art. ix, sec. 76; also Wiggers's Presentation of Augustinism and Pelagianism, chap. xix, p. 268.

be on the left side: for having no more than two hands, and only two places and two sentences, since, then, there are infants which God does not favour, it follows that they will be comprehended in the sentence of the reprobate, which is not only a privation of the sight of God, but also the pain of fire."* Such is the ground, and such the logic, on which St. Augustine and his followers erected that portentous scheme, that awful speculation, which has so long cast a dark cloud over the glory of the Christian world, and prevented it from reflecting the bright, cheering beams of the divine goodness.

But, what! could St. Augustine find rest in his own views,—in his own logic? Did he really banish all non-elect infants into the region of penal fire and everlasting woe? If he adhered to the literal meaning of the words of revelation, as he understood them, he was certainly bound to do so; but did he really and consistently do it? Did he really bind the "poor little" reprobate, because it had sinned in Adam, in chains of adamant, and leave it to writhe beneath the fierce inquisitorial fury of the everlasting flames? Did he really extract the vials of such exquisite and unprovoked wrath from the essence of infinite goodness itself? No: this was reserved for the superior logic and the sterner consistency of an iron age. But since it has been extracted, we may devoutly thank Almighty God, that it is now excluded from the hearts of men calling themselves Christians, and kept safely bottled up in their creeds and confessions.

St Augustine could not endure the insufferable consequences of his own doctrine. Hence, in writing to his great friend, St. Jerome, he said, "in all sincerity: when I come to treat of the punishment of infants, believe *that I find myself in great embarrassment, and I absolutely know not what to reply.*" Writing against Julian, he adds: "*I do not say that those who die without baptism will be punished with a torment such that it would be better for them if they had never been born.*" And again: "Those who, besides original sin which they have contracted, have not committed any other, will be subjected to a pain the most mild of all."† Thus by adopting a wrong interpretation, the principles of which were but little understood in his time, St. Augustine banished all unbaptized infants from the

* Harmonie de la Raison et de la Religion. † Ibid., Almeyda.

kingdom of light; but yet he could hardly find it in his heart to condemn them to the outer darkness. He had too great a regard for the word of God, as he understood it, to permit non-elect infants to reign with Christ in heaven; and, on the other hand, he was too severely pressed by the generous impulses of his nature, nay, by the eternal dictates of truth and goodness, to permit him to consign them really to the "fire prepared for the devil and his angels." Hence, although Christ knew of "but two places," he fitted up a third, to see them in which, was, as Edwards would say, "more agreeable to his imagination."

It was the sublime but unsteady genius of St. Augustine that caused this doctrine of the damnation of infants to be received into the Christian world, and find its way into the council of Trent. That celebrated council not only adopted the views of St. Augustine on this subject, but also most perfectly reflected all his hesitation and inconsistency. Widely as its members differed on other points, they all agreed that unbaptized infants should be excluded from the kingdom of heaven. There was but little unanimity however, as to the best method of disposing of them. The Dominicans fitted up a dark, subterraneous cavern for them, in which there is no fire, at least none such as that of the infernal regions, and in which they might be at least as happy as monks. This place was called *Limbo*—which, we suppose, is to Purgatory, about what the varioloid is to the smallpox. The Franciscans, more humane in their doctrine, determined that "dear little infants," though they had never felt the sanctifying influences of holy water, should yet reside, not in dark caverns and holes of the earth, but in the sweet light and pure air of the upper world. Well done, noble Franciscan! we honour thee for thy sweet fancy! Surely thou wert not, like other monks, made so altogether fierce by dark keeping, that thou couldest not delight to see in God's blessed, beautiful world, a smiling infant!

Others insisted, that unbaptized infants would be condemned to become philosophers, and turn out the authors of great discoveries. This may seem a terrible damnation to some persons; but, for our part, if we had been of that famous council, it is likely we should have been in favour of this decree. As the most agreeable punishment we could imagine, we should have been for condemning them, like the fallen angels of Paradise Lost, to torment themselves with reasonings high,—

> "Of providence, foreknowledge, will, and fate,
> Fix'd fate, free-will, foreknowledge absolute."

And if any of them had been found to possess no very great aptitude for such speculations, then, rather than they should find "no end in wandering mazes lost," we should have condemned them to turn poets and "build the lofty rhyme."

So completely did the spirit of a blind exegesis triumph over the light of reason in the time of Augustine, that even Pelagius and his followers excluded unbaptized infants from the kingdom of heaven, because our Saviour had declared that a man could not enter therein, except he be born of water and of the Spirit. It is true, they did not banish them into "the fire prepared for the devil and his angels," nor into Limbo, nor into dark holes of the earth; on the contrary, they admitted them to the joys of eternal life, but not into the kingdom of heaven.* Thus, the Pelagians brought "poor little infants" as near to the kingdom of heaven as possible, without doing too great violence to the universal orthodoxy of their time.

But as we cannot, like the Church of Rome, determine the fate of infants by a decree, we must take some little pains to ascertain how it has been determined by the Supreme Ruler of the world. For this purpose we shall first show, that there is suffering in the world which is not a punishment for sin, and then declare the great ends, or final causes, of all natural evil.

SECTION IV.

The true ends, or final causes, of natural evil.

We have often wondered that grave divines should declare that there could be no natural evil, or suffering, under the administration of God, except such as is a punishment for sin *in the person upon whom it is inflicted.* We have wondered, that in declaring none but a tyrant could ever permit the innocent to suffer, they have entertained no fears lest they might strengthen the cause of atheism. For if it be impossible to justify the character of God, except on the principle that all

* Wiggers's Presentation of Augustinism and Pelagianism, chap. iv.

suffering is merited on account of sin in the object of it, then it is easy to see, that the atheistical argument against the goodness of God is unanswerable. The atheist might well say: "Do we not see and know that the whole animal creation suffers? Now for what sin are they punished? The inferior animals, you will admit, are not capable of committing actual sin, any more than infants are; and Adam was not their federal head and representative. Hence, unless you can show for what sin they are *punished*, you must admit that, according to your own principles, God is a tyrant." How Dr. Dick, or Dr. Dwight, or President Edwards, or Calvin, would have answered such an argument, we cannot determine. For although they all assume that there can be no suffering under the good providence of God, except it be a punishment for sin in the object of it, yet, so far as we know, they have not made the most distant allusion to the suffering of the inferior animals. Indeed, they seem to be so intently bent on maintaining the doctrine of the imputation of sin to infants, that they pay no attention, in the assumption of the above position, either to the word of God, or to the great volume of nature spread out before them.

But we find the difficulty noticed in a prize essay of three hundred pages, on the subject of native depravity, by Dr. Woods. The author assumes the same ground with Edwards, that all suffering must be justified on the ground of justice; and hence he finds a real and proper sin in infants, in order to reconcile their sufferings with the character of God. This is the only ground, according to Dr. Woods, on which suffering can be vindicated under the administration of a perfect God. Where, then, is the real and proper sin in the inferior animals to justify their sufferings? This difficulty occurs to the distinguished author, and he endeavours to meet it. Let us see his reply. It is a reply which we have long been solicitous to see, and we now have it from one of the most celebrated theologians of the present day.

"Some suppose," says he, "that infants suffer as irrational animals do, without reference to a moral law or the principles of a moral government. A strange supposition indeed, that *human beings* should for a time be ranked with beings which are not human, that is, mere animals." He is evidently shocked at such an insult offered to poor little infants. He will not allow us, for one moment, to take the whole race of man, "during the interesting period of infancy, cut them off from their relation to Adam, degrade them from the dignity of human beings, and put them in the rank of brute animals,—and then say, they *suffer as the brutes do*. . . . . This would be the worst of all theories,—the farthest off from Scripture and reason, and the most revolting to all the noble sensibilities of man."

Now, it is really refreshing to find these allusions to "the dignity of human beings" in a writer of this school; and especially in Dr. Woods, who has so often rebuked others for their pride, when they have imagined that they were only engaged in the laudable enterprise of asserting this very dignity, by raising men from the rank of mere machines. It is so refreshing, indeed, to find such allusions in Dr. Woods, that we could almost forgive a little special pleading and bad logic in his attempt to vindicate the "dignity of human beings," which should have been an attempt to vindicate the goodness of God.

We do not place human beings and brutes in the same rank, except in so far as both are sensitive creatures, and consequently susceptible of pleasure and pain. In this particular, the Creator himself has, to a certain extent, placed them in the same rank, and it is useless to cry out against his appointment. He will not listen to our talk about "the dignity of human beings." He will still leave us, in so far as bodily pain and death are concerned, in the same rank with mere animals. This single point of resemblance between animals and human beings is all that our argument requires; and the *fact* that animals do suffer pain and death cannot be denied, or swept away by declamation. Let this fact be fairly and openly met, and not merely evaded. Let it be shown how the suffering of mere animals may be reconciled with the infinite goodness of God, and we will undertake to show how the suffering of guiltless "human beings" may be reconciled with it. Nay, we will undertake to show that the suffering of infants may be reconciled with the divine goodness, on the same, and also on still higher, grounds. We will place their sufferings on a more solid and a more definite foundation, than upon such vague and misty assertions as that they "suffer with reference to a moral law."

We do not cut off infants from their relation to Adam; nor

could we, if we desired to do so, cut them off from their relation to the animal nature which God has given them. It may be a very humiliating thought, it is true, that *human beings* should ever eat like mere animals, or sleep like mere animals, or suffer like mere animals; but yet we cannot see how any rebellion against so humiliating a thought can possibly alter the fact. We do not deny, indeed, that a theologian may eat, and sleep, and suffer on higher principles than mere animals do; but we seriously doubt if infants ever eat, or sleep, or suffer on any higher principles. It may shock the "noble sensibilities" of man that dear little infants should suffer as *brutes* do, especially when the term *brutes* is so strongly emphasized; but how it can relieve the case to have the poor little creatures arraigned at the bar of divine justice, and condemned to suffer as malefactors and criminals do, is more than we can possibly comprehend. To have them thus arraigned, condemned, and punished as criminals, may dignify their sufferings, and render them more worthy of the rank of human beings; but this is a dignity to which, we trust, they will never aspire.

If we are not mistaken, then, the theory for which we contend is "not the worst of all theories," nor "the most revolting to the noblest sensibilities of man." It is a worse theory to suppose, with Edwards, that they may be arraigned and banished into "eternal misery" for a sin they have not committed, or the possession of a nature they could not possibly have avoided possessing. It is better, we say, to rank the human race "for a time," "during the interesting period of infancy," even with mere animals, than to rank them with the devil and his angels. But, in truth, we rank them with neither; we simply leave them where God hath placed them, as a connecting link between the animal and the angelic natures.

But we may produce many instances of suffering among human beings, which are not a punishment for sin. We might refer to the feeling of compassion, which is always painful, and sometimes wrings the heart with the most exquisite agony; and yet this was not planted in our bosom as a punishment for sin, but, as Bishop Butler has shown,* it was ordained by a God of mercy, to teach us a lesson of mercy, and lead us to mitigate the manifold miseries of man's estate. We might also refer to

* Sermon on Compassion.

an indignation against crime, which, as the same profound thinker has shown in his sermon on resentment, was planted in our natures, not to punish the subject of it, but to insure the punishment of others, that is, of criminals; and thereby to preserve the good order and well-being of the world. This sense of wrong, of injustice, of outrage, by which the soul is so often tortured, is not designed to punish the subject of it, but to promote the happiness and virtue of mankind. We might refer to these, and many other things of the same kind, but it is not necessary to dwell upon particular instances; for the principle against which we contend may be more directly refuted by an appeal to reason, and to the very authors by whom it is advocated; for, although it is adopted by them, and seems plausible at first view, it is often lost sight of when they lose sight of their system, and they give utterance to another principle more in accordance with the voice of nature.

It is evident, that if the government of God requires that no suffering should be inflicted, except as a punishment for sin, then his perfect moral government requires that the punishment should, in all cases, be exactly proportioned to the demerit of those upon whom it falls.

For, as Butler truly says, "Moral government consists in rewarding the righteous and punishing the wicked; in rendering to men according to their actions, considered as good or evil. And the perfection of moral government consists in doing this, with regard to all intelligent creatures, in exact proportion to their personal merits and demerits."* This will not be denied. Hence, if suffering is distributed by God as a punishment for sin in all cases, as Calvin and his followers assert, then it must, on the same principle, be distributed according to the demerit of men. But is this the case? Does this necessary consequence of this principle agree with fact? If so, then every vile deed, every wicked outrage, committed by man, should be regarded as an instrument of divine justice, and deserved by those upon whom they fall. The inquisition itself, with all its unuttered and unutterable horrors, should be regarded, not merely as an exhibition of human wickedness and wrath, but also as an engine of divine justice, to crush the martyr on its wheels, because he refuses to lie to his own soul and to his God! Na-

* Butler's Analogy, part i, chap. iii.

ture itself recoils from such a conclusion. Not one of the writers in question would adopt it. Hence, they should not advocate a principle from which it necessarily flows.

Indeed, they all argue the necessity of a future state of retribution, from the unequal distribution of natural good and evil in this life. But Lord Bolingbroke has refuted this argument by reasoning from their own principles. He insists that such is the justice of God, that there can be no suffering or natural evil in this life, except such as is proportioned to the demerits of men; and hence he rejects the argument from the apparent unequal distribution of pleasure and pain in this world in favour of the reality of a future judgment. He resents the imputation that God could ever permit any suffering which is not deserved, as warmly as it is resented by Dr. Dick himself, and proclaims it to be dishonourable to God. All rewards and punishments, says he, are equal and just in this life; and to say otherwise, is to take an atheistical view of the divine character. Learned divines proceed on the same principle, as we have seen, when they contend for the imputation of sin; but they forget and overlook it, when they come to prove the future judgment to the infidel. Thus, in their zeal to establish their own peculiar dogmas, they place themselves and their cause in the power of the infidel.

But if suffering be not always inflicted, under the administration of God, as a punishment for sin, for what other end is it inflicted? We answer, it is inflicted for these ends: 1. Even when it is inflicted as a punishment for sin, this is not the only end, or final cause of its infliction. It is also intended to deter others from the commission of evil, and preserve the order of the world. 2. In some instances, nay, in very many instances, it is intended to discipline and form the mind to virtue. As Bishop Butler well says, even while vindicating the moral government of the world: "It is not pretended but that, in the natural course of things, happiness and misery appear to be distributed by other rules, than only the personal merit and demerit of character. They may sometimes be distributed by way of mere discipline. And in his profound chapter on a "State of probation, as intended for moral discipline and improvement," he shows that they are actually distributed for this purpose. 3. The unavoidable evils of this life, which are not brought upon us by our faults, are intended to serve as a foil to set off the blessedness of eternity. Our present light afflictions are intended, not merely to work out for us an exceeding and eternal weight of glory, but also to heighten our sense and enjoyment of it by a recollection of the miseries experienced in this life. They are intended to form but a short and discordant prelude to an everlasting harmony. If they should not prove so in fact, the fault will be our own, without the least impeachment of the beneficent design of the great Author and Ruler of the universe.

On these grounds, especially on the first two, we must justify all the natural evil in the world. In regard to the second, Bishop Butler says: "Allurements to what is wrong; difficulties in the discharge of our duties; our not being able to act à uniform right part without some thought and care; and the opportunities we have, or imagine we have, of avoiding what we dislike, or obtaining what we desire, by unlawful means, when we either cannot do it at all, or at least not so easily, by lawful ones; these things, that is, *the snares and temptations of vice, are what render the present world peculiarly fit to be a state of discipline to those who will preserve their integrity;* because they render being upon our guard, resolution, and the denial of our passions, necessary to that end." Thus, the temptations by which we are surrounded, the allurements of those passions by which vice is rendered so bewitching, are the appointed means of moral discipline and improvement in virtue.

The habit of virtue thus formed, he truly observes, will be firm and fixed in proportion to the amount of temptation we have gradually overcome in its formation. "Though actions materially virtuous," says he, "which have no sort of difficulty, but are perfectly agreeable to our particular inclinations, may possibly be done only from those particular inclinations, and so may not be any exercise of the principle of virtue, i. e., not be virtuous actions at all; yet, on the contrary, they may be an exercise of that principle, and, when they are, they have a tendency to form and fix the habit of virtue. But when the exercise of the virtuous principle is more continued, oftener repeated, and more intense, as it must be in circumstances of danger, temptation, and difficulty of any kind, and in any degree, this tendency is increased proportionably, and a more confirmed habit is the consequence."* The greater the temptation, then, the more fixed will be the habit of virtue, by which it is gradually overcome and subdued.

This habit may become so fixed, by a struggle with temptations and difficulties, as to raise the soul above the dangers to which moral agents are exposed. "Virtuous self-government is not only right in itself, but also improves the inward constitution or character; and may improve it to such a degree, that though we should suppose it impossible for particular affections to be absolutely co-incident with the moral principle, and consequently should allow, that *such creatures as have been above supposed would forever remain defectible; yet their danger of actually deviating from right may be almost infinitely lessened, and they fully fortified against what remains of it; if that may be called danger, against which there is an adequate effectual security.*"†

"These several observations," says he, "concerning the active principle of virtue and obedience to God's commands are applicable to passive submission or resignation to his will, which is another essential part of a right character, connected with the former, and very much in our power to form ourselves to." This, then, is the view which we think should be entertained with respect to the natural evils of this life: they are intended by the infinitely wise and good Ruler of the world to detach us from the fleeting things of time and sense, by the gradual formation of a habit of moral goodness, arising from a resistance against the influence of such things and firm adherence to the will of God, and to form our character for a state of fixed eternal blessedness. Such is the beneficent design of God in relation to the human race itself. His design in relation to the more magnificent scheme of the moral universe, in thus planting the human race and striving to train it up to virtue and happiness, we have already considered.‡

We say, then, that it is a principle of the divine government of the world to impose natural evil or suffering as a means of good. It is objected against this principle, that it is to do evil that good may come. "To say that Christ was subjected to *sufferings*," says Dr. Dick, "for the benevolent purpose of conferring important benefits upon mankind, is to give the highest

* Analogy, chap. v. † Id., chap. v, p. 178. ‡ Part i, chap. vi.

sanction to the principle which is so strongly reprobated in the Scriptures, that evil may be done that good may come." The theology of Dr. Dick, and of his school, does not sufficiently distinguish between natural and moral evil. We are nowhere told in Scripture, that it is wrong to do natural evil, or inflict suffering, that good may come. Every good man acts upon this principle every day of his life. Every act of self-denial, and every infliction of parental discipline, are proofs of the justness of this remark. The surgeon who amputates a limb, in order to save the life of his patient, acts upon the same principle. But who ever thought of condemning such conduct? Who ever reminded him that he should not do evil that good may come? It is plain, that neither "the sufferings" of Christ, nor any other sufferings imposed for the real good of the world, are liable to any such objection, or come under the condemnation of any such maxim. This objection lies, as we have seen,* against the doctrine of Edwards and his followers, that *moral evil*, that *sin*, may be chosen as the means of good. The high and holy God never commits, or causes others to commit, moral evil that good may come; but he not only may, but actually does, inflict natural evil in order to promote the good of his creatures. Thus, by applying the language of Scripture to natural evil instead of to moral, Dr. Dick has just exactly inverted the order of things as they actually exist in the constitution and government of the moral world.

SECTION V.

The importance of harmonizing reason and revelation.

For these reasons, we refuse to justify the sufferings of infants, on the ground that the sin of Adam was imputed to them. A sentiment so dark and appalling but ill accords with the sublime and beautiful spirit of the gospel. It partakes more of the weakness and infirmity of human nature than of the divine nature of Him who "spake as never man spake." The best account which Plato could give of the sufferings of infants was that they had sinned in some former state of existence, for which they are punished in this. St. Augustine and his followers, rejecting such a view, and relying on the literal sense of the

* Part i, chap. ii.

words of revelation, advanced the hypothesis that infants sinned, not in a preëxistent state, but in Adam; for which they are justly exposed to pain and death. Others again, not being able to conceive how infants could be really and personally in Adam many thousand years before they were born, so as to sin with him, adopted the hypothesis, that *if they had been in his place they would have sinned*, and are therefore justly exposed to the penalty due to his transgression; according to which theory each soul might be made liable to the guilt of infinitely more sin than any finite being could possibly commit. Another age, rising above such dark notions respecting the nature of sin and the justice of God, maintained the hypothesis that Adam's sin was imputed to all his posterity, by which the fearful penalty due to his sin might be justly inflicted upon them. According to a fifth theory, it is clear that "nothing under the empire of Jehovah" can be sin, except a known transgression of the law; and infants are punished, because, as soon as they come into the world, they knowingly transgress the law of God. They cannot *knowingly* sin, says a sixth theory; but still they really transgress the law of God by those little bubbling emotions of anger, and so forth, as soon as they come into existence; and hence, the penalty of sin is inflicted upon them. Such are some of the hypotheses which have been adopted by Christian theologians to reconcile the suffering of infants with the justice and goodness of God. The more we look into them, the more we are amazed that the great lights of the world should have indulged in reveries so wild and so wonderful; and the more are we convinced, that the speculations of men on these subjects, and the whole theological literature of the world in relation to it, form one of the darkest chapters in the history of the human mind.

How unlike are such views respecting the origin and existence of natural evil to the divine simplicity and beauty of the gospel! "Who did sin, this man or his parents," said the disciples to our Saviour, "that he was born blind?" They made no doubt but that the great evil of natural blindness must have been the punishment of some sin; and merely wished to know whether it were his own sin, committed in some former state of existence, or the sin of his parents. Their minds seem to have hung in a state of vacillation between the theory of Plato and that of imputation. But our Saviour replied: "Neither did this man sin, nor his parents," that he was born blind; but "that the work of God might be made manifest in him." We thank thee, O blessed Master, for that sweet word! How delightful is it, after passing through the dark labyrinths of human folly to sit at thy feet and drink in the lessons of heavenly wisdom! How pleasant to the soul—how inexpressibly cheering is it—to turn from the harsh and revolting systems of men, and listen to the sweet accents of mercy as they fall from thy lips!

The great law of suffering, then, is that it is intended for the benefit of intelligent creatures. This is the case, even when it assumes the character of punishment; for then it is designed to prevent moral evil. Such a view of natural evil, or suffering, does not give that horrid picture of the world which arises from the sentiment that all pain and death must be a punishment for sin. This causes us to see the black scourge of retributive justice everywhere, and the hand of fatherly correction nowhere. It places us, not in a school or state of probation, to train us up for a better and brighter world, but in the midst of inquisitorial fires and penal woe. It teaches that all mankind became guilty by the act of one man; and that for one deed, millions upon millions of human beings are justly obnoxious, not only to temporal and spiritual, but also to eternal death.

We are perfectly aware of all the arguments which have been drawn from Scripture in support of such a doctrine; and we are also perfectly satisfied that they may be most easily and triumphantly refuted. But at present we do not mean to touch this argument; we shall reserve it for another work. In the mean time, we must be permitted to express the sentiment, that a system of theology, so profoundly unphilosophical, so utterly repugnant to the moral sentiments of mankind, can never fulfil the sublime mission of true religion on earth. It may possess the principle of life within, but it is destitute of the form of life without. It may convert the individual soul, and lead it up to heaven; but it has not the radiant form and power of truth, to command the admiration and conquer the intellect of the world. It may elevate and purify the affections, even while it depresses and confounds the understanding; but it cannot transfigure the whole mind, and change it into its own divine image. Nothing but the most fixed and rooted faith, or the most blind and unquestioning submission, can withstand the fearful blasts and dark impulses of such a system.

No wonder, then, that under a system so deplorably deficient in some of the most sublime features of Christianity, infidelity and Pelagianism should so often have sprung up. If we write libels on the divine government, we must expect rebellions and insurrections. This is the natural consequence of the great fundamental heresy which places reason and revelation in opposition to each other. Orthodoxy, as she proudly styles herself, may denounce such rebellions; but she herself is partly responsible for the fatal consequences of them. Reason and revelation can never be dissevered, can never be placed in violent conflict, without a frightful injury to both, and to the best interests of mankind. Reason must find its own internal power and life in revelation, and revelation must find its own external form and beauty in reason. The perfection and glory of each consists in the living union and consentaneous development of both.

If we teach absurdity, it is worse than idle to enforce submission by arrogant and lordly denunciations of human pride, or of "carnal reason." And we shall always find, indeed, that when a theologian or a philosopher begins by abusing and vilifying human reason, he either has some absurdity which he wishes us to swallow, or he wishes to be excused from believing anything in particular. Thus, the dogmatism of the one and the scepticism of the other unite in trampling human reason under foot; the one, to erect an empire of absurdity, and the other, to erect an empire of darkness upon its ruins. It should be the great object of all our labours to effect a reunion and harmony between revelation and reason, whose "inauspicious repudiations and divorces" have so long "disturbed everything in the great family of mankind."*

* This language of Bacon is applied by him to the empirical and rational faculties of the human mind.

CHAPTER III.

THE SUFFERINGS OF CHRIST RECONCILED WITH THE GOODNESS OF GOD.

> O blessed Well of Love! O Flower of Grace!
> O glorious Morning Starre! O Lampe of Light!
> Most lively Image of thy Father's face,
> Eternal King of Glorie, Lord of Might,
> Meeke Lambe of God, before all worlds behight,
> How can we thee requite for all this good?
> Or who can prize that thy most precious blood?—SPENSER.

IN the preceding chapter we have endeavoured to show that natural evil or suffering is not inconsistent with the goodness of God. We were there led to see that God, although he never chooses moral evil, often imposes natural evil, or suffering, in order to secure the well-being of the world. Of this general principle, the sufferings and death of Christ are a particular instance; they are not anomalous, but a striking manifestation of a great principle which pervades the whole economy of divine providence. These sufferings, so far from being inconsistent with the goodness of God, are a stupendous display of that sublime mercy which is over all his works. To illustrate this position, and clear it of sceptical cavils and objections, is the main object of the present chapter.

SECTION I.

The sufferings of Christ not unnecessary.

Because the necessity of Christ's death and sufferings is not manifest at first view, or because the utility of them is not seen, it is concluded by some that they were wholly useless, and consequently inconsistent with the infinite goodness ascribed to the Ruler of the world. We shall content ourselves with disposing of this objection in the words of Bishop Butler. "To object against the expediency or usefulness of particular things revealed to have been done or suffered by him," says he, "because we do not see how they were conducive to those ends, is highly absurd. Yet nothing is more common to be met with than this absurdity. But if it be acknowledged beforehand, that we are not judges in this case, it is evident that no objection can, with any shadow of reason, be urged against any particular part of Christ's mediatorial office revealed in Scripture, till it can be shown positively, not to be requisite, or conducive, to the ends proposed to be accomplished; or that it is in itself unreasonable."*

Again: "It is indeed," says he, "a matter of great patience to reasonable men to find people arguing in this manner; objecting against the credibility of such particular things revealed in Scripture, that they do not see the necessity or expediency of them. For, though it is highly right, and the most pious exercise of our understanding, to inquire with due reverence into the ends and reasons of God's dispensations; yet, when those reasons are concealed, to argue from our ignorance, that such dispensations cannot be from God, is infinitely absurd. The presumption of this kind of objection seems almost lost in the folly of them. And the folly of them is yet greater, when they are urged, as usually they are, against things in Christianity analogous, or like to those natural dispensations of Providence which are matters of experience. Let reason be kept to, and if any part of the Scripture account of the redemption of the world by Christ can be shown to be really contrary to it, let the Scripture, in the name of God, be given up: but let not such poor creatures as we go on objecting against an infinite scheme, that we do not see the necessity or usefulness of all its parts, and call this reasoning; and what heightens the absurdity in the present case, parts which we are not actively concerned in."†

This reply is amply sufficient for such an objection. But although the concession is made, for the sake of argument, it is not true, that we do not see the necessity or usefulness of the sufferings of Christ. For, as the author well says: "What has been often alleged in justification of this doctrine, even from the apparent natural tendency of this method of our redemption—its tendency to vindicate the authority of God's laws, and deter his creatures from sin: *this has never been answered*, and *is, I think, plainly unanswerable;* though I am far from thinking it an account of the whole of the case."‡

It is true, we believe, that the position that the great work

* Butler's Analogy, part ii, chap. v. † Analogy. ‡ Ibid.

of Christ was necessary to maintain the authority of God's law, and to deter his creatures from sin, never has been, and never can be refuted. Yet nearly all of the commonly received systems of theology furnish a principle, a false principle, on which this position may be overthrown, and the sufferings of Christ shown to be unnecessary. For if a necessary holiness be not a contradiction in terms, if God can, as is usually asserted, cause holiness universally to prevail by the mere word of his power, then the work and sufferings of Christ are not necessary to maintain the authority of his law, and deter his creatures from sin. In other words, the sufferings of Christ were "not requisite to the ends proposed to be accomplished," because, on such a supposition, they might have been far more easily and completely accomplished without them.

Those who maintain, then, as most theologians do, that God could easily cause virtue to exist everywhere if he would, really set forth a principle which, if true, would demonstrate the sufferings of Christ to be unnecessary, and consequently inconsistent with the goodness of God. We must strike at this false principle, and restore the truth that a necessary holiness is a contradiction in terms, an inherent and impossible conceit, if we would behold the sublime significancy and beauty of the stupendous sacrifice of the cross. We shall then behold the necessity of that sacrifice, and see the omnipotent yearnings of the divine love in its efforts to overcome an obstacle, which could not be otherwise surmounted.

It is often said, we are well aware, that God might have saved us by a mere word; but he chose not to do so, preferring to give up his Son to death in order to show his love. But how can such a position be maintained? If God could save us by a word, how can it display his love to require such immense sufferings in order to save us? If he could accomplish the salvation of all men by a mere word, how does it show his love to make such wonderful preparations for their salvation; and, after all, permit so large a portion of them to be eternally lost? If we could save the life of a fellow-being by merely putting forth a hand, would it display our love for him if we should choose to travel all around the earth, and incur incredible hardships and sufferings in order to save him? Would this display our love, we ask, or our folly? Is it not evident, then, that the principle that virtue or holiness might be easily caused to exist everywhere, is utterly repugnant to the glory of revelation? Is it not evident that it causes the transcendent glory of the cross to disappear, and reduces the whole complicated system of means and appliances for the salvation of the world to a mere idle mockery of the miseries of man's estate? Does it not show the whole plan of salvation, as conceived and executed by the infinite wisdom of God, to be an awkward and bungling attempt to accomplish an end, which might have been far more easily and perfectly accomplished? And if so, does it not become all Christian theologians to expunge this false principle from their systems, and eradicate it from their thoughts?

SECTION II.

The sufferings of Christ a bright manifestation of the goodness of God.

The reason why the love of God does not appear to all men in the sacrifice of his Son is, that it is often viewed, not as it is in itself, but through the distorting medium of false analogies, or of a vague and ill-defined phraseology. Hence it is that the melancholy spectacle is everywhere presented of men, of rational and immortal beings, living and dying in a determined opposition to a doctrine which they have not taken the pains to understand, and of whose intrinsic grandeur and glory they have not enjoyed the most remote glimpse. So far from beholding the love of God, which shines forth so conspicuously in the cross of Christ, they see in it only an act of injustice and cruelty on the part of God.

One source of this error, we have no doubt, is to be found in the use, or rather in the abuse, of the term *punishment*. In the strict sense of the word, it is not only unjust, but impossible, for God to punish the innocent. The very idea of punishment, according to the strict sense of the word, implies the notion of guilt or ill-desert in the person upon whom it is inflicted. It is suffering inflicted on an offender, on account of his real or supposed personal guilt. Hence, as God regards all things just as they are in themselves, he cannot possibly look upon the innocent as guilty; and consequently he cannot, in the strict sense of the word, inflict punishment upon them. And when we speak of the punishment of Christ, we merely mean, or should merely mean, to convey the idea that he *suffered*, in order to release us from the *punishment* due to our sins. It would be well, perhaps, if this could always be borne in mind; for most men are more under the influence and power of words than they are apt to see, or willing to acknowledge. The mere expression, the *punishment* of the innocent, is apt to awaken associations in the mind which are inconsistent with the dictates of justice; but which the idea of the atonement would never have suggested, if clearly and distinctly viewed in its own clear light, and not through the dark medium of an ill-defined phraseology.

Another source of the error in question is to be found in the ambiguity of the term justice. It is frequently said that the atonement is a satisfaction to divine justice; to which it is replied, that justice requires the punishment of the very individual who offends, and not of another person in his place. Let us consider this subject.

The term *justice* has two distinct significations, which I shall designate by the epithets *retributive* and *administrative*. By retributive justice, I mean that attribute which inclines Him to punish an offender merely on account of the intrinsic demerit and hatefulness of his offence; and which animadverts upon the evil conduct of a moral agent, considered as an individual, and not as a member of the great family of intelligent beings. This attribute seeks to punish sin merely because it deserves punishment, and not because its punishment is necessary to secure the ends of government; and, supposing sin to exist, it would have its object, even if there were only one accountable creature in the universe.

The object of public or administrative justice is quite different. It inflicts punishment, not because it is deserved, but in order to prevent transgression, and to secure the general good, by securing the ends of wise and good government. In the moral government of God, one of the highest objects of this kind of justice, or, if you please, of this phase or manifestation of the divine justice, is to secure in the hearts of its subjects a cordial approbation of the principles according to which they are governed. This is indispensable to the very existence of moral government. The dominion of force, or of power, may be maintained, in many cases, notwithstanding the aversion of those who are subject to it; but it is impossible to govern the heart by love while it disapproves and hates the principles to which it is required to submit, or the character of the ruler by whom those principles are enforced.

Now, it is very true, that Christ has made a satisfaction to divine justice. This is frequently asserted; but it is seldom considered, we apprehend, with any very great degree of distinctness, in what sense the term justice should always be understood in this proposition. It cannot properly refer to the retributive justice of God. This requires the punishment of the offender, and of no one else. It accepts of no substitute. And hence, it is impossible to conceive that it can be satisfied, except by the punishment of the offender himself. The object of this sort of justice, as I have said, is personal guilt; and hence, as our Saviour did not become personally guilty, when he assumed our place and consented to die for us, so it is impossible to conceive that he became liable to the infliction of the retributive justice of God. And we suppose it is this idea, at which the Socinian vaguely and obscurely aims, when he says, that the justice of God requires the punishment of the transgressor alone; and that it is absurd to suppose it can be satisfied by the substitution of the innocent in his stead. He denies the whole doctrine of satisfaction, because he sees and feels that it is not true according to one meaning of the terms in which it is expressed.

In truth and in deed, the sinner is just as guilty after the atonement as he was before; and he is just as obnoxious to the inflictions of the retributive justice of God. He may be most justly punished; for as the claims of retributive justice have not been satisfied, so they may be demanded of him without being a second time exacted. He really deserves the wrath of God on account of his sins, although administrative justice has been satisfied; and hence, when he truly repents and believes, all his sins are freely and graciously remitted. No satisfaction is made to retributive justice.

It is the administrative justice of God that has been satisfied by the atonement. This merely enforces the punishment of the sinner, as I have said, in order to secure the ends of good government; and hence, it is capable of yielding and giving place to any expedient by which those ends may be secured.

In other words, it is capable of being satisfied by whatever method God may be pleased to adopt in order to secure the ends of good government, and to accomplish his own glorious designs, without the punishment of the sinner. All this, as we shall see hereafter, has been most gloriously accomplished by the death and sufferings of Christ. God can now be just, and yet the justifier of him that believes. The great obstacles which the administrative justice of God interposes to the forgiveness of sin, having been taken out of the way and nailed to the cross, that unbounded mercy from which the provision of such a Saviour proceeded, can now flow down upon a lost and ruined world in all the fulness and plenitude of its pardoning and sanctifying power.

As a general thing, those who undertake to vindicate the sufferings of Christ against objections, rest their defence on the ground that they are a satisfaction to the administrative justice of God. This is seen, not from their express declarations, but from the nature of their arguments and defence; as if they unconsciously turned to this position as to their stronghold. On the other hand, those who assail the sacrifice of Christ, almost invariably treat it as if it were a satisfaction to the retributive justice of God. Both sides seem to be right, and both wrong. The whole idea of satisfaction to divine justice by a substitute is not absurd, because the idea of satisfaction to retributive justice is so; nor is the whole justice of God, or the justice of God in every sense of the word, to be conceived of as satisfied by the atonement, because his administrative justice is thus satisfied. When it is thus asserted, then, that the justice of God is satisfied by the atonement; we should be careful, we think, to observe in what precise sense this proposition is true, and in what sense it is false; in order that we may pursue the clear and shining light of truth, neither distracted by the clamour of words nor enveloped in clouds of logomachy.

There is a class of theologians, we are aware, and a very large class, who regard the sufferings of Christ as a satisfaction to the retributive justice of God. But this forms no part of the doctrine which we have undertaken to defend; and, indeed, we think the defence of such a view of the atonement clearly impossible. It is placed on the ground, that the sins of the world, or of those for whom Christ died, have been imputed to him; and hence he really suffers the inflictions of the retributive justice of God. The objections to this scheme, which seek to remove the apparent hardships and injustice of the sufferings of the innocent, by the fiction of the imputation of the sins of the guilty, we shall not dwell upon here; as we so fully considered them in the preceding chapter. To our mind they are plainly unanswerable. We would vindicate the sufferings of Christ no more than those of infants, on the ground that sin was imputed to him, so as to render them just. On the contrary, we hold them to have been wholly undeserved; and instead of vindicating them on the ground of stern justice, we vindicate them on the ground of the infinite, unbounded, and overflowing goodness of God.

It is easy to see that such a view of the atonement does not in the least degree conflict with the justice of God. It merely teaches, that God has provided for the salvation of the world by the sufferings of Jesus Christ, who was without spot or blemish. Surely we cannot find it in our hearts to object, that the sufferings of Christ for such a purpose are not consistent with the justice of God, if we will only read a single page in the great volume of nature and of providence. It has been said by Bishop Butler, that such an objection "concludes altogether as much against God's whole original constitution of nature, and the whole daily course of divine providence, in the government of the world, i. e., against the whole scheme of theism and the whole notion of religion, as against Christianity. For the world is a constitution, or system, whose parts have a mutual reference to each other; and there is a scheme of things gradually carrying on, called the course of nature, to the carrying on of which God has appointed us, in various ways, to contribute. And when, in the daily course of natural providence, it is appointed that innocent people should suffer for the faults of the guilty, this is liable to the very same objection as the instance we are considering. The infinitely greater importance of that appointment of Christianity which is objected against, does not hinder but that it may be, as it plainly is, an appointment of the very same kind with what the world affords us daily examples of. Nay, if there were any force at all in the objection, it would be stronger, in one respect, against natural providence, than against Christianity; because, under the former, we are in many cases commanded, and even necessitated, whether we will or no, to suffer for the faults of others, whereas the sufferings of Christ were voluntary."

Now, how very unreasonable is it in the theist, to object against Christianity, that it represents God as having acted upon a particular principle, i. e., as having appointed the innocent to suffer for the good of the guilty, when we see that he has everywhere recognised and adopted the very same principle in the government of the world? However remote this principle may appear from the conceptions of man, it is not only found in the volume of inspiration; it is deeply engraven by the finger of God himself upon every page of the volume of natural providence. And to question the divine original of revelation, because it contains such a principle or appointment, while we admit that God created and governs the world, is about as unreasonable as it would be to deny that a letter came from a particular person, because it was clearly written in his handwriting, and bore evident traces of his peculiarities of style and thought.

Let us view this general principle in a particular instance. This will set it in a clear and striking light, and seem to vindicate the constitution of the world, as well as the doctrine of the atonement. The principle of compassion has been planted in our bosom by the finger of God. And thus the necessity is laid upon us, by a law of our nature, to suffer on account of the distresses which our fellow-men bring upon themselves by their own crimes and vices; and we are impelled in various ways to undergo inconvenience and loss, and self-denial and suffering, in order to avert from them the consequences of their own misconduct. But have we any reason to complain of this appointment of God? Certainly not: for if we obey the indications of his will, as seen in this part of the constitution of our nature, by doing all in our power to relieve the distresses of our fellow-men, we shall be infinitely more than repaid for all that we may undergo and suffer. However painful may be the feeling of compassion, we only have to obey its dictates by relieving the distressed to the utmost of our ability, and we shall be more than repaid by the satisfaction and delight which never fail to result from such a course of life; to say nothing of those infinite rewards which God has prepared for those who sincerely love and serve him.

Just so it is in relation to the sufferings of Christ. He was led by his boundless compassion to avert from us the awful consequences of sin, by the agony, and the sufferings, and the death, which he endured upon the cross. And, according to the doctrine of atonement, he is infinitely more than repaid for all this. Though he suffered in the flesh, and was made a spectacle to men and angels, yet he despised the shame, seeing the joy that was set before him. We do confess that we can see no insufferable hardship in all this, nor the least shadow of injustice. One thing is certain, if injustice is exhibited here, it is exhibited everywhere in the providence of God; and if the doctrine of the atonement were stricken from the scheme of Christianity, the injustice which is supposed to attend it would still continue to overhang and cloud the moral government of God. And hence, if the deist or the Socinian would escape from this frightful spectre of his own imagination, he must bury himself in the most profound depths and most cheerless gloom of atheism.

The doctrine in question is frequently misrepresented, and made to appear inconsistent with the justice of God, by means of false analogies. The Socinian frequently speaks of it, as if it were parallel with the proceeding of a human government that should doom the innocent to suffer in place of the guilty. Thus the feeling of indignation that is aroused in the human bosom at the idea of a virtuous man's being sentenced to suffer the punishment due to the criminal is sought to be directed against the doctrine of the atonement. But in vain will such rhetoric be employed to excite indignation and horror against the doctrine of the cross, in the mind of any person by whom it is at all understood.

The cases are not at all parallel. In the first place, no human government has a right to doom a virtuous man to bear the punishment due to the criminal; and if he were willing to suffer in the place of the culprit, no government on earth has a right to accept of such a substitute. The life of the virtuous citizen is the gift of God, and no earthly power has the authority to take it for any such purpose. It would be a violation of the will of God for any human government to admit of such a substitution. On the contrary, Christ had the power to lay down his life; and he did so, in perfect accordance with the appointment of God. In submitting to the death of the cross, he did not subvert, he fulfilled the end of his earthly existence.

Secondly, it would overthrow the ends of public justice for any human government to permit a good man, the ornament and blessing of society, to die in the room of the criminal, its scourge and plague. The sufferings of the good citizen in such a case would be pure and unmitigated evil. While they would deprive society of his services, they would throw back upon it the burden of one who deserved to die. They would tend to render the punishment of crime uncertain; they would shock the moral sentiments of mankind, and cover with odium and disgrace the government that could tolerate such a proceeding. But not so in relation to the sufferings of Christ. He assumed his human nature for the express purpose of dying upon the cross. He died, not to deliver an individual and turn him loose to commit further depredations upon society, but to effect the salvation of the world itself, and to deliver it from all the evils under which it groans and travails in pain. He died for sinners, not that they might continue in their sins, but in order to redeem unto himself a peculiar people zealous of good works.

In the third and last place, the death of a good man is the end of his existence, the entire extinction of his being, in so far as all human government is concerned; whereas the death of Christ, in relation to the government of God, was but the beginning of his exaltation and glory. He endured the cross, despising the shame, in view of the unbounded joy that was set before him. The temporal evils which he endured, unutterably great as they were, if viewed merely in relation to himself, were infinitely more than counterbalanced by the eternal satisfaction and delight that resulted from them.

SECTION III.

The objections of Dr. Channing, and other Unitarians, against the doctrine of the atonement.

It is likewise objected against the doctrine of the atonement, that it obscures the freeness and glory of the divine mercy. It is supposed to interfere with the freeness of the favour of God, inasmuch as it requires a sacrifice to procure the remission of sin. This point, no less than the former, the Socinian endeavours to establish by means of analogies drawn from the ordinary transactions of life. "I know it is said," says Dr. Channing, "that Trinitarianism magnifies God's mercy, because it teaches that he himself provided the substitute for the guilty. But I reply, that the work here ascribed to mercy is not the most appropriate, nor the most fitted to manifest it and impress it on the heart. This may be made apparent by familiar illustration. Suppose that a creditor, through compassion to certain debtors, should persuade a benevolent and opulent man to pay him in their stead; would not the debtors see a greater mercy, and feel a weightier obligation, if they were to receive a free, gratuitous release? And will not their chief gratitude stray beyond the creditor to their benevolent substitute? Or suppose that a parent, unwilling to inflict a penalty on a disobedient but feeble child, should persuade a stronger child to bear it; would not the offender see a more touching mercy in a free forgiveness, springing immediately from a parent's heart, than in this circuitous remission?"

If there were any force in such analogies, they would conclude quite as much against the scheme of Dr. Channing as against ours. For he maintains that the sinner can obtain forgiveness only by a sincere repentance of his sins. He teaches that God requires the sinner to humble himself, and take up his cross and follow Christ. Now to return to the case of the debtor. Would he not see a greater kindness, "and feel a weightier obligation," if he were to receive a free release, without any conditions being imposed upon him, than if it was accompanied by any terms or conditions?

But the analogy is false. However well it might serve some purposes, it is misapplied by Dr. Channing. If a creditor is known to love money, as most men are, and he should nevertheless release his debtors; this would undoubtedly be an exhibition of his kindness. And we might measure the extent of his kindness by the amount of the indebtedness which he had forgiven. But although the creditor, who is the most easily moved by the necessities of his debtor, may be the most compassionate man, it does not follow that the governor, who under all circumstances, makes the most free and unrestrained use of the pardoning power, is the best ruler. The creditor has a perfect right to release his debtor; and in so doing, he affects the interest of no one but himself: whereas, by the pardon of offences against public law, the most sacred rights of the community may be disregarded, the protection of law may be removed, and the general good invaded. The penalty of the law does not belong to the supreme executive, as a debt belongs to the creditor to whom it is due; and hence it cannot always be abandoned at his pleasure. It is ordained, not merely for the ruler, but for the benefit and protection of all who are subject to its control. And hence, although a creditor may show his mercy by releasing his necessitous debtors; yet the ruler who undertakes to display his mercy by a free use of the pardoning power, may only betray a weak and yielding compassion for the individual, instead of manifesting that calm and enlightened benevolence which labours to secure the foundations of wise and good government, and thereby to promote the order and happiness of the governed.

This leads me to remark, that the hope and the theology of the Socinian is built upon the most inadequate conceptions of the divine mercy. This is not a weak and yielding thing, as men are so fondly prone to imagine; it is a universal and inflexible law. The most perfect harmony exists among all the attributes of God; and as his justice demands the punishment of the sinner, so also doth his mercy. The bosom of God is not, like that of frail mortals, torn and distracted by conflicting principles. Even to the maintenance of his law, that bright transcript of his eternal justice, his mercy is inviolably pledged. Heaven and earth shall sooner pass away, than his mercy shall withdraw from the support of one jot or one tittle of it. It is not only just and holy, and therefore will be maintained with almighty power; but it is also good, and therefore its immutable foundations are laid in the everlasting and unchanging mercy of God.

For the universal good, it will be inexorably enforced against the individual transgressor. God is not slack concerning his promises. He is free from all human weakness. His mind is not limited, like that of man, to be more affected by partial suffering than by that universal disorder and ruin which must inevitably result from the unrequited violation of his law. The mind of man is unduly affected by the present and the proximate: but to God there is neither remote nor future. And when, in wisdom and in goodness, he first established and ordained the law unto life, he saw the end from the beginning; and he can never sacrifice the universal good by setting aside that law in order to avoid partial evil. His mercy to the whole creation makes the same demand as his justice. The execution of divine justice is, indeed, but a manifestation of that mercy which is over all his works; and which labours, with omnipotent energy, to secure the good of all, by vindicating the majesty and glory of that law, upon the preservation of which inviolate the good of all depends. The fire that is not quenched is kindled by the boundless love of God no less than by his justice; and the very fierceness of its burning is, that it is the "wrath of the Lamb." Let us not be deceived by the vain fancies and the idle dreams which our fond wishes and narrow-minded infirmities are so apt to beget in us. Let us remember that the mercy of God is united with omniscience; and that it is to be found only in the bosom of Him whose empire extends to the utmost bounds of the universe, as well as throughout the endless ages of eternity.

In the genuine spirit of Socinian theology, Dr. Channing, in his illustration, has set before us the mercy of God alone; and that, too, merely in relation to the sinner, and not in relation to his law and government. He entirely overlooks the fact, that it is impossible to exhibit either the justice or the mercy of God in the most affecting manner, except in union with each other. It is frequently said, we are aware, that if God had pardoned the sinner without enforcing the demands of the law, he would have displayed his mercy alone, and not his justice; but in fact this would have been a very equivocal display of mercy. It would have shown only one of two things: either that God regarded the sinner with an eye of compassion, or that he did not regard his sin: either that he was merciful, or that he had no great abhorrence of sin: either that he loved the transgressor, or that he did not hate the transgression.

To illustrate this point, let us take the case of Zaleucus, the king of the Locrians. He passed a certain law, with the penalty that every transgressor of it should lose both his eyes. It so happened that his own son was the first by whom it was violated. Now, any one can see, that although Zaleucus had been a hard-hearted and unfeeling tyrant, he might have pardoned his son, just because he had no regard to the demands of public justice; or, on the other hand, that he might have inflicted the penalty of the law upon his son to the uttermost, not out of a supreme regard to the law, but because he was destitute of mercy and natural affection. Neither by remitting the whole punishment, nor by inflicting it with rigour, could he have made such a display of his justice and mercy as to make a deep moral impression upon his subjects. In other words, if either of these attributes had been left out in the manifestation, the display of the other must have been exceedingly feeble and equivocal. Both must be seen in union, or neither can be seen in the fulness of its glory.

How, then, could Zaleucus have displayed both of these attributes in the most perfect and affecting manner? By doing precisely that which he is said to have done. He directed that one of his own eyes should be put out, and one of his son's. Whose heart is not touched by this most affecting display of the tender pity of the father, in union with the stern justice of the law-giver? His pity would not allow him to inflict the whole penalty upon his beloved son; and his high regard for the demands of public justice would not permit him to set at naught the authority of the law: and but for the possession and manifestation of this last trait of character, the mighty strugglings and yearnings of the first could not have burst forth and appeared with such overwhelming power and transcendent lustre. Hence, every system of redemption which, like that of the Socinian, leaves out of view the administrative justice of God, does not admit of any very impressive display of his goodness and his mercy.

All such illustrations must be imperfect, in some respects; but the one above given conveys a far more adequate view of the atonement than that presented by Dr. Channing. The application of it is easy. Such was the mercy of God, that he could not leave his poor fallen creatures to endure the awful penalty of the law; and such was his regard for the purity and happiness of the universe, that he could not permit his law to be violated with impunity. If his administrative justice had not stood in the way, the offer of pardon to the sinner would have cost him merely a word. And hence the length, the breadth, and the depth of his love could not have been manifested. But he was the Ruler of the universe, and as such his law stood in the way. He owed it to himself not to permit this to be trampled under foot with impunity, nor its violation to be forgiven, until he had provided some way in order to secure the high and holy ends for which it had been established. Hence, as it was not possible for God to deny himself, he sent forth his beloved Son, who had been the companion of his bosom and his blessedness from all eternity, to take upon himself the form of a servant, and by his teaching, and obedience, and sufferings, and death, to vindicate the majesty of the law, and to render it honourable in the sight of the universe. And it is this wonderful union of the goodness and the severity, of the mercy and the justice of God, which constitutes the grand moral tendency and glory of the cross.

The course pursued by the king of the Locrians, in relation to the crime of his son, secured the ends of the law in a much greater degree than they could have been secured by a rigorous execution of its penalty upon the person of his son. It evinced a deep and settled abhorrence of crime, and an inflexible determination to punish it. It cut off all hope from his subjects that crime would be permitted to escape with impunity. And hence, after such a manifestation of his character as a king, he could permit his son to enjoy the unspeakable blessings of sight, without holding out the least encouragement to the commission of crime.

So, likewise, in relation to the sufferings of Christ. These were not, in strictness, the penalty of the law. This was eternal death; whereas the sufferings of Christ, inconceivably great as they were, were but temporal; and there can be no proportion between sufferings which know a period, and those which are without end. Hence, as we have already said, he did not satisfy the punitive justice of God. But the sacrifice of Christ answered all the purposes that could have been answered by the rigorous execution of the law; and it answered them in an infinitely greater degree, than if the human race had been permitted to endure it without remedy.

God's love to his Son was inconceivably greater than that

which any creature ever bore to himself or to any other; and, consequently, by offering him up as a substitute for guilty mortals, in order that he might save them without doing violence to his administrative justice, he manifested the infinite energy of his determination to destroy sin. No account of the indescribable odiousness and deformity of evil, nor of the inconceivable holiness of God, could have made so deep an impression of his implacable abhorrence of sin, as is made by the cross upon which his Son was permitted to expire amid the scorn and contempt of his enemies. The human imagination has no power to conceive of a more impressive and appalling enforcement of the great lesson, "Stand in awe, and sin not," than that which is presented to an astonished universe in the cross and passion of the Son of God.

And besides, it possesses this other unspeakable advantage, that while it manifests an infinite abhorrence of sin, it displays the most heart-subduing love of the sinner. If Zaleucus had exhausted the penalty of the law upon his son, this would have had little or no tendency to reform his heart, or to induce him to acquiesce in the justness of the law. It would have been more apt to lead him to regard the king as an unfeeling father. But when he was made to see, by the manner in which the king had dispensed the law, that he cherished the warmest feelings of affection for him, there was no cause left for a murmur on the part of any, but for the highest admiration on the part of all.

Just so in relation to the sufferings and death of Christ. If God had exhausted the fearful penalty of the law upon poor, suffering, and degraded humanity, this would have been well calculated to inspire his creatures with a servile and trembling awe of him. From their limited and imperfect views of the evil of sin, and of the reasons why it should be punished, they would not have been prepared to acquiesce in such tremendous severity. Thus, one of the great ends of God's moral government would have been subverted: the affections of his creatures would have been estranged from him, through a distrust of his goodness and a dread of his power, instead of having been drawn to him by the sweet and sacred ties of confidence and love. But how different is the case now! Having given for us his beloved Son, who is greater than all things, while we were yet *enemies*, now that we are *reconciled* to him, we are most firmly persuaded that he will freely give us all things that can possibly conduce to our good. Surely, after such a display of his love, it were highly criminal in us, to permit the least shadow of suspicion or distrust to intercept the sweet, and cheering, and purifying beams of his reconciled countenance. Whatever may be his severity against sin, and whatever terror it may strike into the conscience of evil-doers, we can most cordially acquiesce in its justness: for we most clearly perceive, that the penalty of the law was not established to gratify any private appetite for revenge, but to uphold and secure the highest happiness of the moral universe.

CHAPTER IV.

THE ETERNAL PUNISHMENT OF THE WICKED RECONCILED WITH THE GOODNESS OF GOD.

And thus,
Transfigured, with a meek and dreadless awe,
A solemn hush of spirit, he beholds
All things of terrible seeming: yea, unmoved
Views e'en the immitigable ministers,
That shower down vengeance on these latter days.
For even these on wings of healing come,
Yea, kindling with intenser Deity;
From the celestial mercy-seat they speed,
And at the renovating wells of love,
Have fill'd their vials with salutary wrath.—COLERIDGE.

HAVING considered the sufferings of the innocent, it now becomes necessary to contemplate the punishment of the guilty, in connexion with the infinite goodness of God. This conducts us to the consideration of the most awful subject that ever engaged the attention of a rational being,—the never-ending torments of the wicked in another world. Though plausible arguments and objections have been urged against this doctrine, we are perfectly satisfied they will not bear the test of a close examination. They have derived all their apparent force and conclusiveness, it seems to us, from two distinct sources, namely: from the circumstance that this appalling doctrine has been too often placed, by its advocates, upon insecure and untenable grounds; and from the fact, that the supporters of this doctrine have too often maintained principles from which its fallacy may be clearly inferred. In the defence of this doctrine, then, we shall endeavour to point out, first, the false grounds upon which it has been placed; secondly, the unsound principles from which its fallacy may be inferred; and, thirdly, we shall endeavour to show the means by which it may be clearly and satisfactorily reconciled with the goodness of the Supreme Ruler of the world.

SECTION I.

The false grounds upon which the doctrine of the eternity of future punishment has been placed.

Nothing could be more untenable, it seems to us, than the usual argument in favour of future punishments, which seeks to justify their eternity on the ground that every sinful act, because it is committed against an infinite being, is infinite, and therefore deserves to be visited with endless torments. This argument, which seems but little better than a play on the term *infinite*, is perhaps calculated to make no impression upon any mind, which is not already fully persuaded of the truth of the doctrine in question. On the other hand, it may be so easily refuted by a multitude of considerations, that it exposes the doctrine, in one of its defences, to the triumphant attacks of its adversaries. We shall not exhaust the patience of the reader by dwelling upon the refutation which may be given of such an argument. We shall dismiss it with a single reply, and that we shall give in the language of John Foster.

"A common argument has been that sin is an *infinite evil*, that is, of infinite demerit, as an offence against an infinite being; and that, since a finite creature cannot suffer infinitely *in measure*, he must *in duration*. But, surely in all reason, the limited, and in the present instance, *diminutive nature of the criminal*, must be an essential part of the case for judgment. Every act must, for one of its proportions, be measured by the nature and condition of the agent: and it would seem that one principle in that rule of proportion should be, that the offending agent should be capable of being aware of the magnitude (the *amount*, if we might use such a word,) of the offence he commits, by being capable of something like an adequate conception of the being against whom it is committed. A perverse child, committing an offence against a great monarch, of whose dignity it *had some*, but a vastly inadequate apprehension, would not be punished in the same manner as an offender of high endowments and responsibility, and fully aware of the dignity of the personage offended. The one would justly be sharply chastised; the other might as justly be condemned to death. In the present case, the offender does or may know that the Being offended against is of awful majesty, and therefore the offence is one of great aggravation, and he will justly be punished with great severity; but by his extremely contracted and feeble faculties, as the lowest in the scale of strictly rational and accountable creatures in the whole creation, he is *infinitely incapable* of any adequate conception of the greatness of the Being offended against. He is then, according to the argument, obnoxious to a punishment not in any proportion to his own nature, but alone to that infinity of the supreme nature, which is to him infinitely inconceivable and unknown."*

This answer alone, though perhaps not the best which might be made, we deem amply sufficient. Indeed, does not the position, that a man, a poor, weak, fallible creature, deserves an infinite punishment, an eternity of torments, for each evil thought or word, carry its own refutation along with it? And if not, what are we to think of that attribute of justice, which demands an eternity to inflict the infinite pangs due to a single sin? Is it a quality to inspire the soul with a rational worship, or to fill it with a horror which casteth out love?

Another argument to show the infinite ill-desert of some men, is drawn from the *scientia media Dei*. It is said, that if God foresaw that if they had been placed in various other circumstances, and surrounded by other temptations, their dispositions and character would have induced them to commit other sins; for which they are, therefore, as really responsible as if they had actually committed them. If this be a correct principle, it is easy, we must admit, to render each individual of the human race responsible for a greater number of sins than have ever been committed, or than could ever have been committed by all the actual dwellers upon the face of the earth. Nay, by such a process of multiplication, it would be easy to spread the guilt of a single soul over every point of infinite space, and every moment of eternal duration. But such a principle is more than questionable. To say nothing of its intrinsic deformity, it is refuted by the consequences to which it leads. We want arguments on this subject, that will give the mind, not horrid caricatures of the divine justice, but such views of that sublime attribute as will inspire us with sentiments of admiration and love, as well as with a godly fear and wholesome awe.

* Letter on the Duration of Future Punishment, pp. 19, 20.

SECTION II.

The unsound principles from which, if true, the fallacy of the eternity of future punishments may be clearly inferred.

It is a doctrine maintained by Augustine, Calvin, and Luther, as well as by many of their followers, that, in his fallen state, man "is free to evil only." He can do nothing good without the aid of divine grace; and this, in point of fact, is given to but a very small number of the human race; at least, efficacious grace is given to but few, so that the greater part of mankind cannot acquire or possess that holiness without which no man shall see the Lord. Now, if we take our stand upon this platform of doctrine, it will be found utterly impossible, we think, to defend the eternity of future punishments.

It was upon this platform that John Foster erected his tremendous battery against the doctrine in question; and it is believed, that the more closely the argument is examined, the more clearly it will be seen, that he has either demolished the doctrine which was so obnoxious to his feelings, or else the platform which constituted so essential a part of his own creed. In our humble opinion, "the moral argument," as he calls it, "pressed irresistibly upon his mind;" because it was drawn from false premises, of whose correctness he seems not to have entertained the shadow of a doubt. He clung to the conclusion, when he should have abandoned the premises. But we shall give his own words, and permit the reader to judge for himself.

After having endeavoured to impress our feeble powers with "the stupendous idea of eternity," he adds: "Now think of an infliction of misery protracted through such a period, and at the end of it being only *commenced*,—not one smallest step nearer a conclusion,—the case just the same if that sum of figures were multiplied by itself; and then think of *man*,—his nature, his situation, the circumstances of his brief sojourn and trial on earth. Far be it from us to make light of the demerit of sin, and to remonstrate with the Supreme Judge against a severe chastisement, of whatever moral nature we may regard the infliction to be. But still, what is man? He comes into the world with a nature fatally corrupt, and powerfully tending to actual evil. He comes among a crowd of temptations adapted to his innate evil propensities. He grows up (incomparably the greater portion of the race) in great ignorance, his judgment weak, and under numberless beguilements into error; while his passions and appetites are strong, his conscience unequally matched against their power,—in the majority of men, but feebly and rudely constituted. The influence of whatever good instructions he may receive, is counteracted by a combination of opposite influences almost constantly acting on him. He is essentially and inevitably unapt to be powerfully acted on by what is invisible and future. In addition to all which, there is the intervention and activity of the great tempter and destroyer. In short, his condition is such that there is no hope of him, but from a direct, special operation on him, of what we denominate grace. *Is* it not so? *Are* we not convinced? *Is* it not the plain doctrine of Scripture? *Is* there not irresistible evidence, from a view of the actual condition of the human world, that no man can become *good* in the Christian sense,—can become fit for a holy and happy place hereafter,—but by this operation *ab extra?* But this is arbitrary and discriminative on the part of the sovereign Agent, and independent of the will of man. And how awfully evident is it, that this indispensable operation takes place only on a comparatively small proportion of the collective race!

"Now this creature, thus constituted and circumstanced, passes a few fleeting years on earth, a short, sinful course, in which he does often what, notwithstanding his ignorance and ill-disciplined judgment and conscience, he knows to be wrong, and neglects what he knows to be his duty; and, consequently, for a greater or less measure of guilt, widely different in different offenders, deserves punishment. But ENDLESS PUNISHMENT! HOPELESS MISERY, *through a duration to which the enormous terms above imagined will be absolutely* NOTHING! I acknowledge my *inability* (I would say it reverently) *to admit this belief, together with a belief in the divine goodness,*—the belief that 'God is love,' that his tender mercies are over all his works. Goodness, benevolence, charity, as ascribed in supreme perfection to him, cannot mean a quality foreign to all human conceptions of goodness: it must be something analogous in principle to what himself has defined and required as goodness in his moral creatures; that, in adoring the divine goodness, we may not be worshipping an 'unknown God.' But, if so, how would all our ideas be confounded, while contemplating him bringing, of his own sovereign will, a race of creatures into existence, in such a condition that they certainly will and *must—must* by their nature and circumstances—go wrong, and be miserable, unless prevented by especial grace, which is the privilege of only a small proportion of them, and at the same time affixing on their delinquency *a doom of which it is infinitely beyond the highest archangel's faculty to apprehend a thousandth part of the horror!*"*

Now, granting the premises, we hold this argument to be unanswerable and conclusive. But is it not wonderful that it did not occur to so acute a mind as Foster's, that the same premises would furnish a valid argument against the justice of all punishment, as well as against the justice of eternal punishments? Surely, if the utter inability of man to do good without divine grace is any extenuation, when such grace is not given, it is an entire and perfect exoneration. It is either this, or it is nothing. Such are the inevitable inconsistencies of the best thinkers, when the feelings of the heart are at war with the notions of the head. Instead of analyzing this awful subject, and tracing it down to its fundamental principles, upon which his reason might have reposed with a calm and immovable satisfaction, Foster seems to have permitted his great mind to take root in a creed of man's devising, and then to be swayed by the gusts and counter-blasts of passion. Believing that man "must go wrong," that nature and circumstances impose this dire necessity upon him, his benevolence could not contemplate an eternity of torments as due to such inevitable sin. It was repelled by "the infinite horror of the tenet." On the other hand, his abhorrence of evil, and sense of justice, shrank with equal violence from the idea that all punishment is unjust; and hence he could say, "Far be it from us to make light of the demerit of sin, and to remonstrate with the Supreme Judge against a *severe chastisement.*" Thus did his great mind, instead of resting upon truth, perpetually hang in a state of suspense and vacillation between the noblest feelings of his heart and the darkest errors of his creed.

* Letter, &c., pp. 15–18.

Others, who have adopted the same creed, have endeavoured to extricate themselves from the dilemma in which Foster found himself, not by denying the eternity of future punishments, but by inventing a very nice distinction between the natural and moral inability of man. "He can obey the law," say they, "*if he will*;" all that "he wants is the will." All his natural faculties are complete; only let him will aright, and he is safe. But, after all, the question still remains, How is he to get the will,—the good will,—in order to render him acceptable to God? Does he get it from nature—is it a part of his birthright? No: from this he derives a depraved will, "free to evil only." Is it vouchsafed to him from above? Is it a gift from God? Alas! to those who are lost, and perish eternally in their sins, the grace of God is never given! What does it signify thus to tell them, or to tell the world, that they have the natural ability to obey; that none of their natural faculties are lost; that they still have understandings, and affections, and wills? What can all these avail them? Is it not the merest mockery to assure them that they really have hearts, and wills, and feelings, if they "*must* go wrong," if they *must* put forth the volitions for which they shall be tormented forever?

Upon this distinction we shall not dwell, as we have fully considered it in our "Examination of Edwards on the Will." We shall merely add, that it is not an invention of modern times.* It is at least as old as the age of Augustine. "The Pelagians think," says he, "they know some great thing, when they say, '*God would not command what he knew could not be done by man.*' Who does not know this? But he commands what we cannot do, whereby we know what we ought to ask of him. For it is faith which obtains by prayer what the law commands. For true it is that we keep the commandments *if we will*, (*si volumus*;) but as the will is prepared of the Lord, we must seek of him that we may will as much as is sufficient, in order to our doing by volition, (*ut volendo faciamus*.") Truly, we can keep the commandments *if we will* to do so; for, as Augustine immediately says, "certain it is, that we will when we will."† But no man can put forth a volition in conformity

* Robert Hall supposes that Edwards must have found it in Owen. He might have found it in a hundred earlier writers.

† Wiggers's Presentation, p. 210—Note by Translator.

with the commandments, unless it be given him of God, who "causes us to will good;"* and this is never given to the reprobate. How, then, can they be justly consigned to eternal torments? How can they be eternally punished for that which they could not possibly avoid? It is no wonder that a Foster should have shrunk from "the infinite horrors of such a tenet," as seen from this point of view; the only wonder is, that any one can be found who can possibly endure them.

The same distinction, as we have already said, is relied upon by Edwards in order to show that man has an ability to obey the law of God.†

Thus we are gravely taught that we are able to obey the law of God; because if we will to do so, the external act will follow; and because it is certain that *if* we will we do really will. But *how to will* is the question. Can we put forth the requisite volitions? No one doubts that if we put forth the volition which the law of God requires, we then obey him, whether the external act follow or not; nor that if we will, then we do really will. But all this leaves the great question untouched, Can we put forth the requisite volitions without divine aid? And after this question has been answered in the negative, and we have been told that such aid is not given to the reprobate, all this talk about a natural ability, which must forever prove unavailing, is the merest mockery that ever entered into the imagination or the metaphysics of man. However the fact may be disguised by verbal niceties, it as really places eternal life beyond the reach of the reprobate, as is the very sun in the firmament of heaven, and makes eternal death as inevitable to them as is the rising and the setting thereof.

SECTION III.

The eternity of future punishments an expression of the divine goodness.

We have seen in the first chapter of this part of the present work, that God really and sincerely intended the salvation of all men; and that if any are lost, it is because it is impossible in the nature of things to necessitate holiness; and that the impenitent, in spite of all the means employed by infinite wisdom and goodness for their salvation, do obstinately work

* Wiggers's Presentation, p. 210—Note by Trans. † Freedom of the Will, p. 38.

out their own ruin and destruction. Omnipotence cannot confer holiness upon them; they do not choose to acquire it; and hence, they are compelled to endure the awful wages of sin. To those who reject this view of the nature of holiness, the world in which we live must forever remain an inexplicable enigma; and that to which we are hastening must present still more terrific subjects of contemplation. To their minds the eternal agonies of the lost can never be made to harmonize with the infinite perfections of God, by whom the second death is appointed. "How self-evident the proposition," says Foster, "that if the Sovereign Arbiter had *intended* the salvation of the race, it must have been accomplished." Having so summarily settled this position, that God did not intend the salvation of the race, the question which admits of no answer, *Why did he not intend it?* might well spread a mysterious darkness over the whole economy of divine providence. It was that darkness, that perplexing and confounding darkness, by which the mighty soul of Foster was oppressed with so many gloomy thoughts, and filled with so many frightful imaginations.

For our part, if we could believe that God could easily work holiness in the heart of every creature, and that he does not do so simply because he does not intend their salvation, we should not have attempted to vindicate his perfections. We should have believed in them, it is true; but we should have been constrained to confess, that they are veiled in impenetrable clouds and darkness. Hence, if we had not confessed ignorance and inability for all minds and all ages, as so many others have done, we should, at least, have confessed these things for ourselves, and supinely waited for the light of eternity to dispel the awful and perplexing enigmas of time. But we hold no such doctrine; we entertain no such sentiment. We believe that God, in his infinite, overflowing goodness desires, and from all eternity has desired, the salvation of all men. We believe that salvation is impossible to some, because a necessary holiness is impossible, and they do not choose to work out for themselves what cannot be worked out for them, even by omnipotence. It was the bright and cheering light which this truth seemed to cast upon the dark places of the universe, that first inspired us with the thought and determination to produce a theodicy. And it is in the light of this truth, if we mistake not, that the infinite love of God may be seen beaming from the eye of hell, as well as from the bright regions of eternal blessedness. This conclusion we shall endeavour methodically to unfold, and to set in a clear light.

In the first place, then, to begin with our fundamental position, the Creator could not necessitate the holiness of the creature. Hence this holiness, after all the means and the ability were given to him, must be left to the will of the creature himself. All that could be done in such a case was, for God to set life and death before us, accompanied by the greatest of all conceivable motives to pursue the one, and to fly from the other; and then say, "choose ye:" and all this has God actually done for the salvation of all men. Hence, though some should be finally lost, his infinite goodness will be clear. Let us see what objections may be urged against this conclusion.

Supposing it granted, that a necessitated virtue is a contradiction in terms, and that it is indispensably requisite to ordain rewards and punishments in order to prevent sin and secure holiness; it may still be said that the penalty of eternal death is too severe for that purpose, and is therefore inconsistent with the goodness of God. Indeed, after such a concession, this is the only position which can be taken in opposition to the doctrine in question. Let us then look at it, and examine the assumption upon which it rests for support.

If such punishments be too severe, it must be for one of these two reasons: either because no object can justify the infliction of them, or because the end proposed by the Supreme Ruler is not sufficiently great for that purpose.

Let us suppose, then, in the first place, the position to be assumed, that no object can possibly justify the infliction of such awful punishments. Such would be the case, we admit, if such punishments were unjust—were not deserved by the person upon whom they are inflicted. Hence, it becomes indispensable, in order to vindicate the divine benevolence, to show that eternal sufferings are deserved by those upon whom they fall. Otherwise they would be unjust, and consequently unjustifiable; as the end could never justify the means.

We say, then, that eternal sufferings are deserved by the finally impenitent, not because every sinful act carries along with it an infinite guilt, nor because every sinner may be imagined to have committed an infinite number of sins, but because they will continue to sin forever. It will be conceded, that if punishment be admissible at all, it is right and proper that so long as acts of rebellion are persisted in, the rewards of iniquity should attend them. It will be conceded, that if the finally impenitent should continue to sin forever, then they forever deserve to reap the rewards of sin. But this is one part of the Scripture doctrine of future punishments, that those who endure them will never cease to sin and rebel against the authority of God's law.

Foster has attempted a reply to this defence of the doctrine in question, but without success. "It is usually alleged," says he, "that there will be an endless *continuance* of sinning .... and therefore the punishment must be endless." But "the allegation," he replies, "is of no avail in vindication of the doctrine, because the first consignment to this dreadful state *necessitates a continuance of the criminality;* the doctrine teaching that it is of the essence, and is an awful aggravation of the original consignment, that it dooms the condemned to maintain the criminal spirit unchanged forever. The doom *to sin* as well as to suffer, and, according to the argument, to sin *in order* to suffer, is inflicted as the punishment of the sin committed in the mortal state. Virtually, therefore, the eternal punishment is the punishment of the sins of time."*

Even according to the principles of Foster himself, the argument is wholly untenable. For he admits, that such is the evil nature of man, such the circumstances around him, and such the influences of the great tempter, he must inevitably go wrong; and yet he holds that he may be justly punished for such transgressions. Now, if every man who comes into the world be doomed to sin, as this author insists he is, and may be justly punished for sins committed in this life, why should he be excused for the sins committed in another state, because he is doomed to commit them? But this *argumentum ad hominem* is merely by the way, and has more to do with the consistency of the author, than with the validity of his position. We shall proceed to subject this to a more searching and a more satisfactory test.

His argument assumes, that "it is of the essence of the

* Letter, pp. 21, 22.

original consignment, that it dooms the condemned to maintain the criminal spirit unchanged forever." This is an unwarrantable assumption. We nowhere learn, and we are nowhere required to believe, that the guilty are doomed to sin forever, because they have voluntarily sinned in this life; much less that they are necessitated to sin in order to suffer! The doctrine of the eternity of future punishments is not necessarily encumbered with any such ridiculous appendage; and if any one can be found to entertain so absurd a view of the doctrine, we must leave him to vindicate the creation of his own imagination.

We do not suppose that the soul of the guilty will continue to sin forever, because it will be consigned to the regions of the lost; but we suppose it will be consigned to the regions of the lost, because, by its own repeated acts of transgression, it has made sure of its eternal continuance in sinning. God dooms no man to sin—neither by his power nor by his providence. But it is a fact, against which there will be no dispute, that if a man commit a sin once, he will be still more apt to commit the same sin again, under the same or similar circumstances. The same thing will be true of each and every succeeding repetition of the offence; until the habit of sinning may be so completely wrought into the soul, and so firmly fixed there, that nothing can check it in its career of guilt. Neither the glories of heaven, nor the terrors of hell, may be sufficient to change its course. No amount of influence brought to bear upon its feelings, may be sufficient to transform its will. "There is a certain bound to imprudence and misbehaviour," says Butler, "which being transgressed, there remains no place for repentance in the natural course of things." And may we not also add, nor in the supernatural course of things either; and there only remains a certain fearful looking-for of judgment? As this may be the case, for aught we know, nay, as it seems so probable that this is the case, no one is authorized to pronounce endless sufferings unjust, unless he can first show that the object of them has not brought upon himself an eternal continuance in the practice of sin. In other words, unless he can first show that the sinner does not doom himself to an eternity of sinning, he cannot reasonably complain that his Creator and Judge dooms him to an eternity of suffering.

But it may be said, that although the sinner may deserve to suffer forever, because he continues to sin forever; yet it were more worthy the infinite goodness of God, to release him from so awful a calamity. If the sinner deserves such punishment, it is not only just to inflict it upon him, it is a demand of infinite goodness itself that it should be inflicted upon him, provided a sufficiently great good may be attained by such a manifestation of justice. This brings us to the consideration of our second point, namely: Is the object proposed to be accomplished by the infliction of eternal misery sufficiently great to justify the infliction of so severe a penalty? In other words, Is such a penalty disproportioned to the exigencies of the case?

In his attempt to show, that the infliction of eternal misery is too severe to consist with the goodness of God, Mr. Foster does not at all consider the great ends, or final causes, of penal enactments. He merely dwells upon the terrors of the punishment, and brings these into vivid contrast with the weakness and impotency of man in his mortal state. This, it must be confessed, is a most one-sided and partial view of so profound a subject; much better adapted to work upon the feelings than to enlighten the judgment. All that he seems to have seen in the case, is a poor, weak creature, utterly unable to do any good, subjected to eternal torments for the sins of "a few fleeting years on earth." Hence it was, that "the moral argument," which "pressed so irresistibly on his mind," came in "the stupendous idea of eternity."

Indeed, according to his theology, there could be no object sufficiently vast, no necessity sufficiently imperious, to justify eternal punishments. The prevention of sin, and the promotion of universal holiness, could not form such an object or constitute such a necessity; for, according to his creed, all this might have been most perfectly attained by a word. Hence, he was puzzled and confounded in the contemplation of what appeared to him so much unnecessary evil. "I acknowledge my *inability*," said he, "to admit the belief, (the belief in endless punishment,) together with the belief in the divine goodness—the belief that 'God is love,' that 'his tender mercies are over all his works.'"

As we have already seen from another point of view, we must come out from his theology if we would see the harmony and agreement between these beliefs. We must take our stand on the position, that Omnipotence cannot necessitate holiness, and must have recourse to rewards and punishments to secure it. Otherwise all evil and all suffering will remain an inexplicable enigma; all rewards and punishments awkward and clumsy contrivances to attain an end, which might be much better attained without them.

On this high and impregnable ground the moral argument of Foster loses all its irresistible force, and "the stupendous idea of eternity" presses with all its weight in favour of endless punishment. If temporal punishments are justified on the ground that they are necessary to meet the exigencies and uphold the interests of temporal governments, surely eternal punishments may be justified on the same ground in relation to an eternal government. The "stupendous idea of eternity" attaches to the whole, as well as to the part; and hence nothing can be gained to the cause of Universalism by the introduction of this idea, except in the minds of those who take only a one-sided and partial view of the subject.

The spectacle of punishment for a single day, it will be admitted, would be justified on the ground that it was necessary to support for a single day a government; especially if that government were vast in extent and involved stupendous interests. But if suffering for a single day may be justified on such a ground, then the exigencies of such a government for two days would justify a punishment for two days; and so on *ad infinitum.* Hence, the doctrine of eternal punishments in common with the eternal moral government of God, is not a greater anomaly than temporal punishments in relation to temporal governments. If we reject the one, we must also reject the other. Indeed, when we consider not only the eternal duration, *but also the universal extent*, of the divine government, the argument in question, if good for anything, presses with greater force against the little, insignificant governments of men, than against the moral government of God. One reason why Foster was "repelled into doubt by the infinite horrors of the tenet" is, that he merely contemplated the sufferings of the guilty, and saw not how those sufferings were connected with the majesty and glory of God's universal and eternal empire. It is as if an insect should undertake to set bounds to the punishments which human beings have found necessary to meet the exigencies and uphold the interests of human society.

We are told by writers on jurisprudence, that penalties should be proportioned to offences; but, as has been truly said, how this proportion is to be ascertained, or on what principles it is to be adjusted, we are seldom informed. We are usually left to vague generalities, which convey no definite information, and furnish no satisfactory guidance to our minds. If we can ascertain the precise conditions according to which this principle should be adjusted, even by goodness itself, we shall then be the better able to determine whether the eternal suffering of the guilty and impenitent is not a manifestation of the love of God,—of that *tender mercy which is over all his works.*

It is a maxim that punishment should be sufficient to accomplish the great end for which it is imposed, namely, the prevention of offences. Otherwise, if it failed to accomplish this object, "it would be so much suffering in waste."* Now, who can say that the penalty of eternal death is not necessary to this end in the moral government of the universe, or that it is greater than is necessary for its accomplishment? Who can say that a punishment for a limited period would have answered that end in a greater or more desirable degree? Who can say that there would have been more holiness and happiness, with less sin and misery, in the universe, if the punishment of those whom nothing could reclaim had not been eternal? Who can say that it would be better for the universe, on the whole, if the punishment of sin were limited than if it were eternal? Until this question, which so evidently lies beyond the range of our narrow faculties, be answered, it is presumption to object that eternal punishment is inconsistent with the goodness of God. For aught the objector knows, this very penalty is demanded by infinite goodness itself, in order to stay the universal ravages of sin, and preserve the glory of the moral empire of Jehovah. For aught he knows, the very sufferings of the lost forever may be, not only a manifestation of the justice of God, but also a profound expression of that tender mercy which is over all his works. For aught he knows, this very appointment, at which he takes so great offence, may be one of the main pillars in the structure of the intellectual system of the universe; without which its in-

* Jeremy Bentham.

ternal constitution would be radically defective, and its moral government impossible. In short, for aught he knows, his objection may arise, not from any undue or unnecessary severity of the punishment in question, but from his own utter incapacity to decide such a point in relation to the universal and eternal government of God.

It may be said that this is an appeal to human ignorance, rather than a reply to the argument of the Universalist. Surely, it is good to be reminded of our ignorance, when we undertake to base objections against the doctrines of religion upon assumptions about the truth of which we know, and, from the nature of the case, must know, absolutely nothing. If the doctrine in question involved any inherent contradictions, or were it clearly at war with the dictates of justice, or mercy, or truth, there might be some reason in our opposition; but to oppose it because we cannot see how it subserves the highest interests of the universe, seems to be an exceedingly rash and hasty decision; especially as we see that such a penalty must powerfully tend to restrain the wickedness of men, as well as to preserve unfallen creatures in their obedience.

It is not at all strange that beings with such faculties as we possess, limited on all sides, and far more influenced by feeling than by reason, should be oppressed by the stupendous idea of eternal torments. It absolutely overwhelms the imagination of poor, short-sighted creatures like ourselves. But God, in his plans for the universe and for eternity, takes no counsel of human weakness; and that which seems so terrible to our feeble intellects may, to his all-seeing eye, appear no more than a dark speck in a boundless realm of light. Surely, if there ever was, or ever could be, a question which should be reduced to the simple inquiry, "What saith the Scripture?" it is that respecting the future condition of the wicked.

It is truly amazing that a mind like Foster's should have put this inquiry so easily aside, and relied with so much confidence upon what he was pleased to call "the moral argument." This argument, as we have seen, is altogether unsound and sophistical. It bases itself upon the prejudices of a creed, and terminates in dark conjectures merely. He hopes, or rather he "would wish to indulge the hope, founded upon the divine attribute of infinite benevolence, that there will be a period somewhere in the endless futurity, when all God's sinning creatures will be restored by him to rectitude and happiness." Vain hope! delusive wish! How can they be made holy without their own consent and coöperation? And if they could be restored to rectitude and happiness, how can we hope that God would restore them, since he has not been pleased to preserve them in their original state of rectitude and happiness?

But perhaps, says he, there will be, not a restoration of all God's sinning creatures to rectitude and happiness, but an annihilation of their existence. Even this conjecture, if true, "would be a prodigious relief;" for "the grand object of interest is a negation of the perpetuity of misery." Suppose, then, that the universe had been planned according to this benevolent wish of Mr. Foster, and that those who could not be reclaimed should, after a very protracted period of suffering, be forever annihilated; would this promote the order and well-being of the whole creation? How did Mr. Foster know but that such a provision in the government of the universe would oppose so feeble a barrier to the progress of sin, that scenes of mutability, and change, and ruin, would be introduced into the empire of God, from which his benevolence would shrink with infinite abhorrence? How did Mr. Foster know but that the Divine Benevolence itself would prefer a hell in one part of his dominions, to the universal disorder, confusion, and moral desolation which such a provision might introduce into the government of God? Such a conjecture might, it is true, bring a "prodigious relief" to our imagination; but the government of God is intended for the relief of the universe, and not for the relief of our imagination.

Others besides the author in question have sought relief for their minds on this subject, by indulging in vague conjectures respecting the real design of the Supreme Ruler and Judge. Archbishop Tillotson, for example, supposes that although God actually threatened to punish the wicked eternally, he does not intend, and is not bound, to carry this threat into execution. This penalty, he supposes, is merely set forth as a terror to evil-doers, in order to promote the good order and well-being of the world; and after it has subserved this purpose, the Lawgiver will graciously remit a portion of the threatened penalty, and restore all his sinning creatures to purity and bliss. In reply to this extraordinary position, we shall only say that if the Almighty really undertook to deceive the world for its own good, it is a pity he did not take the precaution to prevent the archbishop from detecting the cheat. It is a pity, we say, that he did not deceive the archbishop as well as the rest of men; and not suffer his secret to get into the possession of one who has so indiscreetly published it to the whole world.

Nothing seems more amazing to us than the haste and precipitancy with which most men dispose of subjects so awful as that of the eternity of future punishments. One would suppose that if any subject in the whole range of human thought should engage our most serious attention, and call forth the utmost exertion of our power of investigation, it would be the duration of punishment in a future life. If that punishment be eternal, it is certainly the most momentous question which ever engaged the attention of man, and is to be lightly disposed of only by madmen.*

* On one point we fully concur with Mr. Foster, (see Letter, p. 27:) "As to religious teachers, if this tremendous doctrine be true, surely it ought to be almost continually proclaimed as with the blast of a trumpet, inculcated and reiterated, with ardent passion, in every possible form of terrible illustration; no remission of the alarm to thoughtless spirits."

But if it be so incumbent on religious teachers, who believe this awful tenet, thus to proclaim it to a perishing world, is it not equally incumbent on them not to speak on such a subject at all until they have taken the utmost pains to form a correct opinion concerning it? If the man who merely proclaims this doctrine in the usual quiet way of preachers, while he sees his fellow-men perishing around, is guilty of criminal neglect, what shall we say of the religious teacher who, without having devoted much time to the investigation of the subject, exerts his powers and his influence to persuade his fellow-men that it is all a delusion, and that the idea of endless misery is utterly inconsistent with the goodness of God? How many feeble outcries and warnings of those who are so terribly rebuked by Mr. Foster, may be silenced and forever laid to rest by his eloquent declamation against the doctrine in question, and how many souls may be thereby betrayed and led on to their own eternal ruin! Yet, wonderful as it may seem, Mr. Foster tells us that his opinion on this awful subject has not been the result of "a protracted inquiry." In the very letter from which we have so frequently quoted, he says: "I have perhaps been too content to let an opinion (or impression) admitted in early life dispense with protracted inquiry and various reading." Now, is this the way in which a question of this kind should be decided,—a question which involves the eternal destiny of millions of human beings? Is it to be decided, not by protracted inquiry, but under the influence of an "impression admitted in early life?"

CHAPTER V.

THE DISPENSATION OF THE DIVINE FAVOURS RECONCILED WITH THE GOODNESS OF GOD.

> O God, whose thunder shakes the sky,
> Whose eye this atom globe surveys,
> To thee, my only rock, I fly;
> *Thy mercy in thy justice praise.*
>
> * * * * * * *
>
> Then why, my soul, dost thou complain?
> Why drooping seek the dark recess?
> Shake off the melancholy chain,
> *For God created all to bless.*—CHATTERTON.

In the preceding part, we considered the doctrine of predestination, under the name of necessity, in its relation to the origin of evil. We there endeavoured to show that it denies the responsibility of man, and makes God the author of sin. In the present part, it remains for us to examine the same doctrine in relation to the equality of the divine goodness. If we mistake not, the scheme of predestination, or rather the doctrine of election, which lies at its foundation, is, when rightly understood, perfectly consistent with the impartiality and glory of the goodness of God. On this subject we shall now proceed to unfold our views in as orderly and perspicuous a manner as possible.

SECTION I.

The unequal distribution of favours, which obtains in the economy of natural providence, consistent with the goodness of God.

It has been thought that if the goodness of God were unlimited and impartial, the light and blessings of revelation would be universal. But before we should attach any weight to such an objection, we should first consider and determine two things.

First, we should consider and determine how far the unequal diffusion of the light of revelation has resulted from the agency of man, and how far from the agency of God. For, if this inequality in the spread of a divine blessing has sprung in any degree from the abuse which free, subordinate agents have made of their powers, either by active opposition, or passive neglect, it is in so far no more imputable to a want of goodness in the Divine Being than is any other evil or disorder which the creature has introduced into the world. In so far, the glory of God is clear, and man alone is to blame. It is incumbent upon those, then, who urge this objection against the goodness of God to show that the evil in question has not resulted from the agency of man. This position, we imagine, the objector will not find it very easy to establish; and yet, until he does so, his objection very clearly rests upon a mere unsupported hypothesis.

Secondly, before we can fairly rely upon the objection in question, we should be able to show, that the agency of God might have been so exerted as to spread the light of revelation further than it now extends, without on the whole causing greater evil than good. Light or knowledge, it should be remembered, is not in itself a blessing. It may be so, or it may not; and whether it be a blessing or a curse depends, not upon the beneficence of the giver, but upon the disposition and character of the recipient. Before we should presume to indulge the least complaint, then, against the goodness of divine providence, we should be able to produce the nation, whose character for moral goodness and virtue would, on the whole, and in relation to its circumstances, have been improved by the interposition of God in causing the light of truth to shine in the midst of its corruptions. But we are manifestly incompetent to deal with a question of such a nature. Its infinite complication, as well as its stupendous magnitude, places it entirely beyond the reach of the human mind. So manifold and so multiform are the hidden causes upon which its solution depends, that general principles cannot be brought to bear upon it; and its infinite variety and complication of detail must forever baffle the intellect of man. Hence, an objection which proceeds on the supposition that this question has been solved and determined, is worth nothing.

But, for the sake of argument, let us suppose that the unequal diffusion of religious knowledge has proceeded directly from the agency of God. Still the objection against his goodness, in regard to the dispensation of light, would be no greater than in relation to all the dispensations of his favour. All the gifts of Heaven—health, riches, honour, intelligence, and whatever else comes down from above—are scattered among the children of men with the most promiscuous variety. Hence, the unequal distribution of the blessings of the gospel, or rather of its external advantages, is so far from being inconsistent with the character of God, that it is of a piece with all his other dispensations: it is so far from standing out as an anomaly in the proceedings of the Divine Being, that it falls in with the whole analogy of nature and of providence. Hence, there is no resting-place between the abandonment of this objection, and downright atheism.

Let us see, then, what force there is in this objection, when urged, as it is by the atheist, against the whole constitution and management of the world. It proceeds on the supposition, that if light and knowledge, or any other natural advantage, were bestowed upon one person, it would be bestowed upon all others, and upon all in precisely the same degree. According to his view, there should be no such thing as degrees in knowledge, and consequently no such thing as self-development and progress. To select only one instance out of many: the atheist objects, that it is not worthy of infinite wisdom and goodness to provide us with so complicated an instrument as the eye, as a means of obtaining light and knowlege. Why could not this end be attained by a more simple and direct method? Why leave us, for so great a portion of earthly existence, in comparative ignorance, to grope out our way into regions of light?

In the eye of reason, there is no end to this kind of objecting; and it only stops where the shallow conceit, or wayward fancy, of the objector is pleased to terminate. It is very easy to ask, Why a Being of infinite goodness did not confer light and knowledge upon us directly and at once, without leaving us to acquire them by the tedious use of the complicated means provided by his natural providence. But the inquiry does not stop here. He might just as well ask, Why such a Being was pleased to confer so small an amount of light upon us, and leave us to acquire more for ourselves? Why not confer it upon us without measure and without exertion on our part? The same interrogation, it is evident, may be applied to every other blessing, as well as to knowledge; and hence the objection of the atheist, when carried out, terminates in the great difficulty, why God did not make all creatures alike, and each equal to himself. On the principle of this objection, the insect should complain that it is not a man; the man that he is not an angel; and the angel that he is not a god. Hence, such a principle would exclude from the system of the world everything like a diversity and subordination of parts; and would reduce the whole universe, as a system, to as inconceivable a nonentity as would be a watch, all of whose parts should be made of exactly the same materials, and possessing precisely the same force and properties.

In every system, whether of nature or of art, there must be a variety and subordination of parts. Hence, to object that each part is not perfect in itself, without considering its relations and adaptation to the whole, is little short of madness. And what heightens the absurdity in the present case is, that the parts which fall under observation may, for aught we know, possess the greatest perfection which is consistent with the highest good and beauty of the whole.

If God has endowed man with the attributes of reason and speech; if he has scattered around him, with a liberal hand, the multiplied blessings of life; if, above all, he has made him capable of eternal blessedness, and of an endless progress in glory; this should warm his heart with the most glowing gratitude, and tune his tongue to the most exalted praise. And the man, the rational and immortal being, whose high endowments should lead him to murmur and repine at the unequal dispensations of the divine bounty, because God has created beings of a higher order than himself, and placed them in a world where no cloud is ever seen, and where no sigh is ever heard, would certainly, to say the very least, be guilty of the most criminal ingratitude. Reason and conscience might well cry out, Shall the thing formed say to Him who formed it, Why hast thou made me thus? And God himself might well demand, Is thine eye evil, because I am good?

The case is not altered, if we suppose that the divine favour is unequally bestowed upon different individuals of the same species, instead of the different orders of created beings. The same principle of wisdom and goodness, as Butler remarks, whatever it may be, which led God to make a difference between men and angels, may be the same which induces him to make a difference between one portion of the human family and another—to leave one portion for a season to the dim twilight of nature, while upon another he pours out the light of revelation. The same principle, it may also be, which gives rise to the endless diversity of natural gifts among the different individuals of the same community, as well as to the different situations of the same individual, in regard to his temporal and eternal interests, during the various stages of his earthly existence. And if this be so, we should either cease to object against the goodness of God, because the same powers and advantages are not bestowed upon all, or we should adopt the atheistical principle, in its fullest extent, which has now been shown to be so full of absurdity.

But although we cannot see the particular reasons of such a diversity of gifts, or how each is subservient to the good of the whole; yet every shadow of injustice will disappear, if we consider that God deals with every one, to use the language of Scripture, "according to what he hath, and not according to what he hath not." His bounty overflows, in various degrees, upon his creatures; but his justice equalizes all, by requiring every one to give an account of just exactly as many talents as have been committed to his charge, and no more.

In this respect, all the dispensations of divine providence are clearly and broadly distinguished from the Calvinistic scheme of election and reprobation. According to this scheme, the reprobate, or those who are not objects of the divine mercy, have not, and never had, the ability to obey the law of God; and yet they are condemned to eternal death for their failure to obey it. This is to deal with them, not according to what they have, but according to what they have not, and what they could not possibly have. Hence, to reason from one of these cases to the other, from the inequality of gifts and talents ordained by God to a scheme of election and reprobation, as Calvinists uniformly do, is to confound all our notions of just dealing, and to convert the rightful sovereignty of God into frightful tyranny. The perfect justice of this remark will, we trust, be made to appear the more clearly and fully in the course of the following section of the present work.

SECTION II.

The Scripture doctrine of election consistent with the impartiality of the divine goodness.

We have seen that the election of a nation to the enjoyment of certain external advantages, or the bestowment of superior gifts upon some individuals, is not inconsistent with the perfection of the divine goodness. Beyond the distinctions thus indicated, and which so clearly obtain in the natural providence of God, it is believed that the Scriptural scheme of election does not go; and that the more rigid features of the Calvinistic scheme of election and reprobation can be deduced from revelation only by a violent wresting and straining of the clear word of God. Let us see if this assertion may not be fully established.

The ninth chapter of the Epistle to the Romans, it is well known, is the portion of Scripture upon which the advocates of that scheme have chiefly relied, from Augustine down to Calvin, and from Calvin down to the present day. But, to any impartial mind, we believe, this chapter will not be found to lend the least shadow of support to any such scheme of doctrine. We assume this position advisedly, and shall proceed to give the reasons on which it is based.

Now, in the interpretation of any instrument of writing, it is a universally admitted rule, that it should be construed with reference to the subject of which it treats. What, then, is the subject of which the apostle treats in the ninth chapter of Romans? In regard to this point there is no dispute; and, to avoid all appearance of controversy in relation to it, we shall state the design of the apostle, in this part of his discourse, in the words of one by whom the Calvinistic scheme of election is maintained. "With the eighth chapter," says Professor Hodge, in his Commentary on the Epistle to the Romans, "the discussion of the plan of salvation, and its immediate consequences, was brought to a close. The consideration of the calling of the Gentiles, and the rejection of the Jews, commences with the ninth, and extends to the end of the eleventh." Thus, according to the author, "the subject which the apostle had in view," in the ninth chapter, is "the rejection of the

Jews, and the calling of the Gentiles." Now, if this be his subject, and if the discussion of the plan of salvation was brought to a close in the eighth chapter, how can the doctrine of election and reprobation, which lies at the very foundation of, and gives both shape and colouring to, the whole scheme of salvation, as maintained by Calvinists, be found in the ninth chapter? How has it happened that such important lights have been thrown upon the plan of salvation, and such fundamental positions established in relation to it, after its discussion has been brought to a close? But this only by the way; we shall hereafter see how these important lights have been extracted from the chapter in question.

The precise passage upon which the greatest stress is laid seems to be the following: "The children being not yet born, neither having done any good or evil, that the purpose of God, according to election, might stand, not of works, but of him that calleth; it was said unto her, The elder shall serve the younger. As it is written, Jacob have I loved, but Esau have I hated." Now, the question is, Does this refer to the election of Jacob to eternal life, and the eternal reprobation of Esau; or, Does it refer to the selection of the descendants of the former to constitute the visible people of God on earth? This is the question; and it is one which, we think, is by no means difficult of solution.

The apostle was in the habit of quoting only a few words of a passage of the Old Testament, to which he had occasion to refer; and in the present instance he merely cites the words of the prophecy, "The elder shall serve the younger." But, according to the prophecy to which he refers, it was said to Rebecca, "Two nations are in thy womb, and two manner of people shall be separated from thy bowels; and the one people shall be stronger than the other people, and the elder shall serve the younger." Nothing can be plainer, we think, than that this prophecy relates to the descendants of Jacob and Esau, and not to the individuals themselves.

This view of the above passage, if it needed further confirmation, is corroborated by the fact that Esau did not serve Jacob, and that this part of the prophecy is true only in relation to his descendants. Thus the prophecy, when interpreted by its own express words, as well as by the event, shows that it related to "two nations," to "two manner of people," and not to two individuals.

The argument of St. Paul demands this interpretation. He is not discussing the plan of salvation. The question before him is not whether some are elected to eternal life on account of their works or not; and hence, if he had quoted a *prophecy** from the Old Testament to establish that position, he would have been guilty of a gross solecism, a *non sequitur*, as plain as could well be conceived.

For these reasons, we think there can be but little doubt with respect to the true meaning of the passage in question. And besides, this construction not only brings the language of the apostle into perfect conformity with the providence which God is actually seen to exercise over the world, but also reconciles it with the glory of the divine character.

In regard to the meaning of the terms *loved* and *hated*, used in the prophecy under consideration, there can be no doubt that the interpretation of Professor Hodge is perfectly just. "The meaning is," says he, "that God preferred one to the other, or chose one instead of the other. As this is the idea meant to be expressed, it is evident that in this case the word *hate* means to *love less*, to *regard and treat with less favour*. Thus in Gen. xxix, 33, Leah says, she was hated by her husband; while, in the thirtieth verse, the same idea is expressed by saying, Jacob 'loved Rachel more than Leah.' Matt. x, 37. Luke xiv, 26: 'If any man come to me, and hate not his father and mother,' &c. John xii, 25."

No one will object to this explanation. But how will the language, thus understood, apply to the case of individual election and reprobation, as maintained by Calvinists? We can see, indeed, how it applies to the descendants of Esau, who were in many respects placed in less advantageous circumstances than the posterity of Jacob; but how can God be said to love the elect more than the reprobate? Can he be said to love the reprobate at all? If, from all eternity, they have been eternally damned for not rendering an impossible obedience, should we call this a lesser degree of love than that which is bestowed upon the elect, or should we call it hate? It seems, that the commentator feels some repugnance at the idea of setting apart

* **Surely a very singular doctrine to be found in a prophecy.**

the individual, before he has "done either good or evil," as an object of hate; but not at all at the idea of setting him apart as an object of eternal and remediless woe!

"It is no doubt true," says Professor Hodge, "that the prediction contained in this passage has reference not only to the relative standing of Jacob and Esau, as individuals, but also to that of their descendants. It may even be allowed that the latter was principally intended in the communication to Rebecca. But it is clear: 1. That this distinction between the two races presupposed and included a distinction between the individuals. Jacob, made the special heir to his father Isaac, obtained as an individual the birthright and the blessing; and Esau, as an individual, was cut off."

This may all be perfectly true; it is certainly nothing to the purpose. It is true, that Jacob was made the special heir to his father; but did he thereby inherit eternal life? The distinction between him and Esau was undoubtedly a personal favour; the very fact that his descendants would be so highly blessed, must have been a source of personal satisfaction and joy, which his less favoured brother did not possess. But was this birthright and this blessing the fixed and irreversible boon of eternal life? There is not the least shadow of any such thing in the whole record. The only blessings, of a personal or individual nature, of which the account gives us the least intimation, either by express words or by implication, are like those with which God, in his providence, still continues to distinguish some individuals from others. They are not the gift of eternal life, but of certain external and temporal advantages. Hence they throw no light upon the Calvinistic scheme of election and reprobation. To make out this scheme, or anything in support of it, something more must be done than to show that God distinguishes one nation, or one individual, from another, in the distribution of his favours. This is conceded on all sides; and has nothing to do with the point in dispute. It must also be shown, that the particular favour which he brings home to one by his infinite power, and which he withholds from another, is neither more nor less than the salvation of the soul. It must be shown, that the mere will and pleasure of God makes such a distinction among the souls of men, that while some are invincibly made the heirs of glory, others are stamped with the seal of eternal death. The inheritance of Jacob, and the casting off of Esau, were, so far as we can see, very different from the awful proceeding which is ascribed to God according to the Calvinistic scheme of election and reprobation.

The same remark is applicable to other attempts to show, that God's favour was bestowed upon Jacob, as an individual, in preference to Esau. "As to the objection," says Professor Hodge, "that Esau never personally served Jacob, it is founded on the mere literal sense of the words. Esau did acknowledge his inferiority to Jacob, and was postponed to him on various occasions. This is the real spirit of the passage. This prophecy, as is the case with all similar predictions, has various stages of fulfilment. The relation between the two brothers during life; the loss of the birthright blessing and promises on the part of Esau; the temporary subjugation of his descendants to the Hebrews under David; their final and complete subjugation under the Maccabees; and especially their exclusion from the peculiar privileges of the people of God, through all the periods of their history, are included." Suppose all this to be true, what relation has it to the election of some individuals to eternal life, and the reprobation of others?

We shall not dwell upon other portions of the chapter in question; for, if the foregoing remarks be just, it will be easy to dispose of every text which may, at first view, appear to support the Calvinistic doctrine of election. We shall dismiss the consideration of the ninth chapter of Romans with an extract from Dr. Macknight, who, although a firm believer in the Calvinistic view of election and reprobation, does not find any support for his doctrine in this portion of Scripture. "Although some passages in this chapter," says he, "which pious and learned men have understood of the election and reprobation of individuals, are in the foregoing illustration interpreted of the election of nations to be the people of God, and to enjoy the advantage of an external revelation, and of their losing these honourable distinctions, the reader must not, on that account, suppose the author rejects the doctrines of the decree and foreknowledge of God. These doctrines are taught in other passages of Scripture: see Rom. viii, 29." Thus this enlightened critic candidly abandons the ninth chapter of Romans, and seeks support for his Calvinistic view of the divine decrees elsewhere.

Let us, then, proceed to examine the eighth chapter of Romans, upon which he relies. The words are as follow: "For whom he did foreknow, he also did predestinate to be conformed to the image of his Son, that he might be the first-born among many brethren. Moreover, whom he did predestinate, them he also called: and whom he called, them he also justified: and whom he justified, them he also glorified." We need have no dispute with the Calvinists respecting the interpretation of these words. If we mistake not, we may adopt their own construction of them, and yet clearly show that they lend not the least support to their views of election and reprobation. "As to *know*," says Professor Hodge, "is often to *approve* and *love*, it may express the idea of peculiar affection in the case; or it may mean to *select* or *determine upon*." These two interpretations, as he truly says, "do not essentially differ. The one is but a modification of the other." "The idea, therefore, obviously is, that those whom God peculiarly loved, and by thus loving, distinguished or selected from the rest of mankind; or, to express both ideas in one word, those whom he *elected* he predestinated, &c." Thus, according to this commentator, those whom God elected, he also predestinated, called, justified, and, finally, glorified.

Now, suppose all this to be admitted, let us consider whether it gives any support to the Calvinistic creed of election. It teaches that all those whom God elects shall be ultimately saved; but not one word or one syllable does it say with respect to the principle or ground of his election. It tells us that God, in his infinite wisdom, selects one portion of mankind as the objects of his saving mercy,—the heirs of eternal glory; but it does not say that this selection, this *approbation*, this *peculiar love*, is wholly without foundation in the character or condition of the elect. It tells us that God has numbered the elect, and written their names in the book of life; but it does not tell us that, in any case, he has taken precisely such as he has left, or left precisely such as he has taken. The bare fact of the election is all that is here disclosed. The reason, or the ground, or the principle, of that election is not even alluded to; and we are left to gather it either from other portions of Scripture, or from the eternal dictates of justice and mercy. Hence, as this passage makes no allusion to the ground or reason of the divine election, it does not begin to touch the controversy we have with theologians of the Calvinistic school. Every link in the chain here presented is perfect, except that which connects its first link, the election to eternal life, with the unconditional decree of God; and that link, the only one in controversy, is absolutely wanting. We have no occasion to break the chain; for it is only to the imagination that it seems to be unconditionally bound to the throne of the Omnipotent.

As this passage, then, determines nothing with respect to the ground or reason of election, so we have as much right to affirm, even in the presence of such language, that God did really foresee a difference where he has made so great a distinction, as the Calvinists have to suppose that so great a distinction has been made by a mere arbitrary and capricious exercise of power. That we have a better reason for this position than our opponents can produce for theirs, we shall endeavour to show in the ensuing section.

SECTION III.

The Calvinistic scheme of election inconsistent with the impartiality and glory of the divine goodness.

Having seen that the unequal distribution of favours, which obtains in the wise economy of Providence, distinguishing nation from nation, as well as individual from individual, is not inconsistent with the perfection of the divine goodness; and having also seen that the Scripture doctrine of election makes no other distinctions than those which take place in the providence of God, and is equally reconcilable with the glory of his character, we come now to consider the Calvinistic scheme of election and reprobation. We have shown on what principles the providence of God, which makes so many distinctions among men, may be vindicated; let us now see on what principles the Calvinistic scheme of election and reprobation seeks to justify itself. If we mistake not, this scheme of predestination is as unlike the providence of God in its principles as it is in the appalling distinctions which it makes among the subjects of the moral government of the world.

"Predestination," says Calvin, "we call the eternal decree of God, by which he has determined in himself, what he would have to become of every individual of mankind. For they are not all created with a similar destiny; but eternal life is foreordained for some, and eternal damnation for others. Every man, therefore, being created for one or the other of these ends, we say, he is predestinated either to life or to death."* Again: "In conformity, therefore, to the clear doctrine of Scripture, we assert, that by an eternal and immutable counsel, God has once for all determined, both whom he would admit to salvation and whom he would condemn to destruction."†

The doctrine of predestination is set forth in the Westminster Confession of Faith, in the following terms: "By the decree of God, for the manifestation of his glory, some men and angels are predestinated unto everlasting life, and others foreordained to everlasting death."

"These men and angels, thus predestinated and foreordained, are particularly and unchangeably designed; and their number is so certain and definite, that it cannot be either increased or diminished."

"Those of mankind that are predestinated unto life, God, before the foundation of the world was laid, according to his eternal and immutable purpose, and the secret counsel and good pleasure of his will, hath chosen in Christ unto everlasting glory, out of his mere free grace and love, without any foresight of faith or good works, or perseverance in either of them, or any other thing in the creature, as conditions or causes moving him thereunto; and all to the praise of his glorious grace."

"As God hath appointed the elect unto glory, so hath he, by the eternal and most free purpose of his will, foreordained all the means thereunto. Wherefore, they who are elected, being fallen in Adam, are redeemed by Christ, are effectually called unto faith in Christ by his Spirit working in due season; are justified, adopted, sanctified, and kept by his power through faith unto salvation. Neither are any other redeemed by Christ, effectually called, justified, adopted, sanctified, and saved, but the elect only."

"The rest of mankind, God was pleased, according to the unsearchable counsel of his own will, whereby he extendeth or withholdeth mercy as he pleaseth, for the glory of his sovereign power over his creatures, to pass by, and to ordain to

* Institutes, book iii, ch. xxi. † Ibid.

dishonour and wrath for their sin, to the praise of his glorious justice."

The defenders of this system assume the position, that as "by Adam's sin the whole human race became a corrupt mass, and justly subject to eternal damnation; so that no one can blame God's righteous decision, if none are saved from perdition."* Augustine expressly says: "But why faith is not given to all, need not move the faithful, who believe that by one all came into condemnation, doubtless the most just; *so that there would be no just complaining of God, though no one should be freed.*" And again: "The dominion of death has so far prevailed over men, that the deserved punishment would drive all headlong into a second death likewise, of which there is no end, if the undeserved grace of God did not deliver them from it."† Such is the picture of the divine justice, which the advocates of predestination have presented, from the time of Augustine, the great founder of the doctrine, down to the present day. It surely furnishes a sufficiently dark background on which to display the divine mercy to advantage.

We are told, however, that we should not judge of the proceeding of God, according to our notions of justice. This is certainly true, if the divine justice is fairly represented in the scheme of predestination; for that is clearly unlike all that is called justice among men. If God can create countless myriads of beings, who, because they come into the world with a depraved nature, and "can do nothing but sin," he regards with such displeasure, as to leave them without hope and without remedy; and not only so, but dooms them to eternal misery on account of an unavoidable continuance in sin; it must be confessed, that we should not presume to apply our notions of justice to his dealings with the world. They would more exactly accord with our notions of injustice, cruelty, and oppression, than with any others of which we are capable of forming any conception.

But, if we are not to decide according to our notions of justice, how shall we judge, or form any opinion respecting the equity of the divine proceeding? Shall we judge according to some notion which we do not possess, or shall we not judge at all? This last would seem to be the wiser course; but it is

* Wiggers, ch. xvi. † Wiggers's Presentation, ch. xvi.

one which the Calvinists themselves will not permit us to adopt. They tell us, that the predestination of the greater part of mankind to eternal death is "to the praise of God's glorious justice." But how are we to behold this glorious manifestation of the divine justice, if we may not view it through any medium known to us, or contemplate it in any light which may have dawned upon our minds?

Indeed, although the defenders of this doctrine often declare that the predestination of so many men and angels to eternal misery, displays the justice of God in all its glory; yet their own writings furnish the most abundant and conclusive evidence, that they themselves can see no appearance of justice in such a proceeding. On various occasions they do not hesitate to tell us, that although they cannot recognise the justice of such a proceeding, yet they believe it to be just, because it is the proceeding of God. But how can that be a display of justice to us, which, according to all our notions, wears the appearance of the most frightful injustice? Calvin himself admits, that the justice of God, which is supposed to be so brightly displayed in the predestination of so many immortal beings to endless woe, is, in reality, therein involved in clouds and darkness. Yet he does not fail to deduce an argument in its favour from "the very obscurity which excites such dread."*

It seems clear, that if the divine justice is really displayed in the punishment of the reprobate, it would have been exhibited on a still more magnificent scale by the condemnation of the whole human race. For, according to Calvinism, all were equally deserving of the divine displeasure, and the saved are distinguished from the lost only by the election of God. Hence, this scheme shows the justice of God to be limited, or not displayed on so grand and imposing a scale as it might have been; that is to say, it shows the justice of God to be less than infinite. But if such be the justice of God, we certainly should not complain that it has been limited by his mercy; we should rather rejoice, indeed, to believe that it had been thereby entirely extinguished.

Notwithstanding the claims of divine justice, all were not reprobated and doomed to eternal death. A certain portion of

* Institutes, book iii, ch. xxi.

mankind are elected and saved, "to the praise of his glorious grace." Now, it is conceded by Calvinists, that "all the circumstances which distinguish the elect from others are the fruit of their election."* This proposition is deduced by a Calvinistic divine from the "Westminster Confession of Faith." It is also conceded, that if the same grace which is given to the elect, should be bestowed upon the reprobate, they also would be saved.† Why, then, is it not bestowed? Why this fearful limitation of the divine mercy? Can the justice of God be manifested only at the expense of his mercy, and his mercy only at the expense of his justice? Or, is the everlasting mercy of God, that sublime attribute which constitutes the excellency and glory of his moral nature, so limited and straitened on all sides, that it merely selects here and there an object of its favour, while it leaves thousands and millions, equally within its reach, exposed to the eternal ravages of the spoiler? If so, then are we bound to conclude, that the mercy of God is not infinite; that it is not only limited, but also partial and arbitrary in its operation. But such is not the mercy of God. This is not a capricious fondness, nor yet an arbitrary dictate of feeling; it is a uniform and universal rule of goodness.

To select one here and there out of the mass of mankind, while others, precisely like them in all respects, are left to perish, is not mercy; it is favouritism. The tyrant may have his favourites as well as others. But God is not a respecter of persons. If he selects one, as the object of his saving mercy, he will select all who stand in the like condition; otherwise, his mercy were no more mercy, but a certain capricious fondness of feeling, unworthy of an earthly monarch, and much more of the august Head and Ruler of the moral universe.

These views and feelings are not peculiar to the opponents of Calvinism. They exist in the bosom of Calvinists themselves; only they are so crushed beneath a system, that they cannot find that freedom of development, nor that fulness of utterance, which so rightfully belongs to them, and which is so essential to their entire healthfulness and beauty.

We shall give only one illustration of the justness of this remark, although we might produce a hundred. After having endeavoured to vindicate the mercy of God, as displayed in the

* Hill's Divinity, p. 525. † Id., p. 526.

scheme of predestination, Dr. Hill candidly declares: "Still, however, *a cloud hangs over the subject;* and there is a difficulty in reconciling the mind to a system, which, after laying this foundation, that special grace is necessary to the production of human virtue, adopts as its distinguishing tenet this position, that that grace is denied to many."* Notwithstanding his most elaborate defence of predestination, he may well say, that "a cloud still hangs over the subject," and darkens the mercy of God.

Some of the stereotyped attempts of Calvinists to escape from the cloud which hangs over their doctrine are too weak to deserve a serious refutation. We are often asked, for example, if God may not do what he pleases with his own? Most assuredly he may; but does it please him, according to the high supralapsarian notion of Calvin, to create myriads of men and angels, to the end that they may be eternally damned? Does it please him, according even to the sublapsarian scheme, to leave the great mass of mankind in the helpless and forlorn condition in which they were born, without assistance, and then subject them to eternal misery, because they would not render an obedience beyond their power? Truly, the sovereign Creator and Ruler of the world may do what he pleases with his own; but yet we insist, that it is his supremest pleasure to deal with his creatures according to the eternal principles of justice and mercy.

His power is infinite, we admit, nay, we joyfully believe; but yet it is not a power which works according to the lawless pleasure of an unmitigated despot. It moves within a sphere of light and love. God's infinite wisdom and goodness superintend and surround all its workings; otherwise its omnipotent actings would soon carry the goodly frame of the world, together with all the blessed inhabitants thereof, into a state of utter confusion and chaotic night; leaving occasion for none, save the blind idolaters of power, to exclaim, "May he not do what he pleases with his own?"

We are also told, that "God is under no obligation to his creatures." Supposing this to be true, (though true most certainly it is not,) yet does he not owe it to himself—does he not owe it to the eternal principles of truth and goodness—does he

* Hill's Divinity, p. 562.

not owe it to the glory of his own empire over the world—to deal with his rational and immortal creatures, otherwise than according to the dark scheme of Calvinistic predestination? Nay, is it not due to the creature himself, that he should have some little chance or opportunity to embrace the life which God has set before him? Or, in default of such opportunity, is it not due to him that he should be exempt from the wages of the second death?

Confessing the wisdom and justice of predestination, as maintained by themselves, to be above our comprehension, the Calvinists are accustomed to remind us of the littleness, the weakness, and the blindness of the human mind, and how dangerous it is for beings like ourselves to pry into mysteries. We are aware, indeed, that our faculties are limited on all sides, and that we are exceedingly prone to assume more than belongs to us. We are not sure that the human mind, so little and so assuming, appears to any very great advantage in its advocacy of the Calvinistic scheme of predestination. This scheme is not only found in the ninth chapter of Romans, by a strange misapprehension of the whole scope and design of the apostle's argument, but, after having based it upon this misinterpretation of the divine word, its advocates persist in regarding all opposition to it as an opposition against God. As often as we dispute the doctrine, they cry out, "Nay, but, O man, who art thou that repliest against God?"

This rebuke was well administered by St. Paul. He applied it to those who, understanding his doctrine, did not hesitate to arraign the equity of the divine proceeding in the election of one nation in preference to another to constitute the visible Church on earth. This was not only to reply against God's word, but also against the manifest arrangements and dispensations of his providence. But it is not well applied by Calvinists, unless they possess an infallibility which authorizes them to identify their interpretation of the word of God with the word itself. It is not well applied by them, unless they are authorized to put themselves in the place of God. If they have no right to do this, we must insist upon it that it is one thing to reply against God, and quite another to reply against Calvin and his followers.

SECTION IV.

The true ground and reason of election to eternal life shows it to be consistent with the infinite goodness of God.

We agree with both Calvinistic and Arminian writers in the position, that no man is elected to eternal life on account of his merits. Indeed, the idea that a human being can merit anything, much less eternal life, of God, is preposterous in the extreme. All his gifts are of pure grace. The creation of the soul with glorious and immortal powers was an act of pure, unmixed favour. The duty of loving and serving him, which we are permitted to enjoy, is an exalted privilege, and should inspire us with gratitude, instead of begetting the miserable conceit that our service, even when most perfect, could deserve anything further from God, or establish any claims upon his justice. This view, which we take to be the true one, as completely shuts out all occasion of boasting as does the scheme of election maintained by the Calvinists.

It is objected, that God did not elect individuals to eternal life, because he foresaw that they would repent and believe; since repentance and faith themselves are the fruits of election. If this objection have any force, we are persuaded that it arises from an improper wording, or presentation, of the truth against which it is directed. We cannot suppose that God elected any one because he foresaw his good works, so as to make election to depend upon them, instead of making them to depend upon election. This does not prevent an individual, however, from having been elected, because God foresaw from all eternity that the influences attending upon his election would, by his own voluntary coöperation therewith, be rendered effectual to his salvation. This is the ground on which we believe the election of individuals to eternal life to proceed. Accordingly, we suppose that God never selected, or determined to save, any one who he foresaw would not yield to the influences of his grace, provided they should be given. And we also suppose that such is the overflowing goodness of God, that all were elected by him, and had their names written in the book of life, who he foresaw would yield to the influences of his grace, and, by the coöperation therewith, "make their calling and election sure."

This scheme appears to possess the following very great advantages:—

1. It does not give such a pervading energy to the operations of divine grace as to exclude all subordinate moral agency from the world, and destroy the very foundation of man's accountability.

2. It does not weaken the motives to the practice of a virtuous and decent life, by assuring the worst part of mankind that they are just as likely to be made the objects of the saving grace of God as any others. On the contrary, it holds out this terrible warning, that by an obstinate continuance in evil-doing, the wicked may place themselves beyond the effectual influences of divine grace, and set the seal of eternal death to their own souls.

3. It shows the mercy of God to be infinite. No one, except those who place themselves beyond the possibility of salvation by their own evil deeds, is ever lost. Hence, the mercy of God, which takes in all whose salvation is within the range of possibility, appears in full-orbed and unclouded splendour. It could not possibly appear greater, or more beautiful, than as it presents itself to our view in this scheme.

4. It shows the justice of God to be infinite. This, according to the above view, is neither limited by, nor does it limit, the mercy of God. It acts merely upon those who were not, and never could be made, the objects of mercy; and it acts upon these according to the full measure of their ill-desert, as well as according to the exigencies of the moral empire of God. It has no limits, except those which circumscribe and bound the objects of infinite justice.

5. It not only shows the mercy and justice of God to be as great as can possibly be conceived, but it also shows the perfect harmony and agreement which subsists between these sublime attributes of the Divine Being. It marks out and defines the orbit, in which each revolves in all the perfection and plenitude of its glory, without the least clashing or interference with the other.

In conclusion, we would simply ask the candid and impartial reader, Does any dark or perplexing "cloud still hang over the subject?" Is "there a difficulty in reconciling the mind to a system," which exhibits the character of God, and his government of the world, in so pleasing and so advantageous a light? Does not a system, which gives so glad and joyous a response to the demand of God, "Are not my ways equal?" recommend itself to the affections of the pious mind?

It very clearly seems to us, that, strong as are the convictions of Dr. Chalmers in favour of "a rigid and absolute predestination,"* his affections cannot always be restrained within the narrow confines of so dark a scheme. His language, in pleading for the universality of the gospel offer, contains, it seems to us, as direct, and pointed, and powerful condemnation of his own scheme as can well be found in the whole range of theological literature. "There must be," says he, "a sad misunderstanding somewhere. The commission put into our hands is to go and preach the gospel to every creature under heaven; and the announcement sounded forth in the world from heaven's vault was, Peace on earth, *good-will to men.* There is no freezing limitation here, but a largeness and munificence of mercy boundless as space, free and open as the expanse of the firmament. We hope, therefore, the gospel, the real gospel, *is as unlike the views of some of its interpreters, as creation, in all its boundless extent and beauty, is unlike the paltry scheme of some wretched scholastic in the middle ages.* The middle age of science and civilization is now terminated; but Christianity also had its middle age, *and this, perhaps, is not yet fully terminated.* There is *still a remainder of the old spell,* even the spell of human authority, and by which a certain cramp or confinement has been laid on the genius of Christianity. We cannot doubt that the time of its complete emancipation is coming, when it shall break loose from the imprisonment in which it is held; but meanwhile there is, as it were, a stricture upon it, not yet wholly removed, *and in virtue of which the largeness and liberality of Heaven's own purposes have been made to descend in partial and scanty droppings through the strainers of an artificial theology, instead of falling, as they ought, in a universal shower upon the world.*"†

Is it possible, that this is the language of a man who believes that Heaven's purposes of mercy descend, not upon all men, but only upon the elect? It is even so. Boundless and beautiful as the goodness of God is in itself; yet, through the strainers of

* Institutes of Theology. † Institutes of Theology, vol. ii, ch. vii.

his theology, is it made to descend in partial and scanty droppings merely, and not in one universal shower. It is good-will, not to *men*, but to the *elect*. Such is the "chilling limitation," and such the frightful "stricture," on the genius of Christianity, from which, in the fervour of his imagination, the great heart of Chalmers burst into a higher and a more genial element of light and love.

Alas! how sad and how sudden the descent, when in the very next paragraph he says: "The names and number of the saved may have been in the view, *nay, even in the design and destination of God from all eternity;* and still the distinction is carried into effect, not by means of a gospel addressed partially and exclusively to them, but by means of a gospel addressed generally to all. *A partial gospel, in fact, could not have achieved the conversion of the elect:*" that is to say, though it was the design and destination of God from all eternity to save only a small portion of those whom he might have saved; yet he made the offer of salvation to all, in order to save the chosen few! And if he had not proclaimed this universal offer, by which "the largeness and munificence" of his mercy are made to *appear* as "boundless as space," the elect could not have been saved! If so, is it the real goodness of God, then, or merely the *appearance* of universal goodness, that leadeth men to repentance?

"Any charm," says he, "which there is in Christianity to recall or to regenerate *some*, lies in those of its overtures which are so framed as to hold out the offered friendship of God to all:"* that is, that although God intends and seeks to save only a few, he offers the same salvation to all, to give an efficacious charm to the scheme of redemption! Indeed, if the Calvinistic scheme of an absolute predestination be true, then we admit that there is a charm and a glory in the magnificent delusion, arising from God's offer of friendship to all, which is not to be found in the truth. But that scheme, as we have seen, is not true; and also, that the goodness of God is as boundless and beautiful in reality, as it could possibly be in appearance.

We agree with Dr. Chalmers, that the goodness of God should be viewed, not through the medium of predestination, but as it

* Institutes of Theology, vol. ii, ch. vii.

shines forth in the light of the glorious gospel. We agree with him, that "we ought to proceed on the obvious representations which Scripture gives of the Deity; and *these beheld in their own immediate light, untinged by the dogma of predestination. God waiting to be gracious—God not willing that any should perish, but that all should come to repentance—God swearing by himself that he has no pleasure in the death of a sinner, but rather that all should come unto him and live—God beseeching men to enter into reconciliation, and this not as elect, but simply and generally as men and sinners;*—these are the attitudes in which the Father of the human family sets himself forth unto the world—these the terms in which he speaks to us from heaven." It is precisely in this sublime attitude, and in this transporting light, that we rejoice to contemplate the Father of mercies; and this view, it must be confessed, is wholly "untinged with the dogma of predestination."

CONCLUSION.

A SUMMARY VIEW OF THE PRINCIPLES AND ADVANTAGES OF THE FOREGOING SYSTEM.

There is a lamp within the lofty dome
  Of the dim world, whose radiance clear doth show
Its awful beauty; and, through the wide gloom,
  Make all its obscure mystic symbols glow
With pleasing light,—that we may see and know
  The glorious world, and all its wondrous scheme;
Not as distorted in the mind below,
  Nor in philosopher's, nor poet's dream,
  But as it was, and is, high in the Mind Supreme.

ANON.

CONCLUSION.

I.

SUMMARY OF THE FIRST PART OF THE FOREGOING SYSTEM.

The commonly received systems of theology are, it is confessed by their advocates, attended with manifold inconveniences and difficulties. The habit of mind by which, notwithstanding such difficulties, it clings to the great truths of those systems, is worthy of all admiration, and forms one of the best guarantees of the stability and progress of human knowledge. For in every department of science the great truths which dawn upon the mind are usually attended with a cloud of difficulties, and, but for the habit in question, they would soon be permitted to fade away, and be lost in their original obscurity. Copernicus has, therefore, been justly applauded,* not only for conceiving, but for firmly grasping the heliocentric theory of the world, notwithstanding the many formidable objections which it had to encounter in his own mind. Even the sublime law of the material universe, before it finally established itself in the mind of Newton, more than once fell, in its struggles for acceptance, beneath the apparently insuperable objections by which it was attended; and, after all, the overpowering evidence which caused it to be embraced, still left it surrounded by an immense penumbra of difficulties. These, together with the sublime truth, he bequeathed to his successors. They have retained the truth, and removed the difficulties. In like manner, admirable though the habit of clinging to every sufficiently accredited truth may be, yet, whether in the physical or in the moral sciences, the effort to disencumber the truth of the difficulties by which its progress is embarrassed should never be remitted.

* Whewell's History of the Inductive Sciences, vol. i.

The scientific impulse, by which a great truth is grasped, and established upon its own appropriate evidence, should ever be followed by the subordinate movement, which strives to remove every obstacle out of the way, and cause it to secure a wider and a brighter dominion in the human mind. And in proportion as any scheme, whether in relation to natural or to divine things, shall, without a sacrifice or mutilation of the truth, divest itself of the darkness which must ever accompany all one-sided and partial views, will it possess a decided advantage and superiority over other systems. Since this general principle will not be denied, let us proceed, in conclusion, to take a brief survey of the foregoing scheme of doctrine, and determine, if we can, whether to any truth it has given any such advantage.

It clearly seems free from the stupendous cloud of difficulties that overhang that view of the moral universe which supposes its entire constitution and government to be in accordance with the scheme of necessity. These difficulties pertain, first, to the responsibility of man; secondly, to the purity of God; and, thirdly, to the reality of moral distinctions. These three several branches of the difficulty in question have been respectively considered in the first three chapters of the first part of the present work; and we shall now briefly recapitulate the views therein presented, in the three following sections.

SECTION I.

The scheme of necessity denies that man is the responsible author of sin.

If, according to this scheme, all things in heaven and earth, the volitions of the human mind not excepted, be under the dominion of necessitating causes, then may we well ask, How can man be a free and responsible agent? To this inquiry the most illustrious advocates of the scheme in question have not been able to return a coherent or satisfactory reply. After the search of ages, and the joint labour of all their gigantic intellects, they have found no position in their system on which the freedom of the human mind may be securely planted. The position set up for this purpose by one is pulled down by another, who, in his turn, indicates some other position only to be demolished by some other advocate of his own scheme. The more we look into their writings on this subject, the more irreconcilable seems the conflict of opinion in which they are among themselves involved. The more closely we contemplate the labour of their hands, the more clearly we perceive that all their attempts, in opposition to the voice of heaven and earth, to rear the great metaphysical tower of necessity, have only ended in an utter confusion of tongues. So far, indeed, are they from having found and presented any such view of the freedom and responsibility of man, as shall, by the intrinsic and overpowering lustre of its evidence, stand some chance to disarm the enemies of God, that they have not even found one in which they themselves can rest. The school of the necessitarian is, in reality, a house divided against itself; and that, too, in regard to the most vital and fundamental point of its philosophy.

There seems to be one exception to the truth of this general remark: for there is one scheme or definition of liberty, in which many, if not most, of the advocates of necessity have concurred; that is, the definition of Hobbes. As the current of a river, says he, is free to flow down its channel, provided there be no obstruction in the way; so the human will, though compelled to act by causes over which it has no control, is free, provided there be no external impediment to prevent its volition from passing into effect. This idea of the freedom of the will, though much older than Hobbes, is primarily indebted to his influence for its prevalence in modern times; for it descended from Hobbes to Locke, from Locke to Edwards, and from Edwards to the modern school of Calvinistic divines.

No matter how we come by our volitions, says Edwards, yet are we perfectly free when there is no external impediment to hinder our volitions from passing into effect: that is to say, though our volitions be absolutely produced by the divine omnipotence itself, or in any other way; yet is the will free, provided no external cause interpose to prevent its volition from moving the body. According to this definition of the liberty of the will, it is not a *property* of the soul at all, but only an *accidental* circumstance or condition of the body. In the significant language of Leibnitz, it is not the freedom of the mind; it is merely "elbow-room." It consists not in an attribute, or property, or power of the soul, but only in the external opportunity which its necessitated volitions may have to necessitate an effect. We ask, How can the mind be free? and they tell us, When the body may be so! We inquire about an *attribute* of the spiritual principle within, and they turn us off with an answer respecting an *accident* of the material principle without! An *ignoratio elenchi* more flagrant—a mistaking of the question more palpable—it is surely not possible to conceive. Yet this definition of the freedom of the will, though so superficially false, is precisely that which has found the most general acceptance among necessitarians. Though vehemently condemned by Calvin himself, unanswerably refuted by Leibnitz, sneered at by Edwards the younger, and pronounced utterly inadequate by Dr. John Dick; yet, as we have seen, is it now held up as "the Calvinistic idea of the freedom of the will."

We do not wonder that such a definition of free-will should have been adopted by atheizing philosophers, such as Hume and Hobbes, for example; because we cannot suppose them to have been penetrated with any very profound design to uphold the cause of human responsibility, or to vindicate the immaculate purity of the divine glory. But that it should have been accepted with such unquestioning simplicity by a large body of Christian divines, having the great interests of the moral world at heart, is, we cannot but think, a sufficient ground for the most profound astonishment and regret; for, surely, to plant the great cause of human responsibility on a foundation so slender, on a fallacy so palpable, on a position so utterly untenable, is to expose it to the victorious assaults of its weakest enemy and invader.

SECTION II.

The scheme of necessity makes God the author of sin.

The necessitarian, in his attempts to vindicate the purity of God, has not been more successful than in his endeavours to establish the freedom and accountability of man. If, according to his scheme, the Supreme Ruler of the world be the primal cause of all things, the volitions of men included; it certainly seems exceedingly difficult to conceive, that he is not implicated in the sin of the world. And this difficulty, so appalling at first view, remains just as great after all that the most enlightened advocates of that scheme have advanced as it was before.

We have witnessed the efforts of a Leibnitz, an Edwards, and a Chalmers, to repel this objection to the scheme of necessity; and if we mistake not, we have seen how utterly ineffectual they have proved to break its force, or resist its influence. The sum and substance of that defence is, as we have seen, that God may do evil that good may come; a defence which, instead of vindicating the purity of the divine proceeding, represents it as having been governed by the most corrupt maxim of the most corrupt system of casuistry the world has ever seen. It darkens, rather than illuminates, that profound and portentous obscurity of the system of the world, arising from the origin and existence of moral evil. So far from removing the difficulty from their scheme, they have only illustrated its force by the ineffable weakness of the means and methods which that scheme has necessitated them to employ for its destruction.

SECTION III.

The scheme of necessity denies the reality of moral distinctions.

For, if all things in the world, the acts of the will not excepted, be produced by an extraneous agency, it seems clear that it is absurd to attach praise or blame to men on account of their volitions. Nothing appears more self-evident than the position, that whatever is thus produced in us can neither be our virtue nor our vice. The advocates of necessity, at least those of them who do not admit the inference in question, invoke the aid of logic to extinguish the light of the principle on which it is based. But where have they found, or where can they find, a principle more clear, more simple, or more unquestionable on which to ground their arguments? Where, in the whole armory of logic, can be found a principle more unquestionable than this, that no man can be to praise or to blame for that which is produced in him, by causes over which he had no control?

We have examined those arguments in detail, and exhibited the principles on which they proceed. Those principles, instead of being of such a nature as to subserve the purposes of valid argument, are either insignificant truisms which prove nothing, or else they reach the point in dispute only by means of an ambiguity of words. Of the first description is the celebrated maxim of Edwards, that *the essence of virtue and vice consists in their nature, and not in their cause.* By which he means, that no matter how we come by our virtue and vice, though they be produced in us according to the scheme of necessity, yet are they our virtue and vice. If a horse should fall from the moon, it would be a horse: for no matter where it comes from, *a horse is a horse;* or, more scientifically expressed, the essence of a horse consists in the nature of a horse, and not in its origin or cause. All this is very true. But then, we no more believe that horses fall from the moon, than we do that virtue and vice are produced according to the scheme of necessity.

Of the last description is that other maxim of Edwards, that men are adjudged virtuous or vicious on account of actions proceeding from the will, without considering how they came by their volition. True, we may judge of *external* actions according as their origin is in the will or otherwise, without considering how its volitions come to pass; but then this is because we proceed on the tacit assumption that the will is free, and not under the dominion of necessitating causes. But the question relates, not to external actions or movements of the body, but to the volitions of the mind itself. And this being the case, it does make a vast difference in our estimate, whether we consider those volitions as coming to pass freely; or whether, according to the scheme of necessity, we regard them as being produced by the operation of causes over which we have no control. In this case, it is impossible for the human mind to attach praise or blame to them, or view them as constituting either virtue or vice. For nothing can be plainer than the position, that if anything in us be produced by the mighty and irresistible operation of an extraneous agency, it can neither be our virtue nor vice. This principle is so clear, that logic can neither add to nor detract from the intrinsic lustre of its evidence. And all the cloudy sophistications of an Edwards, ingenious as they are, can obscure it only to the minds of those who have not sufficient penetration to see through the nature of his arguments.

At this point, then, as well as at others, the scheme of necessity, instead of clearing up the old, has introduced new difficulties into the system of the world. Instead of diffusing light, it has actually extended the empire of darkness, by investing in the clouds and mists of its own raising, some of the brightest elements which enter into its organization. By scholastic refinements and sophistical devices, it has sought to overturn and destroy, not the elements of error and confusion, but some of the clearest and most indestructible intuitional convictions of the human head and heart.

But great as these difficulties are, we may still be asked to embrace the scheme from which they flow, on the ground that it is true. Indeed, this is the course pursued by some of the most enlightened Calvinistic necessitarians of the present day. Freely admitting that all the attempts of Leibnitz, of Edwards, and others, to bring the scheme of necessity into an agreement with the dictates of reason, have left its stupendous difficulties pretty much where they found them—wrapped in impenetrable gloom; they nevertheless maintain this scheme, and propose it to our acceptance, on the sole and sufficient ground of its evidence. If we may judge from those of their writings which we have seen, this course of proceeding is getting to be very much the fashion among the Calvinists of the present day; and they have a great deal to say in praise of simply adhering to the truth, without being over-solicitous about its difficulties, or paying too much attention to them. That man, say they, is in imminent danger of heresy who, instead of receiving the truth with the simplicity of a little child, goes about to worry himself with its difficulties. He walks in dark and slippery places. We agree with them in this, and commend their wisdom: for it presents the only chance which their system has of retaining its hold on the human mind. But before accepting this scheme on the ground of its evidence, we have deemed it prudent to look into the very interior of the scheme itself, and weigh the evidence on which it is so confidently recommended.

SECTION IV.

The moral world not constituted according to the scheme of necessity.

In the prosecution of this inquiry, we have appeared to ourselves to find, that this boasted scheme of necessity is neither more nor less than one grand tissue of sophisms. We have found, we believe, that this huge imposition on the reason of man is a vile congregation of pestilential errors, through which, if the glory of God and his marvellous ways be contemplated, they must appear most horribly distorted. We have found that this scheme is as weak and crazy in the mechanism of its internal structure as it is frightful in its consequences. Instead of that closely articulated body of thought, which we were led to expect therein, we have found little more than a jumble of incoherences, a semi-chaotic mass of plausible blunders. We have seen and shown, we trust, that this grand and imposing scheme of necessity is, in reality, based on a false psychology, —directed against a false issue,—supported by false logic,—fortified by false conceptions,—recommended by false analogies, —and rendered plausible by a false phraseology. And, besides, we have ascertained that it originates in a false method, and terminates in a false religion. As such, we deem it far better adapted to represent the little, narrow, dark, crooked, and perverted world within, than the great and all-glorious world of God without. So have we not spared its deformities.

SECTION V.

The relation between the human agency and the divine.

Having got rid of the scheme of necessity, which opposed so many obstacles to the prosecution of our design, we were then prepared to investigate the great problem of evil: but, before entering on this subject, we paused to consider the difficulty which, in all ages, the human mind has found in attempting to reconcile the influence of the Divine Spirit with the freedom of the will. In regard to this difficulty, it has been made to appear, we trust, that we need not understand *how* the Spirit of God acts, in order to reconcile his influence with the free-agency of man. We need to know, not how the one Spirit acts on the other, but only what is done by each, in order to see a perfect agreement and harmony in their coöperation. The inquiry relates, then, to the precise thing done by each, and not to the *modus operandi*. Having, in opposition to the commonly received notion, ascertained this to be the difficulty, we have found it comparatively easy of solution.

For the improved psychology of the present day, which gives so clear and steady a view of the simple facts of consciousness, has enabled us to see what may, and what may not, be produced by an extraneous agency. This again has enabled us to make out and define the sphere of the divine power, as well as that of the human; and to determine the point at which they come into contact, without interfering with or intersecting each other.

The same means have also shown us, that the opposite errors of Pelagianism and Augustinism have a common root in a false psychology. The psychology of the past, which identifies the passive states of the sensibility with the active states of the will, is common to both of these schemes. From this common root the two doctrines branch out in opposite directions; the one on the side of the mind's activity, and the other on that of its passivity. Each perceives only one phase of the complex whole, and denies the reality of the other. With one, the active phase is the whole; with the other, the passive impression is the whole. Hence the one recognises the human power alone; while the other causes this power entirely to disappear beneath the overshadowing influence of the divine.

Now the foregoing system, by availing itself of the psychology of the present day, not only does not cause the one of these great facts to exclude the other, but, by showing their logical coherency and agreement, it removes the temptation that the speculative reason has ever felt to do such violence to the cause of truth. It embraces the half views of both schemes, and moulds them into one great and full-orbed truth. In the great theandric work of regeneration, in particular, it neither causes the human element to exclude the divine, nor the divine to swallow up the human; but preserves each in its integrity, and both in their harmonious union and coöperation. The mutual inter-dependency, and the undisturbed inter-working, of these all-important elements of the moral world, it aims to place on a firm basis, and exhibit in a clear light. If this object has been accomplished, though but in part, or by way of a first approximation only, it will be conceded to be no small gain, or advantage, to the cause of truth.

SECTION VI.

The existence of moral evil consistent with the infinite purity of God.

The relation of the foregoing treatise to the great problem of the spiritual world, concerning the origin and existence of evil, may be easily indicated, and the solution it proposes distinguished from that of others. This may be best done, perhaps, with the aid of logical forms.

The world, created by an infinitely perfect Being, says the sceptic, must needs be the best of all possible worlds: but the actual world is not the best of all possible worlds: therefore it was not created by an infinitely perfect Being. Now in replying to this argument, no theist denies the major premiss. All have conceded, that the idea of an infinitely perfect Being necessarily implies the existence and preservation of the greatest possible perfection in the created universe. In the two celebrated works of M. Leibnitz and Archbishop King, both put forth in reply to Bayle, this admission is repeatedly and distinctly made. This seems to have been rightly done; for, in the language of Cudworth, "To believe a God, is to believe the existence of all possible good and perfection in the universe."*

In this, says Leibnitz, is embosomed all possible good. But how is this point established? "We judge from the event itself," says he; "*since God has made it, it was not possible to have made a better.*"† But this is the language of faith, and not of reason. As an argument addressed to the sceptic, it is radically unsound; for as a medium of proof, it employs the very thing in dispute, namely, that God is infinitely perfect. Hence this is a *petitio principii*, a begging of the question. If this were all that M. Leibnitz had to offer, he might as well have believed, and remained silent.

But this was not all. He endeavours to show, that the world is absolutely perfect, without inferring its perfection from the assumed infinite perfection of its Author. At first view, this does not appear to be so; for the sin and misery which overflow this lower part of the world seem to detract from the perfection and beauty of the whole. Not so, says Leibnitz: "there are some disorders in the parts, which marvellously heighten the beauty of the whole; as certain discords, skilfully employed, render the harmony more exquisite."‡ Considered as an argument, this is likewise quite unsatisfactory. It is, in fact, merely the light of the imagination, playing over the bosom of the cloud; not the concentrated blaze of the intelli-

* Intellectual System, vol. ii, p. 349. † Théodicée, Abrégé de la Controverse.
‡ Ibid.

gence, dispelling its gloom. And besides, this analogy proceeds on a false principle; inasmuch as it supposes that God has himself introduced sin into the world, with a view to its happy effects. We could sooner believe, indeed, that the principle of evil had introduced harmony into the world in order to heighten the frightful effects of its discord, than that the principle of all good had produced the frightful discord of the world, in order to enhance the effects of its harmony. But we shall let all such fine sayings pass. Perhaps they were intended as the ornaments of faith, rather than as the radiant armour and the invincible weapons of reason.

Though Leibnitz frequently insists, that "the permission of evil tends to the good of the universe,"* he does not always seem to mean that evil would be better than holiness in its stead; but that the permission of sin is not so great an inconvenience as would be its universal prevention. "We ought to say," says he, "that God permits sin, because otherwise he would himself do a worse action (*une action pire*) than all the sin of his creatures."† But what is this worse, this more unreasonable action of which God would be guilty, if he should prevent all sin? One bad feature thereof would be, according to Leibnitz, that it would interfere with the freedom of the will. In his "Abrégé de la Controverse," he says: "We have added, after many good authors, that it is in conformity with the general order and good, for God to leave to certain creatures an occasion for the exercise of their liberty." This argument comes with a bad grace from one who has already denied the liberty of the will; and, indeed, from the very form of his expression, Leibnitz seems to have adopted it from authority, rather than from a perception of any support it derives from his own principles. He asserts the freedom of the will, it is true, but he does this, as we have seen, only in opposition to the "absolute necessity" of Hobbes and Spinoza; according to whom nothing in the universe could possibly have been otherwise than it is. In his "Reflexions sur le Livre de Hobbes," he says, that although the will is determined in all cases by the divine omnipotence, yet is it free from an absolute or mathematical necessity, "because *the contrary volition might happen without implying a contradiction.*" True, the contrary volition might happen

* Abrégé de la Controverse. † Reflexions sur le Livre de Hobbes.

without implying a contradiction; for God himself might cause it to exist. And if, by his almighty and irresistible power, he should cause it to exist, the will would still be free in Leibnitz's sense of the word; since its contrary might have happened. Hence, according to this definition of liberty, if God should, in all cases, determine the will to good, it would nevertheless be free; since the contrary determination might have been produced by his power. In other words, if such be the liberty of the will, no operation of the Almighty could possibly interfere therewith; as no volition produced by him would have rendered it impossible for him to have caused the opposite volition, if he had so chosen and exerted his omnipotence for that purpose. This defence of the divine procedure, then, has no foundation in the scheme of Leibnitz; and the only thing he can say in its favour is, that after the authority "of many good authors," we have added it to our own views.

Archbishop King, too, as is well known, assumes the ground that God permits sin, on account of the greater inconvenience that would result to the world from an interference with the freedom of the will. But so extravagant are his views respecting this freedom, that the position in question is one of the weakest parts of his system. The mind chooses objects, says he, not because they please it; but they are agreeable and pleasant to the mind, because it chooses them. Surely, such a liberty as this, consisting in a mere arbitrary or capricious movement of the soul, that owns not the guidance of reason, or wisdom, or anything apparently good, cannot possess so great a value that the moral good of the universe should be permitted to suffer, rather than that it should be interfered with or restrained.

But these are merely *argumenta ad hominem*. There are "many good authors" who, although they maintain neither of the above views of liberty, insist that it is better for God to permit sin, than to interfere with the freedom of his creatures. But is it clear, that greater inconveniences would have arisen from such an interference, than from the frightful reign of all the sin and misery that have afflicted the world? If God can so easily prevent all sin, and secure all holiness, by restraining the liberty of his creatures, is it clear, that in preferring their unrestrained freedom to the highest moral good of the universe, he makes a choice worthy of his infinite wisdom? In other words, is it not more desirable that moral evil should everywhere disappear, and the beauty of holiness everywhere shine forth, than that the creature should be left to abuse his liberty by the introduction of sin and death into the world? Besides, it is admitted by all the authors in question, that God sometimes interposes the arm of his omnipotence, in order to the production of holiness. Now, in such an exertion of his power, he either interferes with the freedom of the creature, or he does not. If he does not interfere with that freedom, why may he not produce holiness in other cases also, without any such interference? And if, in some cases, he does interfere therewith, in order to secure the holiness of his creatures, why should he not, in all cases, prefer their highest moral good to so fatal an abuse of their prerogatives? Is his proceeding therein merely arbitrary and capricious, or is it governed by the best of reasons? Undoubtedly by the best of reasons, say all the authors in question: but then, when we come to this point of the inquiry, they always tell us, that those reasons are profoundly concealed in the unsearchable depths of the divine wisdom; that is to say, they believe them to be the best, not because they have seen and considered them, but because they are the reasons of an infinitely perfect mind. Now, all this is very well; but it is not to the purpose. It is to retire from the arena of logic, and fall back on the very point in dispute for support. It is not to argue; it is simply to drop the weapons of our warfare, and oppose the shield of faith to the shafts of the adversary.

It is also contended by Leibnitz and King, as well as many other good authors, that there is an established order, or system of laws, in the government of the world; into which so great a confusion would be introduced by the interposition of divine power to prevent all sin, that some had better be permitted. This, which Leibnitz so positively asserts, is thrown out as a conjecture by Bishop Butler.* But in the present controversy, it is not to the point. For here the question is concerning the order and government of the moral world itself. And this being the question, it is not admissible for one of the parties to say, that the proposed plan for the government of the world is not the best, because it would interfere with and disturb the

* Analogy, part i, chap. vii.

arrangements of that which is established. This is clearly to beg the question. It is to assume that the established method is the best, and therefore should not have been superseded by another; but this is the very point in dispute.

The truth is, that the theist has assailed the sceptic in his strong and impregnable point, and left the vulnerable part of his system untouched. This may be easily seen. The objection of the sceptic is thus stated by Leibnitz: Whoever can prevent the sin of another, and does not, but rather contributes to it by his concourse and by the occasions he gives rise to, though he possesses a perfect knowledge, is an accomplice. God can prevent the sin of his intelligent creatures: but he does it not, though his knowledge be perfect, and contributes to it by his concourse and the occasions to which he gives rise: therefore he is an accomplice. Now Leibnitz admits the minor, and denies the major, premiss of this argument. He should have done the contrary. For, admitting that God might easily prevent sin, and cause holiness to reign universally, what had he left to oppose to the attacks of the sceptic but the shield of faith? He might say, indeed, as he often does, that God voluntarily permits sin, because it is a part and parcel of the best possible universe. But how easy for the sceptic to demand, What good purpose does it answer? Can it add to the holiness or happiness of the universe? Cannot these high ends, these glorious purposes of the Divine Being, be as well attained by the universal rectitude and purity of his creatures, as by any other means? Cannot the Supreme Ruler of the world, in the resources of his infinite mind, bring as much good out of holiness as can be brought out of sin? And if so, why permit sin in order to the good of the creation? Are not the perfect holiness and happiness of each and every part of the moral world better for each and every part thereof than are their contraries? And if so, are they not better for the whole? By this reply, the theist is, in our opinion, disarmed, and the sceptic victorious. Hence we say, that the former should have conceded the major, and denied the minor, premiss of the above argument; that is, he should have admitted, that whoever can prevent the sin of another, but, instead of so doing, contributes to it by his concourse, is an accomplice: and he should have denied that God, being able to produce holiness in the place of sin, both permits and contributes to the reign of the latter in his dominions. The theist should have denied this, we say, if he would have raised the ever-blessed God above all contact with sin, and placed his cause upon high and impregnable ground, far above the attacks of the sceptic. But as it is, he has placed that cause upon false grounds, and thereby exposed it to the successful shafts of the adversary.

Another reason assigned by Leibnitz* and King† for the permission of moral evil is, that if God should interpose to prevent it, this would be to work a constant and universal miracle. But if such a thing were possible, why should he not work such a miracle? By these authors themselves it is conceded, that the Almighty often works a miracle for the production of moral good; and, this being the case, why should he not exhibit this miracle on the most grand and magnificent scale of which it is possible to conceive? In other words, why should he not render it worthy of his infinite wisdom, and power, and goodness? Is it not by a like miracle, by a like universal interposition of his power, that the majestic fabric of the material globe is upheld, and the sublime movement of all its countless orbs continually carried on? And if so, are not the order and harmony of the moral universe as worthy such an exercise of his omnipotence as are the regularity and beauty of the material? We defend the Divine Author and Preserver of all things on no such grounds. We say that a universal holiness is not produced by the omnipresent energy of his power, not because this would be to work a miracle, but because it would be to work a contradiction.

But we are becoming weary of such replies. The very question is, *Why* is there not a universal interposition of the divine power? and the reply, Because this would be a universal interposition of the divine power! What is all this but a grand attempt to solve the awful mystery of the world, which ends in the assurance that God does not universally interpose to prevent sin, because he does not universally interpose to prevent it? Or, in fewer words, that he does not, because he does not?

Since sin exists, says the sceptic, it follows that God is either unable or unwilling to prevent it. "Able, but *unwilling*," re-

* Remarques sur Le Livre de M. King, sec. xvi.

† Origin of Evil, vol. ii, ch. v, sec. v.

plies the theist. Such is the answer which has come down to us from the earliest times; from a Lactantius to a Leibnitz, and from a Leibnitz to a M'Cosh. No wonder that in all this time they have not been able to find the reason why God is unwilling to prevent sin; since, in truth and reality, he is infinitely more than willing to do so.

But, saying that he is willing, shall we concede that he is unable? By no means: for such language implies that the power of God is limited, and he is omnipotent. We choose to impale ourselves upon neither horn of the dilemma. We are content to leave M. Bayle upon the one, and M. Voltaire upon the other, while we bestow our company elsewhere. In plain English, we neither reply unwilling nor unable.

We do say, however, that although God is infinitely willing to secure the existence of universal holiness, to the exclusion of all sin, yet such a thing is not an object of power, and therefore cannot be produced by omnipotence itself. The production of holiness by the application of power is, as we have seen, an absurd and impossible conceit, which may exist in the brain of man, but which can never be embodied in the fair and orderly creation of God. It can no more be realized by the Divine Omnipotence than a mathematical absurdity can be caused to be true.

Hence, we no longer ask why God permits sin. This were to seek a ground and reason of that which has no existence, except in the imagination of man. God does not permit sin. He chooses it not, and he permits it not, as an essential part of the best possible universe. Sin is that which his soul abhors, and which all the perfections of his nature, his infinite power and wisdom, no less than his holiness, are pledged to wipe out from the face of his creation. He does not cause, he does not tolerate sin, on account of its happy effects, or on account of the uses to which it may be turned. The only word he has for such a thing is *woe;* and the only attitude he bears toward it is one of eternal and inexorable vengeance. All the schemes of men make light of sin; but God is in earnest, infinitely and immutably in earnest, in the purpose to root out and destroy the odious thing, that it may have no place amid the glory of his dominions.

As sin did not originate by his permission, so it does not continue by his sufferance. He permits it, indeed, in that he permits the existence of beings capable of sinning; and he permits the existence of such beings in the very act of permitting the existence of those who are capable of knowing, and loving, and serving him. An infinitely good Being, says M. Bayle, would not have conferred on his creature the fatal power to do evil. But he did not reflect that a power to do good is, *ex necessitate rei*, a power to do evil. Surely, a good Being would bestow on his creature the power to do good—the power to become like himself, and to partake of the incommunicable blessedness of a holy will. But if he would bestow this, he would certainly confer power to do evil; for the one is identical with the other. And sin has arisen, not from any power conferred for that purpose, but from that which constitutes the brightest element in the sublime structure and glory of the moral world. It arises, not from any imperfection in the work of God, but from that without which it would have been infinitely less than perfect.

"All divines admit," says Bayle, "that God can infallibly produce a good act of the will in a human soul without depriving it of the use of liberty."* This is no longer admitted. We call it in question. We deny that such an act can be produced, either with or without depriving the soul of liberty. We deny that it can be produced at all: for whatever God may produce in the human soul, this is not, this cannot be, the moral goodness or virtue of the soul in which it is produced. In other words, it is not, and it cannot be, an object of praise or of moral approbation in him in whom it is thus caused to exist. His virtue or moral goodness can exist only by reason, and in case of an exercise of his own will. It can no more be the effect of an extraneous force than two and two can be made equal to five.

In conclusion, the plain truth is, that the actual universe is not in the best of all possible conditions; for we might conceive it to be better than it is. If there were no sin and no suffering, but everywhere a purity and bliss as great as it is possible to conceive, this would be a vast improvement in the actual state of the universe. Such is the magnificent dream of the sceptic; and, as we have seen, it is not without truth and justice that he thus dreams. But with this dream of his, mag-

* Dictionary, Article Paulicians.

nificent as it is, there is connected another which is infinitely false: for he imagines that the sublime spectacle of a world without sin, that the beatific vision of a universe robed in stainless splendour might have been realized by the Divine Omnipotence; whereas, this could have been realized only by the universal and continued coöperation of the whole intelligent creation with the grand design of God. On the other hand, the theist, by conceding the error and contesting the truth of the sceptic, has inextricably entangled himself in the toils of the adversary.

The only remaining question which the sceptic has to ask is, that since God might have prevented moral evil by the creation of no beings who he foresaw would sin, why did he create such beings? Why did he not leave all such uncreated, and call into existence only such as he foreknew would obey his law, and become like himself in purity and bliss? This question has been fully answered both from reason and revelation. We have shown that the highest good of the universe required the creation of such beings. We have shown that it is by his dealings with the sinner that the foundation of his spiritual empire is secured, and its boundaries enlarged. In particular, we have shown, from revelation, that it is by the redemption of a fallen world that all unfallen worlds are preserved in their allegiance to his throne, and kept warm in the bosom of his blessedness.

If the sceptic should complain that this is to meet him, not with weapons drawn from the armory of reason, but from that of revelation, our reply is at hand: he has no longer anything left to be met. His argument, which assumes that a Being of infinite power could easily cause holiness to exist, has been shown to be false. This very assumption, this major premiss, which has been so long conceded to him, has been taken out of his hands, and demolished. Hence, we do not oppose the shield of faith to his argument; we hold it in triumph over his exploded sophism. We merely recall our faith, and exult in the divine glory which it so magnificently brings to view, and against which his once blind and blundering reason has now no more to say.

II.

SUMMARY OF THE SECOND PART OF THE FOREGOING SYSTEM.

Having reconciled the existence of sin with the purity of God, and refuted the objections against the principles on which that reconciliation is based, we next proceeded to the second part of the work, in which the natural evil, or suffering, that afflicts humanity, is shown to be consistent with his goodness. This part consists of five chapters, of whose leading principles and position we shall now proceed to take a rapid survey in the remaining sections of the present chapter.

SECTION I.

God desires the salvation of all men.

The fact that all men are not saved, at first view, seems inconsistent with the goodness of the Divine Being, and the sincerity of his endeavours for their conversion. We naturally ask, that if God could so easily cause all men to turn and live, why should he in vain call upon them to do so? Is he really sincere in the use of means for the salvation of all, since he permits so many to hold out in their rebellion and perish? In other words, if he really and sincerely seeks the salvation of all, why are not all saved? This is confessedly one of the most perplexing and confounding difficulties which attach to the commonly received systems of theology. It constitutes one of those profound obscurities from which, it is admitted, theology has not been able to extricate itself, and come out into the clear light of the divine glory.

By many theologians this difficulty, instead of being solved, is most fearfully aggravated. Luther, for example, finds it so great, that he denies the sincerity of God in calling upon sinners to forsake their evil ways and live; and that, as addressed to the finally impenitent, his language is that of mockery and scorn. And Calvin imagines that such exhortations, as well as the other means of grace offered to all, are designed, not for the real conversion of those who shall finally perish, but to enhance their guilt, and overwhelm them in the more fearful condemnation. If it were possible to go even one step beyond such doctrines, that step is taken by President Edwards: for he is so far from supposing that God really intends to lead all men into a conformity with his revealed will, that he contends that God possesses another and a secret will by which, for some good purpose, he chooses their sin, and infallibly brings it to pass. If any mind be not appalled by such doctrines, and chilled with horror, surely nothing can be too monstrous for its credulity, provided only it relate to the divine sovereignty.

The Arminian with indignation rejects such views of the divine glory. But does he escape the great difficulty in question? If God forms the design, says he, not to save all men, he is not infinitely good; but yet he admits that God actually refuses to save some. Now, what difference can it make whether God's intention not to save all be evidenced by a preëxisting design, or by a present reality? Is not everything that is done by him, or left undone, in pursuance of his eternal purpose and design? What, then, in reference to the point in question, is the difference between the Arminian and the Calvinist? *Both admit that God could easily save all men if he would;* that is, render all men holy and happy. But the one says that he did not design to save all, while the other affirms that he actually refuses to save some. Surely, if we may assume what is conceded by both parties, the infinite goodness of God is no more disproved by a scheme of salvation limited in its design, than by a scheme of salvation limited in its execution. Hence, it is admitted by many Arminians themselves, that their own scheme merely mitigates and softens down, without removing, the appalling difficulty in question.

There are many exceptions to this remark. One of the most memorable of these is the judgment which Robert Hall* pronounces concerning the solution of this difficulty by the "Wonderful Howe." This solution, as we have seen, labours under the same defect with those of its predecessors, in that it rejects

* It is not exactly just to rank Hall among the Arminians. His scheme of doctrine, if scheme it may be called, is, like that of so many others, a heterogeneous mixture of Calvinism and Arminianism—a *mixture*, and not an *organic compound*, of the conflicting elements of the two systems.

the truth that a necessary holiness is a contradiction in terms. Instead of following the guidance of this truth, he wanders amid the obscurities of the subject, becomes involved in numerous self-contradictions, and is misled by the deceitful light of false analogies.

We shall not here reproduce his inconsistencies and self-contradictions. We shall simply add, that although he, too, attempts to show why it is for the best that all should not be saved, he frequently betrays the feeble and unsatisfactory nature of the impression which his own reasons made upon his mind. For the light of these *reasons* soon fades from his recollection; and, like all who have gone before him, when he comes to contemplate the subject from another point of view, he declares that the reasons of the thing he has endeavoured to explain, are hid from the human mind in the profound depths of the divine wisdom.

If we would realize, then, that God sincerely desires the salvation of all men, we must plant ourselves on the truth, that holiness, which is of the very essence of salvation, cannot be wrought in us by an extraneous force. It is under the guidance of this principle, and of this principle alone, that we can find our way out from the dark labyrinth of error and self-contradiction, in which others are involved, into the clear and beautiful light of the gospel, that God "will have all men to be saved, and come unto a knowledge of the truth." It is with the aid of this principle, and of this alone, that we may hear the sublime teachings of the divine wisdom, unmingled with the discordant sounds of human folly.

SECTION II.

The sufferings of the innocent, and especially of infants, consistent with the goodness of God.

By the Calvinistic school of divines it is most positively and peremptorily pronounced that the innocent can never suffer under the administration of a Being of infinite goodness. They cannot possibly allow that such a Being would permit one of his innocent creatures to suffer; but they can very well believe that he can permit them both to sin and to suffer. Is not this to strain at a gnat, and swallow a camel?

Having predetermined that the innocent never suffer, they have felt the necessity of finding some sin in infants, by which their sufferings might be shown to be deserved, and thereby reconciled with the divine goodness. This has proved a hard task. From the time of Augustine down to the present day, it has been diligently prosecuted; and with what success, we have endeavoured to show. The series of hypotheses to which this effort has given rise, are, perhaps, as wild and wonderful as any to be found in the history of the human mind. We need not again recount those dark dreams and inventions in the past history of Calvinism. Perhaps the hypothesis of the present day, by which it endeavours to vindicate the suffering of infants, will seem scarcely less astonishing to posterity, than those exploded fictions of the past appear to this generation.

According to this hypothesis, the infant world deserves to suffer, because the sin of Adam, their federal head and representative, is imputed to them. It is even contended that this constitution, by which the guilt or innocence of the world was suspended on the conduct of the first man, is a bright display of the divine goodness, since it was so likely to be attended with a happy issue to the human race. Likely to be attended with a happy issue! And did not the Almighty foresee and know, that if the guilt of the world were made to depend on the conduct of Adam, it would infallibly be attended with a fatal result?

We have examined, at length, the arguments of an Edwards to show that such a divine scheme and constitution of things is a display or manifestation of goodness. Those arguments are, perhaps, as ingenious and plausible as it is possible for the human intellect to invent in the defence of such a cause. When closely examined and searched to the bottom, they certainly appear as puerile and weak as it is possible for the human imagination to conceive.

Indeed, no coherent hypothesis can be invented on this subject, so long as the mind of the inventor fails to recognise the impossibility of excluding all sin from the moral system of the universe: for if all sin, then all suffering, likewise, may be excluded; and we can never understand why either should be permitted; much less can we comprehend why the innocent should be allowed to suffer. But having recognised this impossibility, we have been conducted to three grounds, on which, it is believed, the sufferings of the innocent may be reconciled with the goodness of God.

First, the sufferings of the innocent, in so far as they are the consequences of sin, serve to show its terrific nature, and tend to prevent its introduction into the world. If this end could have been accomplished by the divine power, such a provision would have been unnecessary, and all the misery of the world only so much "suffering in waste." Secondly, the sufferings of the innocent serve as a foil to set off and enhance the blessedness of eternity. They are but a short and discordant prelude to an everlasting harmony. Thirdly, difficulties and trials, temptations and wants, are indispensable to the rise of moral good in the soul of the innocent; for if there were no temptation to wrong, there could be no merit in obedience, and no virtue in the world. Suffering is, then, essential to the moral discipline and improvement of mankind. On the one or the other of these grounds, it is believed that every instance in which suffering falls upon the innocent, or falls not as a punishment of sin, may be vindicated and reconciled with the goodness of God.

SECTION III.

The sufferings of Christ consistent with the divine goodness.

The usual defences of the atonement are good, so far as they go, but not complete. The vicarious sufferings of Christ are well vindicated on the ground, that they are necessary to cause the majesty and honour of the divine law to be respected; but this defence, though sound, has been left on an insecure foundation; for it has been admitted that God, by the word of his power, might easily have caused his laws to be universally respected and obeyed. Hence, according to this admission, the sufferings of Christ might have been easily dispensed with, and were not necessary in order to maintain the honour and glory of the divine government. According to this admission, they were not necessary, and consequently not consistent with the goodness of God.

Again: by distinguishing between the *administrative* and the *retributive* justice of God, and showing that the vicarious sufferings of Christ were a satisfaction to the first, and not to the last, we annihilate the objections of the Socinian. By means of this view of the satisfaction rendered to the divine justice, we think we have placed the great doctrine of the atonement in a clearer and more satisfactory light than usual. We have shown that the vicarious sufferings of the INNOCENT are so far from being inconsistent with the divine justice, that they are, in fact, free from the least shadow or appearance of hardship either to him or to the world. Nay, that they are a bright manifestation of the divine goodness both to himself and to those for whom he suffered; the brightest manifestation thereof, indeed, which the universe has ever beheld.

SECTION IV.

The eternity of future punishment consistent with the goodness of God.

The genuine Calvinist, if he reason consecutively from some of the principles of his system, can never escape the conclusion that all men will be saved: for so long as he denies the ability of men to obey without the efficacious grace of God, and affirms that this grace is not given to such as shall finally perish, it must follow that their punishment is unjust, and that their eternal punishment were an act of cruelty and oppression greater than it is possible for the imagination of man to conceive.

It was precisely from such premises, as we have seen, that John Foster denied the eternal duration of future punishment. His logic is good; but even an illogical escape from such a conclusion were better than the rejection of one of the great fundamental doctrines of revealed religion. By having shown his premises to be false, we demolished the very foundation of his arguments. But, not satisfied with this, we pursued those arguments into all their branches and ramifications, and exposed their futility. By these means we have removed the objections and solved the difficulties pertaining to this doctrine of revealed religion. In one word, we have shown that it is not inconsistent with the dictates of reason, or with the principle of the divine goodness.

We have shown that the eternal punishment of the wicked

is deserved, and therefore demanded by the divine justice; that they serve to promote the highest moral interests of the universe, and are consequently imposed by the divine goodness itself. We have shown, that in the administration of his eternal government, the infliction of an endless punishment is even more consistent with goodness than the use of temporal punishment in the management of a temporal government; for the first, besides being eternal in duration, is unbounded in extent. Thus reason itself, when disenchanted of its strong Calvinistic prejudices and its weak Socinian sentimentalities, utters no other voice than that which proceeds from revelation; and this it echoes rather than utters. In plainer words, though reason does not prove or establish the eternity of future punishment, it has not one syllable to say against its wisdom, its justice, or its goodness.

SECTION V.

The true doctrine of election and predestination consistent with the goodness of God.

The Calvinists endeavour to support their scheme of election and predestination by means of analogies drawn from the unequal distribution of the divine favours, which is observable in the natural economy and government of the world. But the two cases are not parallel. According to the one, though the divine favours are unequally distributed, no man is ever required to render an account of more than he receives. Whereas, according to the other, countless millions of human beings are doomed to eternal misery for the non-observance of a law which they never had it in their power to obey. This is to judge them, not according to what they receive, but according to what they receive not, and cannot obtain. It is to call them to give an account of talents never committed to their charge. The difference between the two cases is, indeed, precisely that between the conduct of a munificent prince who bestows his favours unequally, but without making unreasonable demands, and the proceeding of a capricious tyrant who, while he confers the most exalted privileges and honours on one portion of his subjects, consigns all the rest, not more undeserving than they, to hopeless and remediless destruction; and that, too, for the non-performance of an impossible condition. Is it not wonderful that two cases so widely and so glaringly different, should have been so long and so obstinately confounded by serious inquirers after truth?

The Calvinistic scheme of predestination, it is pretended, derives support from revelation. The ninth chapter of Romans which, from the time of Augustine down to the present day, has been so confidently appealed to in its support, has, as we have seen, no relation to the subject. It relates, not to the election of individuals to eternal life, but of a nation to the enjoyment of external privileges and advantages. This is so plain, that Dr. Macknight, though an advocate of the Calvinistic dogma of predestination, refuses to employ that portion of Scripture in support of his doctrine.

Nor does the celebrated passage of the eighth chapter of the same epistle touch the point in controversy. We might well call in question the Calvinistic interpretation of that passage, if this were necessary; but we take it in their own sense, and show that it lends no support to their views. The Calvinists themselves being the interpreters, that passage teaches that God, according to his eternal purpose, chose or selected a certain portion out of the great mass of mankind as the heirs of eternal life. Granted, then, that a certain portion of the human race were thus made the objects of a peculiar favour, and prospectively endowed with the greatest of all conceivable blessings. But *who* were thus chosen, or selected? and on *what principle* was the election made? In regard to this point, it is not pretended by them that the passage in question utters a single syllable. They themselves being the judges, this Scripture merely affirms that a certain portion of mankind are chosen or elected to eternal life; while in regard to the ground, or the reason, of their election, it is most perfectly and profoundly silent.

Hence it leaves us free to assume the position, that those persons were elected or chosen who God foresaw would, by a coöperation with his Spirit, make their calling and election sure. And being thus left free, this is precisely the position in which we choose to plant ourselves, in order to vindicate the divine glory against the awful misrepresentations of Calvinism: for, in the first place, this view harmonizes the passage in question with other portions of the divine record, and allows us, without the least feeling of self-contradiction, to embrace the sublime word, that God "will have all men to be saved;" and that if any are not made the heirs of his great salvation, it is because his grace would have proved unavailing to them.

Secondly, this view not only harmonizes two classes of seemingly opposed texts of Scripture, but it also serves to vindicate the unbounded glory of the divine goodness. It shows that the goodness of God is not partial in its operation; neither taking such as it leaves, nor leaving such as it takes; but embracing all of the same class, and that class consisting of all who, by wicked works, do not place themselves beyond the possibility of being saved. Unlike Calvinism, it presents us, not with the spectacle of a mercy which might easily save all, but which, nevertheless, contenting itself with a few only, abandons the rest to the ravages of the never-dying worm.

Thirdly, at the same time that it vindicates the glory of the divine mercy, it rectifies the frightful distortion of the divine justice, which is exhibited in the scheme of Calvinism. According to this scheme, all those who are not elected to eternal life are set apart as the objects on which the Almighty intends to manifest the glory of his justice. But how is this glory, or his justice, manifested? Displayed, we are told, by dooming its helpless objects to eternal misery for the non-performance of an impossible condition! A *display* of justice this, which, to the human mind, bears every mark of the most appalling cruelty and oppression. *A display of justice stamped with the most terrific features of its opposite;* so that no human mind can see the glory of the one, for the inevitable manifestation of the other! No wonder that Calvinists themselves so often fly from the defence of such a display of the divine justice, and hide themselves in the unsearchable clouds and darkness of the divine wisdom. This being of course a display for eternity, and not for time, they may there await the light of another world to clear away these clouds, and reveal to them the great mystery of such a manifestation of the divine justice. But whether that light will bring to view the great mystery of the divine wisdom therein displayed, or the great secret of human folly therein concealed, we can hardly say remains to be seen.

The view we take presents a glorious display of the divine justice for *time* as well as for eternity.

Fourthly, this view not only shows the justice and the mercy of God, separately considered, in the most advantageous light, but it exhibits the sublime harmony which subsists between them. It presents not, like Calvinism, a mercy limited by justice, and a justice limited by mercy; but it exhibits each in its absolute perfection, and in its agreement with the other: for, according to this view, the claim of mercy extends to all who may be saved, and that of justice to those who may choose to remain incorrigibly wicked. Hence, the claim of the one does not interfere with that of the other; nor can we conceive how either could be more gloriously displayed. We behold the infinite amplitude, as well as the ineffable, unclouded splendour of each divine perfection, without the least disturbance or collision between them. In the very act of punishment, the tender mercy of God, which is over all his works, concurs, and inflicts that suffering which is demanded by the good of the universe. The torment of the lost, is "the wrath of the Lamb." The glory of the redeemed, is the pity of the Judge. Hence, instead of that frightful conflict which the scheme of Calvinism presents, we behold a reconciliation and agreement among the divine attributes, worthy the great principle of order, and harmony, and beauty in the universe.

SECTION VI.

The question submitted.

We must now take leave of the reader. We have honestly endeavoured to construct a Theodicy, or to vindicate the divine glory as manifested in the constitution and government of the moral world. We have endeavoured to reconcile the great fundamental doctrines of God and man with each other, as well as with the eternal principles of truth. It has likewise been our earnest aim, to evince the harmony of the divine attributes among themselves, as well as their agreement with the condition of the universe. In one word, we have aimed to repel the objections, and solve the difficulties which have been permitted to obscure the glory of the Divine Being; whether those difficulties and objections have seemed to proceed from the false philosophy of his enemies, or the mistaken views and misguided zeal of his friends. How far we have succeeded in this attempt, no less arduous than laudable, it is not for us to determine. We shall, therefore, respectfully submit the determination of this point to the calm and impartial judgment of those who may possess both the desire and the capacity to think for themselves.

THE END.

www.ingramcontent.com/pod-product-compliance
Lightning Source LLC
LaVergne TN
LVHW010138110826
845151LV00002B/379

* 9 7 8 1 4 2 5 5 3 9 4 7 4 *